A

PHILOSOPHICAL AND POLITICAL

HISTORY

OF THE

SETTLEMENTS AND TRADE

OF THE

EUROPEANS

IN THE

EAST AND WEST INDIES.

REVISED, AUGMENTED, AND PUBLISHED,

IN TEN VOLUMES,

BY THE ABBE RAYNAL.

NEWLY TRANSLATED FROM THE FRENCH,

BY J. O. JUSTAMOND, F. R. S.

WITH A

New Set of Maps adapted to the Work, and a copious Index.

IN SIX VOLUMES.

VOL. VI.

SECOND EDITION.

NEGRO UNIVERSITIES PRESS
NEW YORK

Originally published in 1798
by J. Mundell & Co., London

Reprinted 1969 by
Negro Universities Press
A DIVISION OF GREENWOOD PUBLISHING CORP.
NEW YORK

Library of Congress Catalogue Card Number 69-18996

SBN 8371-1556-6

CONTENTS.

VOL. VI.

BOOK XVIII.

BOOK XIX.

A

PHILOSOPHICAL AND POLITICAL

HISTORY

OF THE

SETTLEMENTS AND TRADE

OF THE

EUROPEANS

IN THE

EAST AND WEST INDIES.

BOOK XVIII.

Englifh Colonies founded in Pennfylvania, Maryland, Virginia, Carolina, Georgia, and Florida. General Reflections on all thefe Settlements.

No fociety was ever founded on injuftice. A people formed by a compact fo extraordinary, would have been, at the fame time, both the moft degraded and the moft unfortunate of people. Declared enemies of the human race, they would equally have been entitled to compaffion from the fentiments they would have infpired, and thofe they would have experienced. Feared and hated by all furrounding powers, they would have inceffantly been agitated by the fame paffions. Their misfortunes would have excited univerfal joy, and their profperity general affliction. The nations would one day have united to exterminate them; but time would have rendered this league ufelefs. It would have been fufficient for their annihilation, and for the avenging of other nations, that each

BOOK of their members fhould have modelled his conduct
XVIII. upon the maxims of the ftate. Animated with the
fpirit of their inftitution, they would all have been eager to raife themfelves upon the ruin of each other.
No meafure would have appeared too odious for this
purpofe. This would have been realizing the fable
of the race engendered from the teeth of the dragon,
which Cadmus fowed upon the earth, and which was
deftroyed as foon as created.

How different would be the deftiny of an empire
founded on virtue ! Agriculture, the arts, the fciences,
and commerce, improved under the protection of peace,
would have expelled idlenefs, ignorance, and mifery.
The chief of the ftate would have received the different ranks of men in the ftate, and would have been
adored. He would have underftood that not one of
the fociety could fuffer, without fome injury to the
whole body, and therefore he would have attended to
the happinefs of all. Impartial equity would enfure
the obfervation of the treaties which it had dictated,
the ftability of laws, which it had fimplified, and the
diftribution of taxes, which it would have proportioned to the public expences. All the neighbouring
powers, interefted in the prefervation of this people,
would arm in their defence, upon the leaft danger
which fhould threaten them. But in default of foreign fuccours, they might themfelves oppofe, to the
unjuft aggreffor, the impenetrable barrier of a rich
and numerous people, for whom the word Country
would not merely be a nominal idea. This is what
may be called imaginary excellence in politics.

Thefe two forts of government are equally unknown
in the annals of the world ; which prefent us with nothing but imperfect fketches, more or lefs refembling
the atrocious fublimity, or more or lefs diftant from
the affecting beauty, of one or the other of thefe great
portraits. The nations which have made the moft
fplendid figure on the theatre of the world, actuated
by deftructive ambition, have difplayed a greater refemblance to the former. Others, more wife in their

conftitution, more fimple in their manners, more limit- B O O K
ed in their views, and enveloped, if we may ufe the XVIII.
expreffion, with a kind of fecret happinefs, feemed to
be more conformable to the fecond. Among the latter Pennfylvania may be reckoned.

 Lutheranifm, which was deftined to caufe a remark- The Qua-
able change in Europe, either by its own influence, or kers found
by the example it gave, had occafioned a great fer- Pennfylva-
ment in the minds of all men, when there arofe, in the nia. Man-
midft of the commotions it excited, a new religion, fect.
which at firft appeared much more like a rebellion
guided by fanaticifm, than like a fect that was governed by any fixed principle. The generality of innova-
tors in religion follow a regular fyftem, compofed of
doctrines connected with each other, and contend at
firft only to defend them, till perfecution irritates and
ftimulates them to rebellion, fo that at length they
have recourfe to arms. The Anabaptifts, on the contrary, as if they had only looked into the Bible for the
word of command to attack, lifted up the ftandard of
rebellion, before they had agreed upon a fyftem of
doctrine. It is true, indeed, their leaders had taught,
that it was a ridiculous and ufelefs practice to adminifter baptifm to infants, and afferted that their opinion
upon this point was the fame as that of the primitive
church; but they had not yet ever reduced to practice this article of belief, which was the only one that
furnifhed a pretence for their feparation. The fpirit
of fedition prevented them from paying a proper attention to the fchifmatic tenets on which their divifion was founded. To fhake off the tyrannical yoke
of church and ftate, was their law and their faith. To
enlift in the armies of the Lord, to join with the faithful, who were to wield the fword of Gideon, this was
their device, their motive, and their fignal for rallying.

 It was not till after they had carried fire and fword
into a great part of Germany, that the Anabaptifts
thought of giving fome bafis and fome connection to
their creed, and of marking and cementing their confederacy by fome vifible fign of union. Having been

B O O K united at firſt by inſpiration to raiſe a body of troops,
XVIII. in 1525 they were united to compoſe a religious code.

In this mixed ſyſtem of intoleration and mildneſs, the Anabaptiſt church, being the only one in which the pure word of God is taught, neither can nor ought to communicate with any other.

The ſpirit of the Lord blowing whereſoever it liſt-eth, the power of preaching is not limited to one or-der of the faithful, but is diſpenſed to all. Every one likewiſe has the gift of prophecy.

Every ſect which hath not preſerved a community of all things which conſtituted the life and ſpirit of pri-mitive Chriſtianity, has degenerated, and is for that reaſon an impure ſociety.

Magiſtrates are uſeleſs in a ſociety of the truly faith-ful. A Chriſtian never has occaſion for any; nor is a Chriſtian allowed to be one himſelf.

Chriſtians are not permitted to take up arms even in their own defence, much leſs is it lawful for them to enliſt as ſoldiers in mercenary armies.

Both law-ſuits and oaths are forbidden the diſciples of Chriſt, who has commanded them to let their yea, be yea, and their nay, nay.

The baptiſm of infants is an invention of the devil and the pope. The validity of baptiſm depends upon the voluntary conſent of adults, who alone are able to receive it with a conſciouſneſs of the engagement they take upon themſelves.

Such was in its origin the religious ſyſtem of the Anabaptiſts. Though it appears founded on charity and mildneſs, yet it produced nothing but violence and iniquity. The chimerical idea of an equality of ſtations, is the moſt dangerous one that can be adopt-ed in a civilized ſociety. To preach this ſyſtem to the people, is not to put them in mind of their rights, it is leading them on to aſſaſſination and plunder; it is let-ting domeſtic animals looſe, and transforming them into wild beaſts. The rulers of the people muſt be more enlightened, or the laws by which they are go-verned muſt be ſoftened; but there is in fact no ſuch thing in nature as a real equality; it exists only in the system of equity. Even the savages themselves are not equal when once they are collected into hordes. They are only so while they wander in the woods; and even then the man who suffers the produce of his chase to be taken from him, is not the equal of him who deprives him of it. Such has been the origin of all societies.

A doctrine, the basis of which was the community of goods and equality of ranks, was hardly calculated to find partizans any where but among the poor. The peasants therefore adopted it with the greater enthusiasm, in proportion as the yoke from which it delivered them was more insupportable. The far greater part, especially those who were condemned to slavery, rose up in arms on all sides, to support a doctrine, which, from being vassals, made them equal to their lords. The apprehension of seeing one of the first bands of society, obedience to the magistrate, broken, united all other sects against them, who could not subsist without subordination. After having carried on a more obstinate resistance than could have been expected, they yielded at length to the number of their enemies. Their sect, notwithstanding it had made its way all over Germany, and into a part of the North, was nowhere prevalent, because it had been every where opposed and dispersed. It was but just tolerated in those countries, in which the greatest latitude of opinion was allowed; and there was not any state in which it was able to settle a church, authorised by the civil power. This of course weakened it, and from obscurity it fell into contempt. Its only glory is that of having, perhaps, contributed to the foundation of the sect of Quakers.

This humane and peaceable sect arose in England, amidst the confusions of that bloody war, which terminated in a monarch's being dragged to the scaffold by his own subjects. The founder of it, George Fox, was of the lower class of the people; a man who had been formerly a mechanic, but whom a singular and

Origin and character of the Quakers.

contemplative turn of mind had induced to quit his
employment. In order to wean himfelf entirely from
all earthly affections, he broke off all connections with
his own family; and for fear of being tempted to renew them, he determined to have no fixed abode. He
often wandered alone in the woods, without any other
amufement but his Bible. In time he even learned to
go without that, when he thought he had acquired
from it a degree of infpiration fimilar to that of the
apoftles and the prophets.

He then began to think of making profelytes, in
which he found no difficulty in a country where the
minds of all men were filled and difturbed with en-
thufiaftic notions. He was, therefore, foon followed
by a multitude of difciples, the novelty and fingularity
of whofe opinions, upon incomprehenfible fubjects,
could not fail of attracting and fafcinating all thofe
who were fond of the marvellous.

The firft thing by which they caught the eye, was
the fimplicity of their drefs, in which there was no
gold or filver lace, no embroidery, laces, or ruffles, and
from which they affected to banifh every thing that
was fuperfluous or unneceffary. They would not fuffer either a button in the hat or a plait in the coat, becaufe it was poffible to do without them. Such an
extraordinary contempt for eftablifhed modes remind-
ed thofe who adopted it, that it became them to be
more virtuous than the reft of men, from whom they
diftinguifhed themfelves by this external modefty.

All outward marks of deference, which the pride
and tyranny of mankind exact from thofe who are
unable to refufe them, were difdained by the Quakers, who difclaimed the names of mafter and fervant.
They condemned all titles, as being tokens of pride
in thofe who claimed them, and of meannefs in thofe
who beftowed them. They did not allow to any perfon whatever the appellation of eminence or excellence, and fo far they might be in the right; but
they refufed to comply with thofe reciprocal demon-
ftrations of refpect which we call politenefs, and in

this they were to blame. The name of friend, they said, was not to be refused by one Christian or citizen to another, but the ceremony of bowing they confidered as ridiculous and troublefome. To pull off the hat they held to be a want of refpect to a man's felf, in order to fhow it to others. They carried this idea fo far, that even the magiftrates could not compel them to any external mark of reverence; but they addreffed both them and princes according to the ancient majefty of language, in the fecond perfon and in the fingular number; and they juftified this licence by the cuftom of thofe very perfons who were offended at it, and who ufed to addrefs their faints and their God in the fame manner.

The aufterity of their morals ennobled the fingularity of their manners. The ufe of arms, confidered in every light, appeared a crime to them. If it were to attack, it was violating the laws of humanity; if to defend one's felf, it was breaking through thofe of Chriftianity. Univerfal peace was the gofpel they had agreed to profefs. If any one fmote a Quaker upon one cheek, he immediately prefented the other; if any one afked him for his coat, he offered his waiftcoat too. Nothing could engage thefe equitable men to demand more than the lawful price for their work, or to take lefs than what they demanded. An oath, even before a magiftrate, and in fupport of a juft caufe, they deemed to be a profanation of the name of God, in any of the wretched difputes that arife between weak and perifhable beings.

The contempt they entertained for the outward forms of politenefs in civil life, was changed into averfion for the ritual and ceremonial parts of religion. They looked upon churches merely as the oftentatious edifices of prieftcraft; they confidered the Sabbath as a pernicious and idle inftitution, and baptifm and the Lord's Supper as ridiculous fymbols. For this reafon they rejected all regular orders of clergy. Every one of the faithful they imagined received an immediate illumination from the Holy Ghoft, which gave a cha-

BOOK
XVIII.
racter far superior to that of the priesthood. When they were assembled together, the first person who found himself inspired, arose, and imparted the lights he had received from heaven. Even women were often favoured with this gift of speech, which they called the gift of prophecy; sometimes many of these holy brethren spoke at the same time; but much more frequently a profound silence prevailed in their assemblies.

The enthusiasm occasioned both by their meditations and discourses, excited such a degree of sensibility in the nervous system, that it threw them into convulsions, for which reason they were called Quakers. To have cured these people in process of time of their folly, nothing more was requisite than to turn it into ridicule; but instead of this, persecution contributed to make it more general. While every other new sect met with encouragement, this was exposed to every kind of punishment; imprisonments, whippings, pillories, mad-houses, were none of them thought too terrible for bigots, whose only crime was that of wanting to be virtuous and reasonable over much. The constancy with which they bore their sufferings, at first excited compassion, and afterwards admiration for them. Even Cromwell, who had been one of their most violent enemies, because they used to insinuate themselves into his camps, and dissuade his soldiers from their profession, gave them public marks of his esteem. His policy exerted itself in endeavouring to draw them into his party, in order to conciliate to himself a higher degree of respect and consideration; but they either eluded his invitations, or rejected them; and he afterwards confessed, that this was the only religion which was not to be influenced by bribery.

Foundation of Pennsylvania by Penn. Principles of his legislation.
Among the several persons who cast a temporary lustre on the sect, the only one who deserves to be remembered by posterity, is William Penn. He was the son of an admiral, who had been fortunate enough to be equally distinguished by Cromwell, and the two Stuarts, who held the reins of government

after him. This able feaman, more fupple and more infinuating than men of his profeffion ufually are, had made feveral confiderable advances to government in the different expeditions in which he had been engaged. The misfortunes of the times had not admitted of the repayment of thefe loans during his life, and as affairs were not in a better fituation at his death, it was propofed to his fon, that inftead of money, he fhould accept of an immenfe territory in America. It was a country, which, though long fince difcovered and furrounded by Englifh colonies, had always been neglected. A fpirit of benevolence made him accept with pleafure this kind of patrimony, which was ceded to him almoft as a fovereignty, and he determined to make it the abode of virtue, and the afylum of the unfortunate. With this generous defign, towards the end of the year 1681, he fet fail for his new poffeffions, which from that time took the name of Pennfylvania. All the Quakers were defirous to follow him, in order to avoid the perfecution raifed againft them by the clergy, on account of their not complying with the tithes and other ecclefiaftical fees; but from prudential motives he declined taking over any more than two thoufand.

His arrival in the New World was fignalized by an act of equity, which made his perfon and principles equally beloved. Not thoroughly fatisfied with the right given him to his extenfive territory, by the grant he had received of it from the Britifh miniftry, he determined to make it his own property by purchafing it of the natives. The price he gave to the favages is not known; but though fome people accufe them of ftupidity for confenting to part with what they never ought to have alienated upon any terms; yet Penn is not lefs entitled to the glory of having given an example of moderation and juftice in America, which was never thought of before by the Europeans. He rendered himfelf as much as poffible a legal poffeffor of the territory, and by the ufe he made of it supplied any deficiency there might be in the validity of his title. The Americans entertained as great an affection for his colony, as they had conceived an aversion for all those which had been founded in their neighbourhood without their consent. From that time there arose a mutual confidence between the two people, founded upon good faith, which nothing has ever been able to shake.

Penn's humanity could not be confined to the savages only ; it extended itself to all those who were desirous of living under his laws. Sensible that the happiness of the people depended upon the nature of the legislation, he founded his upon those two first principles of public splendour and private felicity, liberty and property. If it were allowed to borrow the language of fable, with respect to an account that seems to be fabulous, we should say, that Astræa, who had been gone up into heaven for so long a time, was now come down upon earth again, and that the reign of innocence and concord was going to be revived among mankind. The mind of the writer and of his reader dwells with pleasure on this part of modern history, and feels some kind of compensation for the disgust, horror, or melancholy, which the whole of it, but particularly the account of the European settlements in America, inspires. Hitherto we have only seen these barbarians depopulating the country before they took possession of it, and laying every thing waste before they cultivated it. It is time to observe the dawnings of reason, happiness, and humanity, rising from among the ruins of a hemisphere, which still reeks with the blood of all its people, civilized as well as savage.

The virtuous legislator made toleration the basis of his society. He admitted every man who acknowledged a God to the rights of a citizen, and made every Christian eligible to state employments. But he left every one at liberty to invoke the Supreme Being as he thought proper, and neither established a reign-

ing church in Pennſylvania, nor exacted contributions B O O K
for building places of public worſhip, nor compelled XVIII.
any perſons to attend them.

Penn, attached to his name, was deſirous that the
property of the ſettlement which he had formed ſhould
remain in perpetuity to his family ; but he deprived
them of any deciſive influence in the public reſolutions, and ordained, that they ſhould not exerciſe any
act of authority without the concurrence of the deputies of the people. All the citizens who had an intereſt in the law, by having one in the object of it,
were to be electors, and might be choſen. To avoid
as much as poſſible every kind of corruption, it was
ordained that the repreſentatives ſhould be choſen by
ſuffrages privately given. To eſtabliſh a law, a plurality of voices was ſufficient ; but a majority of two-
thirds was neceſſary to ſettle a tax. Such a tax as this
was certainly more like a free gift than a ſubſidy demanded by government ; but was it poſſible to grant
leſs indulgences to men who were come ſo far in ſearch
of peace ?

Such was the opinion of that real philoſopher Penn.
He gave a thouſand acres to all thoſe who could afford to pay 450 livres [18l. 15s.] for them. Every
one who could not, obtained for himſelf, his wife,
each of his children above ſixteen years old, and each
of his ſervants, fifty acres of land, for the annual quit-
rent of one ſol ten deniers and a half [about one pen-
ny.] per acre. Fifty acres were alſo given to every
citizen who, when he was of age, conſented to pay
an annual tribute of two livres five ſols [1s. 10¼d.].

To fix theſe properties for ever, he eſtabliſhed tribunals to maintain the laws made for the preſervation
of property. But it is not protecting the property of
lands to make thoſe who are in poſſeſſion of them
purchaſe the decree of juſtice that ſecures them : for
in that caſe every individual is obliged to part with
ſome of his property, in order to ſecure the reſt ; and
law, when protracted, exhauſts the very treaſures it
ſhould preſerve and the property it ſhould defend.

BOOK
XVIII.

Lest any perfons fhould be found whofe intereft it might be to encourage or prolong law-fuits, he forbade, under very ftrict penalties, all thofe who were engaged in the adminiftration of juftice to receive any falary or gratuity whatfoever. And further, every diftrict was obliged to choofe three arbitrators, whofe bufinefs it was to endeavour to prevent, and accommodate, any difputes that might happen, before they were carried into a court of juftice.

This attention to prevent law-fuits fprang from the defire of preventing crimes. All the laws, that they might have no vices to punifh, were calculated to put a ftop to them even in their very fources, poverty and idlenefs. It was enacted that every child above twelve years old, fhould be obliged to learn a profeffion, let his condition be what it would. This regulation, at the fame time that it fecured the poor man a fubfiftence, furnifhed the rich man with a refource againft every reverfe of fortune, preferved the natural equality of mankind, by recalling to every man's remembrance his original deftination, which is that of labour, either of the mind or of the body.

Virtue had never perhaps infpired a legiflation better calculated to promote the felicity of mankind. The opinions, the fentiments, and the morals corrected whatever might be defective in it, and remedied any part of it that might be imperfect. Accordingly, the profperity of Pennfylvania was very rapid. This republic, without either wars, conquefts, ftruggles, or any of thofe revolutions which attract the eyes of the vulgar, foon excited the admiration of the whole univerfe. Its neighbours, notwithftanding their favage ftate, were foftened by the fweetnefs of its manners; and diftant nations, notwithftanding their corruption, paid homage to its virtues. All were delighted to fee thofe heroic days of antiquity realized, which European manners and laws had long taught every one to confider as entirely fabulous.

Profperity
of Pennfyl-
vania.

Pennfylvania is defended on the eaft by the ocean, on the north by New York and New Jerfey, on the

BOOK XVIII.

south by Virginia and Maryland, on the west by the Indians; on all sides by friends, and within itself by the virtue of its inhabitants. Its coasts, which are at first very narrow, extend gradually to 120 miles, and the breadth of it, which has no other limits than its population and culture, already comprehends 145 miles.

Pennsylvania Proper is divided into eleven counties; Philadelphia, Bucks, Chester, Lancaster, York, Cumberland, Berks, Northampton, Bedford, Northumberland, and Westmoreland.

In the same region, the counties of Newcastle, Kent, and Suffex, form a distinct government, but are regulated on the same principles.

The sky of the colony is pure and serene, and the climate, naturally very wholesome, has been rendered still more so by cultivation; the waters, equally salubrious and clear, always flow upon a bed of rock or sand; and the year is tempered by the regular return of the seasons. Winter, which begins in the month of January, lasts till the end of March. As it is seldom accompanied with clouds or fogs, the cold is, generally speaking, moderate; sometimes, however, sharp enough to freeze the largest rivers in a night's time. This change, which is as short as it is sudden, is occasioned by the north-west winds, which blow from the mountains and lakes of Canada. The spring is ushered in by soft rains, and a gentle heat, which increases gradually till the end of June. The heats of the dog-days would be insupportable, were it not for the refreshing breezes of the south-west wind, which afford almost a constant relief.

Though the country be unequal, it is not on that account less fertile. The soil in some places consists of a yellow and black sand, in others it is gravelly, and sometimes it is a greyish ash-colour upon a stony bottom; generally speaking, it is a rich earth, particularly between the rivulets, which, intersecting it in all directions, contribute more to the fertility of the country than navigable rivers would.

BOOK
XVIII.
When the Europeans firſt came into the country, they found nothing but wood for building, and iron mines. In proceſs of time, by cutting down the trees, and clearing the ground, they covered it with innumerable herds, a great variety of fruits, plantations of flax and hemp, many kinds of vegetables, every ſort of grain, and eſpecially wheat and maize, which a happy experience had ſhown to be particularly proper to the climate. Cultivation was carried on in all parts with ſuch vigour and ſucceſs as excited the aſtoniſhment of all nations.

From whence could ariſe this extraordinary proſperity? From that civil and religious liberty which has attracted the Swedes, Dutch, French, and particularly ſome laborious Germans, into that country. It has been the joint work of Quakers, Anabaptiſts, members of the Church of England, Methodiſts, Preſbyterians, Moravians, Lutherans, and Catholics.

Among the numerous ſects which abound in this country, a very diſtinguiſhed one is that of the Dumplers. It was founded by a German, who, weary of the world, retired to an agreeable ſolitude within fifty miles of Philadelphia, in order to be more at liberty to give himſelf up to contemplation. Curioſity brought ſeveral of his countrymen to viſit his retreat; and by degrees his pious, ſimple, and peaceable manners induced them to ſettle near him; and they all formed a little colony, which they called Euphrates, in alluſion to the Hebrews, who uſed to ſing pſalms on the borders of that river.

This little city forms a triangle, the outſides of which are bordered with mulberry and apple-trees, planted with regularity. In the middle of the town is a very large orchard; and between the orchard and theſe ranges of trees are houſes, built of wood, three ſtories high, where every Dumpler is left to enjoy the pleaſures of his meditations without diſturbance. Theſe contemplative men do not amount to above five hundred in all; their territory is about 250 acres in ex-

tent, the boundaries of which are marked by a river, B O O K
a piece of ftagnated water, and a mountain covered XVIII.
with trees.

The men and women live in feparate quarters of the
city. They never fee each other but at places of worfhip, nor are there any affemblies of any kind but for
public bufinefs. Their life is fpent in labour, prayer,
and fleep. Twice every day and night they are called
forth from their cells to attend divine fervice. Like
the Methodifts and Quakers, every individual among
them has the right of preaching when he thinks himfelf infpired. The favourite fubjects on which they
difcourfe in their affemblies, are humility, temperance,
chaftity, and the other Chriftian virtues. They never
violate that day of repofe, which all orders of men,
whether idle or laborious, much delight in. They admit a hell and a paradife, but reject the eternity of future punifhments. They abhor the doctrine of original fin as an impious blafphemy, and in general every tenet that is fevere to man appears to them injurious to the divinity. As they do not allow merit to
any but voluntary works, they only adminifter baptifm to the adult. At the fame time they think baptifm fo effentially neceffary to falvation, that they imagine the fouls of Chriftians in another world are employed in converting thofe who have not died under
the law of the gofpel.

Still more difinterefted than the Quakers, they never allow themfelves any law-fuits. One may cheat,
rob, and abufe them, without ever being expofed to
any retaliation, or even any complaint from them.
Religion has the fame effect on them that philofophy
had upon the Stoics; it makes them infenfible to every kind of infult.

Nothing can be plainer than their drefs. In winter, it is a long white gown, from whence there hangs
a hood, which ferves inftead of a hat, a coarfe fhirt,
thick fhoes, and very wide breeches. The only difference in fummer is, that linen is ufed inftead of wool-

len. The women are dreſſed much like the men, except that they have no breeches.

Their common food confiſts wholly of vegetables,
not becauſe it is unlawful to eat any other, but becauſe that kind of abſtinence is looked upon as more
conformable to the ſpirit of Chriſtianity, which has an
averſion for blood.

Each individual follows with cheerfulneſs the branch
of buſineſs allotted to him. The produce of all their
labours is depoſited in a common ſtock, in order to
ſupply the neceſſities of every one. This union of
induſtry has not only eſtabliſhed agriculture, manufactures, and all the arts neceſſary for the ſupport of
this little ſociety, but hath alſo ſupplied, for the purpoſes of exchange, ſuperfluities proportioned to the
degree of its population.

Though the two ſexes live ſeparate at Euphrates,
the Dumplers do not on that account fooliſhly renounce matrimony; but thoſe who find themſelves
diſpoſed to it leave the city, and form an eſtabliſhment in the country, which is ſupported at the public
expence. They repay this by the produce of their labours, which is all thrown into the public treaſury,
and their children are ſent to be educated in the mother-country. Without this wiſe privilege, the Dumplers would be no better than monks, and in proceſs of
time would become either ſavages or libertines.

The moſt edifying, and at the ſame time the moſt
extraordinary circumſtance, is the harmony that ſubſiſts between all the ſects eſtabliſhed in Pennſylvania,
notwithſtanding the difference of their religious opinions. Though not all of the ſame church, they all
love and cheriſh one another as children of the ſame
father. They have always continued to live like brethren, becauſe they had the liberty of thinking as men.
To this delightful harmony muſt be attributed more
particularly the rapid progreſs of the colony.

At the beginning of the year 1774, the population
of this ſettlement amounted to three hundred and fifty

thoufand inhabitants, according to the calculations of B o o K
the general congrefs. It muft, however, be acknow- XVIII.
ledged, that thirty thoufand Negroes made part of this
numerous population; but truth alfo requires us to
fay, that flavery, in this province, hath not been a
fource of corruption, as it hath always been, and always will be, in focieties that are not fo well regulated.
The manners are ftill pure, and even auftere, in Pennfylvania. Is this fingular advantage to be afcribed to
the climate, the laws, the religion, the emulation conftantly fubfifting between the different fects, or to fome
other particular caufe? Let the reader determine this
queftion.

The Pennfylvanians are in general well made, and
their women of an agreeable figure. As they fooner
become mothers than in Europe, they fooner ceafe
breeding. If the heat of the climate feems on the one
hand to haften the operations of nature, its inconftancy weakens them on the other. There is no place
where the temperature of the fky is more uncertain,
for it fometimes changes five or fix times in the fame
day.

As, however, thefe varieties have neither any dangerous influence upon animals, nor even upon vegetables, and as they do not deftroy the harvefts, there
is a conftant plenty, and an univerfal appearance of
eafy circumftances. The economy which is fo particularly attended to in Pennfylvania does not prevent
both fexes from being well clothed; and their food is
ftill preferable in its kind to their clothing. The families whofe circumftances are the leaft eafy, have all
of them bread, meat, cyder, beer, and rum. A very
great number are able to afford to drink conftantly
French and Spanifh wines, punch, and even liquors
of a higher price. The abufe of thefe ftrong drinks is
lefs frequent than in other places, but is not without
example.

The pleafing view of this abundance is never difturbed by the melancholy appearance of poverty.
There are no poor in all Pennfylvania. All thofe

B O O K whofe birth or fortune have left them without refour-
XVIII. ces, are fuitably provided for out of the public treafury. The fpirit of benevolence is carried ftill further,
and is extended even to the moft engaging hofpitality.
A traveller is welcome to ftop in any place, without
the apprehenfions of giving the leaft uneafy fenfation,
except that of regret for his departure.

The happinefs of the colony is not difturbed by the
oppreffive burden of taxes. In 1766, they did not
amount to more than 280,140 livres [11,672l. 10s.].
Moft of them, even thofe that were defigned to repair
the damages of war, were to ceafe in 1772. If the
people did not experience this alleviation at that period, it was owing to the irruptions of the favages,
which had occafioned extraordinary expences. This
trifling inconvenience would not have been attended
to, if Penn's family could have been prevailed upon
to contribute to the public expences, in proportion to
the revenue they obtained from the province: a circumftance required by the inhabitants, and which in
equity they ought to have complied with.

The Pennfylvanians, happy poffeffors, and peaceable tenants, of a country that ufually renders them
twenty or thirty fold for whatever they lay out upon
it, are not reftrained by fear from the propagation
of their fpecies. There is hardly an unmarried perfon
to be met with in the country. Marriage is the more
happy and the more reverenced for it; the freedom,
as well as the fanctity of it, depends upon the choice
of the parties: they choofe the lawyer and the prieft
rather as witneffes, than as the means to cement their
engagement. Whenever two lovers meet with any
oppofition, they go off on horfeback together: the
man gets behind his miftrefs; and in this fituation they
prefent themfelves before the magiftrate, where the
girl declares fhe has run away with her lover, and that
they are come to be married. So folemn an avowal
cannot be rejected, nor has any perfon a right to give
them any moleftation. In all other cafes, paternal authority is exceffive. The head of a family, whofe af-

fairs are involved, is allowed to fell his children to his
creditors; a punifhment, one fhould imagine, very fufficient to induce an affectionate father to attend to his
affairs. An adult difcharges, in one year's fervice, a
debt of 112 livres 10 fols [4l. 13s. 9d.]; children under twelve years of age are obliged to ferve till they
are one and twenty, in order to pay off the fame fum.
This is an image of the old patriarchal manners of the
Eaft.

Though there be feveral villages, and even fome cities in the colony, moft of the inhabitants may be faid
to live feparately, as it were, within their families.
Every proprietor of land has his houfe in the midft of
a large plantation, entirely furrounded with quickfet
hedges. Of courfe, each parifh is near twelve or fifteen leagues in circumference. This diftance of the
churches makes the ceremonies of religion have little
effect, and ftill lefs influence. Children are not bap-
tifed till a few months, and fometimes not till a year
or two after their birth.

All the pomp of religion feems to be referved for
the laft honours man receives before he is fhut up in
the grave for ever. As foon as any perfon is dead in
the country, the neareft neighbours have notice given
them of the day of the burial. Thefe fpread it in the
habitations next to theirs; and within a few hours the
news is thus conveyed to a diftance. Every family
fends at leaft one perfon to attend the funeral. As
they come in, they are prefented with punch and
cake. When the affembly is complete, the corpfe is
carried to the burying-ground belonging to his fect, or
if that fhould be at too great a diftance, into one of
the fields belonging to the family. There is generally
a train of four or five hundred perfons on horfeback,
who obferve a continual filence, and have all the external appearance fuitable to the melancholy nature
of the ceremony. One fingular circumftance is, that
the Pennfylvanians, who are the greateft enemies to
parade during their lives, feem to forget this character
of modefty at their deaths. They are all defirous that

the poor remains of their fhort lives fhould be attended with a funeral pomp proportioned to their rank or
fortune.   It is a general obfervation, that plain and
virtuous people, even thofe that are favage and poor,
pay great attention to the ordering of their funerals.
The reafon is, that they look upon thefe laft honours
as duties of the furvivors, and the duties themfelves as
fo many diftinct proofs of that principle of love which
is very ftrong in private families while they are in a
ftate neareft to that of nature.   It is not the dying
man himfelf who exacts thefe honours; his parents,
his wife, his children, voluntarily pay them to the
afhes of a hufband and father that has deferved to be
lamented.   Thefe ceremonies have always more numerous attendants in fmall focieties than in larger
ones, becaufe, though there are fewer families upon
the whole, the number of individuals there is much
larger, and all the ties that connect them with each
other are much ftronger.   This kind of intimate union
has been the reafon why fo many fmall nations have
overcome larger ones; it drove Xerxes and the Perfians out of Greece, and it will fome time or other expel the French from Corfica.

But from whence does Pennfylvania get the articles
neceffary for her own confumption, and in what manner does fhe contrive to be abundantly furnifhed with
them?   With the flax and hemp that is produced at
home, and the cotton fhe procures from South America, fhe fabricates a great quantity of ordinary linens;
and with the wool that comes from Europe fhe manufactures many coarfe cloths.   Whatever her own induftry is not able to furnifh, fhe purchafes with the
produce of her territory.   Her fhips carry over to the
Englifh, French, Dutch, and Danifh iflands, bifcuit,
flour, butter, cheefe, tallow, vegetables, fruits, falt
meat, cyder, beer, and all forts of wood for building.
The cotton, fugar, coffee, brandy, and money, received in exchange, are fo many materials for a frefh commerce with the mother country, and with other European nations, as well as with other colonies.   The

Azores, Madeira, the Canaries, Spain, and Portugal, open an advantageous market for the corn and wood of Pennfylvania, which they purchafe with wine and piaftres. The mother-country receives from Pennfylvania, iron, flax, leather, furs, linfeed, mafts and yards, for which it returns thread, fine cloths, tea, Irifh and India linens, hardware, and other articles of luxury or neceffity. But all thefe branches of trade have been hitherto prejudicial to the colony, though it can neither be cenfured nor commiferated on this account. Whatever meafures may be adopted, it is unavoidably neceffary that rifing ftates fhould contract debts; and the one we are now fpeaking of will remain in debt as long as the clearing of the lands requires greater expences than the produce will enable it to anfwer. Other colonies, which enjoy almoft exclufively fome branches of trade, fuch as rice, tobacco, and indigo, muft have grown rich very rapidly. Pennfylvania, the riches of which are founded on agriculture and the increafe of her flocks, will acquire them more gradually; but her profperity will be fixed upon a more firm and permanent bafis.

If any circumftance can retard the progrefs of the colony, it muft be the irregular manner in which the plantations are formed. Penn's family, who are the proprietors of all the lands, grant them indifcriminately in all parts, and in as large a proportion as they are required, provided they are paid 112 livres 10 fols [4l. 13s. 9d.] for each hundred acres, and that the purchafers agree to give an annual rent of 22 fols 6 deniers [18s. 4¼d.]. The confequence of this is, that the province wants that fort of connection which is fo neceffary in all eftablifhments, and that the fcattered inhabitants eafily become the prey of the moft infignificant enemy that ventures to attack them.

There are different ways of clearing the lands which are followed in the colony. Sometimes a huntfman will fettle in the midft of a foreft, or quite clofe to it. His neareft neighbours affift him in cutting down trees, and placing them one above another: and this confti-

tutes a houfe.   Around this fpot he cultivates, without any affiftance, a garden or a field, fufficient to
fubfift himfelf and his family.

A few years after the firft labours are finifhed, fome
more active or richer men arrive from the mother-
country.   They indemnify the huntfman for his labour, and agree with the proprietors of the provinces
for fome lands that have not yet been paid for.   They
build more commodious habitations, and clear a greater extent of territory.

At length fome Germans, who come into the New
World from inclination, or are driven into it by perfecution, complete thefe fettlements that are as yet un-
finifhed.   The firft and fecond order of planters remove into other parts, with a more confiderable ftock
for carrying on agriculture than they had at firft.

In 1767, the exports of Pennfylvania amounted to
13,164,439 livres 5 fols 3 deniers [about 548,518l. 6s.
0¾d.]; and they have fince increafed much more confiderably in that colony than in any other.

Prefent
ftate of
Philadel-
phia,
Philadelphia, or *the City of Brothers*, is the centre of
this great trade.   This famous city is fituated at the
conflux of the Delaware and the Schuylkill, at the diftance of 120 miles from the fea.   Penn, who deftined
it for the metropolis of a great empire, defigned it to
be one mile in breadth and two in length between the
rivers; but its population has proved infufficient to cover this extent of ground.   Hitherto the banks of the
Delaware are only built upon; but without giving up
the ideas of the legiflator, or deviating from his plan.
Thefe precautions are highly proper.   Philadelphia
muft become the moft confiderable city of America,
becaufe the colony muft neceffarily improve greatly,
and its productions muft pafs through the harbour of
the capital before they arrive at the fea.

The ftreets of Philadelphia, which are all regular,
are from fifty to a hundred feet broad.   On each fide
of them there are foot-paths defended by pofts, placed
at different diftances.

The houfes, each of which has its garden and orch- B O O K
ard, are commonly three ftories high, and are built of   XVIII.
brick. The prefent buildings have received an additional decoration from a kind of marble of different
colours, which is found about a mile out of the town.
Of this, tables, chimney-pieces, and other houfehold
furniture, are made ; befides which, it is become rather a confiderable article of commerce with the greateft part of America.

Thefe valuable materials could not have been found
in common in the houfes, unlefs they had been lavifhed in the churches. Every fect has its own church,
and fome of them have feveral. But there are a number of citizens, who have neither churches, priefts, nor
any public form of worfhip, and who are ftill happy,
humane, and virtuous.

The town-houfe is a building holden in as much
veneration, though not fo much frequented, as the
churches. It is conftructed with the greateft magnificence. There the legiflators of the colony affemble
every year, and more frequently if neceffary, to fettle
every thing relative to public bufinefs. Thefe men of
truft are here fupplied with every publication that
may give them any information refpecting government, trade, and adminiftration. Next to the town-
houfe is a moft elegant library, formed in 1732, under the care of the learned Dr. Franklin, and con-
fifting of the beft Englifh, with feveral French and
Latin authors. It is only open to the public on Satur-
days. The founders have free accefs to it at all times.
Others pay a trifle for the loan of the books, and a
forfeit if they be not returned at a ftated time. This
little fund, which is conftantly accumulating, is appropriated to the increafe of the library, to which
have been lately added, in order to make it more
ufeful, fome mathematical and philofophical inftruments, with a very fine cabinet of natural hiftory.

Not far from this there is another monument of the
fame nature. This confifts of a fine collection of
Greek and Latin claffics, with their moft efteemed

commentators, and of the beſt performances that have graced the modern languages. This library was bequeathed to the public, in 1752, by the learned and generous citizen Logan, who had ſpent a long and laborious life in collecting it.

The college, which is intended to prepare the mind for the attainment of all the ſciences, owed its riſe, in 1749, to the labours of Dr. Franklin, whoſe name ſtands always recorded among the great or uſeful things, accompliſhed in this country which gave him birth. At firſt, it only initiated the youth in the belles lettres ; but medicine, chemiſtry, botany, and natural philoſophy, have been ſince taught there. Knowledge of every kind, and maſters in every ſcience, will increaſe, in proportion as the lands, which are become their patrimony, ſhall yield a greater produce. If ever deſpotiſm, ſuperſtition, or war, ſhould plunge Europe again into that ſtate of barbariſm out of which philoſophy and the arts have extricated it, the ſacred fire will be kept alive in Philadelphia, and come from thence to enlighten the world.

This city is amply ſupplied with every aſſiſtance human nature can require, and with all the reſources induſtry can make uſe of. Its quays, the principal of which is two hundred feet wide, preſent a ſuit of convenient warehouſes, and docks ingeniouſly contrived for ſhip building. Ships of five hundred tons may land there without any difficulty, except in times of froſt. There, is taken on board the merchandiſe which has either been brought by the rivers Schuylkill and Delaware, or carried along better roads than are to be met with in moſt parts of Europe. Police has made a greater progreſs in this part of the New World, than among the moſt ancient nations of the Old.

It is impoſſible to determine preciſely the population of Philadelphia, as the bills of mortality are not kept with any exactneſs, and there are ſeveral ſects who do not chriſten their children. It appears, however, that in 1766 it contained 20,000 inhabitants. As moſt of them are employed in the ſale of the productions of the colony, and in supplying it with what they draw from abroad, their fortunes must necessarily be very considerable; and they must increase still further in proportion as the cultivation advances in a country where not above one-sixth of the land has hitherto been cleared.

Philadelphia, as well as the other cities of Pennsylvania, is entirely open. The whole country is equally without defence. This is a necessary consequence of the principles of the Quakers. These sectaries cannot be too much favoured, on account of their modesty, probity, love of labour, and benevolence. One might, perhaps, be tempted to accuse their legislation of imprudence and temerity.

It may, perhaps, be said, that when the founders of the colony established that civil security which protects one citizen from another, they should also have established that political security, which protects one state from the encroachments of another. The authority which hath been exerted to maintain peace and good order at home, seems to have done nothing, if it has not prevented invasion from abroad. To pretend that the colony would never have enemies, was to suppose the world peopled with Quakers. It was encouraging the strong to fall upon the weak, leaving the lamb to the mercy of the wolf, and submitting the whole country to the oppressive yoke of the first tyrant who should think proper to subdue it.

But on the other hand, how shall we reconcile the strictness of the gospel maxims, by which the Quakers are literally governed, with those military preparations, either offensive or defensive, which maintain a continual state of war between all Christian nations? Besides, what could the enemy do, if they were to enter Pennsylvania sword in hand? Unless they massacred, in the space of a night or a day's time, all the inhabitants of that fortunate region, they would not be able totally to extirpate the race of those mild and charitable men. Violence has its boundaries in its very excess; it is consumed and ex-

BOOK
XVIII.
tinguiſhed, as the fire in the aſhes that feed it. But virtue, when guided by humanity and by the ſpirit of benevolence, is revived as the tree under the edge of the pruning-knife. The wicked ſtand in need of numbers to execute their ſanguinary projects. But the Quaker, who is a good man, wants only a brother from whom he may receive, or to whom he may give aſſiſtance. Let then the warlike nations, let people who are either ſlaves or tyrants, go into Pennſylvania; there they will find all avenues open to them, all property at their diſpoſal; not a ſingle ſoldier, but numbers or merchants and farmers. But if theſe inhabitants be tormented, reſtrained, or oppreſſed, they will fly, and leave their lands uncultivated, their manufactures deſtroyed, and their warehouſes empty. They will cultivate, and ſpread population in ſome new land; they will go round the world rather than turn their arms againſt their purſuers, or ſubmit to bear their yoke. Their enemies will have only gained the hatred of mankind, and the execration of poſterity.

May I not be deceived in what I have advanced; and may I not have miſtaken the wiſhes of my heart for a decree of truth! I am diſtreſſed even at the bare ſuſpicion. Fortunate and wiſe country! art thou then one day to experience the fatal deſtiny of other countries? art thou to be ravaged and ſubdued as they have been? Far be it from me to entertain a preſage that might tend to invalidate, in my mind, the moſt comfortable of all ideas; that there exiſts a providence who watches over the preſervation of the good! Nor let the numerous events which ſeem to depoſe the contrary have any influence over me!

It is upon this proſpect that the Pennſylvanians have founded their opinion of their future ſecurity. Beſides, as they do not perceive that the moſt warlike ſtates are the moſt permanent; that miſtruſt, which is ever upon its guard, makes men reſt with greater tranquillity, or that there can be any ſatisfaction in the poſſeſſion of any thing that is kept with ſuch apprehenſions ; they enjoy the preſent moment without B O O K any concern for the future.   The people of Maryland XVIII. are of a different opinion.

    Charles the Firſt, far from having any averſion for Origin of the Catholics, as his predeceſſors, had ſome reaſon to Maryland. Nature of protect them, from the zeal which, in hopes of being its govern- tolerated, they had ſhown for his intereſt.   But when ment. the accuſation of being favourable to popery had alienated the minds of the people from that weak prince, whoſe chief aim was to eſtabliſh a deſpotic government, he was obliged to give the Catholics up to the rigour of the laws enacted againſt them by Henry the Eighth.   Theſe circumſtances induced Lord Baltimore to ſeek an aſylum in Virginia, where he might be indulged in a liberty of conſcience.   As he found there no toleration for an excluſive ſyſtem of faith, which was itſelf intolerant, he formed the deſign of a new ſettlement in that uninhabited part of the country which lay between the river of Potowmack and Pennſylvania.   His death, which happened ſoon after he had obtained powers from the crown for peopling this land, put a ſtop to the project for that time ; but it was reſumed, from the ſome religious motives, by his ſon.   This young nobleman left England in the year 1633, with two hundred Roman Catholics, moſt of them of good families.   The education they had received, the cauſe of religion for which they had left their country, and the fortune which their leader promiſed them, prevented thoſe diſturbances which are but too common in infant ſettlements.   The neighbouring ſavages, won by mildneſs and acts of beneficence, concurred with eagerneſs to aſſiſt the new coloniſts in forming their ſettlement.   With this unexpected help, theſe fortunate perſons, attached to each other by the ſame principles of religion, and directed by the prudent councils of their chief, applied themſelves unanimouſly to every kind of uſeful labour : the view of the peace and happineſs they enjoyed, invited among them a number of men who were either perſecuted

BOOK
XVIII.
for the fame religion, or for different opinions. The Catholics of Maryland gave up at length the intolerant principles, of which they themfelves had been the victims, after having firft fet the example of them, and opened the doors of their colony to all fects, of what religious principles foever. They all enjoyed the rights of a city in the fame extent ; and the government was modelled upon that of the mother-country.

Thefe wife precautions, however, did not fecure Baltimore, at the time of the fubverfion of the monarchy, from lofing all the conceffions he had obtained. Deprived of his poffeffions by Cromwell, he was reftored to them by Charles the Second ; after which they were again difputed with him. Though he was perfectly clear from any reproach of mal adminiftration ; and though he was extremely zealous for the Tramontane doctrines, and much attached to the interefts of the Stuarts ; yet he had the mortification of finding the legality of his charter attacked under the arbitrary reign of James II. and of being obliged to maintain an action at law for the jurifdiction of a province which had been ceded to him by the crown, and which he himfelf had formed at his own expence. This prince, whofe misfortune it had always been not to diftinguifh his friends from his foes, and who had alfo the ridiculous pride to think that regal authority was fufficient to juftify every act of violence, was preparing a fecond time to deprive Baltimore of what had been given him by the two kings, his father and brother, when he was himfelf removed from the throne which he was fo unfit to fill. The fucceffor of this weak defpotic prince terminated this conteft, which had arifen before his acceffion to the crown, in a manner worthy of his political character : he left the Baltimores in poffeffion of their revenues, but deprived them of their authority. When this family, who were more regardlefs of the prejudices of religion, became members of the church of England, they were rein-

stated in the hereditary government of Maryland; B O O K
they began again to conduct the colony, assisted by XVIII.
a council, and two deputies chosen by each district.

Fortunately for itself, Maryland hath been less fruit- Events
ful in events than any other settlement formed in the which have
happened
northern continent. There are only two facts worthy at Mary-
of being recorded in its history. land.

Berkley, extravagantly zealous for the church of
England, expelled from Virginia those among its inhabitants who did not profess this mode of worship;
and they were obliged to seek an asylum in the province we are now speaking of. The Virginians were
highly incensed at the favourable reception which
these people met with; and in the first rage of an
unjust resentment, they persuaded the savages that
their new neighbours were Spaniards. This odious
name entirely changed the sentiments of the Indians;
and, without deliberation, they ravaged the grounds
which they had assisted in clearing; and massacred,
without mercy, those very men whom they had just
received in a brotherly manner. It required a great
deal of time, and patience, and many sacrifices, before these prejudiced minds could be convinced of
their mistake.

Baltimore, attending more to his reason than to the
prejudices of education, granted an equal share in the
government to every different professor of Christianity.
The Catholics were excluded from it, at the memorable period when this nobleman was deprived of his
authority. The British ministry either could not, or
would not, put a stop to this act of fanaticism. It exerted its influence only in preventing the founders of
the colony from being driven out of it, and the penal
laws, which were not even attended to in England,
from being enforced.

The province is very well watered. A number of Present
springs are found in it, and it is intersected by five na- state of
Maryland.
vigable rivers. The air, which is much too damp up- Its cultures.
on the coasts, becomes pure, light, and thin, in propor-

B O O K tion as the foil becomes more elevated. Spring and
XVIII. autumn are moft agreeably temperate; but in the
winter there are fome exceedingly cold days; and in
fummer, fome in which the heat is very troublefome.
The circumftance, however, which is the leaft fupportable in this country, is the great quantity of difgufting infects that are found there.

Maryland is one of the fmalleft provinces of North
America; and accordingly, grants have been made of
almoft all the territory, both in the plains and upon
the mountains. They remained for a long time either
fallow, or very ill cultivated; but the labours have increafed, fince the population, according to the calculation of congrefs, hath amounted to three hundred
and twenty thoufand inhabitants.

Several of thefe are Catholics, and a great many
more are Germans. Their manners have more mild-
nefs than energy; and this may arife from the women
not being excluded from fociety, as in moft of the
other parts of the continent. The men who are free,
and not very rich, who are fettled upon the high
grounds, and who originally bred no flocks, cut no
wood, and cultivated no corn, but for the ufe of the
colony, have gradually furnifhed a great quantity of
thefe articles to the Weft Indies. The profperity,
however, of the colony, hath been more particularly
owing to the flaves employed at a greater or lefs diftance from the fea, in the plantations of tobacco.

This is a fharp cauftic plant; formerly much ufed,
as it ftill is, fometimes in medicine, which, if taken in-
wardly, in fubftance, is a real poifon, more or lefs active, according to the dofe. It is chewed, fmoked in
the leaves, and is in more general ufe as fnuff.

It was difcovered in the year 1520, near Tabafco,
in the Gulf of Mexico, from whence it was carried to
the neighbouring iflands. It was foon after introduced in our climates, where the ufe of it became a matter of difpute among the learned, which even the ignorant took a part in; and thus tobacco acquired ce-

lebrity.   By degrees fashion and custom have greatly B O O K
extended its consumption in all parts of the known   XVIII.
world.

The stem of this plant is straight, hairy, and viscous.
It is three or four feet high. Its leaves, equally downy,
and disposed alternately on the stem, are thick, pulpy,
of a pale green, broad, oval, terminating in a point,
and much larger at the foot than at the summit of
the plant. This summit branches out into clusters of
flowers of a light purple hue. Their tubular calix,
which hath five indentations, encloses a corolla, length-
ened out in form of a funnel, spread out at the top,
divided into five parts, and furnished with as many
stamina. The pistil, concealed at the bottom of the
flower, and terminated by a single style, becomes, as it
ripens, a capsula, with two cavities filled with small
seeds.

Tobacco requires a moderately binding soil, but
rich, even, deep, and not too much exposed to inundations. A virgin soil is very proper for this plant,
which absorbs a great deal of moisture.

The seeds of the tobacco are sown upon beds.
When it is grown to the height of two inches, and
hath got at least half a dozen leaves, it is gently pulled up in damp weather, and transplanted, with great
care, into a well-prepared soil, where the plants are
placed at the distance of three feet from each other.
When they are put into the ground with these precautions, their leaves do not suffer the least injury;
and all their vigour is renewed in four-and-twenty
hours.

The cultivation of tobacco requires continual attention. The weeds which grow round it must be
plucked up; the top of it must be cut off, when it is
two feet and a half from the ground, to prevent it
from growing too high; it must be stripped of all
sprouting suckers; the leaves which grow too near
the bottom of the stem, those that are in the least inclined to decay, and those which the insects have
touched, must all be taken off, and their number re-

BOOK XVIII. duced to eight or ten at moſt. One induſtrious man is able to take care of two thouſand ſix hundred plants, which ought to yield one thouſand weight of tobacco.

The plant is left about four months in the ground. As it advances to maturity, the pleaſant and lively green colour of its leaves is changed into a darker hue ; the leaves are alſo curved, the ſcent of them grows ſtronger, and extends to a diſtance. The plant is then ripe, and muſt be cut up.

The plants, when collected, are laid in heaps upon the ground that produced them, where they are left to exude only for one night. The next day they are laid in warehouſes, conſtructed in ſuch a manner that the air may have free acceſs to them on all ſides. Here they are left ſeparately ſuſpended as long a time as is neceſſary to dry them properly. They are then ſpread upon hurdles, and well covered over, where they ferment for a week or two. At laſt they are ſtripped of their leaves, which are either put into barrels, or made up into rolls. The other methods of preparing the plant, which vary according to the different taſtes of the ſeveral nations that uſe it, have nothing to do with its cultivation.

The inhabitants of the Eaſt Indies, and of Africa, cultivate tobacco only for their own uſe. They neither ſell nor purchaſe any.

Salonica is the great mart for tobacco in the Levant. Syria, the Morea, or the Peloponneſus, and Egypt, ſend there all their ſuperfluous quantity. From this port it is ſent to Italy, where it is ſmoked, after it hath been mixed with the tobacco of Dalmatia and Croatia, to ſoften its cauſtic quality.

The tobacco of theſe two laſt provinces is of a very excellent kind ; but it is ſo ſtrong, that it cannot be uſed till mixed with a milder ſort.

The tobacco of Hungary would be tolerably good, if it had not generally a ſmell of ſmoke which is very diſguſting.

The Ukraine, Livonia, Pruſſia, and Pomerania, cultivate a tolerably large quantity of this production. Its leaves are wider than they are long, are very thin, and have neither flavour nor confiftence. In order to improve it, the court of Ruffia hath caufed fome tobacco feeds, brought from Virginia and from Hamersfort, to be fown in their colonies of Sarratow, upon the Volga; but this experiment hath been attended with little or no fuccefs.

The tobacco of the Palatinate is very indifferent; but it hath the property of mixing with a better kind, and of acquiring its flavour.

Holland alfo furnifhes tobacco. That which is produced in the province of Utrecht, from Hamersfort, and from four or five neighbouring diftricts, is of a fuperior quality. Its leaves are large, fupple, oily, and of a good colour. It hath the uncommon advantage of communicating its delicious perfume to tobacco of an inferior quality. There is a great deal of this latter fort upon the territories of the Republic; but the fpecies which grows in Guelderland is the worft of any.

Tobacco was formerly cultivated in France, and with more fuccefs than any where elfe, near Pont de l'Arche in Normandy, at Verton in Picardy, and at Montauban, Tonneins, and Cleral, in Guyenne. It was prohibited in 1721, except upon fome frontier towns, whofe original terms of capitulation it was not thought proper to infringe. Hainault, Artois, and Franche Compté, profited very little from a liberty which the nature of their foil did not allow them to make ufe of. It has been more ufeful to Flanders and Alface; for their tobaccos, though very weak, may be mixed, without inconvenience, with others of a fuperior kind.

In the beginning, the iflands of the New World attended to the culture of tobacco; but it was fuccefsively fucceeded by richer productions in them all, except at Cuba, which fupplies all the fnuff confumed by the Spaniards of both hemifpheres. Its perfume is exquifite, but too ftrong. The fame crown derives from Caraccas the tobacco which is fmoked by its subjects in Europe. It is likewife ufed in the North, and in Holland, becaufe there is none to be found any where to be compared with it, for this purpofe.

The Brazils cultivated this production very early, and have not fince difdained it. They have been encouraged in this purfuit, by the conftant repute which their tobacco hath enjoyed upon the weftern coafts of Africa. Even in our climates, it is in tolerable requeft among perfons who fmoke. It could not be taken in fnuff, on account of its acrimony, without the preparations which it undergoes. Thefe preparations confift in foaking every leaf in a decoction of tobacco, and of gum copal. Thefe leaves, thus fteeped, are formed into rolls, and wrapped up in the fkin of an ox, which keeps up their moifture.

But the beft tobaccos upon the face of the earth grow in the North of America; and in that part of the New World, the tobacco gathered at Maryland is of the fecond fort. This plant has not, however, an equal degree of perfection throughout the whole extent of the colonies. That of the growth of Chefter and of Chouptan, refembles the Virginia tobacco in quality, and is confumed in France. That which grows in Patapfifco and Potuxant, which is very fit for fmoking, is confumed in the North, and in Holland. Upon the northern fhores of the Potowmack, the tobacco is excellent in the higher parts, and of moderate quality in the lower ones.

Saint Mary, formerly the capital of the ftate, is of no confequence at prefent; and Annapolis, which now enjoys this prerogative, is fcarce more confiderable. It is at Baltimore that almoft all the bufinefs is transacted, the harbour of which can receive fhips that draw feventeen feet of water. Thefe three towns, the only ones which are in the colony, are fituated upon the bay of Chefapeak, which runs two hundred and fifty miles up the country, and the mean breadth of which is twelve miles. There are two capes at its entrance; and in the middle is a fand bank. The channel which

is near Cape Charles can admit none but very small
veffels, while that which runs along-fide Cape Henry
admits the largeft fhips at any feafon of the year.

Few of the lands between the Apalachian mountains and the fea are fo good as thofe of Maryland.
Thefe, however, are in general too light, fandy, and
fhallow, to reward the planter for his labour and expences, in as fhort a time as in our climates. Fertility, which always attends the firft clearing of the foil,
is rapidly followed by an extraordinary decreafe in the
quantity and quality of the corn. The foil is ftill fooner exhaufted by the culture of tobacco. This leaf
lofes much of its ftrength, whenever the fame fpot
hath yielded, without intermiffion, a few crops of tobacco. For this reafon, infpectors were created in
1733, who were empowered to caufe all the tobacco
to be burnt which had not the proper flavour. This
was a prudent inftitution ; but it feems to foretel, that
the moft important production of the province muft
one day be given up, or that it will infenfibly be reduced to very little.

Then, or perhaps before, the iron mines, which are
in great abundance in the colony, will be worked.
This is a fource of profperity which hath not hitherto
been carried beyond the ufe of feventeen or eighteen
forges. A greater degree of liberty, and new wants,
will communicate more ftrength and more activity to
the colonifts.

Other manufactures will alfo undoubtedly arife.
Maryland had never any of any kind. It received
from Great Britain all the articles it wanted for the
moft ordinary purpofes of life. This was one of the
reafons which occafioned its being burdened with
debts. Mr. Stirenwith hath at length eftablifhed manufactures for ftockings, for filk, woollen, and cotton
ftuffs, and for all kinds of hardware, even fire-arms.
Thefe branches of induftry, at prefent united in one
manufacture, at a confiderable expence, and with extraordinary fagacity, will be more or lefs rapidly dif-

In what
manner
Virginia
was efta-
blifhed,
and by
whom.

perfed throughout the province; and, croffing the Potowmack, will be likewife adopted at Virginia.

This other colony, with the fame kind of foil and of climate as Maryland, hath a few advantages over the latter. Its extent is much more confiderable. Its rivers can admit larger fhips, and allow them a longer navigation. Its inhabitants have a more elevated turn of mind, have more refolution, and are more enter-prifing : this may be attributed to their being gene-rally of Englifh extraction.

Virginia was, about two centuries ago, the only country which England intended to occupy on the continent of North America. This name doth not at prefent belong to any thing more than the fpace which is bounded by Maryland on one fide, and by Carolina on the other.

The Englifh landed upon thefe favage fhores in 1606, and their firft fettlement was James Town. Unfortunately, the object that firft prefented itfelf to them was a rivulet, which, iffuing from a fand-bank, carried along with it a quantity of talc, which glitter-ed at the bottom of a clear and running water. In an age when gold and filver were the only objects of men's refearches, this defpicable fubftance was imme-diately taken for filver. The firft and only employ-ment of the new colonifts was to collect it ; and the illufion was carried fo far, that two fhips, which ar-rived there with neceffaries, were fent home fo fully freighted with thefe imaginary riches, that there fcarce remained any room for a few furs. As long as this infatuation lafted, the colonifts difdained to employ themfelves in clearing the lands ; fo that a dreadful famine was at length the confequence of this foolifh pride. Sixty men only remained alive out of five hun-dred who had been fent from Europe. Thefe unfor-tunate few, having only a fortnight's provifion left, were upon the point of embarking for Newfoundland, when Lord Delaware arrived there with three fhips, a frefh colony, and fupplies of all kinds.

Hiſtory has deſcribed this nobleman to us as a man whoſe genius raiſed him above the common prejudices of the times. His diſintereſtedneſs was equal to his knowledge. In accepting the government of the colony, which was ſtill in its infancy, he had no motive but to gratify the inclination a virtuous mind has to do good, and to ſecure the eſteem of poſterity, which is the ſecond reward of that generoſity that devotes itſelf totally to the ſervice of the public. As ſoon as he appeared, the knowledge of his character procured him univerſal reſpect. He firſt endeavoured to reconcile the wretched coloniſts to their fatal country, to comfort them in their ſufferings, and to make them hope for a ſpeedy concluſion of them. After this, joining the firmneſs of an enlightened magiſtrate to the tenderneſs of a good father, he taught them how to direct their labours to an uſeful end. Unfortunately for the reviving colony, Delaware's declining health ſoon obliged him to return to Europe; but he never loſt ſight of his favourite coloniſts, nor ever failed to make uſe of all his credit and intereſt at court to ſupport them.

The colony, however, made but little progreſs; a circumſtance that was attributed to the oppreſſion of excluſive privileges. The company which exerciſed them was diſſolved upon Charles the Firſt's acceſſion to the throne. Before that period, all the authority had been entirely in the hands of the monopoly. Virginia then came under the immediate direction of the crown, which exacted no more than a rent of two livres five ſols [1s. 10½d.] upon every hundred acres that were cultivated.

Till this time the coloniſts had known no true enjoyment of property. Every individual wandered where chance directed him, or fixed himſelf in the place he liked beſt, without conſulting any titles or agreements. At length boundaries were aſcertained; and thoſe who had been ſo long wanderers, now become citizens, had determined limits to their plantations. The eſtabliſhment of this firſt law of ſociety

BOOK
XVIII.
changed the appearance of every thing. Freſh plantations aroſe on all ſides. This activity drew great
numbers of enterpriſing men over to Virginia, who
came either in ſearch of fortune, or of liberty, which
is the only compenſation for the want of it. The memorable troubles that produced a change in the conſtitution of England, added to theſe a multitude of
Royaliſts, who went there with a reſolution to wait,
with Berkley, the governor of the colony, who was
alſo attached to King Charles, the fate of that deſerted
monarch. Berkley ſtill continued to protect them,
even after the king's death; but ſome of the inhabitants, either brought over or bribed, and ſupported by
the appearance of a powerful fleet, delivered up the
colony to the Protector. If the governor was compelled to follow the ſtream againſt his will, he was, at
leaſt, among thoſe whom Charles had honoured with
poſts of confidence and rank, the laſt who ſubmitted
to Cromwell, and the firſt who ſhook off his yoke.
This brave man was ſinking under the oppreſſion of
the times, when the voice of the people recalled him
to the place which his ſucceſſor's death had left vacant; but far from yielding to theſe flattering ſolicita-
tions, he declared that he never would ſerve any but
the legitimate heir of the dethroned monarch. Such
an example of magnanimity, at a time when there
were no hopes of the reſtoration of the royal family,
made ſuch an impreſſion upon the minds of the people, that Charles the Second was proclaimed in Virginia before he had been proclaimed in England.

Obſtacles to
the proſpe-
rity of Vir-
ginia.
The colony did not, however, receive from ſo generous a ſtep all the benefit that might have been expected. The new monarch, either from weakneſs or
corruption, granted to rapacious courtiers immenſe
territories, which abſorbed the poſſeſſions of a great
number of obſcure citizens. The act of navigation,
ſuggeſted by the Protector for the purpoſe of ſecuring
to the mother-country the ſupplying of all their ſettlements in the New World with proviſions, and the
excluſive trade of all their productions, was obſerved

with fuch rigour, as to double almoft the value of the B O O K
articles to be purchafed by Virginia, and leffen ftill XVIII.
more the value of what they had to fell. This double
oppreffion exhaufted all the refources, and difpelled all
the hopes of the colony; and to complete its misfortunes, the favages attacked it with a degree of fpirit
and fkill which they had not manifefted in any of the
preceding wars.

Scarce had the Englifh landed in thefe unknown
regions, than they had difpofed the natives againft
them by the difhonefty they had practifed in their exchanges. This fource of difcord might have been put
a ftop to, had the Englifh confented to take Indian
wives, as they were folicited to do. But although
they had not yet any European women with them,
they rejected this connection with difdain. This contempt exafperated the Americans, already alienated
by their want of faith; and they became irreconcileable enemies. Their hatred was manifefted by fecret
affaffinations, and by public hoftilities, and in 1622,
by a confpiracy, in which three hundred and thirty-
four people loft their lives, and which would even have
deftroyed the whole colony, had not the commanders
been apprifed of the danger a few hours before the
time appointed for a general maffacre.

Since this act of treachery, many atrocious ones
have been committed on both fides. Truces between
the two nations were unfrequent, and ill obferved.
The rupture was ufually begun by the Englifh. The
lefs profit they drew from their plantations, the more
artifice and force did they employ to deprive the favages of their furs. This infatiable avidity, which indifcriminately feized upon all the inhabitants, whether
fettled or wandering, in the neighbourhood of the colony, made the Americans again take up arms towards
the end of the year 1675. They all, by agreement,
fell upon the fettlements, imprudently difperfed, and
at too great a diftance to afford each other any affiftance.

Such a complication of misfortunes drove the Vir-

BOOK ginians to defpair. Berkley, who had fo long been
XVIII. their idol, was accufed of wanting fortitude to refift
the oppreffions of the mother-country, and activity to
repel the irruptions of the favages. The eyes of all
were immediately fixed upon Bacon, a young officer,
full of vivacity, eloquence, and intrepidity, of an infinuating difpofition, and an agreeable perfon. They
chofe him for their general, in an irregular and tumultuous manner. Though his military fucceffes might
have juftified this prepoffeffion of the licentious multitude, yet this circumftance did not prevent the governor, who, with his remaining partifans, had retired
on the borders of the Potowmack, from declaring Bacon a traitor to his country. A fentence fo fevere, and
which was ill-timed, determined Bacon to affume a
power by force, which he had exercifed peaceably,
and without oppofition, for fix months. Death put
an end to all his projects. The malecontents, difunited
by the lofs of their chief, and intimidated by the troops
which were coming from Europe, were induced to fue
for pardon, which was readily granted them. The rebellion, therefore, was attended with no bad confequences, and mercy enfured fubmiffion.

Tranquillity was no fooner reftored, than means
were thought of to reconcile the Indians, with whom
all intercourfe had for fome time been at an end. The
communications were opened again in the year 1678,
by the general affembly; but it was ftipulated, that
the exchanges fhould be made in no other markets,
except fuch as were fettled by themfelves. This innovation difpleafed the favages; and matters foon returned to their former courfe.

The raifing of the value of tobacco was a ftill more
important object, as this was the moft confiderable,
and almoft the only production of the colony. It was
thought that nothing would contribute more effectually to raife it from the ftate of degradation into which
it had fallen, than to refufe the tobaccos which were
brought to Virginia from Maryland and from Carolina, and to fend them to Europe. If the legiflators

had been better informed, they would have under-BOOK stood, that this staple muft neceffarily, fooner or later, XVIII. draw into their own hands the freight of this commodity, and would make them the arbiters of its price. By fending it away from their ports, through an illjudged motive of avarice, they drew upon themfelves, in all the markets, competitors, who convinced them, by dear-bought experience, of the error of their principles.

Thefe arrangements were fcarcely made, before there arrived a new governor to the colony, in the fpring of 1679. This was Lord Colepepper. The troubles with which this fettlement had been fo recently agitated encouraged him to propofe a law, which fhould condemn to one year's imprifonment, or to a fine of 11,250 livres [468l. 15s.], all thofe citizens who fhould fpeak or write any thing againft their governor; and to three months imprifonment, or to a fine of 2250 livres [93l. 15s.], thofe who fhould fpeak or write againft the members of the council, or againft any other magiftrate.

Was this governor apprehenfive then, that the faults of adminiftration, and the difhonefty of its adminiftrators, fhould be fufpected? In what part of the world would not the fame confequences be drawn from the impofing of filence? Is it praife or cenfure that is feared, when the command for filence is iffued? Thefe prohibitions calumniate the government, if it be good, becaufe they tend to perfuade that it is not fo. But what meafures can be adopted to enforce the obfervance of thefe prohibitions? Can we be ignorant, that it is the nature of man to attempt thofe actions, which, by becoming dangerous, have a fenfe of glory attached to them? To opprefs a man, and to prevent him from murmuring and complaining, is an atrocious act of violence againft which he never fails to revolt. But how will the government difcover thofe who are rebellious to their orders? This can only be done by fpies, by informations, and by all thofe meafures which will certainly divide the citizens, and raife miftruft and

BOOK
XVIII.

hatred among them. Whom will government punifh?
The moft honeft and the moft generous men, who will
never be filent when they are perfuaded that it is their
duty to fpeak out. They will certainly bid defiance
to menaces, or will know how to elude them. If they
fhould adopt the firft of thefe refolutions, will government dare to imprifon them? and if it fhould, would
they not foon find perfons to avenge them? If it
fhould not, they would fall into contempt. If thefe
men had been allowed to explain themfelves with
franknefs, they would have blended dignity and moderation in their remonftrances. Conftraint, and the
danger of punifhment, will transform thefe remonftrances into violent, bitter, and feditious libels; and
it is the tyranny of government that will have rendered them guilty. Sovereigns, or you who are depofitaries of their authority, if your adminiftration be a
good one, deliver it up to all the feverity of our examination; it can only enfure our refpect and fubmiffion. If it be a bad one, correct it, or defend it by
force. If you be a fet of abominable tyrants, have at
leaft the courage to acknowledge it. If you be juft,
let the people talk and fleep in peace. If you be oppreffors, tranquillity and fleep are not made for you,
nor will you ever enjoy them, notwithftanding all your
efforts. Remember the fate of him who was willing
to be hated, provided he might be feared. You will
certainly experience the fame, unlefs you be furrounded by vile flaves, fuch as the inhabitants of Virginia
at that time undoubtedly were. The reprefentatives
of this province granted, without hefitation, their confent to a law, which fecured impunity to all the plunders of their governors. The misfortunes of Virginia
were foon aggravated by other calamities.

At the origin of the colony, juftice was adminiftered
with a degree of difinterestednefs which warranted the
equity of the judgments. One fingle court took cognizance of all differences, and decided upon them in a
few days, with a right of appeal to the general affembly, which ufed as much difpatch in fettling them.

This order of things gave the governors too little in- B O O K
fluence over the fortunes of individuals, for them not XVIII.
to endeavour to fuppreſs it. By their manœuvres, and
under feveral pretences, they obtained that the appeals, which till then had been carried before the reprefentatives of the province, fhould be made exclufively to their council.

A ſtill more fatal innovation was ordained in 1692
by another governor, who enacted, that the laws, the
tribunals, the formalities, every thing, in a word, that
contributed to form the chaos of Engliſh jurifpru-
dence, ſhould be eſtabliſhed in his government. Nothing was leſs ſuitable to the planters of Virginia, than
ſtatutes ſo ſingular, ſo complicated, and often ſo contradictory. Accordingly, theſe uninformed men found
themfelves engaged in a labyrinth to which they could
find no iſſue. They were generally alarmed for their
rights and their properties; and this apprehenſion
ſlackened their labours for a long time.

Theſe were not carried on with vigour and ſucceſs,
till after the beginning of the century, at which time
nothing impeded their increaſe; only the frontiers of
the colony were expoſed in the latter times to the de-
vaſtations of the ſavages, whom they had exaſperated
by their acts of atrociouſneſs and injuſtice. Theſe differences were terminated in 1774. They would have
been forgotten, had it not been for the ſpeech made
by Logan, chief of the Shawaneſes, to Lord Dunmore,
governor of the province.

" I now aſk of every white mane, whether he hath
" ever entered the cottage of Logan, when preſſed
" with hunger, and been refuſed food? Whether com-
" ing naked, and ſhivering with cold, Logan hath not
" given him ſomething to cover himſelf with. During
" the courſe of this laſt war, ſo long and ſo bloody,
" Logan hath remained quietly upon his mat, wiſhing
" to be the advocate of peace. Yes, ſuch is my at-
" tachment for white men, that even thoſe of my na-
" tion, when they paſſed by me, pointed at me, ſay-
" ing, *Logan is a friend to white men.* I had even

" thought of living amongft you; but that was before
" the injury which I have received from one of you.
" Laft fummer, Colonel Creffop maffacred in cool blood,
" and without any provocation, all the relations of Lo-
" gan, without fparing either his wife or his children.
" There is not now one drop of my blood in the veins
" of any human creature exifting. This is what has
" excited my revenge. I have fought it; I have kill-
" ed feveral of your people, and my hatred is appeaf-
" ed. I rejoice at feeing the profpect of peace bright-
" en upon my country. But do not imagine that my
" joy is inftigated by fear. Logan knows not what
" fear is. He will never turn his back, in order to fave
" his life. But, alas! no one remains to mourn for
" Logan when he fhall be no more!"

What a beautiful, fimple, energetic, and affecting
fpeech! Are Demofthenes, Cicero, or Boffuet, more
eloquent than this favage? What better proof can
be adduced of the truth of that well-known maxim,
which fays, that *from the abundance of the heart the
mouth fpeaks.*

Population,
trade, and
manners of
Virginia.
Virginia, like moft of the other colonies, was inhabited at firft only by vagabonds, deftitute of family
and fortune. They foon obtained fome kind of wealth
by labour, and they were defirous of fharing the fweets
of it with a female companion. As there were no
women in the province, and that they would have
none but fuch as were decent, they gave 2250 livres
[93*l.* 15s.] for every young perfon brought them from
Europe with a certificate of virtue and chaftity. This
cuftom was not of long duration. As foon as all
doubts refpecting the falubrity and fertility of the
country were removed, whole families, even of refpectable rank, went to Virginia. The population
was increafing with fome degree of rapidity, when its
progrefs was ftopped by fanaticifm.

The religion of the mother-country was the firft,
and foon became the only one which was followed
in this province, when fome Non-conformifts alfo
croffed the feas. Their tenets, or their ceremonies,

difgufted ; and in 1624 a law was made, which expel- B O O K led from the province all thofe inhabitants who did XVIII. not belong to the church of England. The imperious law of neceffity foon caufed the revocation of this fatal decree : but a toleration fo tardy, and which was evidently granted with reluctance, did not produce the great effects that were expected from it. A fmall number only of Prefbyterians, Quakers, and French refugees, ventured to put any truft in this repentance. The religion of Henry VIII. continued to be the prevailing one, and was almoft exclufive.

In procefs of time, however, men multiplied upon this foil, the fertility of which was daily increafing in reputation. The paffion for riches with which the Old Continent was more and more infected, gave citizens inceffantly to this part of the New World. If the calculations of congrefs be not exaggerated, the population amounts to fix hundred and fifty thoufand fouls, including the flaves, whofe number, according to the common opinion, amounts to one hundred and fifty thoufand. The Dutch firft introduced thefe unfortunate people into the colony in 1620.

The labours of thefe white men, and of thefe Negroes, give to the two hemifpheres, corn, maize, dry vegetables, iron, hemp, hides, furs, falt meats, tar, wood, mafts, and efpecially tobacco, which is generally fuperior to that of Maryland, though it be not equally excellent in every part of the province. The preference is given to that of York River ; the fecond beft is reckoned to be that which grows along James's River, and that which grows on the borders of the Rappahanoc, and to the fouth of the Potowmack, is the leaft efteemed.

From 1752 till the end of 1755, Great Britain received from Virginia and Maryland together, three million five hundred and one thoufand one hundred and ten quintals of tobacco, which made for each of the four years, eight hundred and feventy-five thoufand two hundred and fourfcore quintals. Virginia exported two million nine hundred and eighty-nine

BOOK thoufand eight hundred quintals, which reduced its an-
XVIII. nual confumption to one hundred and twenty-feven
thoufand eight hundred and thirty quintals.

From the year 1763, till the end of 1770, the two
colonies fent to the mother-country no more than fix
million five hundred thoufand quintals of tobacco, or
eight hundred and twelve thoufand five hundred quintals each of the eight years. No more was fold to
foreigners than five million one hundred and forty-
eight thoufand quintals, or fix hundred and forty-three
thoufand five hundred quintals per annum ; the nation
therefore annually confumed one hundred and fixty-
nine thoufand quintals.

In the interval between thefe two periods the importation, therefore, decreafed annually, one year with
another, fixty-two thoufand feven hundred and fourfcore quintals, and the exportation one hundred and
three thoufand nine hundred and fifty quintals ; while
the confumption in England increafed forty-one thoufand one hundred and feventy quintals every year.

The ufe of tobacco hath not decreafed in Europe ;
the paffion for this fuperfluity hath even increafed, notwithftanding the heavy duties with which it hath been
burdened by all governments. If the tobacco, furnifhed by North America be daily lefs fought after among
us, it is becaufe Holland, Alfatia, the Palatinate, and
principally Ruffia, have carried on this culture with
great induftry.

In 1769, Virginia and Maryland together fold to
the amount of 16,195,577 livres 4 fols 7 deniers [about
674,815l. 14s. 4¼d.] of their productions. Two-thirds
of this fum belonged to the firft of thefe fettlements.
Tobacco was the principal of thefe productions ; fince
one of the colonies exported fifty-feven million three
hundred and thirty-feven thoufand feven hundred and
ninety-five pounds weight of it ; and the other, twenty-
five million feven hundred and eighty-one thoufand
feven hundred and fixty nine pounds weight.

In Virginia, veffels employed for the exportation of
thefe productions do not find them collected in a fmall

number of staples, as in the other commercial states of B O O K
the globe. They are obliged to form their cargo by XVIII.
detail from the plantations themselves, which are situated at a greater or less distance from the ocean, upon
navigable rivers, of one or two hundred miles in length.
This custom fatigues the navigators, and makes their
voyage tedious. Great Britain, which is always attentive to the preservation of her seamen, and is par-
ticulary careful of lessening the number of their voyages, wished, and even ordered, that some towns should
be built at the mouth of the rivers, where the productions of the province might be sent. But neither
insinuations, nor the constraint of the laws, were of
any avail. A few small villages only were built, which
could scarce fulfil even the least part of the views of
the mother-country. Williamsburg itself hath no more
than two thousand inhabitants, though it be the resi-
dence of the governor, the place where the national
assemblies and the courts of justice are holden, and
where colleges are instituted ; though it be decorated
with the finest public edifices on the northern continent ; and though it be the capital of the colony,
since the ruin of James-town.

Men, who prefer the tranquillity of a rural life to
the tumultuous abode of cities, ought naturally to be
economical and laborious ; but this was never the
case in Virginia. Its inhabitants were always very
expensive in the furniture of their houses ; they were
always fond of entertaining their neighbours with ostentation. They always liked to display the greatest
luxury before the English navigators, whom business
brought to their plantations. They always gave themselves up to that effeminacy, and to that negligence, so
common in countries where slavery is established. Accordingly, the engagements of the colony became habitually very considerable. At the beginning of the
troubles, they were supposed to amount to 25,000,000
of livres [1,041,666l. 13s. 4d.]. This prodigious sum
was due to the merchants of Great Britain, for Negroes, or for other articles which they had furnished.

B O O K The confidence of thefe bold lenders was particularly
XVIII. founded upon an unjuſt law, which ſecured their payment in preference to every other debt, though pre-
vioſly contracted.

The colony hath great powers to extricate itſelf
from a ſituation apparently ſo deſperate. It will ſucceed, when more ſimplicity ſhall prevail in the manners, and more moderation in the expences; when
availing itſelf of the reſources offered by an immenſe
and fertile territory, it ſhall vary and improve its cultures; it will ſucceed, when it ſhall no longer receive
from foreigners the moſt ordinary houſehold furniture,
and that which is in moſt general uſe; when its manufactures ſhall no longer be confined to the employing of ſome ſmall quantities of cotton, which is of too
indifferent a quality to be ſought for in the European
manufactures; and when its public coffers, leſs plundered, and better regulated, ſhall admit of the diminution of the taxes, which are much more conſiderable in that province than in any other of this continent. Several of theſe counſels may concern the
two Carolinas.

Origin of
the two
Carolinas.
Their firſt
and their
laſt govern-
ment, both
civil and
religious.

The vaſt country which theſe provinces occupy, was
diſcovered by the Spaniards, ſoon after their firſt expeditions in the New World; they deſpiſed it, becauſe
it did not offer any gold to their avarice. Admiral
Coligny, more wiſe, and more able, opened there a
ſource of induſtry to the French Proteſtants; but fanaticiſm, which purſued them, ruined their hopes by
the aſſaſſination of this juſt, humane, and enlightened man. They were ſucceeded by a few Engliſhmen
towards the end of the ſixteenth century; who by an
inexplicable caprice forſook this infant ſettlement, to
go and cultivate a harſher ſoil, under a leſs temperate
climate.

There was not a ſingle European ſeen in Carolina,
when the lords Berkley, Clarendon, Albemarle, Cra-
ven, Aſhley, and Meſſrs. Carteret, Berkley, and Colle-
ton, obtained from Charles II. in 1663, a grant of
this fine country. The plan of government for this

new colony was drawn up by the famous Locke. A B O O K philofopher, who was a friend to mankind, and to that XVIII. moderation and juftice which fhould be the only rule of their actions, ought to have deftroyed the very foundations of that fanaticifm, which in all countries hath excited divifions among them, and which will induce them to take up arms againft each other to the end of time.

Intoleration, however horrid it may appear to us, is a neceffary confequence of the fpirit of fuperftition. Will it not be acknowledged, that punifhments fhould be proportioned to the nature of offences? What crime then can be greater than that of infidelity, in the eyes of him who confiders religion as the fundamental bafis of morality? According to thefe principles, the irreli- gious man is the common enemy of all fociety; the breaker of the only tie that connects men with each other; the promoter of all the crimes that may efcape the feverity of the laws. It is he who ftifles every re- morfe, who fets the paffions loofe from every reftraint, and who keeps, as it were, a fchool of wickednefs. What! fhall we lead to the gibbet an unfortunate man, whom indigence conceals upon the highway, who rufhes out upon the traveller with a piftol in his hand, and demands a fmall pittance that may be neceffary for the fubfiftence of his wife and children, who may be expiring with mifery; and fhall we pardon a rob- ber infinitely more dangerous? We think meanly of the man who fuffers his friend to be ill fpoken of in his prefence; and fhall we require that the religious man fhall fuffer the infidel to blafpheme his Mafter, his Father, and his Creator with impunity? We muft ei- ther admit that all faith is abfurd, or we muft put up with intoleration as a neceffary evil. Saint Lewis rea- foned very confiftently when he faid to Joinville, *If thou fhouldft ever hear any one fpeak ill of God, draw thy fword and ftab him through the heart; I allow thee to do it.* So important it is in all countries, as we are af- fured is the cafe in China, that fovereigns, and the depofitaries of their authority, fhould not be attached

BOOK to any tenet, to any sect, nor to any form of religious
XVIII. worship.

Every thing induces us to imagine that such was the opinion of Locke. But not daring to attack too openly the prejudices of the times, founded equally on virtues and vices, he wished to conciliate them as much as could ·be consistent with a principle dictated by reason and humanity. As the savage inhabitants of America, said he, have no idea of a revelation, it would be the height of folly to torment them for their ignorance. Those Christians who should come to people the colony, would undoubtedly come in quest of a liberty of conscience, which priests and princes deny them in Europe: it would therefore not be consistent with good faith to persecute, after having received them. The Jews and the Pagans did not more deserve to be rejected, for an infatuation which mildness and persuasion might have put a stop to.

Thus it was that the English philosopher reasoned with men whose minds were imbued and prejudiced with tenets which it had not yet been allowed to discuss. Out of regard to their weakness, he placed the system of toleration which he was establishing under the following restriction: that every person above seventeen years of age, who should claim the protection of the laws, should cause his name to be registered in some communion. This was a breach made in his system. The liberty of conscience admits of no kind of modification. This is an account which man owes to God alone. In whatever manner the magistrate may be made to interfere in it, it is an act of injustice. A Deist could not possibly subscribe to such terms.

Civil liberty, however, was much less favoured by Locke. Whether this proceeded from motives of complaisance for those who employed him, a kind of meanness which we are averse from suspecting him of; or whether, being more of a metaphysician than a statesman, he had pursued philosophy only in those tracts which had been opened by Descartes and Leibnitz, it is certain, that the fame man who had diffipated and deftroyed fo many errors in his theory concerning the origin of ideas, made but very feeble and uncertain advances in the paths of legiflation. The author of a work, the permanency of which will render the glory of the French nation immortal, even when tyranny fhall have broken all the fprings, and all the monuments of the genius of a people efteemed by the whole world for fo many brilliant and amiable qualities; even Montefquieu himfelf did not perceive that he was making men for governments, inftead of governments for men.

The code of Carolina, by a fingularity not to be accounted for in an Englifhman and in a philofopher, gave to the eight proprietors who founded the fettlement, and to their heirs, not only all the rights of fovereignty, but all the powers of legiflation.

The firft ufe thefe fovereigns made of their authority was to create three orders of nobility. Thofe to whom they gave no more than twelve thoufand acres of land were called barons; thofe who received twenty-four thoufand were called caciques, and the title of landgrave was beftowed on thofe two who obtained fourfcore thoufand each. Thefe conceffions could never be alienated in detail, and their fortunate poffeffors were alone to form the houfe of peers. The houfe of commons was compofed of the reprefentatives of the towns and counties, but with privileges lefs confiderable than in the mother-country. The affembly was called a court palatine. Every tenant was obliged to pay annually 1 livre 2 fols 6 deniers [$11\frac{1}{4}$d.] per acre, but he was allowed to redeem this duty.

The progrefs of this great fettlement was for too long a time impeded by powerful obftacles.

The colony had from its origin been open indifcriminately to all fects, which had all enjoyed the fame privileges. It had been underftood, that this was the only way to make an infant ftate acquire rapid and great profperity. The members of the church of England being afterwards jealous of the non-conformifts, wanted to exclude them from government, and even to oblige them to fhut up the houfes where they performed divine fervice. Thefe acts of folly and of violence were annulled in 1706 by the mother-country, as being contrary to humanity, to juftice, to reafon, and to policy. From the collifion of thefe opinions arofe cabals and tumults, which diverted the inhabitants from ufeful labours, and turned their attention to a multitude of abfurdities, which will be never fo much defpifed as they deferve to be.

Two wars, which were carried on againft the favages, were almoft as extravagant and as deftructive of every improvement. All the wandering or fixed nations between the ocean and the Apalachian mountains, were attacked and maffacred without any intereft or motive ; thofe who efcaped being put to the fword, either fubmitted or were difperfed. In the meanwhile, a form of conftitution ill-arranged, was the principal caufe of an almoft general indolence. The lords who were proprietors, imbued with defpotic principles, ufed their utmoft efforts to eftablifh an arbitrary government. The colonifts, on the other hand, who were not ignorant of the rights of mankind, exerted themfelves with equal warmth to avoid fervitude. It was neceffary either to eftablifh a new order of things, or to fuffer, that a vaft country, from which fuch great advantages had been expected, fhould remain in perpetual humiliation, mifery, and anarchy. The Britifh fenate at length took the refolution, in 1728, to reftore this fine country to the nation, and to grant to its firft mafters 540,000 livres [22,500l.] in compenfation. Granville alone, from motives which are unknown to us, was left in poffeffion of his eighth fhare, which was fituated on the confines of Virginia : but even this part was not long before it recovered its independence. The Englifh government, as it was already eftablifhed in the other provinces of the New World, was fubftituted to the whimfical arrangement, which, in times of extreme corruption, had been extorted from an indolent and weak mo-

narch by infatiable favourites. The country might
then expect to profper. It was divided into two diftinct governments, under the names of North and
South Carolina, in order to facilitate the adminiftration of it.

The two countries united occupy more than four
hundred thoufand miles upon the coaft, and about
two hundred thoufand miles in the inland parts. It
is a plain, in general fandy, which is rendered very
marfhy by the overflowing of the rivers, and by heavy
and frequent rains. The foil doth not begin to rife,
till at the diftance of fourfcore or a hundred miles
from the fea; and it continues rifing as far as the A-
palachian mountains. Upon thefe latitudes, and in
the midft of pine-trees, which are irregularly placed
there by nature, a few fheep, extremely degenerated,
both in their flefh and in their fleece, feed upon a
ftrong and coarfe grafs; there are alfo a number of
horned cattle, who have not preferved all their ftrength
and all their beauty; and an innumerable quantity
of hogs, who appear to have improved.

The country is watered by a great number of rivers, fome of which are navigable. They would be
fo for a longer fpace, were it not for the rocks and
the water-falls which interrupt the navigation.

Though the climate be as variable as the reft of
North America, it is commonly agreeably temperate.
A piercing cold is never felt but in the evening and
morning, and there are feldom any exceffive heats.
Though fogs be frequent, they are at leaft difpelled in
the middle of the day. Unfortunately, in the months
of July, Auguft, September, and October, intermittent fevers prevail in the plains, and are fometimes
fatal to the natives themfelves, and, too often, deftroy
foreigners.

Such is the natural organization of the two Carolinas; let us fee what diftinguifhes them from each
other.

North Carolina is one of the largeft provinces of
the continent; it unfortunately doth not offer advan-

tages proportioned to its extent.   Its foil is generally
flatter, more fandy, and more marfhy, than that of
South Carolina.   Thefe melancholy plains are covered with pines or cedars, which announce a barren foil;
and are interfected at intervals by a fmall number of
oaks, too full of fap to be employed in the conftruction of fhips.   The coafts, generally blocked up by
a fand bank, which keeps navigators at a diftance,
are not more favourable to population than the inland countries.   Finally, the country is more expofed than the neighbouring regions to the hurricanes
that come from the fouth-eaft.

Thefe were undoubtedly the motives which prevented the Englifh of North Carolina from fettling
there, though that country was the firft which they
difcovered in the New World.   None of the numerous people who were driven to that part of the hemifphere, either from inclination or neceffity, carried
there their mifery or their reftleffnefs.   It was long
after, that a few vagabonds, without friends, without
laws, and without plan to fix themfelves, fettled there.
But, in procefs of time, the lands in the other colonies
became fcarce, and then men who were not able to
purchafe them, betook themfelves to a country where
they could get lands without purchafe.   According to
the account of congrefs, three hundred thoufand fouls,
in which few flaves are included, are ftill found in the
province.   There are but few of thefe inhabitants
which are either Englifh, Irifh, or German.   Moft of
them are of Scotch origin, and for this reafon :

Thefe Highlanders, whofe character has been fo
boldly defcribed by a mafterly hand, were never enflaved either by the Romans, the Saxons, or the
Danes.   They bravely repulfed every invafion, and
no foreign cuftoms could penetrate beyond the foot
of their inacceffible habitations.   Separated from the
reft of the globe, they difplayed in their manners the
politenefs of courts, without having any of their vices;
their countenance fhowed the pride with which the
nobility of their origin had infpired them ; and they

were poffeffed of all the delicacy of our point of ho- B O O K
nour, but without its fufpicious minutiæ. As induftry XVIII.
had not transformed them into mere machines, and as
the nature of their foil and climate did not require the
labours of the fields for more than two feafons in the
year, they had a great deal of leifure time, which they
employed in war, in hunting, in dancing, or in converfations animated by picturefque expreffions, and
original ideas. Moft of them were muficians. Schools
were every where opened for the inftruction of youth.
Under every roof was found one hiftorian, to recal to
their minds great events, and a poet to celebrate them.
The lakes, the forefts, the caves, the cataracts, the ma-
jeftic grandeur of all the objects that furrounded them,
infpired them with an elevation of mind, caft a fhade
of melancholy over their characters, and kept up in
their hearts a facred enthufiafm. Thefe people efteemed themfelves, without defpifing other nations. Their
afpect ftruck the civilized man with awe, in whom
they only beheld one of their equals, whatever title
he might be decorated with. They received all foreigners who came to them with a fimple and cordial
affection. They kept a long time in their memory a
refentment for any injury offered to any of them;
which was rendered common to them all by the ties
of blood. After an engagement they dreffed their
enemies wounds before their own. As they were always armed, the habitual ufe of deftructive weapons
prevented them from having any fear of them. They
believed in fpirits; and if the lightning fhone during
the night, if thunder rolled over their heads, if the
ftorm rooted up the trees around their houfes, or
fhook their roofs, they imagined that it was fome forgotten hero reproaching them for their filence: they
then took up their inftruments, and fang a hymn to
his honour; they affured him that his memory would
never be forgotten among the children of men. They
believed in prefages and in divination. They all fubmitted to the eftablifhed form of worfhip; fuperftition

never excited quarrels among them, nor caufed the effufion of one drop of blood.

Thefe manners were never altered ; nor could they
be fo. The Scotch formed a great number of tribes,
called *clans ;* each of which bore a different name, and
lived upon the eftate of fome particular lord. It was
the hereditary patriarch of a family, from whom they
all claimed their defcent, and they all knew to what
degree.

The caftle was in fome meafure a common property, where every perfon was fure of meeting with an
honourable reception, and where they all reforted upon the firft rumour of war. They all revered their
own dignity in their chief ; they had a brotherly affection for the other members of the confederation.
They all patiently fupported their fate, becaufe it never had any thing humiliating in it. The head of the
clan, on his fide, was the common father of them all,
as well from gratitude as from intereft.

This order of things fubfifted during a long feries of
ages without the leaft alteration. At laft the noblemen contracted the habit of fpending a great part of
their lives in travelling, at London, or at court. Thefe
repeated abfences detached from them their vaffals,
who faw them lefs frequently, and were no longer affifted by them. Thefe men, who were no longer reftrained by any tie of affection in their barren and favage mountains, then difperfed themfelves. Several
of them went in fearch of another country in divers
provinces of America. The greateft number took refuge in North Carolina.

Thefe colonifts are feldom affembled together, and
they are therefore the leaft informed of the Americans,
and the moft indifferent to the public intereft. Moft
of them live difperfed upon their plantations, without
ambition or forefight. They are but little inclined to
labour, and they are feldom good planters. Though
they have the Englifh form of government, the laws
have very little force among them. Their domeftic

are better than their social manners; and there is B O O K
scarce an instance of any one of them having had any XVIII.
connection with a slave. Their food consists of pork,
milk, and maize; and they can be accused of no other
kind of intemperance than an inordinate passion for
spirituous liquors.

The first unfortunate people whom chance dispersed along these savage coasts confined themselves to
the cutting of wood, which they delivered to the navigators, who came to purchase it. In a short time
they collected from the pine tree, which covered the
country, turpentine, tar, and pitch. To collect the
turpentine, it was sufficient to make incisions in the
trunk of the tree, which being carried on to the foot
of it, terminated in vessels placed there to receive it.
When they wanted tar, they raised a circular platform
of potter's earth, on which they laid piles of pines; to
these they set fire, and the resin distilled from them
into casks placed underneath. The tar was converted into pitch, either in great iron pots, in which they
boiled it, or in pits formed of potter's earth, into which
it was poured while in a fluid state. In process of
time, the province was enabled to furnish Europe with
hides, a small quantity of wax, a few furs, ten or
twelve millions weight of an inferior kind of tobacco;
and the West Indies, with a great quantity of salt pork,
maize, dried vegetables, a small quantity of indifferent
flour, and several objects of less importance. The exportations of the colony did not, however, exceed
twelve or fifteen hundred thousand livres [from 50,000l.
to 62,500l.].

North Carolina hath not yet attended to the exportation of its own productions. What its soil furnishes
to the New Hemisphere, hath been hitherto taken
away by the navigators of the North of America, who
brought in exchange rum, of which it hath still continued to make an immense consumption. The articles
which the colony delivers to the Old World, have
passed through the hands of the English, who supplied

B O O K it with clothes, inftruments for agriculture, and fome
   XVIII. Negroes.

Through the whole extent of the coafts, there is no
port but that of Brunfwick, which can receive the veffels deftined for thofe tranfactions. Thofe which draw
no more than fixteen feet water anchor at that town,
which is built almoft at the mouth of the river of Cape
Fear, towards the fouthern extremity of the province.
Wilmington, its capital, fituated higher up upon the
fame river, admits only much fmaller veffels.

What di-   South Carolina furnifhes to the trade of both hemi-
ftinguifhes   fpheres as North Carolina, but in lefs quantity. Its
South Ca-
rolina.   labours have been chiefly turned towards rice and indigo.

Rice is a plant very much refembling wheat in fhape
and colour, and in the figure and difpofition of its
leaves. The panicle which terminates the ftem is
compofed of fmall flowers, diftinct from each other,
which have four unequal fcales, fix ftamina, and one
piftil, furrounded with two ftyles. This piftil becomes
a white feed, extremely farinaceous, covered with two
interior fcales, which are larger, yellowifh, covered
with light afperities, and furnifhed with feveral falient
coftæ, the middle one of which terminates in an elon-
gated extremity. This plant thrives only in low, damp,
and marfhy lands, when they are even a little over-
flowed. The period of its difcovery is traced to the
remoteft antiquity.

Egypt, unfortunately for itfelf, firft attended to it.
The pernicious effect of this culture rendered the
country the moft unhealthy in the known world;
conftantly ravaged by epidemical diforders, and afflicted with cutaneous difeafes, which paffed from that
region to the others, where they have been perpetuated during whole centuries, and where they have only been put a ftop to by the contrary caufe to that
which had occafioned them, to wit, the drying up of
the marfhes, and the reftoring of falubrity to the air
and to the waters. China and the Eaft Indies muft

experience the fame calamities, if art doth not oppofe B O O K
prefervatives to nature, whofe benefits are fometimes XVIII.
accompanied with evils, or if the heat of the torrid
zone doth not quickly difpel the damp and malignant
vapours which are exhaled from the rice grounds. It
is a known fact, that in the rice grounds of the Milanefe, the cultivators are all livid and dropfical.

Opinions differ about the manner in which rice hath
been naturalized in Carolina. But whether the province may have acquired it by a fhipwreck, or whether it may have been carried there with flaves, or
whether it be fent from England, it is certain that the
foil feemed favourable for it. It multiplied, however,
very flowly, becaufe the colonifts, who were obliged
to fend their harvefts into the ports of the mother-
country, by which they were fent into Spain and Portugal, where they were confumed, acquired fo fmall a
profit from their productions, that it was fcarcely fufficient to defray the expences of cultivation. In 1730,
a more enlightened adminiftration permitted the direct
exportation of this grain beyond Cape Finifterre. Some
years afterwards it was allowed to be carried to the
Weft Indies; and then the provinces, being fure of
felling the good rice advantageoufly in Europe, and
the inferior or fpoiled rice in America, attended ferioufly to the cultivation of it. This production grows, by
the care of the Negroes, in the moraffes which are
near the coafts. At a great diftance from the ocean,
indigo is cultivated by the fame hands, but with lefs
danger.

This plant, which originally comes from Indoftan,
fucceeded at firft at Mexico, afterwards at the Antil-
les, and laftly in South Carolina. The firft experiments made in this province yielded only a produce
of an exceedingly inferior quality; but this dye acquires daily a greater degree of perfection. Its cultivators do not even defpair of fupplanting, in time, the
Spaniards and the French in all the markets. Their
hopes are founded upon the extent of their foil, upon

B O O K the abundance and the cheapnefs of fubfiftence, and
  XVIII. efpecially upon the cuftom which they have of ploughing their grounds with animals, and of fowing the indigo in them in the fame manner as corn ; while, on
the contrary, in the Weft Indies they are the flaves
who prepare the grounds, and who throw the feed into holes, difpofed at different diftances to receive it.

If, contrary to all probability, this revolution in
trade fhould ever happen, South Carolina, which at
prefent reckons two hundred and fifty thoufand inhabitants, half white people and half Negroes, and the
exportations of which, including thofe of North Carolina, amounted, in the year 1769, to 10,601,336 livres
[44,722l. 6s. 8d.], would foon double its population
and its cultures. It is already the richeft of all the
provinces of the northern continent. Accordingly,
the tafte for the conveniencies of life is generally prevalent, and the expences are carried as far as luxury.
This magnificence was more particularly remarked
fome time ago in the funerals. As many citizens as
it was poffible to colleft were affembled at them ; expenfive difhes were ferved up, and the moft exquifite
wines and the fcarceft liquors were lavifhed. To the
plate which the family had, was added that of the relations, the neighbours, and the friends. It was common to fee fortunes either much encroached upon, or
even deranged, by thefe obfequies. The fanguinary
and ruinous contefts between the mother-country and
the colonies have put a ftop to thefe profufions, but
without abolifhing a cuftom perhaps ftill more extravagant.

From the origin of the fettlement, the minifters of
religion adopted the cuftom of pronouncing indifcriminately, in the churches, an eulogium upon every
one of their flock after death. The praife was never
in proportion to the aftions and virtues of the deceaf-
ed, but to the greater or lefs reward which they were
to receive for the funeral oration. So that while, in
our countries, the Catholic priefts were making a traf-

fic of prayer, the clergy of the church of England B O O K
were carrying on, in the other hemisphere, the more XVIII.
odious traffic of the praises of the dead.

Could there be a more effectual method of degrading virtue, of diminishing the horror of vice, and of corrupting in men's minds the true notions of each? Could there be any thing more scandalous to a whole Christian audience, than the impudence of an orator, of a preacher of the gospel extolling a citizen who had been abhorred for his avarice, his cruelty, and his debauchery; a bad father, an ungrateful son, or married persons who had led a life of dissoluteness; and placing in heaven those whom the Almighty Judge had precipitated into the depth of the infernal regions?

South Carolina hath only three cities worthy of being called so; and these are also ports.

George Town, situated at the mouth of the Black River, is still very inconfiderable; but its situation must render it one day more important.

Beaufort, or Port Royal, will never emerge from a state of mediocrity, though its road be capable of receiving and securing the largest ships.

It is Charlestown, the capital of the colony, which is at present the most important staple, and which must necessarily become still more so.

The channel which leads up to it is full of breakers, and embarrassed with a sand-bank: but with the assistance of a good pilot, a ship arrives safely in the harbour. It can receive three hundred sail; and ships of three hundred and fifty or four hundred tons burden can enter it at all times, with their entire cargo.

The town occupies a great space, at the confluence of the two navigable rivers, Ashley and Cooper. Its streets are very regular, and most of them large; it hath two thousand convenient houses, and a few public buildings, which would be reckoned handsome even in Europe. The double advantage which Charlestown enjoys, of being the staple for the productions of the colony which are to be exported, and of all the foreign merchandise that can be consumed there, keeps up a conftant activity in it, and hath fucceffively been the caufe of making fome confiderable fortunes.

The two Carolinas are ftill very far from attaining to that degree of fplendour to which they have a right to afpire. North Carolina doth not cultivate all the productions of which its foil is fufceptible, and thofe which it feems to attend a little to are in a manner left to chance. The inhabitants of South Carolina are more intelligent and more active: but they have not yet found out, at leaft not fufficiently, how far they might improve their fortune by the culture of the above tree, and of filk. Neither of thefe provinces have cleared one quarter of their territory which may be ufefully employed. This labour is referved for future generations, and for an increafe of population. Then, undoubtedly, fome kind of induftry will be eftablifhed in provinces, where there would not exift the leaft appearance of any, if the French refugees had not brought a linen manufactory to them.

By whom, upon what occafion, and in what manner, Georgia was founded. Between Carolina and Florida, there is a flip of land, which extends fixty miles along the fea-fide, which acquires, by degrees, a breadth of one hundred and fifty miles, and hath three hundred miles in depth, as far as the Apalachian mountains. This country is limited on the North by the Savannah river, and to the South by the river Alatamaha.

The Englifh miniftry had been long defirous of erecting a colony on this tract of country, that was confidered as dependent upon Carolina. One of thofe inftances of benevolence, which liberty, the fource of every patriotic virtue, renders more frequent in England than in any other country, ferved to determine the views of government with regard to this place. A rich and humane citizen, at his death, left the whole of his eftate to fet at liberty fuch infolvent debtors as were detained in prifon by their creditors. Where fhall we find, either in France or in other parts, any perfon who fhall thus propofe to expiate a long abufe of profperity? Several will die, after having fquandered away millions, without being able to recollect one good action they have done. Several will die, and will leave behind them, to heirs who are anxious for their death, treafures acquired by ufury and concuffion, without repairing, by fome honourable and ufeful in-ftitution, the crime of their opulence. Is it then one of the neceffary effects of gold, to harden the heart to the laft, and to ftifle remorfe; fince there is fcarce any man who hath known how to make a good ufe of it during his life; fcarce any man who has employed it in procuring tranquillity to himfelf in his laft moments? Prudential reafons of policy concurred in the perform-ance of this will dictated by humanity; and the go-vernment gave orders, that fuch unhappy prifoners as were releafed fhould be tranfplanted into that defert country, that was now intended to be peopled. It was named Georgia, in honour of the reigning fove-reign.

This inftance of refpect, the more pleafing, as it was not the effect of flattery; and the execution of a de-fign of fo much real advantage to the ftate, were en-tirely the work of the nation. The parliament added 225,000 livres [9375l.] to the eftate left by the will of the citizen; and a voluntary fubfcription produced a much more confiderable fum. General Oglethorpe, a man who had diftinguifhed himfelf in the houfe of commons by his tafte for great defigns, by his zeal for his country, and his paffion for glory, was fixed upon to direct thefe public finances, and to carry into exe-cution fo excellent a project. Defirous of maintain-ing the reputation he had acquired, he chofe to con-duct himfelf the firft colonifts that were fent to Geor-gia; where he arrived in January 1733, and fixed his people on a fpot ten miles diftant from the fea, in an agreeable and fertile plain on the banks of the Savan-nah. The river gave its name to this feeble fettle-ment, which might one day become the capital of a flourifhing colony. It confifted at firft of no more than one hundred perfons; but before the end of the year the number was increafed to fix hundred and eighteen, of whom one hundred and twenty-feven had emigrated at their own expence. Three hundred men, and one hundred and thirteen women, one hundred and two lads, and eighty-three girls, formed the beginning of this new population, and the hopes of a numerous posterity.

This settlement was increased in 1735 by the arrival of some Scotch Highlanders. Their national courage induced them to accept an establishment offered them upon the borders of the Alatamaha, to defend the colony, if necessary, against the attacks of the neighbouring Spaniards. Here they built the town of Darien, five leagues distant from the island of St. Simon, where the hamlet of Frederica was already established.

In the same year, a great number of Protestants, driven out of Saltzburg by a fanatical priest, embarked for Georgia, to enjoy peace and liberty of conscience. Ebenezer, situated upon the river Savannah, sixteen leagues from the ocean, owed its rise to these victims of an odious superstition.

Some Switzers followed the example of these wise Saltzburghers, though they had not, like them, been persecuted. They also settled on the bank of the Savannah, but three leagues lower, and upon a spot which subjected them to the laws of Carolina. Their colony, consisting of a hundred habitations, was named Purysburg, from Pury their founder, who having been at the expence of their settlement, was deservedly chosen their chief, in testimony of their gratitude to him.

In these four or five colonies, some men were found more inclined to trade than agriculture. These, therefore, separated from the rest, in order to build the city of Augusta, one hundred and forty-five miles distant from the ocean. The goodness of the soil was not the object they had in view; but they wished to share with Virginia and the Carolinas the peltries which these provinces obtained from the Creeks, the Chickasaws, and the Cherokees, which were the most numerous savage nations of this continent. Their project was so successful, that as early as the year 1739, six hundred people were employed in this commerce. The sale of thefe furs was with much greater facility carried on, from the circumftance of the Savannah admitting, during the greateft part of the year, fhips from twenty to thirty tons burden as far as the walls of Augufta.

The mother-country ought, one would imagine, to have formed great expectations from a colony which had received, in a very fhort fpace of time, five thoufand inhabitants, which had coft the treafury 1,485,000 livres [61,875l.], and the zealous patriots a great deal more. What muft not, therefore, have been their aftonifhment, when, in 1741, they were informed, that moft of the unfortunate people who had fought an afylum in Georgia had fucceffively withdrawn themfelves from it; and that the few who remained there feemed only defirous to fix in a lefs infupportable fpot? The reafons of this fingular event were inquired into, and difcovered.

This colony, even in its origin, brought with it the feeds of its decay. The government, together with the property of Georgia, had been ceded to individuals. The example of Carolina ought to have prevented this imprudent fcheme; but nations, any more than individuals, do not learn inftruction from their paft mifconduct. Facts are generally unknown; and if they fhould not be, ftill bad confequences are imputed to unable predeceffors, or elfe fome trifling difference in circumftances, or in fome frivolous precautions, afford a pretence for giving a falfe colouring to meafures that are faulty in themfelves. Hence it happens, that an enlightened government, though checked by the watchful eye of the people, is not always able to guard againft every mifufe of its confidence. The Englifh miniftry, therefore, facrificed the public intereft to the rapacious views of interefted individuals.

The firft ufe which the proprietors of Georgia made of the unlimited power they were invefted with, was to eftablifh a fyftem of legiflation, that made them entirely mafters, not only of the police, juftice, and finances of the country, but even of the lives and eftates of its inhabitants. Every fpecies of right was withdrawn from the people, who are the original poffeffors of every right. Obedience was required of them, though contrary to their intereft and knowledge; and it was confidered as their duty and their fate.

As great inconveniences had been found to arife in other colonies from large poffeffions, it was thought proper in Georgia to allow each family only fifty acres of land at firft, and never more than five hundred, which they were not permitted to mortgage, or even to difpofe of by will to their female iffue. This laft regulation, of making only the male iffue capable of inheritance, was foon abolifhed; but there ftill remained too many obftacles to excite a fpirit of emulation.

When a man is neither purfued by the laws, nor driven away to avoid ignominy, nor tormented by religious tyranny, by the perfecutions of his creditors, by fhame or mifery, or by the want of every kind of refource in his own country, he doth not renounce his relations, his friends, and his fellow-citizens; he doth not banifh himfelf, he doth not crofs the feas, he doth not go in fearch of a diftant land, unlefs he be attracted there by hopes which are more powerful than the allurements of his native foil, than the value he fets upon his exiftence, and the dangers to which he expofes himfelf. To go on board of fhip, in order to be landed on an unknown region, is the act of a defperate man, unlefs the imagination be influenced by the profpect of fome great happinefs; a profpect which the leaft alarm will diffipate. If the vague and unlimited confidence the emigrant hath in his induftry, in which his whole fortune confifts, be fhaken by any means whatever, he will remain upon the fhore. Such muft neceffarily have been the effect of the boundaries affigned to every plantation. Several other errors ftill affected the original plan of this country, and prevented its increafe.

The taxes impofed upon the moft fertile of the Englifh colonies are very inconfiderable, and even thefe are not levied till the fettlements have acquired fome degree of vigour and profperity. From its infant ftate,

Georgia had been fubjected to the fines of a feudal go- B o o k
vernment, with which it had been, as it were, fettered. XVIII.
The revenues raifed by this kind of fervice muft have
increafed beyond meafure in procefs of time. The
founders of it, blinded by a fpirit of avidity, did not
perceive, that the fmalleft duty impofed upon a populous and flourifhing province would much fooner enrich them, than the heavieft taxes laid upon a barren
and uncultivated country.

To this fpecies of oppreffion was added an arrangement which became a frefh caufe of inactivity. The
diforders which were the confequence of the ufe of fpirituous liquors throughout all the continent of North
America, occafioned the importation of rum to be prohibited in Georgia. This prohibition, however laudable the motive for it might be, deprived the colonifts of the only drink which could correct the bad effects of the water of the country, which they found
everywhere unhealthy, and of the only means they
had of repairing their ftrength, exhaufted by continual
perfpiration. It alfo fecluded them from the trade of
the Weft Indies, where they were no more allowed to
exchange for thefe liquors the wood, the feeds, and
the cattle, which ought to have conftituted their firft
riches.

Weak as thefe refources were, they muft have increafed very flowly, on account of a prohibition which
would deferve recommendation, had it been dictated
by a fentiment of humanity, and not by policy. The
planters of Georgia were not allowed the ufe of flaves.
Other colonies having been eftablifhed without their
affiftance, it was thought that a country, deftined to
be the bulwark of thofe poffeffions, ought not to be
peopled by a fet of flaves, who could not be in the
leaft interefted in the defence of their oppreffors. But
would this prohibition have taken place, had it been
forefeen that colonifts, who were lefs favoured by the
mother-country than their neighbours, who were fituated in a country lefs fufceptible of culture, and in
a hotter climate, would want ftrength and fpirit to un-

B O O K dertake a cultivation that required greater encourage-
   XVIII. ment?

The demands of the people, and the refufals of the
government, may be equally extravagant. The people liften only to their wants, and fovereigns confult
only their perfonal intereft. The former, commonly very indifferent, efpecially in diftant countries, with
refpect to the powers to which they belong, and thofe
which they may receive by an invafion, neglect their
political fecurity, in order to attend only to their perfonal welfare. The latter, on the contrary, will never hefitate between the felicity of the people, and
the folidity of their poffeffions; and will always prefer a fteady and permanent authority over a fet of
miferable beings, to an uncertain and precarious fway
over men who are happy. Their miftruft, which a
long feries of vexations hath too well juftified, will
induce them to confider the people as flaves, ever
ready to efcape from them by revolt or by flight;
and it will not enter into the thoughts of any one of
them, that this habitual fentiment of hatred, which
they fuppofe to exift againft them becaufe they have
deferved it, and which is but too real, would be extinguifhed, if they could experience a few years of a
mild and paternal adminiftration: for nothing is alienated with fo much difficulty as the affection of the
people. It is founded on the advantages rarely felt,
but always acknowledged, of a fupreme authority,
whatever it may be, which directs, which is watchful,
which protects, and which defends. For the fame
reafon, nothing is more eafily recovered, when alienated. The delufive hope of a change for the better
is alone fufficient to quiet our imaginatation, and to
prolong our miferies without end. What I here advance is confirmed by the almoft univerfal example
of the whole world. At the death of a tyrant all nations flatter themfelves with the hopes of a king. The
tyrants continue their fyftem of oppreffion, and die in
peace; and the people ftill continue to groan under
it, and to expect with patience a king who never ap-

pears. The fucceffor, educated as his father or his
grandfather, is prepared from his infancy to model
himfelf after their example, unlefs he fhould have received from nature a ftrength of genius, a firmnefs of
foul, a rectitude of judgment, and a fund of benevolence and equity, which may correct the defect of his
education. Without this fortunate difpofition, he will
not inquire, in any circumftance, what is proper to be
done, but what hath been done before him. He will
not afk what is moft fuitable to the good of his fubjects, whom he will confider as his neareft enemies, on
account of the parade of guards that furround him;
but he will ftudy what will increafe his defpotifm and
their fervitude. He will remain ignorant during life
of the moft fimple and moft evident of truths; which
is, that their ftrength and his are infeparable from each
other. The example of the paft will be his only rule
of conduct, both on thofe occafions when it may be
prudent to follow it, and on thofe it would be proper to deviate from it. The meafure which the miniftry will adopt in politics, will always be that which
fhall be moft analogous to the fpirit of tyranny, the
only one which has been decorated with the title of
the great art of governing. When, therefore, the inhabitants of Georgia afked for flaves, in order to know
whether they fhould have been granted or refufed to
them, it was only neceffary to examine whether they
were required for the better cultivation of the lands,
and the greater fecurity of the property of the colony.

In the meanwhile, the truly defperate fituation of
the new fettlement proclaimed too forcibly the imprudence of the miniftry, to make it poffible to perfevere in fuch fatal meafures. At length the province
received the fame form of government which made
the other colonies profper. When it ceafed to be a
fief belonging to individuals, it became a truly national
poffeffion.

Since this fortunate revolution, Georgia hath improved confiderably, though not fo rapidly as was expected. It is true, that neither the vine, the olive-

B O O K
XVIII.

Situation
and expec-
tations of
Georgia.

B O O K tree, nor filk, have been cultivated, as the mother-
XVIII.   country wifhed; but its marfhes have furnifhed a tolerable quantity of rice; and indigo, fuperior in quality to that of Carolina, hath been produced upon the
higher grounds.   Before the 1ft January 1768, a grant
had been made of fix hundred thirty-feven thoufand
one hundred and feventy acres of land.   Thofe which,
in 1763, were worth no more than 3 livres 7 fols 6 deniers [2s. 9¼d.], were fold in 1776 for 67 livres 10 fols
[2l. 16s. 3d.].   In 1769, the exportations of the colony amounted to 1,625,418 livres 9 fols 5 deniers [a-
bout 67,725l. 15s. 4¾d.]; and fince that time they
have confiderably increafed.

This profperity will undoubtedly be augmented. In
proportion as the forefts fhall be felled, the air will become more falubrious, and the productions will increafe
with the population, which at prefent doth not exceed
thirty thoufand men, moft of whom are flaves.   However, as the lands are not fo extenfive in Georgia as in
moft of the other provinces, and that in the fame proportion lefs of them are fufceptible of culture, the
riches of that colony will always be limited.   Let us
fee whether Florida hath a right to expect a more brilliant deftiny.

Florida be-   Under this name the ambition of Spain compre-
comes a   hended formerly all that tract of land in America,
Spanifh
poffeffion. which extended from the Gulf of Mexico to the moft
northern regions.   But fortune, which fports with the
vanity of nations, hath long fince confined this unlimited denomination to the peninfula formed by the
fea, between Georgia and Louifiana.

It was Luke Velafquès, whofe memory ought to be
holden in execration in this world, as he deferves to be
punifhed in the next; it was that monfter, to whom I
can fcarce give the name of man, who firft landed upon this region, with the intention of obtaining flaves
either by ftratagem or by force.   The novelty of the
fpectacle attracted the neighbouring favages.   They
were invited to come on board the fhips; they were
intoxicated, put in irons, and the anchor was weighed,

while the guns were fired upon the reft of the Indians, who remained upon the fhore. Several of thefe unfortunate people, fo cruelly torn from their own country, refufed to take the food which was offered them, and perifhed from inanition. Others died of grief; and thofe who furvived their defpair, were buried in the mines of Mexico.

Thefe infatiable gulfs required more victims. The perfidious Velafquès went in fearch of them again in the fame country. He was known, and half of his infamous companions were murdered on their arrival. Thofe who fled from a juftly implacable enemy, were fhipwrecked; he himfelf only efcaped the fury of the waves, to lead the remainder of his detefted life in fhame, mifery, and remorfe.

Spain had forgotten that part of the New World, when the memory of it was revived by a fettlement made there by the French. The court of Madrid thought proper to drive from their rich poffeffions fo active a nation; and they accordingly gave orders for the deftruction of the infant colony. This command was put in execution in 1565; and the conquerors re-occupied the place, which was rendered an abfolute defert by their cruelties. They were threatened with a lingering death, when they were relieved by the culture of faffafras.

This tree, which is an evergreen, is peculiar to America, and is better at Florida than in any other part of that hemifphere. It grows equally on the borders of the fea and upon the mountains, but always in a foil which is neither too dry nor too damp. Its roots are even with the furface of the ground. Its trunk, which is very ftraight, without leaves, and not high, is covered with a thick and dirty bark, of an afh colour, and throws out at its fummit fome branches which fpread out on the coafts. The leaves are difpofed alternately, green on the upper, and white on the under furface, and are divided into three lobes. Sometimes they are found entire, efpecially in young plants. The branches are terminated by clusters of small yellow flowers. They are of the same kind as those of the laurel or cinnamon tree. The fruits, which succeed, are small, blue, pendent berries, fixed to a red pedicle, and to a calix of the same colour.

Its flower is taken in infusion, as mullein and tea is. The decoction of its root is used with effect in intermittent fevers. The bark of the trunk hath an acrid and aromatic taste, and a smell similar to that of fennel and aniseed. The wood is whitish and less odoriferous. They are both used in medicine to promote perspiration, to attenuate thick and viscid humours, to remove obstructions, to cure the gout and the palsy. Saffafras was also formerly much prescribed in the venereal disease.

The first Spaniards who settled there would probably have fallen a sacrifice to this last disorder, at least they would not have recovered from those dangerous fevers with which most of them were attacked on their arrival in Florida, either in consequence of the food of the country, or of the badness of the waters. But the savages taught them, that by drinking fasting, and at their meals, water in which the root of saffafras had been boiled, they might depend upon a speedy recovery. The experiment upon trial proved successful.

What can be the reason that this medicine and so many others which produce extraordinary cures in those distant countries, seem to have lost almost all their efficacy when transplanted into ours? It must probably be owing to the climate being more favourable for perspiration, to the nature of the plant which degenerates and loses some part of its strength during a long voyage, and especially to the nature of the disease, when joined to our intemperate way of living; and the obstinacy of which increases from the numberless disorders prevailing in our constitutions.

The Spaniards established some small posts at San Matheo, at Saint Marc, and at Saint Joseph; but it

was only Saint Auguftine and at Penfacola that they
properly formed fettlements; the former on their arrival in the country, and the latter in 1696.

Penfacola was attacked and taken by the French
during the fhort contefts which divided the two houfes
of Bourbon in 1718; but it was foon reftored.

In 1740, the Englifh befieged the former of thefe
fettlements in vain. The Scotch Highlanders, in endeavouring to cover the retreat of the affailants, were
beaten and flain. One of their ferjeants only was
fpared by the favage Indians, who, while they were
fighting for the Spaniards, referved him to undergo
thofe torments which they inflict upon their prifoners. This man, it is faid, on feeing the horrid tortures that awaited him, addreffed the blood-thirfty
multitude in the following manner:

" Heroes and patriarchs of the weftern world, you
" were not the enemies that I fought for; but you
" have at laft been the conquerors. The chance of
" war has thrown me in your power. Make what ufe
" you think proper of the right of conqueft. This is
" a right I do not call in queftion. But as it is cuf-
" tomary in my country to offer a ranfom for one's
" life, liften to a propofal not unworthy of your no-
" tice.

" Know then, valiant Americans, that in the coun-
" try of which I am a native, there are fome men who
" poffefs a fuperior knowledge of the fecrets of nature.
" One of thofe fages, connected to me by the ties of
" kindred, imparted to me, when I became a foldier,
" a charm to make me invulnerable. You muft have
" obferved how I have efcaped all your darts. With-
" out fuch a charm would it have been poffible for me
" to have furvived all the mortal blows you have aim-
" ed at me? For I appeal to your own valour, to tef-
" tify that mine has fufficienty exerted itfelf, and has
" not avoided any danger. Life is not fo much the ob-
" ject of my requeft, as the glory of communicating
" to you a fecret of fo much confequence to your fafe-
" ty, and of rendering the moft valiant nation upon the

" earth invincible.   Suffer me only to have one of my
" hands at liberty, in order to perform the ceremonies
" of enchantment, of which I will now make trial
" on myfelf before you."

The Indians liftened with eagernefs to this difcourfe,
which was flattering both to their warlike character,
and their turn for the marvellous.   After a fhort con-
fultation, they untied one of the prifoner's arms.   The
Highlander begged that they would put his broad
fword into the hands of the moft expert and ftouteft
man among them ; and at the fame time laying bare
his neck, after having rubbed it, and muttering fome
words accompanied with magic figns, he cried aloud
with a cheerful countenance, " Obferve now, O vali-
" ant Indians, an inconteftible proof of my honefty.
" Thou warrior, who now holdeft my keen cutting
" weapon, do thou now ftrike with all thy ftrength :
" far from being able to fever my head from my bo-
" dy, thou wilt not even wound the fkin of my neck."

He had fcarcely fpoken thefe words, when the Indian aiming the moft violent blow, ftruck off the head
of the ferjeant, to the diftance of twenty feet.   The
favages aftonifhed, ftood motionlefs, viewing the bloody
corpfe of the ftranger ; and then turned their eyes upon one another, as if to reproach each other with
their blind credulity.   But admiring the artifice the
prifoner had made ufe of to avoid the torture by
haftening his death, they beftowed on his body the
funeral honours of their country.   If this fact, the
date of which is too recent to admit of credit, has
not all the marks of authenticity it fhould have, it will
only be one falfehood more to be added to the accounts of travellers.

Florida is
ceded to
Great Bri-
tain by the
court of
Madrid.
The treaty of peace of 1763, put in the power of
Great Britain, that fame Florida which had refifted
the ftrength of their arms twenty-three years before.
At that time there were no more than fix hundred inhabitants.   It was with the fale of their hides, and
with the provifions they furnifhed to their garrifon,
that they were to provide themfelves with clothes,

and to supply a small part of their wants, which were exceedingly confined. These miserable people went all to Cuba, though convinced that they would be obliged to beg their bread, if their monarch, moved with such an instance of affection, did not provide for their subsistence.

What motive could induce the Spaniards to prefer an oppressive to a free government? Was it superstition, which cannot suffer the altars of the heretics near its own? Was it prejudice, which renders suspicious the morals and the probity of those who profess a different religion? Was it the fear of seduction for themselves, and still more for their children? Long accustomed to idleness, did they imagine that they should be compelled to labour? Or hath man so bad an opinion of man, that he should rather choose to dispose of himself and his fate, than to abandon it to the mercy of his fellow-creature? However it may be, nothing but a desert remained to the power that obtained the possession ; but was it not an acquisition to lose inhabitants not inured to fatigue, and who would never have been well affected?

Great Britain congratulated itself upon the acquisition of the property of an immense province, the limits of which were still extended as far as the Mississippi, by the cession of one part of Louisiana. That power had for a long time been desirous of settling on a territory which would open an easy communication to them with the richest of the Spanish colonies. They did not give up the hopes of a smuggling trade, but they were aware that this precarious and momentary advantage was not sufficient to render their conquests flourishing, and they turned their labours and expectations principally towards cultivation.

The new acquisition was divided into two governments. It was thought that this would be a powerful inducement to carry on with greater zeal, and to direct with more vigour, the cultivation of the lands. Ministry might also have determined upon this divi- What hath been done by England, and what she may expect to do in Florida.

fion, in expectation of always finding more fubmiffion in two feparate provinces than in one alone.

Saint Auguftine became the capital of Eaft Florida,
and Penfacola of Weft Florida. Thefe capitals, which
were at the fame time tolerable good harbours, did
not undoubtedly unite all the conveniences they were
fufceptible of, but it was ftill a very fortunate circumftance to find thofe which they really did poffefs. The
other colonies did not enjoy this advantage at their
origin.

The firft colonifts who fettled in thefe countries were
half-pay officers and difbanded foldiers. All thofe
among them who had ferved in America and were
fettled there, obtained the grant of a piece of land
proportionable to their rank. This favour was not
extended to all the army that had fought in the New
World. It would have been apprehended, that the
military men of the three kingdoms who were in the
fame fituation, might be tempted to forfake the mother-country, already too much exhaufted by the laft
hoftilities.

The new colony received alfo cultivators from the
neighbouring fettlements, from the mother-country,
and from feveral Proteftant ftates. It alfo obtained
fome, whofe arrival was a matter of aftonifhment to
both hemifpheres.

The Greeks groan under the Ottoman tyranny, and
muft be inclined to fhake off this detefted yoke. This
was the opinion of Dr. Turnbull, when, in 1767, he
went to offer an afylum in Britifh America to the inhabitants of the Peloponnefus. Several of them yielded to his folicitations; and for the fum of one hundred
guineas he obtained leave from the government of the
place to embark them at Modon. He landed in Corfica and at Minorca, and prevailed alfo upon fome of
the inhabitants of thofe two iflands to follow him.

The emigrants, to the number of a thoufand, arrived in Eaft Florida with their prudent conductor, where
fixty thoufand acres of land were granted to them.

This would have been an immenfe poffeffion, even if the climate had not deftroyed any of them; but they had unfortunately been fo much thwarted by the winds as to prevent their landing before fummer, which is a dangerous feafon, and which deftroyed one quarter of their number. They were moftly the old people who perifhed. They were numerous, becaufe the judicious Turnbull chofe to carry none with him but whole families.

Thofe who efcaped this firft difafter have fince enjoyed perfect health, which has only been affected by a few fevers. The men are become ftronger in their conftitutions, and the women, who, on account of the change of climate, did not breed often at firft, are at prefent very fruitful. It is prefumed that the children will be taller than they would have been in the country from whence their parents came.

The fmall colony have received from their founder inftitutions, which they have themfelves approved, and which are obferved. They are ftill no more than one entire family, where the fpirit of concord muft be kept up for a long time. On the firft of January 1776, they had already cleared two thoufand three hundred acres of a tolerably fertile foil. They had animals fufficient for their fubfiftence and for their labour. Their crops were fufficient for their own confumption, and they fold 67,500 livres [2812l. 10s.] worth of indigo. The induftry and activity by which they are diftinguifhed, give great expectations from time and experience.

Why fhould not Athens and Lacedemon be one day revived in North America? Why fhould not the city of Turnbull become in a few centuries the refidence of politenefs, of the fine arts, and of eloquence? The new colony is lefs diftant from this flourifhing ftate than were the barbarous Pelafgians from the fellow-citizens of Pericles. What difference there is between a fettlement conceived and founded by a wife and pacific man, and the conquefts of a long feries of avaricious, extravagant, and fanguinary men; between

the prefent ftate of South America and what it might
have been, had thofe who difcovered it, took poffeffion
of it and laid it wafte, been animated with the fame
fpirit as the worthy Turnbull? Will not nations learn
by his example, that the foundation of a colony requires more wifdom than expence? The univerfe hath
been peopled by one man and one woman only.

The two Floridas, which in 1769 did not export
productions to the amount of more than 673,209 livres
18 fols 9 deniers [about 28,045l. 8s. 3¼d.], have a remarkable advantage over the reft of this great continent.   Situated in a great meafure between two feas,
they have nothing to fear from the frozen winds, nor
from the unforefeen variations in the temperature of
the air, which at all feafons occafion fuch frequent
and fatal devaftations in the neighbourhood.   It is
therefore to be hoped that the vine, the olive, the cotton tree, and other delicate plants, will profper there
fooner and better than in any of the adjacent provinces.   In 1774, the fociety inftituted in London for
the encouragement of arts, manufactures, and fciences,
gave a gold medal to Mr. Strachey, for his having
produced as fine indigo as that which comes from
Guatimala.   Although, in the firft paroxyfms of enthufiafm, the qualities of this production have been
but moderately attended to, yet it will become a
fource of riches for the colony.

The foil of Eaft Florida, however, being a great
deal too fandy, conftantly drove away all men who
were defirous of making a rapid fortune.   It would
fcarce have been peopled, except by fome extraordinary event.   The troubles with which North America hath been agitated, have driven to that commonly barren foil a few peaceful citizens, who had a fettled averfion for difputes, and a ftill greater number of
men, who, either from ambition, habit, or prejudice,
were devoted to the intereft of the mother-country.

The fame inducements have given colonifts to the
other Florida, which is much more fertile, efpecially
on the pleafant borders of the Miffiffippi.   This pro-

vince hath had the advantage to furnifh Jamaica, and B O O K
feveral of the Britifh iflands in the Weft Indies, with XVIII.
wood, and with various articles, which they formerly
received from the feveral countries of New England.
This population would have been ftill more rapid if
the coafts of Penfacola had been more accefsible, and
if its harbours had been lefs infefted with worms. How
greatly might the improvements of the two provinces
be accelerated, if the new fovereigns of North America would depart from the maxims they have uni-
formly purfued, and would condefcend to intermar-
riages with Indian families! And for what reafon
fhould this method of civilizing the favage tribes,
which has been fo fuccefsfully employed by the moft
enlightened politicians, be rejected by a free people,
who, from their principles, muft admit a greater equality than other nations? Would the Englifh then be
ftill reduced to the cruel alternative of feeing their
crops burnt, and their hufbandmen maffacred, or of
perfecuting without intermiffion, and exterminating
without pity, thofe wandering bands of natives?
Ought they not to prefer to fanguinary and inglori-
ous hoftilities a humane and infallible method of dif-
arming the only enemy that remains to difturb their
tranquillity?

The Englifh flatter themfelves, that, without the affiftance of thefe alliances, they fhall foon be freed from
the little interruption that remains. It is the fate of
favage nations, fay they, to wafte away in proportion
as the people of civilized ftates come to fettle among
them. Unable to fubmit to the labour of cultivation,
and failing of their ufual fubfiftence from the chafe,
they are reduced to the neceffity of abandoning all
thofe tracts of lands which induftry and activity have
undertaken to clear. This is actually the cafe with
all the natives bordering on the European fettlements.
They keep daily retiring further into the woods; they
fall back upon the Affenipouals and Hudfon's Bay,
where they muft neceffarily encroach upon each other,
and in a fhort time muft perifh for want of fubfiftence.

But before this total deſtruction is brought about, events of a very ſerious nature may occur. We have not yet forgotten the generous Pondiack. That formidable warrior had broken with the Engliſh in 1762. Major Roberts, who was employed to reconcile him, ſent him a preſent of brandy. Some Iroquois, who were ſtanding round their chief, ſhuddered at the ſight of this liquor. Not doubting but that it was poiſoned, they inſiſted that he ſhould not accept ſo ſuſpicious a preſent. *How can it be*, ſaid their leader, *that a man, who knows my eſteem for him, and the ſignal ſervices I have done him, ſhould entertain a thought of taking away my life?* Saying this, he received and drank the brandy with a confidence equal to that of the moſt renowned hero of antiquity.

By many inſtances of magnanimity ſimilar to this, the eyes of the ſavage nations had all been fixed upon Pondiack. His deſign was to unite them in a body for the defence of their lands and independence. Several unfortunate circumſtances concurred to defeat this grand project; but it may be reſumed, and it is not impoſſible that it may ſucceed. The uſurpers would then be under a neceſſity of protecting their frontier againſt an enemy that hath none of thoſe expences to ſuſtain, or evils to dread, which war brings with it among civilized nations; and will find the advantages they have promiſed themſelves from conqueſts made at the expence of ſo much treaſure and ſo much blood, conſiderably retarded at leaſt, if not entirely loſt. Should the Engliſh diſdain an advice dictated to them through me by juſtice and humanity, may another Pondiack ariſe from his aſhes, and conſummate his plan.

Extent of the Britiſh dominions in North America.
The two Floridas, part of Louiſiana, and all Canada, obtained at the ſame era, either by conqueſt or treaty, rendered the Engliſh maſters of all that ſpace which extends from the river St. Lawrence to the Miſſiſſippi; ſo that without reckoning Hudſon's Bay, Newfoundland, and the other iſlands of North America, they would have been in poſſeſſion of the moſt exten-

five empire that ever was formed upon the face of the
globe.

This vast territory is divided from north to south by
a chain of high mountains, which alternately receding
from and approaching to the coast, leave between them
and the ocean a tract of land of a hundred and fifty,
two hundred, and sometimes three hundred miles in
breadth. Beyond these Apalachian mountains is an
immense desert, into which some travellers have ventured as far as eight hundred leagues, without finding
an end to it. It is supposed that the rivers at the extremity of these uncultivated regions have a communication with the South Sea. If this conjecture, which
is not destitute of probability, should be confirmed by
experience, England would unite in her colonies all
the branches of communication and commerce of the
world. As her territories extend from one American
sea to the other, she may be said to join the four quarters of the world. From all her European ports, from
all her African settlements, she freights and sends out
ships to the New World. From her maritime settlements in the east she would have a direct channel to
the West Indies by the Pacific Ocean. She would
discover those slips of land, or branches of the sea, the
isthmus of the strait, which lies between the northern
extremities of Asia and America. By the vast extent
of her colonies, she would have in her own power all
the avenues of trade, and would secure all the advantages of it by her numerous fleets. Perhaps, by having
the empire of all the seas, she might aspire to the supremacy of both worlds. But it is not in the destiny
of any single nation to attain to such a pitch of greatness. Is then extent of dominion so flattering an object, when conquests are made only to be lost again?
Let the Romans speak! Does it constitute power, to
possess such a share of the globe, that some part shall
always be enlightened by the rays of the sun, if while
we reign in one world we are to languish in obscurity
in the other? Let the Spaniards answer!

The English will be happy if they can preserve, by

the means of culture and navigation, an empire, which muſt ever be found too extenſive, when it cannot be maintained without bloodſhed. But as this is the price which ambition muſt always pay for the ſuccefs of its enterprifes, it is by commerce alone that conqueſts can become valuable to a maritime power. Never did war procure for any conqueror a territory more improveable by human induſtry than that of the northern continent of America. Although the land in general be ſo low near the ſea, that in many parts it is ſcarcely diſtinguiſhable from the top of the mainmaſt, even after anchoring in fourteen fathom, yet the coaſt is very eaſy of accefs, becauſe the depth diminiſhes inſenſibly as you advance. From this circumſtance, it is eaſy to determine exactly by the line the diſtance of the main land. Beſide this, the mariner has another ſign, which is the appearance of trees, that, ſeeming to rife out of the ſea, form an inchanting object to his view upon a ſhore, which prefents roads and harbours without number, for the reception and preſervation of ſhipping.

The productions of the earth arife in great abundance from a ſoil newly cleared; but, on the other hand, they are a long time before they come to maturity. Many plants are even ſo late in flower, that the winter prevents their ripening; while, on our continent, both the fruit and the ſeed of them are gathered in a more northern latitude. What can be the cauſe of this phenomenon? Before the arrival of the Europeans, the North Americans, living upon the produce of their hunting and fiſhery, left their lands totally uncultivated. The whole country was covered with woods and thickets. Under the ſhade of theſe foreſts grew a multitude of plants. The leaves, which fell every winter from the trees, formed a bed three or four inches thick. Before the damps had quite rotted this ſpecies of manure, the ſummer came on; and nature, left entirely to herſelf, continued heaping inceſſantly upon each other theſe effects of her fertility. The plants buried under wet leaves, through which they with difficulty made their way in a long courſe

of time, became accuftomed to a long vegetation. B O O K
The force of culture has not yet been able to fubdue XVIII.
the habit fixed and confirmed by ages, nor have the
difpofitions of nature given way to the influence of
art. But this climate, fo long unknown or negleded
by mankind, prefents them with advantages which
fupply the defects and ill confequences of that omif-
fion.

It produces almoft all the trees that are natives of Trees peculiar to
our climate. It has alfo others peculiar to itfelf, a- North A-
mong which are the fugar maple, and the candleburry merica.
myrtle.

The latter, thus named on account of its produce,
is a branching, tortuous fhrub, rather irregular, and
which delights in a moift foil. It is therefore feldom
found at any diftance from the fea, or from large rivers. Its leaves, alternately difpofed, are narrow, entire, or denticulated, and always covered with fmall
gilded points, which are almoft imperceptible. It
bears male and female flowers, upon two different
plants. The firft form a bezil, every fcale of which
bears fix ftamina. The fecond, difpofed alike on
young fprigs, have, inftead of ftamina, an ovary, furmounted with ftyles, which becomes a very fmall,
hard, and fpherical fhell, which is covered with a gra-
nulated, white, and unctuous fubftance. Thefe fruits,
which together appear like a bunch of grapes, are gathered at the end of the autumn, and thrown into
boiling water. The fubftance with which they are
covered detaches itfelf, fwims at the top, and is fkim-
med off. As foon as this is grown cold, it is commonly of a dirty green colour. To purify it, it is boiled a
fecond time, when it becomes tranfparent, and acquires
an agreeable green colour.

This fubftance, which in quality and confiftence is a
medium between tallow and wax, fupplied the place of
both to the firft Europeans who landed in this country.
The dearnefs of it has occafioned it to be lefs ufed, in
proportion as the number of domeftic animals hath
increafed. Neverthelefs, as it burns flower than tal-

low, is lefs fubject to melt, and has not that difagreeable fmell, it is ftill preferred, wherever it can be procured at a moderate price. If it be mixed with a
fourth part of tallow, it burns much better; but this
is not its only property. It ferves to make excellent
foap and plafters for wounds: it is even employed for
the purpofe of fealing letters. The fugar maple merits no lefs attention than the candleburry myrtle, as
may be conceived from its name.

This tree, the nature of which is to flourifh by the
fide of ftreams, or in marfhy places, grows to the height
of the oak. Its trunk is ftraight and cylindrical, and
covered with a tolerably thin bark. Its branches,
which are always oppofite, are covered with leaves
difpofed in the fame manner, which are whitifh underneath, and are divided into five acute lobes. Its
flowers, collected in clufters, have a calix, with five
divifions, charged with as many petals, and eight ftamina, which are fometimes abortive. In the centre of
them is a piftil, which becomes a fruit, compofed of
two pods, preffed together, and clofed at the bottom,
open and alated at the top, and filled with a fingle
feed.

In the month of March, an' incifion, of the depth
of three or four inches, is made at the lower part of
the trunk of the maple. A pipe is put into the ori-
fice, through which the juice that flows from it is conveyed into a veffel placed to receive it. The young
trees are fo full of this liquor, that in half an hour they
will fill a quart bottle. The old ones afford lefs, but
of much better quality. No more than one incifion,
or two at moft, can be made, without draining and
weakening the tree. If three or four pipes be applied,
it foon dies.

The fap of this tree has naturally the flavour of honey. To reduce it to fugar, it is evaporated by fire,
till it has acquired the confiftence of a thick fyrup. It
is then poured into moulds of earthen ware, or bark
of the birch tree. The fyrup hardens as it cools, and
becomes a red kind of fugar, almoft tranfparent, and

pleafant enough to the tafte. To give it a whitenefs, B O O K
flour is fometimes mixed up with it in the making; XVIII.
but this ingredient always changes the flavour of it.
This kind of fugar is ufed for the fame purpofes as
that which is made from canes; but eighteen or twenty pounds of juice go to the making of one pound of
fugar, fo that it can be of no great ufe in trade. Honey is the fugar of the favages of our countries; the
maple is the fugar of the favages of America. Nature
difplays in all parts its fweets and its wonders.

Amidft the multitude of birds which inhabit the fo- Birds pe-
refts of North America, there is one extremely fingu- culiar to North A-
lar in its kind; this is the humming bird; a fpecies of merica.
which, on account of its fmallnefs, is called *l'oifeau
mouche*, or the fly bird. Its beak is long and pointed
like a needle, and its claws are not thicker than a
common pin. Upon its head it has a black tuft of
incomparable beauty. Its breaft is of a rofe colour,
and its belly white as milk. The back, wings, and
tail, are grey, bordered with filver, and ftreaked with
the brighteft gold. The down, which covers all the
plumage of this little bird, gives it fo delicate a caft,
that it refembles a velvet flower, the beauty of which
fades on the flighteft touch.

The fpring is the only feafon for this charming bird.
Its neft, perched on the middle of a bough, is covered
on the outfide with a grey and greenifh mofs, and on
the infide lined with a very foft down gathered from
yellow flowers. This neft is half an inch in depth, and
about an inch in diameter. There are never found more
than two eggs in it, about the fize of the fmalleft peas.
Many attempts have been made to rear the young
ones; but they have never lived more than three
weeks or a month at moft.

The humming bird lives entirely on the juice of
flowers, fluttering from one to another, like the bees.
Sometimes it buries itfelf in the calix of the largeft
flowers. Its flight produces a buzzing noife like that
of a fpinning-wheel. When tired, it lights upon the
neareft tree or ftake; refts a few minutes, and flies

B O O K again to the flowers. Notwithstanding its weakness,
  XVIII. it does not appear timid ; but will suffer a man to approach within eight or ten feet of it.

Who would imagine, that so diminutive an animal
could be malicious, passionate, and quarrelsome? These
birds are often seen fighting together with great fury
and obstinacy. The strokes they give with their beak
are so sudden and so quick, that they are not distin-
guishable by the eye. Their wings move with such
agility, that they seem not to have any kind of motion. They are more heard than seen ; and their
noise resembles that of a sparrow.

These little birds are all impatience. When they
come near a flower, if they find it faded and wither-
ed, they tear all the leaves asunder. The precipitation with which they peck it, betrays, as it is said,
the rage with which they are animated. Towards
the end of the summer, thousands of flowers may be
seen stript of all their leaves by the fury of the humming birds. It may be doubted, however, whether
this mark of resentment is not rather an effect of hunger than of an unnecessarily destructive instinct.

Every species of beings hath another that is an enemy to it. That of the fly-bird is a large spider, which
is very greedy of its eggs. This is the sword which is
continually suspended over the tyrant's head.

North America was formerly devoured by insects.
As the air was not then purified, the ground cleared,
the woods cut down, nor the waters drained off, these
little animals destroyed, without opposition, all the
productions of nature. None of them were useful
to mankind. There is only one at present, which is
the bee ; but this is supposed to have been carried
from the Old to the New World. The savages call
it the English fly ; and it is only found near the coasts.
These circumstances announce it to be of foreign original. The bees fly in numerous swarms through the
forests of the New World. Their numbers are continually increasing, and their honey, which is converted to several uses, supplies many persons with food.

Their wax becomes daily a confiderable branch of trade.

The bee is not the only prefent which Europe has had it in her power to make to America. She has enriched her alfo with a breed of domeftic animals, for the favages had none. America had not yet affociated beafts with men in the labours of cultivation, when the Europeans carried over thither oxen, fheep, and horfes. They were all, at firft, expofed, as well as man, to epidemical difeafes. If the contagion did not attack them, as it did their proud fovereign, in the fource even of their generation, feveral of their fpecies were at leaft reproduced with much difficulty. All of them, except the hog, loft much of their ftrength and fize. It was not till late, and that only in fome places, that they recovered their original properties. Without doubt, it was the climate, the nature of the air, and the foil, which prevented the fuccefs of their tranfplantation. Such is the law of climates, which wills every people, every animal and vegetable fpecies, to grow and flourifh in its native foil. The love of their country feems an ordinance of nature prefcribed to all beings, as the defire of preferving their exiftence.

Europe
fupplies
North A-
merica with
domeftic
animals.

Yet there are certain correfpondences of climate, which form exceptions to the general rule againft the tranfplanting of animals and plants. When the Englifh firft landed on the North American continent, the wandering inhabitants of thofe defolate reigions had fcarcely arrived at the cultivation of a fmall quantity of maize, a plant which refembles a reed. Its leaves, which are large, and very long, furround, at their bafis, the ftem, which is round and knotty at intervals. It is terminated by a panicle of male flowers. Each of the bunches which compofe it, hath two flowers, covered with two common fcales; and each flower hath three ftamina, enclofed between two fcales proper to them. At the axilla of the inferior leaves, the female flowers are found, difpofed in a very clofe clufter, upon a thick and flefhy axis, con-

European
grain hath
been culti-
vated in
North A-
merica.

cealed under feveral coverings. The piftil of thefe
flowers, furrounded with fome fmall fcales, and furmounted with a long ftyle, becomes a farinaceous feed,
almoft fpherical, and half funk into the common axis.
Its maturity is known by its colour, and by the feparation of the covering, through which the blade of
corn may be feen.

This fpecies of corn, unknown at that time in Europe, was the only one known in the New World.
The culture of it was by no means difficult. The favages contented themfelves with taking off the turf,
making a few holes in the ground with a ftick, and
throwing into each of them a fingle grain, which produced two hundred and fifty or three hundred. The
method of preparing it for food was not more complicated. They pounded it in a wooden or ftone mor-
tar, and made it into a pafte, which they baked under
embers. They often ate it toafted merely upon the
coals.

The maize has many advantages. Its leaves are
ufeful in feeding cattle; a circumftance of great moment where there are very few meadows. A hungry,
light, fandy foil, agrees beft with this plant. The feed
may be frozen in the fpring two or three times without impairing the harveft. In fhort, it is of all plants
the one that is leaft injured by the excefs of drought
or moifture.

Thefe caufes, which introduced the cultivation of it
in that part of the world, induced the Englifh to preferve and even promote it in their fettlements. They
fold it to the fouthern part of Europe, and to the .Eaft
Indies, and employed it for their own ufe. They did
not, however, neglect to enrich their plantations with
European grains, all of which fucceeded, though not
fo perfectly as in their native foil. With the fuperfluity of their harvefts, the produce of their herds, and
the clearing of their forefts, the colonifts formed a
trade with all the wealthieft and moft populous provinces of the New World.

The mother-country, finding that her northern co-

lonies had fupplanted her in her trade with South A- BOOK
merica, and fearing that they would foon become her XVIII.
rivals, even in Europe, at all the markets for falt provifions and corn, endeavoured to divert their induftry
to objects that might be more ufeful to her. An opportunity foon prefented itfelf.

The greateft part of the pitch and tar the Englifh North A-
wanted for their fleet, ufed to be furnifhed by Sweden. merica hath
fupplied
In 1703, that ftate was fo blind to its true intereft, as Europe
to lay this important branch of commerce under the with naval
ftores.
reftrictions of an exclufive charter. The firft effect of
this monopoly was a fudden and confiderable increafe
of price. England, taking advantage of this blunder
of the Swedes, encouraged, by confiderable premiums,
the importation of all forts of naval ftores which North
America could furnifh.

Thefe rewards did not immediately produce the effect that was expected from them. A bloody war,
raging in each of the four quarters of the world prevented both the mother-country and the colonies from
giving to this beginning revolution in commerce, the
attention which it merited. The northern nations,
which had all the fame motives of intereft, taking this
inaction, which was only occafioned by the hurry of
a war, for an abfolute proof of inability, thought they
might without danger lay every reftrictive claufe upon the exportation of marine ftores, that could contribute to enhance the price of them. For this purpofe
they entered into mutual engagements which were
made public in 1718, a time, when all the maritime
powers ftill felt the effects of a war that had continued
fourteen years.

England was alarmed at fo odious a convention. She
difpatched to America men of fufficient ability to convince the inhabitants how neceffary it was for them to affift the views of the mother-country; and of fufficient
experience to direct their firft attempts towards great objects, without making them pafs through thofe minute
details, which quickly extinguifh an ardour excited
with difficulty. In a very fhort time, fuch quantities

BOOK XVIII. of pitch, tar, turpentine, yards and mafts, were brought into the harbours of Great Britain, that fhe was enabled to fupply the nations around her.

This fudden fuccefs blinded the Britifh government. The cheapnefs of the naval ftores furnifhed by the colonies, in comparifon of thofe which were brought from the Baltic, gave them an advantage, which feemed to enfure a conftant preference. Upon this the miniftry concluded that the bounties might be withdrawn. But they had not taken into their calculation the difference of freight, which was entirely in favour of their rivals. A total ftop enfued in this branch of trade, and made them fenfible of their error. In 1729, they revived the bounties; which, though they were not laid fo high as formerly, were fufficient to give to the vent of American ftores the greateft fuperiority, at leaft in England, over thofe of the northern nations.

The woods, though they conftituted one of the principal riches of the colonies, had hitherto been overlooked by the governors of the mother-country. The produce of them had long been exported by the Englifh to Spain, Portugal, and the different markets in the Mediterranean, where it was bought up for building and other ufes. As thefe traders did not take in return merchandife fufficient to complete their cargoes, it had been a practice with the Hamburghers, and even the Dutch, to import on their bottoms the produce of the moft fertile climates of Europe. This double trade of export, and carrying the merchandife of other nations, had confiderably augmented the Britifh navigation. The parliament, being informed of this advantage, in the year 1722, immediately exempted the timber of the colonies from all thofe duties of importation to which Ruffian, Swedifh, and Danifh timber are fubject. This firft favour was followed by a bounty, which, at the fame time that it comprehended every fpecies of wood in general, was principally calculated for thofe which are employed in fhip-building. Unfortunately the materials of the

New World were found to be very inferior in quali- B O O K
ty to thofe of the Old; they were, however, employ- XVIII.
ed preferably to the latter by the Englifh navy. England drew its yards and its mafts from North America, and was likewife defirous of getting fails and
rigging from thence.

The French Proteftants, who, when driven from
their country by a prince, become infected with a fpirit of bigotry, carried their national induftry into all
the countries of his enemies, and taught England the
value of flax and hemp, two commodities of the utmoft
importance to a maritime power. Both thefe plants
were cultivated with fuccefs in Scotland and Ireland;
but the manufactures of the nation were chiefly fupplied with them from Ruffia. To put a ftop to this
foreign importation, it was propofed to grant a bounty
to North America of 135 livres [5l. 12s.] for every
ton of thefe articles. This was doing a great deal;
and yet fo confiderable an encouragement had no great
fuccefs. There were not many lands in that part of
the New World which were good enough for a production which profpers only upon an excellent foil.
This region abounds more in iron, that metal which is
deftined to conquer the gold and filver of the fouth.

This moft ferviceable of metals, fo neceffary to man- The iron of
kind, was unknown to the Americans, till the Europe- North A-
ans taught them the moft fatal ufe of it, that of mak- merica hath
ing weapons. The Englifh themfelves long neglected been con-
the iron mines, which nature had lavifhed on the con- veyed into
tinent where they were fettled. That channel of mates.
wealth had been diverted from the mother-country
by being clogged with enormous duties. The proprietors of the national mines, in concert with thofe
of the coppice woods, which are ufed in the working
of them, had procured impofts to be laid on them
that amounted to a prohibition. By corruption, intrigue, and fophiftry, thefe enemies to the public good
had ftifled a competition which would have been fatal
to their interefts. At length the government took the
firft ftep towards a right conduct. The importation of

American iron into the port of London was granted duty free; but at the fame time it was forbidden to be carried to any other ports, or even more than ten miles inland. This whimfical reftriction continued till 1757. At that time the general voice of the people called upon the parliament to repeal an ordinance fo manifeftly contrary to every principle of public utility, and to extend to the whole kingdom a privilege which had been granted exclufively to the capital.

Though nothing could be more reafonable than this demand, it met with the ftrongeft oppofition. Combinations of interefted individuals were formed, to reprefent, that the hundred and nine forges worked in England, not reckoning thofe of Scotland, produced annually eighteen thoufand tons of iron, and employed a great number of able workmen; that the mines, which were inexhauftible, would have fupplied a much greater quantity, had not a perpetual apprehenfion prevailed, that the duties on American iron would be taken off; that the iron works carried on in England confumed annually one hundred and ninety-eight thoufand cords of underwood, and that thofe woods furnifhed, moreover, bark for the tanneries, and materials for fhip-building; and that the American iron, not being proper for fteel, for making fharp inftruments, or many of the utenfils of navigation, would contribute very little to leffen the importation from abroad, and would have no other effect than that of putting a ftop to the forges of Great Britain.

Thefe groundlefs reprefentations had no weight with the parliament, who faw clearly, that, unlefs the price of the original materials could be leffened, the nation would foon lofe the numberlefs manufactures of iron and fteel, by which it had fo long been enriched; and there was no time to be loft in putting a ftop to the progrefs other nations were making in thefe works. It was therefore refolved, that the free importation of iron from America fhould be permitted in all the ports of England. This wife refolution was accompanied with an act of juftice. The proprietors of coppices were, by a ſtatute of Henry the Eighth, forbidden to clear their lands ; but the parliament took off this pro-hibition, and left them at liberty to make uſe of their eſtates as they ſhould think proper.

Previous to theſe regulations, Great Britain uſed to pay annually to Spain, Norway, Sweden, and Ruſſia, ten millions of livres [416,666l. 13s. 4d.] for the iron ſhe purchaſed of them. This tribute is greatly leſſen-ed, and will ſtill decreaſe. The ore is found in ſuch quantities in America, and is ſo eaſily ſeparated from the ground, that the Engliſh did not deſpair of having it in their power to furniſh Portugal, Turkey, Africa, the Eaſt Indies, and every country in the world with which they had any commercial connections.

Perhaps the Engliſh might be too ſanguine in their repreſentations of the advantages they expected from ſo many articles of importance to their navy. But it was ſufficient for them, if by the aſſiſtance of their co-lonies they could free themſelves from that dependence in which the northern powers of Europe had hitherto kept them, with regard to the equipment of their fleets. Nothing appeared to them more capable of checking their natural ardour for the empire of the ſea, which alone could enſure to them the empire of the New World.

After having paved the way to that grand object, by forming a free, independent navy, ſuperior to that of every other nation, England has adopted every meaſure that could contribute to her enjoyment of a ſpecies of conqueſt ſhe had made in America, not ſo much by the force of her arms, as by her induſtry. In proportion as the ſettlements, from their natural ten-dency, advanced from the north to the ſouth, freſh projects and enterpriſes, ſuitable to the nature of the ſoil and of the climate, ſuggeſted themſelves. To the wood, the grains, and the cattle, which had been the former productions, were added ſucceſſively rice, to-bacco, indigo, and other riches. The Engliſh, who had no wine of their own growth in Europe, reſolved

Can it be expected that wine and ſilk will proſper in North America?

to endeavour to procure that alſo from the New Hemiſphere.

Upon the northern continent of North America are
found prodigious quantities of wild vines, which bear
grapes, different in colour, ſize, and quantity, but all
of a four and diſagreeable flavour. It was ſuppoſed
that good management would give theſe plants that
perfection which unaſſiſted nature had denied them;
and French vine-dreſſers were invited into a country,
where neither public nor private impoſitions took away
their inclination to labour, by depriving them of the
fruits of their induſtry. The repeated experiments
they made, both with American and European plants,
were all equally unſucceſsful. The juice of the grape
was too watery, too weak, and too difficult to preſerve.
The country was too full of woods, which attract and
confine the moiſt and hot vapours; the ſeaſons were
too unſettled, and the inſects too numerous near the
foreſts, to ſuffer a production to grow up and proſper,
of which the Engliſh, and all other nations who have
it not, are ſo ambitious. The time will come, perhaps, when this country will furniſh a liquor, in the
preparation of which moſt parts of the globe are employed, and the uſe of which many other parts are ſo
much attached to: but this event will not happen for
ſeveral centuries, and after ſeveral repeated experiments. It is moſt probable that the harveſt of the vine
will be preceded by that of ſilk; the work of that little worm which clothes mankind with the leaves of
trees digeſted in its entrails.

A very conſiderable ſum of money was annually exported from Great Britain for the purchaſe of this rich
production; it was therefore determined to obtain it
from Carolina, which, from the mildneſs of the climate, and the great abundance of mulberry trees,
ſeemed favourable to the project. Some attempts
made by the government to attract ſome Switzers into
the colony were yet more ſucceſsful than could have
been expected. Yet the progreſs of this branch of

trade has not been anſwerable to ſo promiſing a be- B O O K
ginning. The blame has been laid on the inhabitants, XVIII.
who buying only Negro men, from whom they received an immediate and certain profit, neglected to have
women, who with their children might have been employed in bringing up ſilk-worms, an occupation ſuitable to the weakneſs of that ſex, and to the tendereſt
age. But it ought to have been conſidered, that men,
coming from another hemiſphere into a rude uncultivated country, would apply their firſt care to the cultivation of eſculent plants, breeding cattle, and the
toils of immediate neceſſity. This is the natural and
conſtant proceeding of well-governed ſtates. From
agriculture, which is the ſource of population, they riſe
to the arts of luxury; and the arts of luxury nouriſh
commerce, which is the child of induſtry and parent
of wealth. In 1769, the parliament were of opinion
that this period was at length arrived; and they granted a bounty of 25 per cent. for ſeven years on all raw
ſilks imported from the colonies, a bounty of 20 per
cent. for ſeven years following, and for ſeven years after that a bounty of 15 per cent. This encouragement would neceſſarily be followed by the cultivation
of cotton and olive trees, and of ſeveral other plants.
The nation thought that there are few productions,
either of Europe or Aſia, which might not be tranſ-
planted and cultivated with more or leſs ſucceſs on
ſome of the vaſt countries of North America. Men
only were wanting; and no proper precautions were
neglected to increaſe their number.

The firſt perſons who landed in this deſert and ſa- With what
vage region were Engliſhmen, who had been perſe- kind of men
cuted at home for their civil and religious opinions. the provinces of
It was not to be expected that this firſt emigration North A-
would be attended with important conſequences. The merica
inhabitants of Great Britain are ſo ſtrongly attached pled.
were peo-
to their native ſoil, that nothing leſs than civil wars or
revolutions can incline thoſe among them who have
any property, character, or induſtry, to a change of
climate and country: for which reaſon, the re-eſta-

B O O K blifhment of public tranquillity in the mother country
  XVIII.   was likely to put an infurmountable bar to the progrefs
         of American cultivation.

Add to this, that the Englifh, though naturally active, ambitious, and enterprifing, were ill adapted to
the bufinefs of clearing the foil of the New World.
Accuftomed to a quiet life, eafe, and many conveniencies, nothing but the enthufiafm of religion or politics could fupport them under the labours, miferies,
wants, and calamities, infeparable from new plantations.

It is further to be obferved, that, though England
might have been able to overcome thefe difficulties,
fhe ought not to have wifhed to do it. Without
doubt, the founding of colonies, rendering them flourifhing, and enriching herfelf with their productions,
was an advantageous profpect to her; but thofe advantages would be dearly purchafed at the expence of
her own population.

Happily for her, the intolerant and defpotic fpirit
that prevailed in moft countries in Europe, forced
numberlefs victims to take refuge in an uncultivated
tract, which, in its ftate of defolation, feemed to implore that affiftance for itfelf which it offered to the
unfortunate. Thefe men, who had efcaped from the
rod of tyranny, in croffing the feas, abandoned all the
hopes of return, and attached themfelves for ever to a
country, which at the fame time afforded them an afylum and an eafy quiet fubfiftence. Their good fortune
could not remain for ever unknown. Multitudes, particularly from Germany, flocked to partake of it. One
of the advantages which the emigrants propofed to
themfelves was the becoming citizens throughout the
whole extent of the Britifh dominions, after a refidence
of feven years in any of the colonies.

While tyranny and perfecution were deftroying and
exhaufting population in Europe, Englifh America
was beginning to be filled with three forts of inhabitants. The firft clafs, which is the moft numerous,
confifts of freemen.

The Europeans, who overrun and defolate the globe for thefe three centuries paft, have fcattered colonies in moft of the points of its circumference; and their race hath more or lefs degenerated everywhere. The Englifh fettlements of North America appeared to have undergone a fimilar fate. The inhabitants were univerfally thought to be lefs robuft in labour, lefs powerful in war, and lefs adapted to the arts, than their anceftors. Becaufe the care of clearing the lands, of purifying the air, of altering the climate, and of improving nature, had abforbed all the faculties of this people; tranfplanted under another fky, it was concluded that they were degenerated, and unable to elevate their minds to any complicated fpeculations.

In order to difpel this fatal prejudice, it became neceffary that a Franklin fhould teach the philofophers of our continent the art of governing the thunder. It was neceffary that the pupils of this illuftrious man fhould throw a ftriking light upon feveral branches of the natural fciences. It was neceffary that eloquence fhould renew, in that part of the New World, thofe ftrong and rapid impreffions which it had made in the proudeft republics of antiquity. It was neceffary that the rights of mankind, and the rights of nations, fhould be firmly eftablifhed there, in original writings, which will be the delight and the confolation of the moft diftant ages.

Works of imagination, and of tafte, will foon follow thofe of reafoning and obfervation. New England will foon, perhaps, be able to quote its Homer, its Theocritus, and its Sophocles. Neither affiftance, nor mafters, nor models, are now wanting. Education is diffufed, and improves daily. There are, in proportion, more perfons well brought up, and they have more leifure for profecuting the bent of their genius, than men have in Europe, where the education, even of youth, is often contrary to the progrefs and to the unfolding of genius and of reafon.

By a fingular contraft with the Old World, in which the arts have paffed from the fouth towards the north,

we fhall find that in the New World the north will
ferve to enlighten the fouthern parts. Hitherto, the
mind, as well as the body, hath appeared enervated in
the Weft Indies. Men in thofe parts, endowed with
vivacity and early penetration, have a quick conception, but they do not perfevere in ftudy, nor do they
ufe themfelves to long-continued thought. Moft of
them have a great facility for acquiring every kind of
knowledge, but have no decifive turn for any particular fcience. As they are forward, and come to maturity before us, they are far from perfection, and we
are almoft as near to it as we can be. The glory and
happinefs of producing a change in their difpofitions
muft be the work of Englifh America. But it is neceffary that it fhould take fteps conformable to this
noble defign, and aim, by juftice and laudable means,
to form a fet of people fit for the creation of a New
World. This is what hath not yet been done.

The fecond clafs of colonifts was formerly compofed
of malefactors which the mother country tranfported,
after condemnation, to America, and who were bound
to a fervitude of feven or fourteen years to the planters who had purchafed them from the cours of juftice.
Thefe corrupt men, always difpofed to commit frefh
crimes, have at length been univerfally neglected.

They have been replaced by indigent perfons, whom
the impoffibility of fubfifting in Europe has driven into the New World. After having bought and fold
the Negro, there was but one crime which could go
beyond this : this was, to fell one's countryman, without having bought him ; and to find fome perfon who
would buy him : accordingly this has been done.
Having embarked without being able to pay for their
paffage, thefe wretched men are at the difpofal of their
captain, who fells them to whom he choofes. This
fort of flavery is for a longer or fhorter time ; but it
can never exceed eight years. If among thefe emigrants there are any who are not of age, their fervitude lafts till they arrive at that period, which is fixed
at twenty-one for the boys, and eighteen for the girls.

None of thofe who are contracted for have a right
to marry without the approbation of their mafter, who
fets what price he choofes on his confent. If any one
of them fhould run away, and be retaken, he is to
ferve a week for each day's abfence, a month for every week, and fix months for one. The proprietor
who does not think proper to receive again one who
has deferted from his fervice, may fell him to whom
he choofes; but that is only for the term of the firft
contract. Befides, this fervice doth not carry any ignominy with it; and the purchafer does all that lies
in his power to leffen the ftain received by this kind
of fale and purchafe. At the end of his fervitude, the
contracted perfon enjoys all the rights of a free citizen. With his freedom, he receives from the mafter
whom he has ferved, either implements for hufbandry,
or utenfils proper for his work.

But with whatever appearance of juftice this fpecies of traffic may be coloured, the greateft part of
the ftrangers who go over to America under thefe
conditions, would never go on board a fhip, if they
were not inviegled away. Some artful kidnappers
from the fens of Holland fpread themfelves over the
Palatinate, Suabia, and the cantons of Germany,
which are the beft peopled, or the leaft happy. There
they fet forth with raptures, the delights of the New
World, and the fortunes eafily acquired in that country. Simple men, feduced by thefe magnificent pro-
mifes, blindly follow thefe infamous brokers, engaged
in this fcandalous commerce, who deliver them over
to factors at Amfterdam or Rotterdam. Thefe, who
are in the pay of companies who have undertaken to
ftock the colonies with inhabitants, give a gratuity to
the men employed in this fervice. Whole families
are fold, without their knowledge, to mafters at a diftance, who impofe the harder conditions upon them,
as hunger and neceffity do not permit the fufferers
to give a refufal. America acquires its fupplies of
men for hufbandry, as princes do for war, by the
fame artifices; but with a lefs honeft, and perhaps a

more inhuman defign; for who knows the number of
thofe who die, or who furvive their expectations? The
deception is perpetually carried on in Europe, by
carefully fuppreffing all correfpondence with America, which might unveil a myftery of impofture and
iniquity, too well difguifed by the interefted principles which gave rife to it.

But, in a word, there would not be fo many dupes,
if there were fewer victims. It is the oppreffion of
government which makes thefe chimerical ideas of
fortune be adopted by the credulity of the people.
Men, unfortunate in their private affairs, vagabonds,
or contemptible at home, have nothing worfe to fear,
in a foreign climate, and eafily purfue the profpect of
a better lot. The means made ufe of to retain them
in a country where chance has given them birth, are
only calculated to excite in them a defire to quit it.
It is vainly fuppofed that they are to be confined by
prohibitions, menaces, and punifhments : thefe do but
exafperate them, and drive them to defertion by the
very forbidding of it. They fhould be attached by
milder means, and by future expectations ; whereas
they are imprifoned and bound : man, born free, is
reftrained from attempting to exift in regions, where
heaven and earth offer him an afylum. It has been
thought better to ftifle him in his cradle, than to let
him feek for his fubfiftence in fome favourable climate.
It is not judged proper even to leave him the choice
of his burial-place.—Tyrants in policy ! thefe are the
effects of your laws ! People, where then are your
rights ?

Is it then become neceffary to lay open to the nations the fchemes that are formed againft their liberty ? Muft they be told, that by a confpiracy of the
moft odious nature, certain powers have lately entered into an agreement, which muft deprive even defpair itfelf of every refource ? For thefe two centuries paft, all the princes of Europe have been fabri-
cating, in the fecret receffes of the cabinet, that long
and heavy chain with which the people are encom-

paſſed on every fide. At every negotiation freſh links
were added to the chain fo artificially contrived. Wars
tended not to make ſtates more extenſive, but ſubjects
more ſubmiſſive, by gradually ſubſtituting military government to the mild and gentle influence of laws and
morality. The ſeveral ſovereigns have all equally
ſtrengthened themſelves in their tyranny by their conqueſts or by their loſſes. When they were victorious
they reigned by their armies ; when humbled by defeat, they held the command by the miſery of their
puſillanimous ſubjects ; if they were either competitors or adverſaries from motives of ambition, they
entered into league or alliance, only to aggravate the
ſervitude of their people. Whether they meant to excite war or to preſerve peace, they were certain of
turning to the advantage of their authority, either
the aggrandiſement or the humiliation of their people. If they ceded a province, they exhauſted every
other, that they might either recover it or indemnify
themſelves for the loſs. If they acquired a new one,
the haughtineſs they affected out of it was the occafion of cruelty and extortion within. They borrowed one of another, by turns, every art and invention,
whether of peace or of war, that might concur ſometimes to foment natural antipathy and rivalſhip, ſometimes to obliterate the character of the nations ; as if
there had been a tacit agreement among the rulers
to ſubject the nations, one by means of another, to
the deſpotiſm they had conſtantly been preparing for
them. Ye people, who all groan more or leſs ſecret-
ly, be not blinded with reſpect to your condition ;
thoſe who never entertained any affection for you,
are come now not to have any fear for you. In the
extremity of wretchedneſs one ſingle reſource remained for you ; that of eſcape and emigration.—Even
that has been ſhut againſt you.

Princes have agreed among themſelves to reſtore to
one another deſerters, who, for the moſt part, enliſted
by compulſion or by fraud, have a right to eſcape ;
not only villains, who, in reality, ought not to find a

refuge anywhere; but indifferently all their fubjects,
whatever may be the motive that obliged them to quit
their country.

Thus all ye unhappy labourers, who find neither
fubfiftence nor work in your own countries, after they
have been ravaged and rendered barren by the exactions of finance; thus ye die where ye had the misfortune to be born; ye have no refuge but in the
grave. All ye artifts and workmen of every fpecies,
haraffed by monopolies, who are refufed the right of
working at your own free difpofal, unlefs you have
purchafed the privileges of your calling : ye who are
kept for your whole life in the workfhop, for the purpofe of enriching a privileged factor : ye whom a court-
mourning leaves for months together without bread or
wages! never expect to live out of a country where
foldiers and guards keep you imprifoned; go, wander
in defpair, and die of regret. If ye venture to complain, your cries will be re-echoed and loft in the
depth of a dungeon; if ye make your efcape, ye will
be purfued even beyond mountains and rivers : ye
will be fent back, or given up, bound hand and foot,
to torture, and to that eternal reftraint, to which you
have been condemned from your birth. Do you likewife, whom nature has endowed with a free fpirit, independent of prejudice and error, who dare to think
and talk like men, do you erafe from your minds every
idea of truth, nature, and humanity! Applaud every
encroachment made on your country and your fellow-
citizens, or elfe maintain a profound filence in the receffes of obfcurity and concealment. All ye who
were born in thofe barbarous ftates, where the condition for the mutual reftoration of deferters has been
entered into by the feveral princes, and fealed by a
treaty; recollect the infcription Dante has engraven
on the gate of his infernal region : *Voi ch' entrate, laf-
ciate omai ogni fperanza: You who enter here, leave behind you every hope.*

What! is there then no afylum remaining beyond
the feas? Will not England open her colonies to thofe

wretches who voluntarily prefer her dominion to the insupportable yoke of their own country? What occasion has she for that infamous band of contracted slaves, seduced and debauched by the shameful means employed by every state to increase their armies? What need has she of those beings still more miserable, of whom she composes another class of her inhabitants?

Yes, by an antiquity, the more shocking as it is apparently the less necessary, the northern provinces have had recourse to the traffic and slavery of the Negroes. It will not be disowned, that they may be better fed, better clothed, less ill treated, and less overburdened with toil, than in the islands. The laws protect them more effectually, and they seldom become the victims of the barbarity or caprice of an odious tyrant. But still, what must be the burden of a man's life who is condemned to languish in eternal slavery? Some humane sectaries, Christians who look for virtues in the gospel, more than for opinions, have often been desirous of restoring to their slaves that liberty for which they cannot receive any adequate compensation; but they have been a long time withholden by a law, which directed that an assignment of a sufficiency for subsistence should be made to those who were set at liberty.

Let us rather say, they have been prevented from doing this by the convenient custom of being waited on by slaves; by the fondness they have for power, which they attempt to justify by pretending to alleviate their servitude; and by the opinion so readily entertained that the slaves do not complain of a state, which is by time changed into nature: these are the sophisms of self love, calculated to appease the clamours of conscience. The generality of mankind are not born with evil dispositions, or prone to do ill by choice; but even among those whom nature seems to have formed just and good, there are but few who possess a soul sufficiently disinterested, courageous, and great, to do any good action, if they must sacrifice some advantage for it.

B O O K   But ſtill the Quakers have lately ſet an example
  XVIII.   which ought to make an epocha in the hiſtory of religion and humanity. In one of their aſſemblies, where
every one of the faithful, who conceives himſelf moved by the impulſe of the Holy Spirit, has a right of
ſpeaking ; one of the brethren, who was himſelf undoubtedly inſpired on this occaſion, aroſe and ſaid :
" How long then ſhall we have two conſciences, two
" meaſures, two ſcales ! one in our own favour, one
" for the ruin of our neighbour, both equally falſe ?
" Is it for us, brethren, to complain at this moment,
" that the parliament of England wiſhes to enſlave
" us, and to impoſe upon us the yoke of ſubjects,
" without leaving us the rights of citizens ; while for
" this century paſt, we have been calmly acting the
" part of tyrants, by keeping in bonds of the hardeſt
" ſlavery men who are our equals and our brethren ?
" What have thoſe unhappy men done to us, whom na-
" ture hath ſeparated from us by barriers ſo formidable,
" whom our avarice has ſought after through ſtorms and
" wrecks, and brought away from the midſt of their
" burning ſands, or from their dark foreſts inhabited
" by tygers ? What crime have they been guilty of,
" that they ſhould be torn from a country which fed
" them without toil, and that they ſhould be tranſ-
" planted by us to a land where they periſh under the
" labours of ſervitude ? Father of heaven, what fami-
" ly haſt thou then created, in which the elder born,
" after having ſeized on the property of their bre-
" thren, are ſtill reſolved to compel them with ſtripes,
" to manure with the blood of their veins and the
" ſweat of their brow that very inheritance of which
" they have been robbed ? Deplorable race, whom we
" render brutes to tyrannize over them ; in whom we
" extinguiſh every power of the ſoul, to load their
" limbs and their bodies with burdens ; in whom we
" efface the image of God and the ſtamp of man-
" hood. A race mutilated and diſhonoured as to the
" faculties of mind and body, throughout its exiſtence,
" by us who are Chriſtians and Engliſhmen ! Engliſh-

" men, ye people favoured by Heaven, and refpect- B O O K
" ed on the feas, would ye be free and tyrants at the XVIII.
" fame inftant? No, brethren! it is time we fhould
" be confiftent with ourfelves. Let us fet free thofe
" miferable victims of our pride : let us reftore the
" Negroes to that liberty which man fhould never
" take from man. May all Chriftian focieties be in-
" duced, by our example, to repair an injuftice au-
" thorifed by the crimes and plunders ^f two centu-
" ries! May men too long degraded, at length raife
" to heaven their arms freed from chains, and their
" eyes bathed in tears of gratitude! Alas! thefe un-
" happy mortals have hitherto fhed no tears but thofe
" of defpair."

This difcourfe awakened remorfe, and the fmall
number of flaves who belonged to the Quakers were
fet at liberty. If the fetters of thefe unfortunate people were not broken by the other colonifts of North
America, yet Pennfylvania, New Jerfey, and Virginia,
warmly folicited that this infamous traffic of men
fhould be prohibited. Every colony of this vaft continent appeared difpofed to follow this example ; but
they were prevented by an order from the mother-
country to its delegates, to reject every propofal tending to this humane project. This cruel prohibition
would not have been furprifing, if it had come from
thofe countries which are as deep funk in barbarifm
by the fhackles of vice, as they have formerly been
by thofe of ignorance. When a government, both
facerdotal and military, has brought every thing, even
the opinions of men, under its yoke ; when man, become an impoftor, has perfuaded the armed multitude
that he holds from Heaven the right of oppreffing the
earth, there is no fhadow of liberty left for civilized
nations. Why fhould they not take their revenge on
the people of the torrid zone? But I fhall never comprehend by what fatality that legiflation, which is the
moft happily planned of any that hath ever exifted,
hath been capable of preferring the intereft of a few

B O O K of its merchants to the dictates of nature, of reason,
XVIII   and of virtue.

To what   The population of North America consists of four
degree the hundred thousand Negroes, and of two millions five
population
of North or six hundred thousand white people, if the calcula-
America tions of congress be not exaggerated. The number
hath arisen.
of citizens doubles every fifteen or sixteen years in
some of those provinces, and every eighteen or twenty
years in others.   So rapid an increase must have two
sources ; the first is, that a number of Irishmen, Jews,
Frenchmen, Switzers, Palatines, Moravians, and Saltzburghers, after having been worn out with the political and religious troubles they had experienced in Europe, have gone in search of peace and quietness in
these distant climates. The second source of that a-
mazing increase arises from the climate itself of the
colonies, where experience has shown that the people
naturally doubled their numbers every five-and-twenty years. The observations of Mr. Franklin will make
these truths evident.

The numbers of the people, says that philosopher,
increase every where in proportion to the number of
marriages ; and that number increases as the means of
subsisting a family are rendered more easy. In a country where the means of subsistence abound, more people marry early.   In a society, whose prosperity is a
mark of its antiquity, the rich, alarmed at the expences which female luxury brings along with it, engage as late as possible in a state, which is difficult to
enter into, and expensive to maintain ; and the persons who have no fortunes pass their days in a celibacy which disturbs the married state. The masters
have but few children, the servants have none at all,
and the artisans are afraid of having any. This circumstance is so evident, especially in great towns, that
the population in them is not kept up to its usual stan-
dard, and that we constantly find there a greater number of deaths than births. Happily for us this decrease
has not yet penetrated into the country, where the

constant practice of making up the deficiency of the B O O K
XVIII. towns gives a little more scope for population. But the lands being every where occupied, and let at the highest rate, those who cannot acquire property of their own, are hired by those who are in possession of it. Competition, which arises from the multitude of workmen, lowers the price of labour, and the small-ness of profit takes away the desire and the hope of, as well as the abilities requisite for, increase by mar-riage. Such is the present state of Europe.

That of America presents an appearance of a quite contrary nature. Tracts of land, waste and unculti-vated, are either given away, or may be obtained for so moderate a price, that a man of the least turn for labour is furnished in a short time with an extent, which, while it is sufficient to rear a numerous family, will maintain his posterity for a considerable time. The inhabitants, therefore, of the New World, marry in greater numbers, and at an earlier time of life, than the inhabitants of Europe. Where one hundred en-ter into the married state in Europe, there are two hundred in America; and if we reckon four children to each marriage in our climates, we should allow at least eight in the New Hemisphere. If we multiply these families by their produce, it will appear, that, in less than two centuries, North America will arrive at an immense degree of population, unless its natural progress should be impeded by obstacles which it is not possible to foresee.

It is now peopled with healthy and robust men, of Manners prevailing at present in North America. a stature above the common size. These Creoles come to their full growth sooner than the Europeans, but do not live so long. The inhabitants are supplied with great plenty of every thing requisite for food, by the low price of meat, fish, grain, game, fruits, cyder, and vegetables. Clothing is not so easily procured, that being still very dear, whether it be brought from Eu-rope or made in the country. Manners are in the state they should be among young colonies, and peo-ple given to cultivation, who are not yet polished nor

BOOK XVIII. corrupted by refiding in great cities. Throughout the families in general, there reigns economy, neatnefs, and regularity. Gallantry and gaming, the paffions of indolent opulence, feldom interrupt that happy tranquillity. The female fex are ftill what they fhould be, gentle, modeft, compaffionate, and ufeful; they are in poffeffion of thofe virtues which perpetuate the empire of their charms. The men are engaged in their firft occupations, the care and improvement of their plantations, which will be the fupport of their pofterity. One general fentiment of benevolence unites every family. Nothing contributes to this union fo much as a certain equality of ftation, a fecurity that arifes from property, hope, and a general facility of increafing it; in a word, nothing contributes to it fo much as the reciprocal independence in which all men live, with refpect to their wants, joined to the neceffity of focial connections for the purpofes of their pleafures. Inftead of luxury, which brings mifery in its train, inftead of this afflicting and fhocking contraft, an univerfal eafe, wifely dealt out in the original diftribution of the lands, has, by the influence of induftry, given rife in every breaft to the mutual defire of pleafing; a defire, without doubt, more fatisfactory than the fecret difpofition to injure our brethren, which is infeparable from an extreme inequality of fortune and condition. Men never meet without fatisfaction, when they are neither in that ftate of mutual diftance which leads to indifference, nor in that way of rivalfhip which borders on hatred. They come nearer together and unite in focieties; in fhort, it is in the colonies that men lead fuch a rural life as was the original deftination of mankind, beft fuited to the health and increafe of the fpecies: probably they enjoy all the happinefs confiftent with the frailty of human nature. We do not, indeed, find there thofe graces, thofe talents, thofe refined enjoyments, the means and expence of which wear out and fatigue the fprings of the foul, and bring on the vapours of melancholy, which fo naturally follow the difguft arifing from fenfual enjoyment; but there are the pleafures B o o k of domeſtic life, the mutual attachments of parents and children, and conjugal love, that paſſion ſo pure and ſo delicious to the ſoul that can taſte it, and deſpiſe all other gratifications. This is the inchanting proſpect exhibited throughout North America. It is in the wilds of Florida and Virginia, even in the foreſts of Canada, that men are enabled to continue to love, during their whole life, what was the object of their firſt affection, that innocence and virtue, which never entirely loſe their beauty.

B o o k XVIII.

If there be any circumſtance wanting to the happineſs of Britiſh America, it is that of forming one entire nation. Families are there found ſometimes reunited, ſometimes diſperſed, originating from all the different countries of Europe. Theſe coloniſts, in whatever ſpot chance or diſcernment may have placed them, all preſerve, with a prejudice not to be worn out, their mother-tongue, the partialities and the cuſtoms of their own country. Separate ſchools and churches hinder them from mixing with the hoſpitable people who afforded them a place of refuge. Still more eſtranged from this people by worſhip, by manners, and probably by their feelings, they harbour ſeeds of diſſenſion that may one day prove the ruin and total overthrow of the colonies. The only preſervative againſt this diſaſter depends entirely on the conduct of the governments they belong to.

By governments muſt not be underſtood thoſe ſtrange conſtitutions of Europe, which are an abſurd mixture of ſacred and profane laws. Engliſh America was wiſe or happy enough not to admit any eccleſiaſtical power : being from the beginning inhabited by Preſbyterians, ſhe rejected with horror every thing that might revive the idea of it. All affairs which in the other parts of the globe are determined by the eccleſiaſtical courts, are here brought before the civil magiſtrate, or the national aſſemblies. The attempts made by the members of the Engliſh church to eſtabliſh their hierarchy in that country, have ever

Nature of the governments eſtabliſhed in North America.

been abortive, notwithſtanding the ſupport given them by the mother-country : but ſtill they are equally concerned in the adminiſtration as well as thoſe of other ſects. None but Catholics have been excluded, on account of their refuſing thoſe oaths which the public tranquillity ſeemed to require. In this view American government has deſerved the greateſt commendation ; but in other reſpects it is not ſo well regulated.

Policy, in its aim and principal object, reſembles the education of children. They both tend to form men, and ſhould be in ſeveral reſpects ſimilar to each other. Savage people, firſt united in ſociety, require, as much as children, to be ſometimes led on by gentle means, and ſometimes reſtrained by compulſion. For want of experience, which alone forms our reaſon, as theſe ſavages are incapable of governing themſelves in the ſeveral changes of things and the various concerns that belong to a riſing ſociety, the government that conducts them ſhould itſelf be enlightened, and guide them by authority to years of maturity. Thus it is that barbarous nations are naturally ſubject to the oppreſſive yoke of deſpotic power, till in the advanced ſtate of ſociety their intereſts teach them to connect themſelves.

Civilized nations, like young men, more or leſs advanced, not in proportion to their abilities, but from the conduct of their early education, as ſoon as they become ſenſible of their own ſtrength and right, require to be managed, and even attended to by their governors. A ſon well educated ſhould engage in no undertaking without conſulting his father : a prince, on the contrary, ſhould make no regulations without conſulting his people : further, the ſon, in reſolutions where he follows the advice of his father, frequently hazards nothing but his own happineſs : in all that a prince ordains, the happineſs of his people is concerned. The opinion of the public, in a nation that thinks and ſpeaks, is the rule of the government ; and the prince ſhould never thwart that opinion without public reaſons, nor oppoſe it without having firſt convin-

ced the people of their error. Government is to mo- BOOK
del all its forms according to public opinion : this, it XVIII.
is well known, varies with manners, habits, and information. So that one prince may, without finding the
leaft refiftance, do an act of authority, not to be revived by his fucceffor, without exciting the public indignation. From whence does this difference arife?
The firft cannot have thwarted an opinion that was
not fprung up in his time, but the latter may have
openly counteracted it a century after. The firft, if
I may be allowed the expreffion, may, without the
knowledge of the public, have taken a ftep, the violence of which he may have foftened or made amends
for by the happy fuccefs of his government; the other
fhall, perhaps, have increafed the public calamities by
fuch unjuft acts of wilful authority, as may perpetuate
its firft abufes. Public remonftrance is generally the
refult of opinion ; and the general opinion is the rule
of government : and becaufe the public opinion governs mankind, kings, for this reafon, become the rulers of men. Governments then, as well as opinions,
ought to improve and advance to perfection. But
what is the rule for opinions among an enlightened
people ? It is the permanent intereft of fociety, the
fafety and advantage of the nation. This intereft is
modified by the turn of events and fituations ; public
opinion and the form of the government follow thefe
feveral modifications. This is the fource of all the
forms of government eftablifhed by the Englifh, who
are rational and free, throughout North America.

The government of Nova Scotia, of one of the provinces in New England, New York, New Jerfey, Virginia, the two Carolinas, and Georgia, is ftyled royal,
becaufe the king of England is there invefted with
the fupreme authority. Reprefentatives of the people
form a houfe of commons, as in the mother-country :
a felect council, approved by the king, intended to
fupport the prerogatives of the crown, reprefents the
houfe of peers, and maintains that reprefentation by
the fortune and rank of the moft diftinguifhed perfons

B O O K in the country, who are members of it.   A governor
XVIII. convenes, prorogues, and diffolves their affemblies;
gives or refufes affent to their deliberations, which receive from his approbation the force of law, till the
king, to whom they are tranfmitted, has rejected them.

The fecond kind of government which takes place
in the colonies, is known by the name of proprietary
government.   When the Englifh firft fettled on thofe
diftant regions, a rapacious and active court favourite
eafily obtained in thofe waftes, which were as large as
kingdoms, a property and authority without bounds.
A bow and a few fkins, the only homage exacted by
the crown, purchafed for a man in power the right of
fovereignty, or of governing at pleafure in an unknown
country : fuch was the origin of government in the
greater part of the colonies.   At prefent, Maryland
and Pennfylvania are the only provinces under this
fingular form of government, or rather this fingular
foundation of fovereignty.   Maryland, indeed, differs
from the reft of the provinces only by receiving its
governor from the family of Baltimore, whofe nomi-
nation is to be approved by the king.   In Pennfylvania, the governor named by the proprietary family,
and confirmed by the crown, is not fupported by a
council, which gives a kind of fuperiority, and he is
obliged to agree with the commons, in whom is naturally vefted all authority.

A third form, ftyled by the Englifh charter government, feems more calculated to produce harmony in
the conftitution.   At prefent this fubfifts only in Connecticut and Rhode Ifland ; but it was formerly extended to all the provinces in New England.   It may
be confidered as a mere democracy.   The inhabitants
of themfelves elect and depofe all their officers, and
make whatever laws they think proper, without being
obliged to have the affent of the king, or his having
any right to annul them.

At length the conqueft of Canada, joined to the
acquifition of Florida, has given rife to a form of legiflation hitherto unknown throughout the realm of

Great Britain. Thofe provinces have been put or left
under the yoke of military, and confequently abfolute authority. Without any right to affemble in a national body, they receive immediately from the court of London every order of government.

This diverfity of governments is not the work of the mother country. We do not find in it the traces of a reafonable, uniform, and regular legiflation. It is chance, climate, the prejudices of the times, and of the founders of the colonies, that have produced this motley variety of conftitutions. It is not the province of men, who are caft by chance upon a defert coaft, to conftitute legiflation.

All legiflation, in its nature, fhould aim at the happinefs of fociety. The means by which it is to attain this great end, depend entirely on its natural qualities. Climate, that is to fay, the fky and the foil, are the firft rule for the legiflator. His refources dictate to him his duties. In the firft inftance, the local pofition fhould be confulted. A number of people thrown on a maritime coaft, will have laws more or lefs relative to agriculture or navigation, in proportion to the influence the fea or land may have on the fubfiftence of the inhabitants who are to people that defert coaft. If the new colony be led by the courfe of fome large river far within land, a legiflator ought to have regard to the quality of the foil and the degree of its fertility, as well as to the connections the colony will have either at home or abroad by the traffic of commodities moft conducive to its profperity.

But the wifdom of legiflation will chiefly appear in the diftribution of property. It is a general rule, which obtains in all countries, that, when a colony is founded, an extent of land be given to every perfon fufficient for the maintenance of a family : more fhould be given to thofe who have abilities to make the neceffary advances towards improvement; and fome fhould be referved for pofterity, or for additional fettlers, with which the colony may in time be augmented.

The firft object of a rifing colony is fubfiftence and
population : the next is the profperity likely to flow
from thefe two fources.   To avoid occafions of war,
whether offenfive or defenfive ; to turn induftry towards thofe objects which are moft advantageous; not
to form connections around them, except fuch as are
unavoidable, and may be proportioned to the ftability
which the colony acquires by the numbers of its inhabitants and the nature of its refources; to introduce, above all things, a partial and local fpirit in a
nation which is going to be eftablifhed, a fpirit of
union within, and of peace without ; to refer every
inftitution to a diftant but fixed point ; and to make
every occafional law fubfervient to the fettled regulation which alone is to effect an increafe of numbers,
and to give ftability to the fettlement : thefe circumftances make no more than a fketch of a legiflation.

The moral fyftem is to be formed on the nature of
the climate ; a large field for population is at firft to
be laid open by facilitating marriage, which depends
upon the facility of procuring fubfiftence. Sanctity
of manners fhould be eftablifhed by opinion. In a
barbarous ifland, which is to be ftocked with children,
no more would be neceffary than to leave the principles of truth to unfold themfelves with the natural
progrefs of reafon. By proper precautions againft
thofe idle fears which proceed from ignorance, the
errors of fuperftition fhould be removed, till that period when the warmth of the natural paffions, fortunately uniting with the rational powers, diffipates every phantom. But when people already advanced in
life are to be eftablifhed in a new country, the ability
of legiflation confifts in removing every injurious opinion or habit which may be cured or corrected. If
we wifh that thefe fhould not be tranfmitted to pofterity, we fhould attend to the fecond generation, by
inftituting a general and public education of the children. A prince or legiflator fhould never found a colony, without previoufly fending thither fome proper
perfons for the education of youth ; that is, fome go-

vernors rather than teachers : for it is of lefs moment
to teach them what is good, than to guard them from
evil. Good education is ineffectual, when the people
are already corrupted. The feeds of morality and virtue, fown in the infant ftate of a generation already
vitiated, are annihilated in the early ftages of man-
hood by debauchery, and the contagion of fuch vices
as have already become habitual in fociety. The beft
educated young men cannot come into the world
without making engagements and forming connections, which will wholly influence them during the
remainder of their lives. If they marry, follow any
profeffion or purfuit, they find the feeds of evil and
corruption rooted in every condition ; a conduct entirely oppofite to their principles ; example and difcourfe which difconcerts and combats their beft refolutions.

But in a rifing colony, the influence of the firft generation may be corrected by the manners of the fucceeding one. The minds of all are prepared for virtue by labour. The neceffities of life remove all vices
proceeding from want of employment. The overflowing of its population hath a natural tendency towards
the mother-country, where luxury continually invites
and feduces the rich and voluptuous planter. A legiflator, who intends to refine the conftitution and
manners of a colony, will meet with every affiftance
he can require. If he be only poffeffed of abilities
and virtue, the lands and the people he has to manage
will fuggeft to his mind a plan of fociety, that a writer
can only mark out in a vague manner, liable to all the
uncertainty of hypothefes that are varied and complicated by an infinity of circumftances too difficult to
be forefeen and combined.

But the chief bafis of a fociety for cultivation or
commerce, is property. It is the feed of good and
evil, natural or moral, confequent on the focial ftate.
Every nation feems to be divided into two irreconcileable parties. The rich and the poor, the men of property and the hirelings, that is to fay, mafters and

BOOK
XVIII.
flaves, form two claffes of citizens, unfortunately, in oppofition to one another. In vain have fome modern authors wifhed by fophiftry to eftablifh a treaty of peace between thefe two ftates. The rich on all occafions are difpofed to obtain a great deal from the poor at little expence, and the poor are ever inclined to fet too high a value on their labour; while the rich man muft always give the law in this too unequal bargain. Hence arifes the fyftem of counterpoife eftablifhed in fo many countries. The people have not wifhed to attack property which they confidered as facred, but they have made attempts to fetter it, and to check its natural tendency to univerfal power. Thefe counterpoifes have almoft always been ill applied, as they were but a feeble remedy againft the original evil in fociety. It is then to the repartition of lands that a legiflator will turn his principal attention. The more wifely that diftribution fhall be managed, the more fimple, uniform, and exact, will be thofe laws of the country which chiefly conduce to the prefervation of property.

The Englifh colonies partake, in this refpect, of the radical vice inherent in the ancient conftitution of the mother-country. As its prefent government is but a reformation of that feudal fyftem which had oppreffed all Europe, it ftill retains many ufages, which being originally nothing more than abufes of fervitude, are ftill more fenfibly felt by their contraft with the liberty which the people have recovered. It has, therefore, been found neceffary to join the laws which left many rights to the nobility, to thofe which modify, leffen, abrogate, or foften the feudal rights. Hence fo many laws of exception for one original law; fo many of interpretation for one fundamental; fo many new laws that are at variance with the old. Hence it is agreed, there is not in the whole world a code fo diffufe, fo perplexed, as that of the civil law of Great Britain. The wifeft men of that enlightened nation have often exclaimed againft this diforder. They have either not been heard, or the changes which have been produced by their remonftrances have only ferved to increafe the confufion.

By their dependence and their ignorance, the colonies have blindly adopted that deformed and ill-digefted code, the burden of which oppreffed their anceftors : they have added to that obfcure heap of materials by every new law that the times, manners, and place could introduce. From this mixture has refulted a chaos the moft difficult to put in order; a collection of contradictions that requires much pains to reconcile. Immediately there fprang up a numerous body of lawyers, to prey upon the lands and inhabitants of thofe new fettled climates. The fortune and influence they have acquired in a fhort time, have brought into fubjection to their rapacioufnefs the valuable clafs of citizens employed in agriculture, commerce, in all the arts and labours moft indifpenfably neceffary for every fociety, but almoft fingularly effential to a rifing community. To the fevere evil of chicane, which has fixed itfelf on the branches, in order to feize on the fruit, has fucceeded that of finance, which deftroys the heart and the root of the tree.

In the origin of the colonies, the coin bore the fame value as in the mother-country. The fcarcity of it foon occafioned a rife of one-third. That inconvenience was not remedied by the abundance of fpecie which came from the Spanifh colonies; becaufe it was neceffary to tranfmit that into England in order to pay for the merchandife wanted from thence. This was a gulf that abforbed the circulation in the colonies. It was, however, neceffary to eftablifh a mode of exchange; and every province, except Virginia, fought for it in the creation of a paper currency.

The coin that has been current in the Englifh colonies in North America.

The general government made at firft but a moderate ufe of this expedient; but the difputes of the favages increafing, as well as the wars againft Canada, occafioned men of an enterprifing fpirit to form complicated and extenfive projects; and the management of the public treafury was intrufted to rapacious or unfkilful hands. This refource was then more freely

employed than was proper.   In vain were taxes levied
at firſt, in order to pay the intereſt of the paper, and
and to take up the paper itſelf at a ſtipulated period.
New debts were contracted to ſatisfy freſh wants, and
engagements were generally carried beyond all exceſs.
In Pennſylvania alone, the paper currency of the ſtate
preſerved unremittingly its entire value.   The credit
of it was ſhaken in two or three other colonies, though
it was not entirely loſt.   But in the two Carolinas, and
in the four provices which conſtitute what is commonly called New England, it fell into ſuch diſcredit from
the multiplicity of it, that it could no longer be circulated at any rate.   Maſſachuſet's Bay, which had
conquered Cape Breton from the French, received from
the mother-country 4,050,000 livres [168,750l.] of indemnification.   With this ſum they paid off twelve
times the value in their paper, and thoſe who received
the money thought they had made a very good bargain.   The parliament, aware of this miſchief, made
ſome attempts to remedy it ; but their meaſures were
only very imperfectly ſucceſsful.   It would certainly
have been a more effectual ſtep, than any of thoſe
which had been invented by either a good or bad
policy, to have broken the fetters with which the internal induſtry, and the external commerce, of ſo many great ſettlements were ſhackled.

Regula-
tions to
which the
internal in-
duſtry and
the external
trade of
North A-
merica had
been ſub-
jected.
The firſt coloniſts who peopled North America applied themſelves ſolely to agriculture.   They ſoon perceived that their exports did not enable them to buy
what they wanted, and they therefore found themſelves in a manner compelled to ſet up ſome rude manufactures.   The intereſts of the mother-country ſeemed to be affected by this innovation ; which was made
a matter of parliamentary inquiry, and diſcuſſed with
all the attention it deſerved.   There were men bold
enough to defend the cauſe of the coloniſts.   They
urged, that as the buſineſs of tillage did not employ
men all the year, it was tyranny to oblige them to
waſte in idleneſs the time which the land did not require : that as the produce of agriculture and hunt-

ing did not furnifh them to the extent of their wants,
the preventing them from providing againft them by
a new fpecies of induftry, was in fact reducing them
to the greateft diftrefs : in a word, that the prohibition of manufactures only tended to enhance the price
of all provifions in a rifing ftate, to leffen, or, perhaps, ftop the fale of them, and to deter fuch perfons as might intend to fettle in it.

The evidence of thefe principles was not to be con-
troverted : they were complied with after great debates. The Americans were permitted to manufacture their own clothes themfelves, but with fuch reftrictions as betrayed how much avarice regretted,
what an appearance of juftice could not but allow.
All communication from one province to another on
this account was feverely prohibited. They were forbidden, under the heavieft penalties, to traffic with
each other for wool of any fort, raw or manufactured. However, fome manufacturers of hats ventured
to break through thefe reftrictions. To put a ftop
to what was termed a heinous diforderly practice, the
parliament had recourfe to the mean and cruel expedient of law. A workman was not at liberty to fet
up for himfelf till after feven years apprenticefhip ; a
mafter was not allowed to have more than two ap-
prentices at a time, nor to employ any flave in his
work-fhop.

Iron mines, which feem to put into men's hands the
inftruments of their own independence, were laid under
reftrictions ftill more fevere. It was not allowed to carry iron in bars, or rough pieces, anywhere but to the
mother-country. Without being provided with cru-
cibles to melt it or machines to bend it, without ham-
mers or anvils to fafhion it, they had ftill lefs liberty
of converting it into fteel.

Importation was fubjected to ftill further reftraints.
All foreign veffels, unlefs in evident diftrefs or danger of wreck, or freighted with gold or filver, were
not to come into any of the ports of North America.
Even Englifh veffels were not admitted there, unlefs

they came immediately from some port of the country. The ships of the colonies going to Europe, were to bring back no merchandise but from the mother-country. Every thing was included in this proscription, except wine from the Madeiras, the Azores, and the Canaries, and salt for the fisheries.

All exportations were originally to terminate in England; but important reasons determined the government to relax and abate this extreme severity. The colonists were allowed to carry directly south of Cape Finisterre, grain, meal, rice, vegetables, fruit, salt fish, planks, and timber. All other productions were reserved for the mother-country. Even Ireland, which afforded an advantageous mart for corn, flax, and pipe-staves, has been shut against them by an act of parliament.

The parliament, which represents the nation, assumed the right of directing commere in its whole extent throughout the British dominions. It is by this authority it pretends to regulate the connections between the mother-country and the colonies, to maintain a communication, an advantageous reciprocal re-action between the scattered parts of an immense empire. There should, in fact, be one power to appeal to, in order to determine finally upon the concerns that may be useful or prejudicial to the general good of the whole society. The parliament is the only body that can assume such an important power. But it ought to employ it to the advantage of every member of society. This is an inviolable maxim, especially in a state where all the powers are formed and directed for the preservation of national liberty.

That principle of impartiality was unattended to, which alone can maintain an equal state of independence among the several members of a free government; when the colonies were obliged to vent in the mother-country all their productions, even those which were not for their own consumption; when they were obliged to take from the mother-country all kinds of merchandise, even those which came from foreign nations. This imperious and useless restraint, loading the fales and purchafes of the Americans with unne- ceffary and ruinous charges, has neceffarily leffened their induftry, and confequently diminifhed their profits; and it has been only for the purpofe of enriching a few merchants, or fome factors at home, that the rights and interefts of the colonies have thus been facrificed. All they owed to England for the protection they received from her, was only a preference in the fale and importation of all fuch of their commodities as fhe fhould confume; and a preference in the purchafe and in the exportation of all fuch merchandife as came from her hands: fo far all fubmiffion was a return of gratitude: beyond it all obligation was violence.

Thus it is that tyranny has given birth to contraband trade. Tranfgreffion is the firft effect produced by unreafonable laws. In vain has it frequently been repeated to the colonies, that fmuggling was contrary to the fundamental intereft of their fettlements, to all reafon of government, and to the exprefs intentions of law. In vain has it been continually laid down in public writings, that the fubject who pays duty is oppreffed by him who does not pay it; and that the fraudulent merchant robs the fair trader by difappointing him of his lawful profit. In vain have precautions been multiplied for preventing fuch frauds, and frefh penalties inflicted for the punifhment of them. The voice of intereft, reafon and equity, has prevailed over all the numberlefs clamours and various attempts of finance. Foreign importations fmuggled into North America, amount to one-third of thofe which pay duty.

An indefinite liberty, or merely reftrained within proper limits, would have put a ftop to the prohibited engagements of which fo much complaint had been made. Then the colonies would have arrived to a ftate of affluence, which would have enabled them to difcharge a load of debt due to the mother-country, amounting to one hundred and twenty, or one hundred and thirty millions of livres [from 5,000,000l.

B O O K to 5,416,666l. 13s. 4d.]. They would then have drawn
XVIII. from thence annually goods to the amount of forty-
five millions of livres [1,875,000l.], the fum to which
their wants had been raifed in the moft fuccefsful periods. But inftead of having their deftiny alleviated,
as they were inceffantly demanding, thefe great fettlements faw themfelves threatened with a tax.

Diftreffed   England had juft emerged from a long and bloody
ftate of   war, during which her fleets had been victorious in all
England in   the feas, and her conquefts had enlarged her domi-
1763.   nions, already too extenfive, with an immenfe acquifition of territory in the Eaft and Weft Indies. This
fplendour might perhaps externally dazzle the nations;
but the country was continually obliged to lament
its acquifitions and its triumphs. Oppreffed with a
load of debt to the amount of 3,330,000,000 of
livres [138,750,000l.], that coft her an intereft of
111,577,490 livres [4,649,062l. 1s. 8d.] a year; fhe
was fcarce able to fupport the neceffary expences of
the ftate, with a revenue of 130,000,000 of livres
[5,416,666l. 13s. 4d.]; and that revenue was fo far
from increafing, that it was not even certain it would
continue.

The lands were charged with a heavier tax than had
ever been impofed in time of peace. New duties were
laid on houfes and windows; and the controul of the
acts was oppreffive on all kinds of property. Wine,
plate, cards, dice, and every thing which was confidered as an object of luxury or amufement, paid more
than it could have been thought poffible. To compenfate for the facrifice which had been made for the
prefervation of the citizens, by prohibiting fpirituous
liquors, duties were laid on the ordinary drink of the
common people, on malt, cyder, and beer. The
ports difpatched nothing for foreign kingdoms, and
received nothing from them, but what was loaded
with duties, both of export and import. Materials
and workmanfhip had fo prodigioufly rifen in price
in Great Britain, that her merchants were fupplanted
even in the countries where they had not till then

met with any competitors. The commercial pro- B O O K
fits of England with every part of the world, did XVIII.
not amount annually to more than 56,000,000 livres
[2,333,333l. 6s. 8d.] ; but of this balance 35,000,000
livres [1,458,333l. 6s. 8d.] were to be deducted, to
pay the arrears of the fums which foreigners had
placed in the public funds.

The fprings of the ftate were all ftrained. The
mufcles of the body politic being in a ftate of extreme
tenfion, were in fome meafure thrown out of their
place. The crifis was a violent one. The people
fhould have been allowed time to recover. They
could not be eafed by a diminution of expences ; for
thofe made by government were neceffary, either for
the purpofe of improving the conquefts, purchafed at
the price of fo much blood and treafure, or to reftrain
the refentment of the houfe of Bourbon, irritated by
the humiliations of the late war and the facrifices of
the late peace. As other means did not occur, which
might fecure the prefent as well as future profperity of
the nation, it was thought proper to call in the colonies to the aid of the mother-country. Thefe views
were prudent and juft.

The members of a confederate body muft all of them England
contribute to its defence and its fplendour, in propor- calls its
tion to their refpective abilities ; as it is only by public its affiſt-
ftrength that each clafs is enabled to preferve the en- ance.
tire and peaceful enjoyments of its poffeffions. The
poor are certainly lefs interefted in this than the wealthy ; but yet their tranquillity is concerned in it, in
the firft place, and in the fecond place, the national
riches, which they are called upon to fhare by their
induftry. There can be no focial principle more evident, and yet the infringement of it is the moft ordinary of all political faults. From whence can arife
this perpetual contradiction between the conviction and
the conduct of government?

It arifes from the fault of the legiflative power, in
exaggerating the means for maintaining the public
ftrength, and in employing for its own caprices part

of the funds deſtined for this purpoſe. The wealth
of the merchant and of the farmer, and the ſubſiſtence
of the poor, taken from them in the country places and
in the towns in the name of the ſtate, and proſtitut-
ed in the courts to the purpoſes of intereſt and vice,
are employed to increaſe the pomp of a number of
men, who flatter, deteſt, and corrupt their maſter ; or
paſs into ſtill baſer hands than theſe, to pay for the
ſcandal and ſhame of his pleaſures. Theſe treaſures
are laviſhed for a parade of grandeur, the vain decoration of thoſe who can have no real grandeur; and
for feſtivals, the reſource of idleneſs, unable to exert
itſelf, in the midſt of the cares and labours which the
government of an empire would require. A portion of
them, it is true, is given to the public wants : but theſe,
from incapacity or inattention, are applied without judgment as without economy. Authority deceived, and
diſdaining even to endeavour to be otherwiſe, admits
of an unjuſt diſtribution of the tax, and of a mode of
collecting it, which is itſelf an additional oppreſſion.
Then every patriotic ſentiment becomes extinct. A
war is excited between the prince and his ſubjects.
Thoſe who levy the revenues of the ſtate, appear nothing but the enemies of the citizen. He defends his
fortune from the impoſt, as he would defend it from
encroachment. Every thing which cunning can take
from power appears a lawful gain ; and the ſubjects,
corrupted by the government, make uſe of the re-
priſals againſt a maſter who plunders them. They
do not perceive that, in this unequal conflict, they
are themſelves both dupes and victims. The inſati-
able and eager treaſury, leſs ſatisfied with what is given to them than irritated for what is refuſed, perſecutes
every individual delinquent by a variety of means.
They join activity to intereſt ; and vexations are multiplied. They go under the denomination of puniſhment and juſtice ; and the monſter, who reduces to
poverty all thoſe whom he proſecutes, returns thanks
to Heaven for the number of culprits whom he pu-
niſhes, and for the multiplicity of offences by which

he enriches himfelf. Happy is the fovereign who, to B O O K prevent fo many abufes, would not difdain to give his XVIII. people an exact account of the manner in which all the fums he had required of them were employed. But this fovereign hath not yet appeared ; nor indeed will he ever appear. Neverthelefs, the debt due by the protected perfon to the ftate which protects him, is equally neceffary and facred ; and has been acknowledged by all people. The Englifh colonies of North America had not difavowed this obligation ; and the Britifh miniftry had never applied to them without obtaining the affiftance they folicited.

But thefe were gifts and not taxes, fince the grant was preceded by free and public deliberations in the affemblies of each fettlement. The mother-country had been engaged in expenfive and cruel wars. Tumultuous and enterprifing parliaments had difturbed its tranquillity. It had a fet of bold and corrupt minifters, unfortunately inclined to raife the authority of the throne on the ruin of all the powers and all the rights of the people. Revolutions had fucceeded each other, while the idea had never fuggefted itfelf, of attacking a cuftom, confirmed by two centuries of fortunate experience.

The provinces of the New World were accuftomed to confider as a right this mode of furnifhing their contingent in men and money. Whether this claim had been doubtful or erroneous, prudence would have required that it fhould not have been too openly attacked. The art of maintaining authority is a delicate one, which requires more circumfpection than is generally thought. Thofe who govern are perhaps too much accuftomed to defpife men. They confider them as flaves, bowed down by nature, whereas they are only fo by habit. If they be opprefled with a frefh weight, take care left they fhould rife up again with fury. Let it not be forgotten, that the lever of power hath no other fupport but that of opinion ; and that the ftrength of thofe who govern is really nothing more than the ftrength of thofe who fuffer themfelves

BOOK
XVIII.
to be governed. Let not the people, who are diverted by their employments, or who sleep in their chains, be instructed to pry into truths which are too formidable for government; and when they obey, let them not be made to recollect that they have the right to command. As soon as the instant of this terrible alarm shall arrive; as soon as they shall think that they are not made for their chiefs, but that their chiefs are made for them; as soon as they shall have been able to collect together, and to hear each other unanimously exclaim, *We will not have this law, the custom is displeasing to us;* there is then no alternative left, but either to submit or to punish, to be weak or to be tyrants; and from that time the authority of government being detested or despised, whatever measures they may take, they will have nothing to expect from the people but open insolence or concealed hatred.

The first duty of a prudent administration is, therefore, to respect the prevailing opinions of a country; for opinions are the kind of property to which the people are more attached than even to that of their fortune. It may, indeed, endeavour to rectify them by knowledge, or alter them by persuasion, if they should be prejudicial to the strength of the state. But it is not allowable to contradict them without necessity; and there never was any to reject the system adopted by North America.

In fact, whether the several countries of the New World were authorised, as they wished to do, to send representatives to parliament, in order to deliberate with their fellow-citizens on the exigencies of the British empire; or whether they continued to examine within themselves what contribution it was convenient for them to grant; the treasury could not have experienced any embarrassment from either of these modes. In the first instance, the remonstrances of their deputies would have been lost in the multitude, and the provinces would have been legally charged with part of the burden intended for them to bear. In the second, the ministry disposing of the dignities, of the

employments, of the penfions, and even of the elec- B O O K
tions, would not have experienced more oppofition to XVIII.
their will in the other hemifphere, than they do in this.

But the maxims which were holden facred in America had fome other foundation befide prejudice. The
people relied upon the nature of their charters; they
relied ftill more firmly upon the right which every
Englifh citizen hath, not to be taxed without his confent, or that of his reprefentatives. This right, which
ought to belong to all people, fince it is founded on
the eternal code of reafon, was traced to its origin as
far back as the reign of Edward I. Since that period,
the Englifh never loft fight of it. In peace and in
war, under the dominion of ferocious kings, as well as
under that of weak monarchs, in times of flavery as
in periods of anarchy, they never ceafed to claim it.
The Englifh, under the Tudors, were feen to abandon their moft valuable rights, and to deliver up their
defencelefs heads to the ftroke of the tyrant; but they
were never feen to renounce the right of taxing themfelves. It was in defence of this right that they fhed
torrents of blood, that they dethroned or punifhed
their kings. Finally, at the revolution of 1688, this
right was folemnly acknowledged by the famous act,
in which Liberty, with the fame hand that fhe was
expelling a defpotic king, was drawing the conditions
of the contract between the nation and the new fovereign they had juft chofen. This prerogative of the
people, much more facred, undoubtedly, than fo many imaginary rights which fuperftition hath endeavoured to fanctify in tyrants, was at once in England
the inftrument and the bulwark of its liberty. The
nation thought and perceived that this was the only
dyke which could for ever put a ftop to defpotifm;
that the moment which deprives a people of this privilege condemns them to oppreffion; and that the
funds, raifed apparently for their fafety, are employed
fooner or later to ruin them. The Englifh, when they
founded their colonies, had carried thefe principles

B O O K beyond the feas, and the fame ideas were tranfmitted
XVIII. to their pofterity.

    Alas! if in thofe countries even of Europe, where
flavery feems for a long time to have taken up its refidence in the midft of vices, of riches, and of the arts;
where the defpotifm of armies maintains the defpotifm
of courts ; where man, fettered from his cradle, and
bound by the twofold bands of fuperftition and policy,
hath never breathed the air of liberty ; if, even in
thofe countries, perfons who have reflected once in
their lives on the deftiny of ftates, cannot avoid the
adopting of thefe maxims, and envying the fortunate
nation which hath contrived to make them the foundation and the bafis of its conftitution ; how much
more muft the Englifh, the children of America, be
attached to them ; they who have received this intelligence from their anceftors, and who know at what
price they have purchafed it ? Even the foil they inhabit muft keep up in them a fentiment favourable to
thefe ideas. Difperfed over an immenfe continent, free
as nature, which furrounds them, amidft the rocks, the
mountains, the vaft plains of their deferts, and on the
fkirts of thofe forefts where every thing is ftill wild,
and where nothing calls to mind neither the fervitude
nor the tyranny of man, they feem to receive from natural objects leffons of liberty and independence. Befides, thefe people, who are almoft all of them devoted
to agriculture, to commerce, and to ufeful labours,
which elevate and ftrengthen the mind by giving fimplicity to the manners, who have been hitherto as far
removed from riches as from poverty, cannot yet be
corrupted either by an excefs of luxury or by a multiplicity of wants. It is this ftate more efpecially, that
man who enjoys liberty can maintain it, and can fhow
himfelf jealous of defending an hereditary right which
feems to be the fure guarantee of all the other rights.
Such was the refolution of the Americans.

England
exacts from
her colonies
    Whether the Britifh miniftry were yet unacquainted
with thefe difpofitions, or whether they hoped that

their delegates would succeed in altering them, they
however embraced the opportunity of a glorious peace
to exact a forced contribution from the colonies. For
let it be well observed, that a war, whether fortunate
or unfortunate, serves always as a pretence to the
usurpations of government, as if the views of the chiefs
of the belligerent powers were less to conquer their
enemies than to enslave their subjects. The year 1764
gave birth to the famous stamp act, which forbade the
admission into the tribunals of any claim which had
not been written upon paper stamped and sold for the
benefit of the treasury.

The English provinces of the North of America
were all incensed at this usurpation of their most valuable and most sacred rights. By unanimous consent,
they refused to consume what was furnished them by
the mother-country, till this illegal and oppressive bill
was withdrawn. The women, whose weakness might
have been feared, were the most eager in sacrificing
what served for their ornament; and the men, animated by this example, gave up on their parts other
enjoyments. Many cultivators quitted the plough, in
order to accustom themselves to the work of manufactures; and the woollen, linen, and cotton, coarsely
wrought, were bought up at the price that was previously given for the finest cloths and most beautiful
stuffs.

This kind of combination surprised the government,
and their anxiety was increased by the clamours of the
merchants, who found no market for their goods.
These discontents were supported by the enemies of
the ministry; and the stamp act was repealed after two
years of a commotion, which in other times would
have kindled a civil war.

But the triumph of the colonies was of short duration. The parliament, which had retracted only with
extreme reluctance, ordained in 1767, that the revenue which they had not been able to obtain by means
of the stamp, should be collected by the glass, the lead,
the pasteboard, the colours, the figured paper, and the

tea, which were conveyed from England to America.
The people of the northern continent were not lefs in-
cenfed with this innovation than with the former.   In
vain was it reprefented to them, that no one could
conteft with Great Britain the power of fettling upon
her exports fuch duties as were fuitable to her interefts ; fince fhe did not deprive her eftablifhments beyond the feas of the liberty of manufacturing themfelves the commodities which were fubjected to the
new taxes.   This fubterfuge appeared a mark of deri-
fion to men, who, being merely cultivators, and compelled to have no communication except with the mother-country, could neither procure for themfelves by
their own induftry, nor by foreign connections, the articles that were taxed.   Whether the tribute were paid
in the Old or in the New World, they underftood that
the name made no alteration in the thing, and that
their liberty would be no lefs attacked in this manner
than it had been in the former, which had been repulfed with fuccefs.   The colonifts faw clearly that
the government meant to deceive them, and they
would not be impofed upon.   Thefe political fophifms
appeared to them as they really are, the mafk of tyranny.

Nations in general are more adapted to feel than to
think.   Moft of them have never thought of analyzing
the nature of the power which governs them.   They
obey without reflection, and becaufe they are in the
habit of obeying.   The origin and object of the firft
national affociations being unknown to them, every
refiftance to their will appears to them a crime.   It is
chiefly in thofe ftates where the principles of legiflation
are blended with thofe of religion, that this error was
common.   The habit of believing is favourable to the
habit of fuffering.   Man doth not renounce with impunity one fingle object.   It feems as if Nature avenged herfelf of him who ventures thus to degrade her.
This fervile difpofition of the foul extends to every
thing ; it makes a duty of refignation as of meannefs,
and refpecting every chain that binds it, trembles to

enter into an examination of the laws as well as of the
tenets. In the fame manner as one fingle extravagance in religious opinions is fufficient to induce minds
that are once deceived to adopt numberlefs others, fo
the firft ufurpation of government opens the door to
all the reft. He who believes the moft believes alfo
the leaft, and he who can exert the moft power can
exert alfo the leaft. It is by this double abufe of credulity and of authority, that all the abfurdities in matters of religion and politics have been introduced in
the world to crufh mankind. Accordingly, the firft
fignal of liberty among the nations hath excited them
to fhake off thefe two yokes at once ; and the period
in which the human mind began to difcufs the abufes
of the church and of the clergy is that when reafon
became at length fenfible of the rights of the people,
and when courage endeavoured to fix the firft limits to
defpotifm. The principles of toleration and of liberty
eftablifhed in the Englifh colonies had made them a
people very different from others. There it was
known what the dignity of man was; and when it
was violated by the Britifh miniftry, it neceffarily followed, that a people, compofed entirely of citizens,
fhould rife againft this attempt.

Three years elapfed, and none of the taxes which
had fo much offended the Americans were yet levied.
This was fomething, but it was not all that was expected from men jealous of their prerogatives. They
wanted a general and formal renunciation of what had
been illegally ordained, and this fatisfaction was granted to them in 1770. The tea only was excepted. The
intent, indeed, of this referve, was merely to palliate
the difgrace of giving up entirely the fuperiority of the
mother-country over its colonies; for this duty was
not more exacted than the others had been.

The miniftry, deceived by their delegates, certainly
imagined that the difpofitions of the people were altered in the New World, when in 1773 they ordered the
tax on the tea to be levied.

At this news the indignation became general

England,
after hav-
ing given
way, wifhes
to be obey-
ed by its
colonies.

B O O K
XVIII.

Meafures
which they
take to re-
fift its au-
thority.
throughout North America. In fome provinces,
thanks were decreed to thofe navigators who had refufed to take any of this article on board. In others,
the merchants to whom it was addreffed refufed to receive it. In one place, whoever fold it was declared
an enemy to his country ; in another, the fame mark
of ignominy was beftowed upon thofe who fhould
keep it in their warehoufes. Several diftricts folemnly
renounced the ufe of this liquor, and a greater number of them burnt all the tea they had remaining,
which had hitherto been in fuch high eftimation
among them. The tea fent to this part of the globe
was valued at five or fix millions of livres [from
208,333l. 6s. 8d. to 250,000l.], and not a fingle cheft
of it was landed. Bofton was the chief fcene of this
infurrection. Its inhabitants deftroyed in the harbour
three cargoes of tea, which had arrived from Europe.

This great city had always appeared more attentive
to their rights than the reft of America. The leaft attempt againft their privileges was repulfed without dif-
cretion. This refiftance, fometimes accompanied with
troubles, had for fome years paft difturbed the government. The miniftry, who had fome motives of revenge
to gratify, too haftily feized upon the circumftance of
this blameable excefs, and demanded of the parliament a fevere punifhment.

Moderate people wifhed that the guilty city fhould
be condemned to furnifh an indemnity proportioned
to the damage done in its harbour, and which it deferved for not having punifhed this act of violence.
This penalty was judged too flight ; and on the 13th
of March 1774, a bill was paffed, which fhut up the
port of Bofton, and which forbade that any thing
fhould be carried there.

The court of London congratulated itfelf upon this
rigorous law, and doubted not but that it would bring
the Boftonians to that fpirit of fervitude with which it
had been hitherto attempted in vain to infpire them.
If, contrary to every appearance, thefe bold men
fhould perfevere in their pretenfions, their neighbours

would eagerly avail themſelves of the prohibition B O O K
thrown upon the principal port of the colonies. At XVIII.
the worſt, the other colonies which had been for a
long time jealous of that of Maſſachuſet's Bay, would
abandon it with indifference to its melancholy fate,
and would colleɛt the immenſe trade which theſe miſ-
fortunes would cauſe to flow in upon them. In this
manner the union of the ſeveral ſettlements, which, in
the opinion of the mother-country, had for ſome years
paſt acquired too much conſiſtence, would be broken.

The expeɛtations of the miniſtry were in general
fruſtrated. An aɛt of rigour ſometimes ſtrikes awe.
The people who have murmured while the ſtorm was
only preparing at a diſtance, ſubmit when it comes to
fall upon them. It is then that they weigh the advantages and diſadvantages of reſiſtance, that they meaſure their ſtrength with that of their oppreſſors : it is
then that a panic terror ſeizes thoſe which have every
thing to loſe, and nothing to gain; that they raiſe their
voices, that they intimidate, and that they bribe ; that
diviſion is excited in the minds of men, and that ſociety is divided between two faɛtions which irritate
each other, which ſometimes take up arms and ſlay
each other in the view of their tyrants, who behold
with complacency and ſatisfaɛtion the effuſion of their
blood. But tyrants ſcarcely find any accomplices, unleſs among people already corrupt. It is vice which
gives them confederates among thoſe whom they oppreſs. It is effeminacy which takes the alarm, and
cannot venture to exchange its tranquillity for honourable dangers. It is the vile ambition of commanding
which lends its aſſiſtance to deſpotiſm, and conſents to
be a ſlave for the ſake of acquiring dominion, to give
up a people in order to divide their ſpoils, and to renounce the ſenſe of honour in order to obtain honours
and titles. It is eſpecially that indifferent and cold
perſonality, the laſt of the crimes of the people, the
laſt of the vices of governments ; for it is government
which always gives riſe to them ; it is government
which, from principle, ſacrifices a nation to a man, and

B O O K the happiness of a century and of posterity to the en-
XVIII. joyment of a day and of a moment. All these vices,
which are the fruits of an opulent and voluptuous society, of a society grown old and come to its last period, do not belong to recent people engaged in the
toils of agriculture. The Americans remained united
among themselves. The carrying into execution a
bill which they called inhuman, barbarous, and destructive, served only to confirm them in the resolution
of supporting their rights with more unanimity and
steadiness.

The minds of men grew more and more exalted at
Boston. The cry of liberty was reinforced by that of
religion. The churches resounded with the most violent exhortations against England. It was undoubtedly an interesting spectacle for philosophy, to see that
in the temples and at the feet of the altars, where superstition had so often blessed the chains of the people,
where the priests had so often flattered the tyrants,
that liberty should raise its voice to defend the privileges of an oppressed nation; and if we believe that
the Deity condescends to cast an eye upon the unfortunate contests of mankind, it preferred certainly to
see its sanctuary consecrated to this use, and to hear
hymns to liberty become part of the worship addressed
to it by its ministers. These discourses must have produced a great effect; and when a free people invokes
the aid of Heaven against oppression, they soon have
recourse to arms.

The other inhabitants of Massachuset's Bay disdain-
ed even the idea of taking the least advantage of the
disasters of the capital. They thought of nothing but
tightening the bands which connected them with the
Bostonians, and were inclined to bury themselves under the ruins of their common country, rather than
suffer the least encroachment upon rights which they
had learned to cherish more than life.

All the provinces attached themselves to the cause
of Boston, and their attachment increased in proportion to the calamities and sufferings of that unfortunate

city. Being almoft guilty of the fame refiftance which
had been fo feverely punifhed, they were fenfible that the vengeance of the mother-country againft them was only delayed, and that all the grace which the moft favoured of them can poffibly expect will be to be the laft object of its revenge.

Thefe difpofitions to a general infurrection were increafed by the act againft Bofton, which was circulated throughout the continent upon paper edged with black, as an emblem of the mourning of liberty. Anxiety foon communicates from one houfe to another. The citizens affemble and converfe in the places. All the preffes teem with writings full of eloquence and vigour.

" The feverities of the Britifh parliament againft
" Bofton ought to make all the American provinces
" tremble. They have now only to choofe between
" fire and the fword, between the horrors of death
" and the yoke of a fervile and bafe obedience. The
" period of an important revolution is at length ar-
" rived, the fortunate or unfortunate fuccefs of which
" will for ever determine the regret or admiration of
" pofterity.

" Shall we be free, or fhall we be flaves? It is up-
" on the folution of this great problem, that the de-
" ftiny of three millions of men will depend for the
" prefent and for the future, the happinefs or mifery
" of their numberlefs defcendants.

" Roufe yourfelves up, therefore, O you Americans!
" for the regions you inhabit were never covered with
" fuch dreadful clouds : you are called rebels, becaufe
" you will be taxed only by your reprefentatives. Juf-
" tify this claim by your courage, or feal the lofs of it
" with your blood.

" It is no longer time to deliberate, when the hand
" of the oppreffor is inceffantly at work in forging
" chains for you; filence would be a crime, and in-
" action infamy. The prefervation of the rights of
" the republic, that is the fupreme law. He would
" be the loweft of flaves, who, in the danger which

" now threatens the liberty of America, would not
" exert his utmoft efforts to preferve it."

Such was the general difpofition : but the moft important object, and the moft difficult matter to effect
in the midft of the general tumult, was to bring about
a calm, by means of which a harmony of inclinations
might be produced, which might give dignity, ftrength,
and confiftence to the refolutions. It is this kind of
harmony, which, from a number of loofe and fcattered
parts, all of them eafily broken, compofes one complete whole, which it is impoffible to fubdue, unlefs
one can fucceed in dividing it either by ftrength or
by policy. The neceffity of this great union was perceived by the provinces of New Hampfhire, of Maffachufet's Bay, of Rhode Ifland, of Connecticut, of New
York, of New Jerfey, of the three counties of the Delaware, of Pennfylvania, of Maryland, of Virginia, and
of the two Carolinas. Thefe twelve colonies, to which
Georgia hath fince acceded, fent deputies to Philadelphia in the month of September 1774, who were appointed to defend their rights and their interefts.

The difputes between the mother-country and its
colonies acquired at this period a degree of importance
which they had not had before. It was no more a few
individuals who oppofed a ftubborn refiftance to imperious mafters. It was the ftruggle between one body of men and another, between the congrefs of America and the parliament of England, between one nation and another. The refolutions taken on each fide
inflamed the minds of men ftill more and more, and
increafed the animofity. Every hope of reconciliation
was diffipated. The fword was drawn on both fides ;
Great Britain fent troops into the New World, and
this other hemifphere prepared for its defence. Its citizens became foldiers. The materials for the conflagration are collected, and the fire will foon break out.

General Gage, who commanded the royal troops,
fent a detachment from Bofton on the night of the
18th of Auguft 1775, with orders to deftroy a magazine of arms and provifions collected by the Americans

at Concord. This detachment met with some militia at Lexington, whom they difperfed without much difficulty, continued their march with rapidity, and executed the orders they had received. But they had fcarcely refumed the road to the capital, before they were affailed in a fpace of fifteen miles by a furious multitude, whom they deftroyed, and by whom they were alfo flain. The blood of Englifhmen, fo often fpilt in England by the hands of Englifhmen, was now fpilt in America, and the civil war was begun.

More regular engagements were fought upon the fame field of battle in the enfuing months. Warren was the victim of thefe deftructive and unnatural actions. The congrefs did honour to his remains.

" He is not dead," faid the orator; " this excellent
" citizen fhall not die. His memory will be eternally
" prefent, eternally dear to all good men, to all lovers
" of their country. He hath difplayed, in the limited
" career of a life of thirty-three years, the talents of
" a ftatefman, the virtues of a fenator, and the foul of
" a hero.

" All you who are animated with the fame intereft,
" approach the bloody corpfe of Warren. Bathe his
" honourable wounds with your tears; but do not re-
" main too long over this inanimate body. Return
" to your habitations to infpire a deteftation of the
" crime of tyranny. Let the hair of your children
" ftart upon their heads at this horrible reprefentation;
" let their eyes fparkle, let their brows become threa-
" tening, and let their voices exprefs their indignation;
" then you will give them arms, and your laft wifh
" will be, that they may either return conquerors, or
" perifh like Warren."

The troubles with which Maffachufet's Bay was agitated were extended to the other provinces. The tranfactions were not, indeed, bloody in them, becaufe there were no Britifh troops; but in all parts the Americans feized upon the forts, the arms, and the provifions; they expelled their chiefs and the other agents of government, and ill-treated the inhabitants

who appeared to favour the caufe of the mother-country. Some enterprifing men carried their boldnefs fo
far as to feize upon the works formerly erected by the
French near lake Champlain, between New England
and Canada, and even made an irruption into that vaft
region.

While private individuals, or feparate diftricts, were
fo ufefully ferving the common caufe, the congrefs
was employed in the care of affembling an army, the
command of which was given to George Wafhington,
a native of Virginia, and known by a few fuccefsful
actions in the preceding wars. The new general immediately flew to Maffachufet's Bay, drove the royal
troops from one poft to another, and compelled them
to fhut themfelves up in Bofton. Six thoufand of his
old foldiers, who had efcaped the fword, ficknefs, and
every other kind of diftrefs, preffed either by hunger
or by the enemy, embarked on the 24th of March
1776, with a precipitation which had all the appearance of flight. They went to feek an afylum in Nova
Scotia, which, as well as Florida, had remained faithful
to its former mafters.

The colo-
nies had a
right to fe-
parate
themfelves
from their
mother-
country,
even if
they had
no caufe of
difcontent.
This fuccefs was the firft ftep of Englifh America
towards the revolution. It began to be openly wifhed
for, and the principles which juftified it were univerfally diffufed. Thefe principles, which originated in
Europe, and particularly in England, had been tranfplanted by philofophy into America. The knowledge
of the mother-country was turned againft itfelf; and
it was faid :

One muft be very careful not to confound focieties
and government with each other. Let us inveftigate
their origin, in order to diftinguifh them.

Man, thrown upon the globe as it were by chance,
furrounded with all the evils of nature, obliged to defend and protect his life againft the ftorms and hurricanes of the air, againft the inundations of the waters,
againft the fires and the conflagrations of volcanos, a-
gainft the intemperature of the zones, either torrid or
frozen, againft the barrennefs of the earth, which re-

fufes to yield him any fubfiftence, or againft its unfor- B O O K
tunate fertility, which produces poifons under his feet, XVIII.
againft the teeth of ferocious animals, who difpute
with him his abode and his prey, and, by combating
him themfelves, feem to intend to acquire the dominion of the globe, of which he thinks himfelf the mafter ; man, in this ftate alone, and abandoned to himfelf, could do nothing for his own prefervation. It was
therefore neceffary that he fhould unite and affociate
with his fellow-creatures, in order to make a common
ftock of their ftrength and underftanding. It is by this
union that he hath been able to triumph over fo many
evils, that he hath fafhioned the globe to his own ufe,
kept the rivers within their boundaries, fubdued the
feas, enfured his fubfiftence, conquered one part of the
animals, by compelling them to ferve him, and driven
away the reft to a diftance from his empire, in the
midft of deferts or of forefts, where their numbers diminifh from one century to another. Men, united
among themfelves, have carried into execution what
one man alone could never have accomplifhed ; and
they all together concur in preferving their work.
Such is the origin, fuch are the advantages and the
end of fociety.

Government owes its rife to the neceffity of preventing and of repelling the injuries which the affo-
ciates had to fear from each other. It is the centinel
who watches to prevent the common labours from being difturbed.

Society hath therefore arifen from the neceffities of
mankind, and government owes its origin to their
vices. Society always tends to good ; government
ought always to tend towards repreffing evil. Society
is the firft, and in its origin independent and free ; government hath been inftituted for it, and is only its
inftrument. The former has the right of commanding, the latter muft obey. Society hath created public ftrength, and government, which hath received it
from its hands, ought to confecrate it entirely to its
ufe. In a word, fociety is effentially good ; govern-

ment, as it is well known, may be, and is but too often bad.

It hath been said that we were all born equals; but that is not true. That we had all the same rights: I do not know what rights are, where there is an inequality of talents and of ftrength, and no guarantee nor fanction. That Nature hath offered to us all the fame habitation and the fame refources; that is not true. That we were indifcriminately endowed with the fame means of defence; that is not true: nor do I know in what fenfe it can be true that we enjoy the fame qualities of body and of mind.

There is an original inequality between men which nothing can remedy. It muft laft for ever; and all that can be obtained from the beft legiflation will not be to deftroy it, but to prevent its abufes.

But hath not Nature herfelf produced the feeds of tyranny, by dealing with her children like a ftepmother, and by creating fome children weak, and others ftrong? It is fcarce poffible to deny this, efpecially if we go back to a period previous to all legiflation, when we fhall fee men as paffionate and as unreafonable as brutes.

What views then can the founders of nations and the legiflators have had? To obviate all the difafters of this detefted principle, by a kind of artificial equality, which fhould fubject the members of a fociety, without exception, to one fingle impartial authority. It is a fword which is indifcriminately fufpended over every head; but this fword was only ideal. It was neceffary that fome hand, fome natural being, fhould hold it.

The refult of this hath been, that the hiftory of civilized man is nothing more than the hiftory of his mifery. All the pages of it are ftained with blood; fome with that of the oppreffors, the reft with that of the oppreffed.

In this point of view, man appears more wicked and more unfortunate than animals. The different fpecies of animals fubfift at the expence of each other; but the focieties of men have never ceafed to attack each other. There is no condition in the fame fociety, which doth not either devour, or hath not itfelf devoured, whatever may have been, or whatever may be the form of government, or of artificial equality, which hath been oppofed to the primitive or natural inequality.

But thefe forms of government, freely chofen by our forefathers, whatever fanction they may have received, either from oath, or from unanimous confent, or from permanency, are they to be confidered as binding to their defcendants? Certainly not: and it is impoffible that you, Englifhmen, who have fuccef-fively undergone fo many different revolutions in your political conftitution; who have been driven from monarchy to tyranny, from tyranny to ariftocracy, from ariftocracy to democracy, and from democracy to anarchy; it is impoffible, I fay, that you can think differently from me, without accufing yourfelves of rebellion and perjury.

We examine things as philofophers; and it is well known that our fpeculations have not occafioned civil wars. No fubjects are more patient than we are. I fhall therefore purfue my object without any apprehenfion for the confequences. If people be happy under their form of government, they will maintain it. If they be wretched, it will be neither your opinion nor mine, but the impoffibility of fuffering any more, or for any longer time, which will determine them to change. A falutary commotion, which the oppreffor will call revolt, though it be no more than the legal exercife of an unalienable and natural right of the man who is oppreffed, and even of him who is not oppreffed.

Man has a will and a choice of his own; but he can neither have a will nor a choice for another: and it would be an extravagance to exercife his will and his choice for him who is not yet born, for him who will not exift for many centuries after. There is no individual who hath not a right to feek elfewhere a

better form of government, if he be diffatisfied with
that of his own country.   There is no fociety which
hath not the fame liberty of altering its own form of
government, as its anceftors had to adopt it.   Upon
this point, focieties are in the fame ftate as in the firft
inftant of their civilization.   It would be a great evil
if it were not fo ; and indeed in that cafe there could
be no remedy againft the greateft of all evils.   Millions
of men muft have been condemned to endlefs misfortune.   It will therefore be admitted, in conformity to
my principles,

That there is no form of government, the prerogative of which is to be immutable.

That there is no political authority, created either
yefterday or a thoufand years ago, which cannot be
abrogated, either ten years hence, or to-morrow.

Whoever thinks otherwife is a flave ; he is the ido-
later of the works of his own hands.

Whoever thinks otherwife is a madman, who devotes himfelf, as well as his family, his children, and
his children's children, to everlafting mifery, by granting to his anceftors the right of ftipulating for him
when he was not in being, and by arrogating to himfelf the right of ftipulating for his defcendants, who
are not yet in being.

All authority in this world hath begun either by
the confent of the fubjects, or by the ftrength of the
mafter.   It may be legally put a ftop to in either of
the cafes.   There is nothing which favours tyranny
againft liberty.

The truth of thefe principles is the more effential,
as every power tends by its nature to defpotifm, even
in that nation which is the moft jealous of its rights,
even in England.

I have heard a Whig fay, that as long as a bad fovereign, or at leaft a bad minifter, could not be fent
to Tyburn with as little formality, parade, tumult, and
furprife, as the moft obfcure malefactor, the nation
would never either have a proper idea, nor the full
enjoyment of its rights, in a manner fuitable to a peo-

ple who venture to think, and to call themfelves a free people. This man was perhaps a fanatic; but madmen fometimes utter words of profound fenfe. Neverthelefs, an adminiftration which you yourfelves own to be ignorant, corrupt, and audacious, fhall imperioufly precipitate you with impunity into the deepeft abyfs of misfortune.

The quantity of fpecie circulating among you is not very confiderable. You are overburdened with paper-currency, under every denomination. All the gold of Europe, heaped up in your treafury, would be fcarce fufficient to pay off your national debt. It is not known by what kind of incredible illufion this fictitious coin is kept up. The moft trifling event may in a moment bring it into difcredit. One fingle alarm is fufficient to induce a fudden bankruptcy. The dreadful confequences of this breach of faith are beyond our imagination. And this is the moment which hath been chofen to make you declare againft your colonies, that is to fay, to involve yourfelves in an unjuft, fenfelefs, and ruinous war. What will become of you, when one important branch of your commerce fhall be annihilated; when you fhall have loft one third of your poffeffions; when you fhall have maffacred one or two millions of your fellow-citizens; when your ftrength fhall be exhaufted, your merchants ruined, your manufacturers' reduced to perifh for want; when your debt fhall be increafed, and your revenue diminifhed? Beware! the blood of the Americans will fooner or later fall upon your own heads. Its effufion will be revenged by your own hands; and the moment is at hand.

But, you fay, *they are rebels.*—Why are they fo? Becaufe they will not be your flaves? A people who are fubject to the will of another, who can difpofe at pleafure of their government, of their laws, and of their commerce, who can tax them according to their own fancy, limit their induftry, and fetter it by arbitrary prohibitions, are flaves, and their fervitude is worfe than that which they would experience under a ty-

BOOK rant; becaufe a tyrant may be got rid of, either by
XVIII. expulfion or by affaffination. Both thefe acts have
been done by you. But a nation can neither be put
to death nor expelled. Liberty can be expected only
from a rupture, the confequence of which muft be the
ruin of one or the other of the nations, and fometimes
of both. A tyrant is a monfter with only one head,
which may be ftricken off at a blow. A defpotic nation is a hydra with a thoufand heads, which can only be fmitten off by a thoufand fwords at once. The
crime of the oppreffion exercifed by a tyrant excites
univerfal indignation againft himfelf alone. The fame
crime, committed by a numerous fociety, fpreads the
horror and the fhame of it amongft a multitude, which
is never afhamed. It is the crime of every body and
of no body; and the fentiment of mifguided defpair
knows not upon what object to fix its refentment.

But they are our fubjects.—Your fubjects! not more
than the inhabitants of the province of Wales are the
fubjects of the county of Lancafter. The authority
of one nation over another can only be founded upon
conqueft, upon general confent, or upon propofed and
accepted conditions. Conqueft is no more binding
than robbery; the confent of anceftors cannot compel defcendants; and no conditions can be confiftent
with the facrifice of liberty. Liberty cannot be bartered for any thing, becaufe no equivalent can be given for it. This is the fpeech you have made to your
tyrants, and we now addrefs it to you in favour of your
colonifts.

The land which they occupy is ours.—Yours! It is
thus you call it, becaufe you have invaded it. But
fuppofing it be fo, doth not the charter of conceffion
oblige you to treat the Americans as your countrymen? and do you comply with this obligation? But
to what purpofe are conceffions and charters, which
grant what one is not mafter of, and which confequently one hath no right of granting to a fmall number of feeble men, compelled by circumftances to receive as a gratuity what they have a natural right to?

Befides, have the defcendants, who are now alive, been invited to accede to a compact, figned by their anceftors? The truth of this principle muft be acknowledged, or the defcendants of James muft be recalled. What right was there to drive him away, which we had not equally to feparate from you? fay the Americans. And what anfwer can be made to them?

They are ungrateful; we are their founders; we have been their defenders; we have indebted ourfelves for them. —For yourfelves, you may fay, as much, or more than for them. If you have defended them, it is in the fame manner as you would have defended the fultan of Conftantinople, if your ambition or your intereft had required it. But have they not repaid this obligation, by delivering to you their productions, by exclufively receiving your merchandife, at the exorbitant price you have chofen to put upon it, by fubmitting to the prohibitions which thwarted their induftry, and to the reftrictions with which you have oppreffed their property? Have they not affifted you, and indebted themfelves for you? Have they not taken up arms, and fought for you? Have they not acceded to your demands, when you have made them in a manner fuitable to freemen? When have they ever refufed you any thing, unlefs when prefenting your bayonets to their breafts, you have faid to them, *Your treafure, or your life; die, or be our flaves.* What! becaufe you have been beneficent, have you the right to become oppreffors? Will the nations alfo convert their expectations of gratitude into a barbarous pretence to difgrace and infult thofe who have had the misfortune to receive their benefits? Individuals, perhaps, though it be not their duty, may in their benefactors bear with their tyrants. In them, undoubtedly, it is great, it is magnanimous, to confent to be unhappy, rather than be ungrateful. But the fyftem of morality among nations is different. The public felicity is the firft law, as it is the firft duty. The primary obligation of thefe great bodies is towards themfelves. They

BOOK
XVIII.

owe, above all things, liberty and juſtice to thoſe who compoſe them. Every child who is born in a ſtate, every citizen who comes to breathe the air of a country which he hath choſen for himſelf, or which Nature hath given him, has a right to the greateſt degree of happineſs he can poſſibly enjoy. Every obligation which cannot be reconciled with that principle is void. Every contrary claim is an encroachment upon his rights. Of what concern is it to him, if his anceſtors have been favoured, when he himſelf is deſtined to be the victim? By what right can we exact the payment of this uſurious debt of benefits, which he hath not even experienced? No. To arrogate to one's ſelf a ſimilar claim, againſt a whole nation and its poſterity, is to ſubvert all the ideas of order and policy; it is to betray all the laws of morality, while we invoke their countenance. What hath not England done for Hanover? But is Hanover ſubject to your command? All the republics of Greece were connected with each other by mutual ſervices? Did any one of them exact, as a token of gratitude, the right of diſpoſing of the adminiſtration of the republic that had received the obligation?

But our honour is compromiſed.—Say rather, the honour of your bad miniſters, and not your own. In what conſiſts the real honour of him who is in an error? Is it to perſiſt in it, or to acknowledge it? The man who returns to ſentiments of juſtice hath no occaſion to be aſhamed. Engliſhmen, you have been too precipitate. Why did you not wait till riches had corrupted the Americans, as you are corrupted? Then they would have been as little concerned for their liberty as you for yours. Then, ſubdued by wealth, your arms would have been uſeleſs. But you have attacked them in an inſtant, when what they had to loſe, liberty, could not be balanced by what they had to preſerve.

But in later times they would have become ſtill more numerous.—I acknowledge it. You have therefore only attempted the enſlaving of a people, whom time would

have fet free in fpite of you. In twenty or thirty B o o k
years, the remembrance of your atrocious deeds will XVIII.
be recent ; and the fruit of them will be taken away
from you : then nothing but fhame and remorfe will
remain to you. There is a decree of nature which
you cannot change ; it is, that great bodies always
give law to fmaller ones. But if the Americans fhould
then undertake againft Great Britain what you have
undertaken againft them, would you not fay to them
exactly what they fay to you at this inftant ? Wherefore fhould motives which affect you but little, coming from them, appear more folid when coming from
you?

They will neither obey our parliament, nor adopt our con-
ftitution.—Have they made, or can they change them?

We obey them without having had, either in paft times,
or without having at prefent any influence over them.—
That is to fay, that you are flaves, and that you cannot
fuffer freemen. Neverthelefs, do not confound the pofition of the Americans with yours. You have reprefentatives, and they have none ; you have voices which
fpeak for you, and no one ftipulates for them. If the
voices be bought and fold, this is an excellent reafon
for them to difclaim this advantage.

They would be independent of us.—Are not you fo of
them?

They will never be able to fupport themfelves without
us.—If that be the cafe, keep quiet ; neceffity will
bring them back to you.

But what if we could not fubfift without them ?—This
would be a great misfortune : but to cut their throats,
in order to prevent it, is a fingular expedient.

It is for their intereft, it is for their good, that we are
angry with them, as we are with children who behave
improperly.—Their intereft and their good ! Who hath
appointed you the judges of thefe two points which
touch them fo nearly, and which they ought to know
better than you ? If it fhould happen that a citizen
fhould enter by force into the houfe of another, upon
a pretence that he was a man of great underftanding,

and that no one was more capable of maintaining
good order and peace at his neighbour's houfe; would
not his neighbour have a right to defire him to withdraw, and concern himfelf about his own affairs? But
what fhall we fay if the affairs of this officious hypo-
crite were much in diforder? If he were nothing more
than an ambitious man, who, under pretence of governing, wanted to ufurp; if under the mafk of benevolence he concealed only views full of injuftice,
fuch, for inftance, as the endeavour to relieve his own
difficulties at the expence of his fellow-citizens?

We are the mother-country.——What, are the moft facred names always to ferve as veils to ambition and
to intereft? If you be the mother-country, fulfil the
duties of it.   Moreover, the colony is formed of different nations, among whom fome will grant and o-
thers will refufe you this title.   While all of them
will fay to you at once, there is a time when the authority of parents over their children is to ceafe, and
this time is that when children can provide for themfelves.   What term have you fixed for our emancipa-
tion? Be honeft, and confefs you flattered yourfelves
that you fhould have kept us under perpetual tutelage.   This tutelage however might be fupportable, if
it were not changed for us into an unbearable conftraint; if our advantage were not inceffantly facrificed to yours; if we were not obliged to fuffer a multitude of oppreffions in detail from the governors, the
judges, the financiers, and the military men whom
you fend to us; if moft of them at their arrival in
our climates did not bring with them degraded characters, ruined fortunes, rapacious hands; and the infolence of fubaltern tyrants, who, tired with obeying
the laws in their own country, come to indemnify
themfelves in a New World, by exercifing there a
power which is too frequently arbitrary.   You are
the mother-country, but far from encouraging our
progrefs, you ftand in awe of it.   You confine our
induftry, and you counteract our rifing ftrength.   Nature, in favouring us, difappoints your fecret wifhes;

or rather, it is your defire that fhe fhould remain in a ftate of eternal infancy, with refpect to every thing that may be ufeful to us; and notwithftanding this, that we fhould ftill be robuft flaves to ferve you, and inceffantly to fupply your avidity with new fources of wealth. Is this being a mother? Is this being our country? Alas! in the forefts that furround us, Nature hath beftowed a milder inftinct on the wild beaft, who, when fhe is become a mother, doth not at leaft devour thofe to whom fhe hath given birth.

If we agreed to all their pretenfions, they would foon be happier than we are.—And why not? If you be corrupted, why fhould they be fo? If you incline to flavery, muft they alfo imitate your example? If you were their mafter, why fhould you not confer the property of another power to your fovereign? Why fhould you not make him your defpot, as you have declared him by a folemn act the defpot of Canada? Muft they then have ratified this extravagant conceffion? and if they had ratified it, muft they have obeyed the fovereign you would have given them? and muft they have taken up arms againft you in obedience to his orders? The king of England hath a negative power. No law can be enacted there without his confent. This power, the inconvenience of which you daily experience, why fhould the Americans grant it to him among themfelves? Would it be to deprive him of it one day by taking up arms, as it will happen to you if your government fhould be improved? What advantage can you find in fubjecting them to a vicious conftitution?

Vicious or not, this conftitution is ours, and it muft be generally acknowledged and accepted by all who bear the Englifh name; otherwife, each of our provinces governing itfelf in its own way, having its own laws, and pretending to independence, we fhould ceafe to form a national body, and fhould be nothing more than a collection of fmall infulated republics divided, inceffantly at war with each other, and eafily invaded by a common enemy. The

*sagacious and powerful Philip, capable of undertaking this
enterprise, is near us.*

Suppoſing him to be near you, he is at a diſtance
from the Americans. A privilege which may be attended with ſome inconvenience to you, is not the
leſs a privilege. But, ſeparated as they are from Great
Britain, by immenſe ſeas, of what concern is it to you
whether your colonies accept or rejeᴄt your conſtitutions ? What has this to do either for or againſt your
ſtrength, or for or againſt your ſecurity ? That·unity,
of which you exaggerate the advantages, is alſo nothing more than a vain pretence. You urge your
laws to them when they are oppreſſed by them,. and
you trample upon them yourſelves when they appeal
to them in their favour. You tax yourſelves, and you
want to tax them. When the leaſt encroachment is
attempted upon this privilege, you exclaim with rage,
you take up arms, and you are ready to devote yourſelves to death, and yet you put the poniard to the
throat of your fellow-citizen to compel him to renounce it. Your ports are open to all nations, and
you ſhut up thoſe of the coloniſts from them. Your
merchandiſe is conveyed to all parts where you chooſe
to ſend it, and theirs is forced to be ſent to you. You
manufaᴄture, and you will not ſuffer them to do the
ſame. They have hides and they have iron, and you
compel them to deliver theſe hides and this iron to you
in the rough ſtate. What you get at a low price, they
muſt purchaſe from you at the price which your
rapaciouſneſs exaᴄted. You ſacrifice them to your
merchants ; and becauſe your Eaſt India Company was
in danger, it was neceſſary that their loſſes ſhould be
repaired by the Americans. And yet you call them
your fellow-citizens, and it is thus you invite them to
accept your conſtitution. This unity, this league
which ſeems ſo neceſſary to you, is nothing more than
the league of the fooliſh animals in the fable, among
which you have reſerved to yourſelf the part of the lion.

Perhaps you have only ſuffered yourſelves to be in-

duced to fill the New World with blood and ravages, B O O K
merely from a falfe point of honour.　We like to per- XVIII.
fuade ourfelves, that fo many enormities have not been
the confequence of a project coolly concerted.　You
have been told, that the Americans were nothing more
than a bafe herd of cowards, whom the leaft threat
would induce with fear and confternation to comply
with every thing you chofe to exact.　Inftead of thofe
pufillanimous men, who had been defcribed to you,
and whom you had been taught to expect, you
met with brave people, true Englifhmen, and fellow-
citizens worthy of you.　Was this a reafon for increafing your anger?　What! have your anceftors ad-
mired the Dutch fhaking off the Spanifh yoke; and
fhall you be aftonifhed that your defcendants, your
countrymen, your brethren, thofe who felt your blood
circulating in their veins, fhould rather choofe to fpill
it than fubmit to the yoke, and fhould prefer death to
a life of flavery?　A ftranger, over whom you would
affume the fame pretenfions, would have difarmed you;
if laying bare his breaft he had faid, *Bury your dagger
here, or leave me free.*　And yet you murder your brother, and you murder him without remorfe, becaufe
he is your brother!　Englifhmen! what can be more
ignominious than the ferocioufnefs of a man proud of
his liberty, and encroaching upon that of another?
Muft we be taught to believe, that the greateft enemy of liberty is the man who enjoys it?　Alas! we
are but too much difpofed to believe it.　Enemies to
kings, you have all their haughtinefs.　Enemies to the
royal prerogative, you difplay it in all parts.　You
fhow yourfelves tyrants everywhere.　Tyrants of nations and of your colonies; if you fhould prevail in
this conteft, it is becaufe Heaven will have been inattentive to the vows that are addreffed to it from all
regions of the earth.

　　Since the feas have not fwallowed up your proud fatellites, tell me what will become of them, if there
fhould arife in the New World an eloquent man, who
fhould promife eternal falvation to thofe who fhould

perifh fword in hand, the martyrs of liberty. Americans, let your priefts be inceffantly feen in your pul-
pits, with crowns in their hands, and fhowing you the
heavens opened. Priefts of the New World, it is time
to expiate the ancient fanaticifm, which hath defolated and ravaged America, by a fanaticifm more fortunate, the offspring of politics and of liberty. But
you will not deceive your fellow citizens. God, who
is the firft principle of juftice and of order, abhors tyrants. God hath imprinted in the heart of man the
facred love of liberty, and will not fuffer that fervitude fhould degrade and disfigure the moft beautiful
of his works. If apotheofis be due to man, it is certainly to him who fights and dies for his country.
Place his image in your churches, and put it near your
altars. It will be the worfhip of the country. Compofe a political and religious kalendar, in which every
day fhall be marked with the name of fome one of
thofe heroes who fhall have fpilt his blood to make
you free. Your pofterity will read them one day with
a holy refpect ; they will fay, thefe are the names of
thofe who have fet half the world at liberty, and who,
exerting themfelves for our happinefs before we exifted, have prevented that at our birth we fhould hear
the rattling of chains over our cradles.

What mea-
fures would
it have fuit-
ed England
to adopt,
when fhe
faw the fer-
ment raifed
in her colo-
nies.
When the caufe of the colonies was debated in the
national affemblies, we have heard many excellent
pleadings pronounced in their favour. But perhaps
the following would have been the moft proper to addrefs to them :

    " I will fay nothing to you, Gentlemen, of the juf-
" tice or injuftice of your pretenfions. I am not fo
" much a ftranger to public affairs, to be ignorant that
" this preliminary examination, which is facred in all
" other circumftances of life, would be improper and
" ridiculous in this. I will not enter into what ex-
" pectations you may have of fuccefs, nor will I exa-
" mine whether you will prevail in this caufe, although
" this fubject might appear of fome importance to you,
" and might probably engage your attention. Nor

" will I even compare the advantages of your fituation B O O K
" if you fhould fucceed, with the confequences that XVIII.
" will follow if you fhould fail. But I will fuppofe at
" once, that you have reduced the colonies to the de-
" gree of fervitude which you require. I only wifh to
" be informed how you will maintain them in it. Will
" it be by a ftanding army ? But this army, which will
" exhauft you of men and money, will it follow or
" not the increafe of population ? There are but two
" anfwers to be made to this queftion, and of thefe
" two anfwers one feems to me to be abfurd, and the
" other brings you back to the fituation in which
" you now are. I have reflected much upon the mat-
" ter, and if I miftake not, I have difcovered the only
" reafonable and fure meafure you have to purfue.
" This is, as foon as you fhall have made yourfelves
" mafters of them, to ftop the progrefs of population,
" fince it appears to you more advantageous, more ho-
" nourable, and more proper, to rule over a fmall num-
" ber of flaves, than to have a nation of freemen for
" your equals and friends.

" But you will afk me, how is the progrefs of po-
" pulation to be ftopped ? The expedient might per-
" haps difguft men of weak and pufillanimous minds;
" but fortunately there are none fuch in this auguft
" affembly. This expedient is to put to death, with-
" out mercy, the greateft part of thefe unworthy re-
" bels, and to reduce the reft to the condition of Ne-
" groes. The brave and generous Spartans, fo cele-
" brated in ancient and modern hiftory, have fet you
" the example. Like them, with their faces muffled
" up in their cloaks, let our fellow-citizens and fatel-
" lites go out clandeftinely in the night-time, and maf-
" facre the children of our Helots by the fide of their
" fathers and on the breafts of their mothers, leaving
" only a fufficient number of them alive for the la-
" bours, and for our fecurity."

Englifhmen, you fhudder at this horrid propofal,
and you afk what meafure might be adopted; either
conquerors or conquered, this is what you have to

BOOK XVIII. do: If the refentment excited by your barbarities can be calmed, if the Americans can fhut their eyes upon the ravages that furround them, if when walking over the ruins of their cities reduced to afhes, and of their habitations deftroyed, over the bones of their fellow-citizens fcattered in the field; if while they breathe the fcent of blood which your hands have fpilt in all parts, it can be poffible that they fhould forget the enormities of your defpotifm; if they can allow themfelves to put the leaft truft in your difcourfes, and can perfuade themfelves that you have ferioufly renounced the injuftice of your pretenfions, begin by recalling the affaffins who are in your pay; reftore liberty to their ports, which you now keep blocked up; let your veffels depart from their coafts; and if there be a wife citizen among you, let him take an olive branch in his hand, let him prefent himfelf to them and fay:

" O you, our fellow-citizens and our old friends,
" allow us to ufe this title; we have indeed profaned
" it, but our repentance makes us worthy of refuming
" it, and we fhall hereafter afpire to the glory of pre-
" ferving it; we confefs, in the prefence of Heaven,
" and of this earth, which have been witneffes of it,
" that our pretenfions have been unjuft, and our pro-
" ceedings barbarous. Forget them as we do. Build
" up your ramparts and your fortreffes. Affemble
" yourfelves again in your peaceable habitations. Let
" us wipe out from our memory even the laft drop of
" blood that has been fpilt. We admire the generous
" fpirit which hath directed you. It is the fame to
" which, in fimilar circumftances, we have owed our
" falvation. It is particularly by thefe figns that we
" know you to be our fellow-citizens and our bre-
" thren: your wifh is liberty, and you fhall be free.
" You fhall be free in all the extent that we ourfelves
" have attached to this facred name. It is not from
" us that you hold this right; we can neither give it
" nor take it away from you. You have received it
" as we have, from nature, which the crime and the

" fword of tyrants can fight againſt, but cannot de-
" ſtroy. We pretend not to any kind of ſuperiority
" over you; the honour of aſpiring to an equality is
" ſufficiently glorious for us. We are too well ac-
" quainted with the ineſtimable advantage of govern-
" ing ourſelves, to be deſirous hereafter of depriving
" you of it.

" Maſters and ſupreme arbitrators of your own le-
" giſlation, if in your ſtates you can create a better
" form of government than ours is, we congratulate
" you previouſly upon it. Your happineſs will inſpire
" us with no other ſentiment than the deſire of imi-
" tating you. Form for yourſelves conſtitutions adapt-
" ed to your climate, to your ſoil, and to the New
" World, which you are civilizing. Who can be bet-
" ter acquainted with your own wants than yourſelves?
" Proud and virtuous ſouls, ſuch as yours are, ought
" not to obey any laws except thoſe which they give
" themſelves. Every other yoke would be unworthy
" of them. Regulate your taxes yourſelves. We only
" aſk of you to conform to our cuſtom in the levying
" of the impoſt. We will preſent you with a ſtate of
" our wants, and you will determine yourſelves the
" juſt proportion between your ſupplies and your
" riches.

" Moreover, exerciſe your own induſtry as we do
" ours, and that without any reſtraint. Make the beſt
" advantage of the benefits of Nature, and of the fer-
" tile regions which you inhabit. Let the iron of your
" mines, the fleeces of your flocks, the ſkins of the
" wild animals wandering in your foreſts, be prepared
" in your own manufactures, and acquire in your
" hands an additional value. Let your ports be free.
" Let your commodities, and the productions of your
" arts, be conveyed to all parts of the world, from
" whence you may alſo derive all thoſe which you are
" in want of. This is one of our privileges, let it alſo
" be yours. The empire of the ocean, which we have
" ſubdued by two centuries of grandeur and glory,
" belongs to you as well as to us. We will be united

" by the ties of commerce. You will bring your pro-
" ductions to us, which we will accept in preference
" to thofe of all other people ; and we hope that you
" will prefer ours to thofe of foreign nations, without,
" however, being reftrained to it by any law, unlefs by
" that of the common intereft, and by the title of fel-
" low-citizens and friends.

" Let your fhips and ours, decorated with the fame
" flag, cover the feas ; and when thefe friendly veffels
" fhall meet in the midft of the deferts of the ocean,
" let fhouts of joy be heard on both fides. Let peace
" be renewed, and let concord laft for ever between
" us. We underftand at length, that the chain of re-
" ciprocal benevolence is the only one that can con-
" nect empires at fuch a diftance, and that every other
" principle of union would be unjuft and precarious.

" According to this new plan of everlafting friend-
" fhip, let agriculture, induftry, legiflation, the arts,
" and that firft of all fciences, that of doing the great-
" eft good to ftates and to mankind, be improved
" among us. Let the account of your happinefs in-
" vite around your dwellings all the unfortunate men
" upon the face of the earth. Let tyrants of all coun-
" tries, and all oppreffors, whether political or reli-
" gious, know, that there exifts a place upon the earth
" where one may efcape from their chains ; where hu-
" manity difgraced hath raifed its head again ; where
" the harvefts grow for the poor ; where the laws are
" no more than the guarantee of happinefs ; where re-
" ligion is free, and confcience hath ceafed to be a
" flave ; where Nature, in a word, feems to wifh to
" juftify herfelf for having created man ; and where
" government, for fo long a time guilty over all the
" earth, at length makes ample reparation for its
" crimes. Let the idea of fuch an afylum alarm the
" defpots, and ferve as a reftraint to them ; for if the
" happinefs of mankind be a matter of indifference to
" them, they are at leaft ambitious and avaricious, and
" are therefore anxious to preferve both their power
" and their riches.

" We ourfelves, O! our fellow-citizens and our
" friends, we ourfelves will profit by your example.
" If our conftitution fhould be impaired ; if public
" wealth fhould corrupt the court, and the court the
" nation ; if our kings, to whom we have given fo
" many terrible leffons, fhould at length forget them ;
" if we, who were an auguft people, were threatened
" with becoming the meaneft and vileft of all herds
" by felling ourfelves ; the fight of your virtues and
" of your laws might perhaps reanimate us. It would
" recal to our degraded minds both the value and the
" grandeur of liberty : and if this example fhould be
" ineffectual ; if flavery, the confequence of venal cor-
" ruption, fhould one day eftablifh itfelf in that fame
" country, which hath been deluged with blood in
" the caufe of liberty, and where our fathers have feen
" fcaffolds erected for tyrants ; we will then abandon
" this ungrateful land devoted to defpotifm, and we
" will leave the monfter to reign over a defert. You
" will then receive us as friends and brethren. You
" will partake with us that foil, that air, as free as the
" fouls of its generous inhabitants ; and thanks to
" your virtues, we fhall find England and a country
" again.

" Such are, brave fellow-citizens, both our hopes
" and our wifhes. Receive, therefore, our oaths as
" the pledges of fo holy an alliance. Let us invoke,
" to render this treaty more folemn, let us invoke our
" common anceftors, who have all been animated with
" the fpirit of liberty as you are, and who have not
" feared to die in its defence. Let us call to witnefs
" the memory of the illuftrious founders of your colo-
" nies, that of your auguft legiflators, of the philofo-
" pher Locke, who was the firft man upon earth who
" made a code of toleration, and of the venerable
" Penn, who firft founded a city of brothers. The
" fouls of thefe great men, whofe eyes are undoubted-
" ly in this moment fixed upon us, are worthy to pre-
" fide at a treaty which is to fecure the peace of two
" worlds. Let us fwear in their prefence, and upon

BOOK
XVIII.

" thofe arms with which you have fought us, to re-
" main ever united and faithful; and when we have
" pronounced all together an oath of peace, then let
" thefe fame arms be taken up, and let them be con-
" veyed into a facred depofit, where fathers will fhow
" them to every rifing generation: and there let them
" be kept faithfully from age to age, in order to be
" one day turned againft the firft man, whether Eng-
" lifh or American, who fhall dare to propofe the
" breaking off of this alliance, equally ufeful and
" equally honourable to both nations."

At this difcourfe methinks I hear the cities, the
hamlets, the fields, and all the fhores of North America, refound with acclamations, and repeating with
emotion the name of their Englifh brethren, the name
of the mother-country. Joyful fireworks fucceed to
the conflagrations of difcord; and in the meanwhile,
the nations, jealous of your power, will remain filent
in aftonifhment and defpair.

The parliament is going to affemble, and what have
we to expect? Will the voice of reafon be heard there,
or will they perfevere in their folly? Will they be the
defenders of the people, or the inftrument of the tyranny of minifters? Will their acts be the decrees of a
free nation, or edicts dictated by the court? I attend
at the debates. Thefe revered places refound with ha-
rangues full of moderation and wifdom. Soft perfuafion feems to flow from the lips of the moft diftinguifhed orators. They draw tears from the audience. My
heart is elated with hope, when fuddenly a voice, the
organ of defpotifm and of war, fufpends this delightful
emotion.

" Englifhmen," faith this furious declaimer, " can
" you hefitate one moment? They are your rights,
" your moft important interefts; it is the glory of
" your name which muft be defended. Thefe great
" benefits are not attacked by a foreign power, but
" threatened by a domeftic enemy. The danger is
" the greater, the outrage more fenfibly felt.

" Between two rival nations in arms for mutual

" pretenfions, policy may fometimes fufpend the fight. B O O K
" Againft rebellious fubjects the greateft fault is delay. XVIII.
" All moderation is weaknefs. The ftandard of rebel-
" lion was raifed by boldnefs; let it be pulled down
" by force. Let the fword of juftice fall upon thofe
" who have unfheathed it. Let us lofe no time : to
" ftifle revolutions, there is a firft moment which muft
" be feized upon. Let us not leave to aftonifhed
" minds the leifure to accuftom themfelves to their
" crime; to the chiefs, the time to confirm their pow-
" er; nor to the people, that of learning to obey new
" mafters. The people in a rebellion are almoft al-
" ways drawn away by fome foreign impulfe; neither
" their fury, nor their hatred, nor their attachment,
" belong to them. Their paffions are given to them
" as their weapons. Let us difplay before their eyes
" the ftrength and majefty of the Britifh empire. They
" will foon fall down at our feet; they will pafs on,
" in an inftant, from terror to remorfe, and from re-
" morfe to obedience. If we muft have recourfe to
" the feverity of arms, let there be no quarter. In ci-
" vil war, mercy is the moft falfe of all virtues. When
" once the fword is drawn, it fhould never be fheath-
" ed till fubmiffion be attained. Henceforward it is
" theirs to anfwer to heaven and to earth for their own
" misfortunes. Let us confider, that a temporary fe-
" verity, exercifed in thefe rebellious regions, muft fe-
" cure to us obedience and peace for ages to come.

" To fufpend our exertions, and to difarm us, we
" are repeatedly told, that this country is peopled with
" our fellow-citizens, our friends, and our brothers.
" What, fhall we invoke in their favour names which
" they have outraged, and ties which they have bro-
" ken? Thefe names, and thefe facred ties, are the
" things that accufe them, and pronounce them guil-
" ty. Since when do thofe titles, fo revered, impofe
" duties only upon us? Since when have rebellious
" children the right of taking up arms againft their
" mother, of depriving her of her inheritance, and of
" tearing her to pieces? They talk of liberty. I re-

BOOK
XVIII.
" fpeᵭ the name as much as they do: but, is this li-
" berty independence? Is it the right of fubverting a
" legiflation, eſtabliſhed and founded for two centu-
" ries paſt? Is it the right of uſurping all our rights?
" They talk of liberty; and I talk of the fupremacy
" and the fovereign power of England.

" What, if they had any complaints to make, if
" they refuſed to bear with us a ſmall portion of the
" burden which oppreſſes us, and to ſhare in our ex-
" pences, as we make them ſhare in our grandeur, had
" they no other way of doing this but by rebellion,
" but by arms? They are called our fellow-citizens,
" and our friends; but I behold in them nothing more
" than our perfecutors, and the moſt cruel enemies of
" our country. Undoubtedly, we have had common
" anceſtors; but theſe reſpeᵭable forefathers I myſelf
" call upon with confidence. If their ſhades could
" refume their place here, their indignation would be
" equal to ours. With what refentment would thefe
" virtuous citizens hear, that thofe of their defcendants
" who had fettled beyond the feas, had no fooner felt
" their own ſtrength, than they had made the guilty
" trial of it againſt their country; and that they have
" turned her own benefits againſt her? All of them,
" yes, all of them, even that pacific fet into whom
" their founder inſtilled the duty of never ſteeping
" their hands in blood; they who had refpeᵭed the
" rights and the lives of favage people; they who, in
" the enthufiafm of humanity, have broken the fetters
" of their ſlaves; at prefent, equally faithleſs to their
" country and to their religion, take up arms for the
" purpoſe of carnage, and to uſe them againſt you.
" They treat all men as their brethren; and you alone,
" of all people, are excluded from this title. They
" have taught the world, that the favage Americans,
" and the Negroes of Afiica, are henceforth leſs ſtran-
" gers to them than the citizens of England.

" Arm yourſelves, therefore; avenge your offended
" rights, avenge your greatneſs betrayed. Diſplay
" that power, which makes itſelf be feared in Europe,

" in Africa, and in India; and which hath fo often
" aftonifhed America itfelf: and fince between a fo-
" vereign people, and the fubject that rebels, there
" can henceforth be no other treaty than that of force,
" let force determine the matter. Preferve and retake
" that univerfe which belongs to you, and which in-
" gratitude and boldnefs would deprive you of."

The fophifms of a vehement orator, fupported by
the influence of the crown, and by national pride, extinguifhed in moft of the representatives of the people
the defire of a pacific arrangement. The new refolutions are fimilar to the former. Every thing in them
even bears, in a more decifive manner, the ftamp of
ferocioufnefs and defpotifm. Armies are raifed, and
fleets are equipped. The generals and the admirals
fail towards the New World, with deftructive and fanguinary orders and plans. Nothing but unreferved
fubmiffion can preferve or put a ftop to the ravages ordained againft the colonies.

Till this memorable period, the Americans had confined themfelves to a refiftance authorifed by the Englifh laws themfelves. They had fhown no other ambition, but that of being maintained in the very limited rights which they had always enjoyed. Their
chiefs, even, who might be fuppofed to have more extenfive views, had not yet ventured to fpeak to the
people of any thing more than an advantageous accommodation. By going further, they would have
been apprehenfive of lofing the confidence of the people, attached by habit to an empire under the protection of which they had profpered. The report of the
great preparations that were making for war in the Old
Hemifphere, either to enflave or to reduce the New
one to afhes, extinguifhed what remains there might
be of affection for the original government. It now
remained only to infpire the minds of men with energy. This effect was produced by a work entitled Common Senfe. We fhall here give an account of the
ground-work of this doctrine, without confining ourfelves precifely to the order the writer hath adopted.

Never, fays the author of this celebrated work, never did an intereft of greater importance engage the
attention of the nations. It is not the concern of a
city, or of a province; it is that of an immenfe continent, and of a great part of the globe. It is not the
concern of a day, it is that of ages. The prefent period will determine the fate of a long futurity; and
many hundred years after the ceffation of our exiftence, the fun, in giving light to this hemifphere, will
fhine either upon our fhame or our glory. We have
for a long time talked of reconciliation and peace; but
every thing is changed. As foon as arms are taken
up, as foon as the firft drop of blood is fpilt, the time
for debate is paft. One day hath given rife to a revolution. One day hath tranfported us into a new age.

Men of timorous minds, and who judge of the future by the paft, think we are in want of the protection of England. She may be ufeful to a rifing colony; fhe is become dangerous to a nation completely
formed. Infancy ftands in need of fupport, but youth
muft walk free, and with the elevation that is fuitable
to it. Between one nation and another, as between
man and man, he who can have the power and the
right to protect me, may alfo have the power and the
will to do me an injury. I give up the protector, in
order that I may not have a mafter to fear.

In Europe, the people are too clofely preffed together to admit this part of the globe to enjoy conftant
peace. The interefts of courts and of nations are always clafhing with each other. As the friends of England, we are obliged to have all her enemies. The
dowry which this alliance will bring to America is perpetual war. Let us, therefore, feparate. Neutrality,
trade, and peace; fuch are the foundations of our
grandeur.

The authority of Great Britain muft fooner or later
have an end. This is the operation of nature, of neceffity, and of time. The Englifh government, therefore, can only give us a temporary conftitution; and
we fhall only bequeath to our pofterity an American

ſtate, burdened with diſſenſions and debts. If we be
deſirous of ſecuring our happineſs, let us ſeparate. If
we be fathers, and if we love our children, let us ſeparate. Laws and liberty, ſuch is the inheritance we owe
them.

England is at too great a diſtance from us to govern
us. What, ſhall we always croſs two thouſand leagues
to demand the protection of laws, to claim juſtice, to
juſtify ourſelves of imaginary crimes, and meanly to
ſolicit the court and the miniſtry of a foreign climate?
Muſt we wait whole years for every anſwer, ſuppoſing
it were not even too often injuſtice that we were obliged to go in ſearch of acroſs the ocean? No; for a
great ſtate, the centre and the ſeat of power muſt neceſſarily be in the ſtate itſelf. Nothing but the deſpotiſm of the Eaſt can poſſibly have accuſtomed the people thus to receive laws from diſtant maſters, or from
baſhaws, who are the repreſentatives of inviſible tyrants. But remember, that the more the diſtance increaſes, the heavier is the weight of deſpotiſm; and
that the people, then deprived of almoſt all the benefits of government, have none but the misfortunes and
vices of it.

Nature hath not created a world, in order to ſubject
it to the inhabitants of an iſland in another hemiſphere.
Nature hath eſtabliſhed laws of equilibrium, which ſhe
follows in all parts, in the heavens as on the earth. By
the rule of quantity and of diſtance, America can belong only to itſelf.

There is no government without a mutual confidence between him who commands and him who
obeys; otherwiſe all is over, the communication is
interrupted, and cannot poſſibly be renewed. England hath ſhown too evidently that ſhe wanted to
command us as ſlaves; America, that ſhe was equally
ſenſible of her rights and her ſtrength. Each of them
hath betrayed its ſecret; and from that moment no
treaty can take place. It would be ſigned by hatred
and miſtruſt; hatred which cannot forgive, and miſtruſt, which in its nature is irreconcileable.

Would you know what would be the confequence of an accommodation? Your ruin. You ftand in need of laws, and will not obtain them. Who is to give them to you? The Englifh nation? But fhe is jealous of your increafe. The king? He is your ene- my. Yourfelves, in your affemblies? Do you not re- collect, that every legiflation is fubject to the negative right of the monarch who wifhes to fubdue you? This right would be a terrible one, inceffantly militating againft you. Should you make demands, they will be eluded; fhould you form plans of grandeur and commerce, they would become an object of alarm for the mother-country. Your government would be no- thing more than a clandeftine war, fuch as that of an enemy who wifhes to deftroy without fighting; it would be, in political economy, a flow and concealed affaffination, which gives rife to languor, which pro- longs and entertains weaknefs, and which, by a de- ftructive art, keeps the body equally fufpended be- tween life and death. If you fhould fubmit to Eng- land, fuch will be your fate.

We have a right to take up arms. Our rights are neceffity, a juft defence; our misfortunes, thofe of our children, the enormities committed againft us. Our rights are our auguft title of nation. The fword muft decide between us. The tribunal of war is henceforth the only tribunal that exifts for us. If we muft fight, let it at leaft be for a caufe that is worthy, and which will reward us for the lavifhment of our riches and our blood. What! fhall we expofe ourfelves to fee our cities deftroyed, our countries ravaged, our fami- lies put to the fword, merely to obtain an honourable accommodation; that is to fay, to entreat for new chains, and to cement ourfelves the edifice of our flavery? What! fhall it be by the light of conflagra- tions; fhall it be over the graves of our fathers, of our children, and of our wives, that we fhall fign a treaty with our oppreffors? And will they, covered over with our blood, condefcend to forgive us? Alas! we fhould then be nothing more than a vile object of aftonifh-

ment to Europe, of indignation to America, and of
contempt even to our enemies.   If we can obey, we
have had no right to contend.   Liberty alone can ab-
folve us.   Liberty, and entire liberty, is the only aim
worthy of our efforts and of our perils.   What do I
fay ? It belongs to us from this moment.   It is in the
bloody plains of Lexington that our claims are regi-
ftered ; it is there that England hath torn in pieces
that contract which united us to her.   Yes, at the inftant when England fired the firft fhot againft us, Nature herfelf proclaimed us free and independent.

Let us avail ourfelves of the benefits we receive
from our enemies.   The youth of nations is the age
the moft favourable to their independence.   It is the
period of energy and vigour.   Our minds are not yet
furrounded with that parade of luxury which ferves as
a hoftage to tyranny.   Our limbs are not yet enervated by the arts of effeminacy.   There is none of that
nobility bearing fway among us, which, even by its
conftitution, is allied to kings ; which is no further attached to liberty, than when it can make it the means
of oppreffion ; that nobility, eager of rights and titles,
for whom, in times of revolution and crifis, the people
are nothing more than an inftrument, and for whom
the fupreme power is a corrupter always at hand.

Your colonies are formed of plain and courageous,
laborious and proud men ; men who are at once the
proprietors and the cultivators of their lands.   Liberty
is the firft of their wants.   Ruftic labours have previoufly inured them to war.   Public enthufiafm will
bring forth talents unknown.   It is in revolutions that
the minds of men are enlarged, that heroes make their
appearance, and take their poft.   Recal Holland to
your memory, and the multitude of extraordinary
men to whom the conteft for her liberty gave birth :
fuch is your example.   Recollect her fuccefs : fuch is
your prefage.

Let our firft meafure be to form a conftitution that
may unite us.   The moment is come.   Later than this,

it would be abandoned to an uncertain futurity, and to the caprices of chance. The more we acquire men and riches, the more barriers will arife between us. How fhall we then conciliate fo many interefts and fo many provinces? For a union of this kind, it is necef-fary that every people fhould be fenfible at once of the weaknefs and ftrength of the whole. Great cala-mities or great apprehenfions muft prevail. Then it is, that among nations, as among individuals, thofe vi-gorous and rooted friendfhips take place, which reci-procally bind the fouls and the intereft of men. Then it is, that one fingle fpirit univerfally prevailing, forms the genius of ftates ; and that all the fcattered forces become, by being collected, one fole and terrible force. Thanks to our perfecutors, we are now at that period ; and if we have courage, it will be a fortunate one for us. Few nations have feized the favourable moment for the formation of their government. If this mo-ment fhould once efcape, it never returns ; and men are confequently punifhed with ages of anarchy and flavery. Let not a fimilar fault prepare fimilar regrets for us, which would be ineffectual.

Let us therefore feize upon the moment which is the only one for us. It is in our power to form the fineft conftitution that ever exifted among men. You have read in your facred writings the hiftory of man-kind buried under a general deluge of the globe. One fingle family furvived, and was commiffioned by the Supreme Being to renew the earth. We are that fa-mily. Defpotifm hath overwhelmed every thing ; and we can renew the world a fecond time.

At this inftant, we are going to determine the fate of a race of men more numerous, perhaps, than all the people of Europe taken together. Shall we wait till we become the prey of the conqueror, and till the hopes of the univerfe fhall be fruftrated? Let us fup-pofe, that all the future generations of the world have at this moment their eyes fixed upon us, and are afk-ing us for liberty. We are going to fettle their def-

tiny. If we betray them, they will one day walk over
our graves with their chains, and perhaps load us with
imprecations.

Remember a work that hath appeared among us,
and the motto of which was, UNION OR DEATH.

Let us therefore unite, and begin by declaring our
INDEPENDENCE. That alone can efface the title of rebellious fubjects, which our infolent oppreffors dare to
beftow upon us. That alone can make us rife to that
dignity that is our due, enfure us allies among the
powers, and imprint refpect even on our enemies; and
if we treat with them, that alone can give us the right
of treating with that right and majefty which belongs
to a nation.

But I will repeat it: Let us lofe no time. Our uncertainty occafions our weaknefs. Let us dare to be
free, and we are fo. When we are ready to get over
this ftep, we ftart back. We all look at each other
with anxious curiofity. It feems as if we were afto-
niſhed at our boldnefs, and frightened at our courage.
But it is no longer time to calculate. In great affairs,
and where there is but one great meafure to adopt, too
much circumfpection ceafes to be prudence. Whatever is extreme demands an extreme refolution. Then
the moft enterprifing fteps are the moft prudent; and
the excefs of boldnefs becomes even the means and
the warrant of fuccefs.

Such was the bafis of the fentiments and ideas diffufed in this work. They confirmed in their principles thofe bold men, who for a long time paft had
aſked to be entirely detached from the mother-country. The timid citizens, who had hitherto hefitated,
at length determined on this great feparation. The
wiſh for independence had a fufficient number of partifans, to enable the general congrefs to declare it on
the 4th of July 1776.

The colo-
nies break
the ties
which unit-
ed them to
England,
and declare
themfelves
indepen-
dent of that
country.

O that I had received from nature the genius and
eloquence of the celebrated orators of Athens and
Rome! With what fublimity, with what enthufiafm
ſhould I not fpeak of thofe generous men, who, by

BOOK
XVIII.

their patience, their wifdom, and their courage, have erected this grand edifice. Hancock, Franklin, and the two Adamfes, were the principal perfons in this interefting fcene; but they were not the only ones. Pofterity will be acquainted with them all. Their celebrated names will be tranfmitted to it by a more fortunate pen than mine. The marble and the bronze will exhibit them to the remoteft ages. At fight of them, the friend of liberty will feel his eyes filled with pleafing tears, and his heart will bound with joy. Under the buft of one of them has been written, HE TOOK FROM HEAVEN ITS THUNDER, AND FROM TYRANTS THEIR SCEPTRE. They will all partake with him the laft words of this encomium.

Heroic region! mine advanced age will not allow me to vifit thee! I fhall never be prefent amidft the refpectable perfons who compofe your Areopagus. I fhall never affift at the deliberations of your congrefs. I fhall die without having feen the refidence of toleration, of morality, and of found laws; of virtue, and of liberty. A free and facred land will not cover my afhes; but I could have wifhed it: and my laft words fhall be vows addreffed to Heaven for your profperity.

Although America was affured that her conduct would meet with univerfal approbation, yet fhe thought it her duty to lay before the nations the motives of it. She publifhed her manifefto *, in which we read; the hiftory of the Englifh nation, and of its king, will offer to pofterity, in fpeaking of them and of us, nothing but a heap of outrages and ufurpations, all equally tending to the eftablifhment of abfolute tyranny in thefe provinces.

This hiftory will fay, that its monarch hath refufed to give his confent to laws which were the moft falutary and the moft neceffary for the public good.

That he hath transferred the affemblies to inconvenient places, at a diftance from the records, in order to bring the deputies more eafily into his views.

---

* The Englifh reader will eafily perceive that this account is not taken literally from the original manifefto publifhed by the Americans.

That he hath feveral times diffolved the chamber of the reprefentatives, becaufe the rights of the people were ftrenuoufly defended there.

That after the diffolution, the ftates have been left too long without reprefentatives, and were confequently expofed to the inconveniences refulting from the want of an affembly.

That he hath endeavoured to put a ftop to population, by making it difficult for a foreigner to be naturalized, and by requiring too much for the lands of which he granted the property.

That he hath put the judges too much under his dependence, by enacting that they fhould hold their offices and their falaries from him alone.

That he hath created new places, and filled thofe regions with a multitude of agents, who devoured our fubftance, and difturbed our tranquillity.

That in time of full peace he hath kept up confiderable forces in the midft of us, without the confent of the legiflative power.

That he hath rendered the military power independent of, and even fuperior to, the civil law.

That he hath fettled with corrupt men to lodge armed foldiers in our houfes, and to fhelter them from punifhment for the murders which they might commit in America; to deftroy our trade in all the parts of the globe; to impofe taxes on us without our confent; to deprive us in feveral cafes of our trials by juries; to tranfport us beyond feas, that we might be brought to trial there; to take away our characters, fupprefs our beft laws, and alter the bafis and the form of our government; to fufpend our own legiflation, in order to give us other laws.

That he hath himfelf abdicated his government over the provinces of America, by declaring that we had forfeited his protection, and by waging war againft us.

That he hath caufed our coafts to be ravaged, our ports to be deftroyed, and our people to be maffacred,

That he hath compelled our fellow-citizens, taken prisoners at sea, to bear arms against their country, to become the assassins of their friends and their brethren, or to perish themselves by those beloved hands.

That he hath fomented intestine divisions amongst us, and endeavoured to excite against our peaceful inhabitants barbarous savages, accustomed to massacre, without distinction of rank, of sex, or of age, every person they met with.

That at this time mercenary and foreign armies have arrived on our shores, who were intended to consummate the work of desolation and of death.

And that a prince, whose character was thus marked by all the features of tyranny, was not fit to govern a free people.

A proceeding which dissolved the ties formed by consanguinity, by religion, and by habit, ought to have been supported by a great unanimity, and by prudent and vigorous measures. The united states of America gave themselves a confederate constitution, which added all the exterior strength of the monarchy to all the interior advantages of a republican government.

Each province had an assembly formed by the representatives of the different districts, and who were entrusted with the legislative power. The executive power was vested in the president. It was his right and his duty to hear the complaints of all the citizens, to convene them when circumstances required it, to provide for the equipment and subsistence of the troops, and to concert the operations with their chiefs. He was placed at the head of a secret committee, whose business it was to keep up a constant intercourse with the general congress. The time of his administration is limited to two years, but the laws allowed it to be prolonged.

The provinces were not obliged to give an account of their administration to the great council of the nation, although it was composed of the deputies of all

the colonies. The fuperiority of the general congrefs B o o k
over each particular congrefs was limited to what con- XVIII.
cerned policy and war.

But fome people have judged that the inftitution of
this body was not fo well planned as the legiflation of
the provinces. It fhould feem, indeed, that confederate ftates, who emerge from the condition of fubjects to rife to independence, cannot without danger
entruft their delegates with an unlimited power of making peace or war. For if thefe were either faithlefs or
not much enlightened, they might again fubject the
whole ftate to the fame yoke from which it attempts
to free itfelf. It feems that in the inftant of a revolution, the public wifhes cannot be too much known,
nor too literally explained. It is undoubtedly neceffary, fay they, that all the meafures, all the operations
which concur to the common attack or defence, fhould
be decided by the common reprefentatives of the body
of the ftate ; but the continuation of the war, and the
conditions of peace, ought to be debated in each province ; and the deliberations fhould be tranfmitted to
the congrefs by the deputies, who fhould fubmit the
opinion of their provinces to the majority of votes.
Laftly, it is added, that if it be right in eftablifhed governments for the people to confide in the wifdom of
the fenate, it is neceffary in a ftate where the conftitution is forming, where the people, ftill uncertain of
their fate, require their liberty fword in hand, that all
the citizens fhould continually attend at the councils
in the army, and in the public places, and that they
fhould always keep a watchful eye over the reprefentatives to whom they have entrufted their deftiny.

Though thefe principles be generally true, it may
however be anfwered, that it was difficult perhaps to
apply them to the new republic formed by the Americans. The cafe is not with them as with the confederate republics we fee in Europe, I mean Holland and
Switzerland, which only occupy a territory of fmall extent, and where it is an eafy matter to eftablifh a rapid
communication between the feveral provinces. The

BOOK
XVIII.
 fame thing may be faid of the confederacies of ancient Greece. Thefe ftates were fituated at a fmall diftance from each other, almoft entirely confined within the limits of the Peloponnefus, or within the circuit of a narrow Archipelago. But the united ftates of America, difperfed over an immenfe continent, occupying in the New World a fpace of near fifteen degrees, feparated by deferts, mountains, gulfs, and by a vaft extent of coafts, cannot enjoy fo fpeedy a communication. If congrefs were not empowered to decide upon political interefts without the particular deliberations of each province; if upon every occafion of the leaft importance, and every unforefeen event, it were neceffary for the reprefentatives to receive new orders, and as it were a new power, this body would remain in a ftate of inactivity. The diftances to be traverfed, together with the length and the multiplicity of the debates, might be too frequently prejudicial to the general good.

Befides, it is never in the infancy of a conftitution, and in the midft of the great commotions for liberty, that we need apprehend that a body of reprefentatives fhould betray, either from corruption or weaknefs, the interefts with which they are entrufted. The general fpirit will rather be inflamed and exalted in fuch a body. There it is that the genius of the nation refides in all its vigour. Chofen by the efteem of their fellow-citizens, chofen at a time when every public function is dangerous, and every vote an honour; placed at the head of thofe who will eternally compofe this celebrated Areopagus, and on that account naturally induced to confider public liberty as the work of their own hands, they muft be poffeffed with the enthufiafm of founders, whofe pride it is to engrave for future centuries their names upon the frontifpiece of the auguft monument which is erecting. The apprehenfions which the favourers of the contrary fyftem might have upon this account, appear therefore to be ill-founded.

I will go further ftill. It might happen that a peo-

ple who fight for their liberty, fatigued with a long
and painful ftruggle, and more affected with the dangers of the moment than with the idea of their future happinefs, might feel their courage damped, and
might one day, perhaps, be tempted to prefer dependence and peace to a tempeftuous independence,
which would expofe them to dangers and blood-
fhed. It is then that it would be advantageous to
thofe people to have deprived themfelves of the power of making peace with their oppreffors, and to have
vefted that power in the hands of a fenate which
they had chofen to be the organ of their will at a
time when that will was free, haughty and courageous. It feems as if they had told their fenate at the
time of their inftitution, we raife the ftandard of war
againft our tyrants; if our arms fhould grow weary
of the fight, if we fhould ever be capable of degrading ourfelves fo far as to fue for repofe, fupport us
againft our weaknefs: do not attend to wifhes unworthy of ourfelves, which we previoufly difavow;
and do not pronounce the name of peace till our
chains fhall be entirely broken.

Accordingly, if we confult the hiftory of republics,
we fhall find that the multitude have almoft always the
impetuofity and the ardour of the firft moment; but
that it is only in a fmall number of men chofen and
fit to ferve as chiefs, in whom refide thofe conftant
and vigorous refolutions which proceed with a firm
and certain ftep towards a great aim, and which are
never altered, but obftinately ftruggle againft calamities, fortune, and mankind.

However this may be, and whatever fide we may
take in this political difcuffion, the Americans had
not yet formed their fyftem of government, when in
the month of March, Hopkins was carrying off from
the Englifh iflands of Providence a very numerous
artillery, and a great quantity of warlike ftores; when
at the beginning of May, Carleton drove away from
Canada the Provincials who were employed in reducing Quebec, in order to finifh the conqueft of that

War begins
between
the United
States and
England.

BOOK great poffeffion; when in June, Clinton and Parker
XVIII. were fo vigoronfly driven back upon the coafts of
South America. The declaration of independence
was followed by greater fcenes.

Howe had fucceeded the feeble Gage. It was even
the new general who had evacuated Bofton. Received
in Halifax on the fecond of April, he quitted it the
tenth of June to go to Staten Ifland, where he was
fucceffively joined by the land and fea forces which
he expected; and on the 28th of Auguft he landed
without oppofition upon Long Ifland, under the protection of a fleet commanded by the admiral his brother. The Americans did not difplay much more vigour in the inland countries than upon the coafts.
After a trifling refiftance and confiderable loffes they
took refuge on the continent, with a facility which a
conqueror, who had known how to improve his advantages, would never have given them.

The new republicans forfook the city of New York
with ftill greater facility than they had evacuated
Long Ifland, and they had retired to Kingfbridge,
where every thing feemed difpofed for an obftinate
refiftance.

Had the Englifh followed up their firft fucceffes
with that activity which the circumftances required,
the new levies which were oppofed to them would infallibly have been difperfed or obliged to lay down
their arms. Six weeks were allowed them to recover
themfelves, and they did not abandon their intrenchments till the night of the 2d of November, when
they were convinced, by the motions which were
made under their eyes, that their camp was going to
be attacked.

Wafhington their chief did not choofe to truft the
fate of his country to an action which might have been,
and which muft naturally have been, decifive againft
the great interefts he was entrufted with. He knew
that delays are always favourable to the inhabitants of
a country and fatal to ftrangers. This conviction determined him to fall back upon the Jerfeys with the

intention of protracting the war. Favoured by the winter, by the knowledge of the country, by the nature of the territory, which deprived difcipline of part of its advantages, he might flatter himfelf that he fhould be able to cover the greateft part of this fertile province, and to keep the enemy at a diftance from Pennfylvania. All of a fudden he found his colours forfaken by foldiers, who were engaged for no more than fix or even three months, and from an army of five-and-twenty thoufand men, he fcarcely kept together two thoufand-five hundred, with whom he found himfelf very fortunate to efcape beyond the Delaware.

Without lofing a moment the royal troops ought to have croffed the river in purfuit of this fmall number of fugitives, and to have completed the difperfion of them. If the five thoufand men deftined for the conqueft of Rhode Ifland had gone up the river upon the fhips they were on board of, the junction of the two corps would have been made without oppofition in Philadelphia itfelf, and the new republic would have been extinguifhed in the famous and interefting city which had given it birth.

The Englifh general was perhaps cenfured at that time for having been too timorous and too circumfpect in the operations of the field. It is however certain, that he was rafh in the diftribution of his winter-quarters. He fettled them as if there had not been a fingle individual in America, who either had the power or the inclination to moleft them.

This prefumption emboldened the militia of Pennfylvania, of Maryland, and of Virginia, who had united for their common fafety. The 25th of December they croffed the Delaware, and fell unawares upon Trentown, which was occupied by fifteen hundred of the twelve thoufand Heffians who had been fo bafely fold to Great Britain by their avaricious mafter. This corps was either maffacred, taken, or entirely difperfed. A week after, three Englifh regiments were alfo driven out of Princes Town, but not without having

BOOK fhown more courage than the foreign troops in their
XVIII. pay. Thefe unexpected events reduced the enemies
of America in Jerfey to the pofts of Amboy and of
Brunfwick; and they were even much haraffed there
during the remainder of the bad feafon. The effect
of great paffions and great dangers is frequently to
aftonifh the foul, and to plunge it in a kind of ftupor
which deprives it of the ufe of its powers. By degrees it comes to itfelf and recovers. All its faculties,
fufpended for a moment, exert themfelves with greater
energy. It ftrains all its fprings, and its ftrength becomes equal to its fituation. In a great multitude fome
individuals firft experience this effect, and it is quickly
communicated to all. This revolution had been accomplifhed in the confederate ftates, and armed men
iffued forth from all quarters of them.

The campaign of 1777 was opened very late. The
Englifh army defpairing of making a road to Pennfylvania through the Jerfeys, embarked at length on
the 23d of July, and arrived by Chefapeak Bay, in a
country which their generals might be cenfured for
not having invaded the preceding year. Their march
was not interrupted till they came to Brandewine,
where they attacked and defeated the Americans on
the 11th of September, and arrived on the 30th at
Philadelphia, which had been abandoned by congrefs
on the 25th, and by a great number of the inhabitants
fome days fooner or later.

This conqueft was attended with no confequences.
The conquerors beheld nothing but hatred and devaftation around them. Confined in a very circumfcrib-
ed fpace, they met with unfurmountable obftacles in
extending themfelves upon an uncultivated territory.
Their gold even did not furnifh them with refources
from the neighbouring diftricts, and they could only
acquire their fubfiftence from acrofs the feas. Wearied with a confinement which had lafted nine months,
they determined to regain New York by the Jerfeys;
and this long and dangerous retreat was accomplifhed
under the command of Clinton, who had fucceeded

Howe, with lefs lofs than they would have fuffered from a more experienced enemy.

While the Englifh were languifhing in Pennfylvania a vaft fcene was opening in the more northern countries of America. In the month of May 1776, Carleton had driven away the provincials from Canada, and deftroyed in October the fhips of war which had been conftructed upon lake Champlain. This fuccefs carried Burgoyne to Ticonderago, in the month of July of the enfuing year. At his approach, the garrifon of four thoufand men abandoned this important poft with the lofs of their artillery, ammunition, and rear guard.

The Englifh general was naturally prefumptuous, and his boldnefs was increafed by thefe evident figns of weaknefs. He had conceived the defign of uniting the troops of Canada with thofe of New York by the fhores of Hudfon's Bay. This project was great and daring. Had it fucceeded it would have divided South America into two parts, and perhaps have ended the war. But in order to make it fucceed, it was neceffary that while one army was going down the river another fhould be coming up it. This plan having failed, Burgoyne ought to have perceived from the firft that his enterprife was chimerical. It became more fo every march. His communications became more diftant and his provifions were diminifhing. The courage of the Americans being revived, they affembled and clofed him on all fides. At length this unfortunate army found itfelf furrounded on the 13th October at Saratoga, and the nations heard with aftonifhment, that fix thoufand of the beft difciplined troops of the Old Hemifphere, had laid down their arms before the hufbandmen of the New Hemifphere, under the conduct of the fortunate Gates. Thofe who recollected that the Swedes of Charles XII. who had till then been invincible, had capitulated to the Ruffians, who were ftill in a ftate of barbarifm, did not cenfure the Englifh troops, and only blamed the imprudence of their general.

B O O K
XVIII.
This event, so decisive in the opinion of our politicians, was attended with no greater consequences
than had resulted from actions less favourable to the
American arms.   After three years spent in battles,
devastation, and massacres, affairs were much in the
same situation as they were a fortnight after the commencement of hostilities.   Let us endeavour to inves-
tigate the cause of this strange singularity.

What is the
reason that
the English
have not
succeeded
in subduing
the confe-
derate pro-
vinces.
England, accustomed to stormy times in her own
country, did not at first perceive all the dangerous
tendency of the tempest which was rising in her distant possessions.   Her troops had been a long time
insulted at Boston.   An authority independent of her
own had been formed in Massachuset's Bay ; the other
colonies were preparing to follow that example before
administration had seriously attended to those great
objects.   When they were laid before parliament they
excited much clamours in both houses, and there was
no end to the debates.   The senate of the nation at
length determined, that the country which rebelled
against its decrees should be compelled by force to
submit to them.   But this violent resolution was carried into execution with that delay which is but too
common in free states.

England was generally of opinion, that defenceless
coasts and countries, which were entirely laid open,
could not long resist her fleets and her armies.   It did
not appear to her, that this expedition would continue
long enough to give the peaceful cultivators of America time to instruct themselves in the art of war.   She
did not take into consideration the climate, the rivers,
the defiles, the woods, the morasses, the want of subsistence increasing in proportion as one advanced in
the inland countries, together with an infinite number
of other natural obstacles which would impede any rapid progress in a country three-fourths of which were
uncultivated, and which ought to be considered as a
recent one.

The successes were still more retarded by the influence of moral causes.

Great Britain is the region of parties. Her kings B O O K XVIII. have moſt generally been convinced of the neceſſity of abandoning the direction of affairs to the prevailing faction, by which they were commonly conducted with intelligence and vigour, becauſe the principal agents who compoſed it were animated with one common intereſt. At that time, to the public ſpirit which prevails more in England than in any European government, was added the ſtrength of faction, and that ſpirit of party which is perhaps the firſt ſpring of a republic, and which ſo powerfully agitates the ſoul, becauſe it is always the effect of ſome paſſion. George III. in order to free himſelf from this long tutelage, compoſed his council of members unconnected with each other. This innovation was not attended with great inconveniences, as long as events moved on in their ordinary circle. But when the American war had complicated a machine which was already too intricate, it was perceived that it had no longer that power and that union ſo neceſſary to accompliſh great things. The wheels, too much divided, wanted, as it were, one common impulſe and a centre of motion. Their progreſſion was alternately tardy and precipitate. The adminiſtration reſembled too much that of an ordinary monarchy, when the principle of action doth not come from the head of an active and intelligent monarch, who himſelf collects under his own management all the ſprings of government. There was no longer any harmony in the enterpriſes, nor was there any more in the execution of them.

A miniſtry without-harmony and without concord was expoſed to the attacks inceſſantly renewed of an adverſe body of men united and compacted together. Their reſolutions, whatever they might be, were oppoſed with ridicule and with argument. They were cenſured for having acted with violence againſt citizens at a diſtance; and they would have been equally cenſured, had they treated them with more circumſpection. Even thoſe who in parliament exclaimed the moſt vehemently againſt the treatment the Americans

had met with, thofe who encouraged them the moft
to refiftance, thofe who perhaps fent them fecret fuccours, were as much averfe from their independence,
as the minifter whom they were inceffantly endeavouring to degrade or to render odious. If the oppofition
had fucceeded in difgufting the prince of his confi-
dents, or had prevailed upon him to facrifice them on
account of the clamours of the nation, the project of
conquering America would ftill have been purfued ;
but with more dignity, with more ftrength, and with
meafures perhaps better adapted. But as the reduc-
tion of the provinces was not to be accomplifhed by
them, they chofe rather that this immenfe part of the
Britifh empire fhould be feparated from it, than that
it fhould remain attached to it by any other means
than theirs.

The generals did not repair, by their activity, the
errors of thefe contradictions, and of the delays which
were the confequence of them. They granted too
long repofe to the foldiers ; they wafted in deliberation
the time which they fhould have employed in action ;
they marched up to new raifed troops with as much
precaution as they would have taken againft veterans.
The Englifh, who are fo impetuous in their factions,
difplay on all other occafions a calm and cool character. They require violent paffions to agitate them.
When this ftimulus is wanting, they calculate all their
motions. Then they conduct themfelves according to
the tenor of their character, which in general, except
in the arts of imagination and tafte, is univerfally mechanical and prudent. In war, their valour never
lofes fight of military principles, and leaves little to
chance. They fcarce ever leave upon their flanks, or
in their rear, any thing that can give them uneafinefs.
This fyftem hath its advantages, efpecially in a narrow
and confined country, in a country thick fet with fortreffes or military pofts. But in the prefent circumftances, and on the vaft continent of America, againft
a people to whom one fhould not have allowed time
to fortify themfelves, nor to inure themfelves to war,

the perfection of the art would perhaps have been, to
lay it entirely afide; to fubftitute to it an impetuous
and rapid march, and that boldnefs which at once aftonifhes, ftrikes, and overthows. It was in the firft inftances efpecially, that it would have been proper to
imprefs the Americans, not with the terror of ravages,
which irritate rather than they frighten a people armed for their liberty; but with that which arifes from
the fuperiority of talents and of arms, and which a
warlike people of the Old World ought naturally to
have carried into the New one. The confidence of
victory would foon have been victory itfelf. But by
too much circumfpection, by too fervile an attachment to principles and to rules, commanders of little
fkill failed in rendering that fervice to their country
which fhe expected, and had a right to expect from
them.

The troops, on the other hand, did not prefs their
officers to lead them on to action. They arrived from
a country, where the caufe which had obliged them
to crofs fo many feas excited no concern. It was, in
the eyes of the people, an effervefcence which would
have no confequences. They confounded the debates
which it occafioned in parliament, with other debates,
which were often of little importance. It was not
talked of; and if any perfon happened to mention it,
they appeared to be no more interefted in it, than in
that kind of news which, in great cities, employs the
lounging hours of every day. The indifference of the
nation had communicated itfelf to thofe who were to
defend their rights. Perhaps even they were apprehenfive of gaining too decifive an advantage over fellow-citizens, who had only taken up arms to prevent
flavery. In all the monarchies of Europe, the foldier
is only the inftrument of defpotifm, and his fentiments
are analogous. He thinks he belongs to the throne,
and not to his country; and a hundred thoufand men
in arms are nothing more than one hundred thoufand
difciplined and terrible flaves. The habit even of exercifing the empire of force, to which every thing

BOOK XVIII. gives way, contributes to extinguifh in them all idea of liberty. Finally, the difcipline, and military fub-ordination, which, at the command of one fingle man, puts thoufands in motion; which doth not fuffer the foldier either to fee or to afk queftions; and which, on the firft fignal, makes it a rule to kill or to die, tends completely to change in them thofe fentiments into principles, and makes them as it were the moral fyf-tem of their condition. It is not the fame in England. The influence of the conftitution is fo powerful, that it extends even to the troops. A man there is a citi-zen before he is a foldier. Public opinion agreeing with the conftitution, honours one of thefe titles, and thinks little of the other. Accordingly, we fee from the hiftory of the revolutions that have happened in this turbulent ifland, that the Englifh foldier, though enlifted for life, preferves a paffion for political liberty, the idea of which cannot be eafily conceived in our regions of flavery.

How is it poffible that the ardour which was want-ing to the Britifh troops fhould have animated the Heffians, the Brunfwickers, and the other Germans, ranged under the fame ftandards, and all of them equally diffatisfied with the fovereigns who had fold them, diffatisfied with the prince who had purchafed them, diffatisfied with the nation that paid them, and diffatisfied with their comrades, who defpifed them as mercenaries? Befides, they had alfo in the enemy's camp, brothers whom they were afraid of deftroying, and by whofe hands they would not have wifhed to be wounded.

The fpirit of the Britifh armies was alfo changed, in confequence of a revolution which had taken place in the manners of the nation for about fifteen or eighteen years paft. The fucceffes of the laft war; the exten-fion commerce had received after the peace; the great acquifitions made in the Eaft Indies; all thefe means of wealth had accumulated uninterruptedly prodigious riches in Great Britain. Thefe treafures kindled the defire of frefh enjoyments. The great went in fearch of this art in foreign countries, efpecially in France, and brought with them the poifon of it into their own country. From the men of high rank, it foon diffufed itfelf among all orders of men. To a haughty, fimple, and referved character, fucceeded the tafte for parade, diffipation, and gallantry. The travellers who had formerly vifited this ifland, fo celebrated, thought themfelves under another fky. The contagion had even gained the troops; they carried into the New Hemifphere that paffion they had contracted in the Old one, for play, the inclination for all the conveniences of life, and for high living. In quitting the coafts, they fhould have renounced all the fuperfluities to which they were attached; and that tafte for luxury, that ardour, fo much the more violent as it was recent, did not encourage them to follow into the inland parts, men who were always ready to fall back upon them. Ye new politicians, who advance with fo much confidence, that the manners have no kind of influence upon the deftiny of ftates; that for them the meafure of their grandeur is that of their riches; that the luxury of peace, and the voluptuous purfuits of the citizen, cannot weaken the effect of thofe great machines which are called armies, and the fenfible and terrible impulfe of which European difcipline hath brought to fo great perfection: you who, to fupport your opinion, turn your eyes away from the afhes of Carthage and the ruins of Rome, fufpend at leaft your judgment at the account I am giving you, and acknowledge that there may perhaps be opportunities of fuccefs, which luxury prevents us from availing ourfelves of. Acknowledge that for troops even that are brave, it has been often the firft fource of victory, that they had no wants. It is too eafy a matter, perhaps, to have nothing but death to face. Nations corrupted by wealth have a more difficult trial to undergo; that of fupporting the privation of their pleafures.

Let us add to all thefe reafons, that the inftruments of war do not often arrive acrofs the feas in the proper feafons for action. Let us add, that the councils of

George III. had too much influence over military operations, which were to be carried on at fo great a diftance from them; and we fhall then comprehend moft
of the obftacles which impeded the fuccefs of the ruinous efforts of the mother-country againft the liberty of
the colonies.

Why have
not the con-
federate
provinces
fucceeded
in driving
the Englifh
from the
continent
of Ameri-
ca?
But wherefore did not America herfelf repulfe from
her fhores the Europeans who were bringing death or
flavery to her?

This New World was defended by regular troops,
which at firft had been enlifted only for three or fix
months, and afterwards for three years, or even for all
the time hoftilities might laft.   It was defended by citizens, who only took the field when their particular
province was either invaded or threatened.   Neither
the ftanding army, nor the militia affembled for a
time, breathed the military fpirit.   They were planters, merchants, lawyers, exercifed only in the arts of
peace, and led on to danger by commanders as little
verfed as their fubalterns in the very complicated fcience of military actions.   In this ftate of things, what
hope was there of their acting with advantage againft
men grown old in difcipline, trained to evolutions,
fkilled in tactics, and abundantly provided with all the
inftruments neceffary for a brifk attack, and for an obftinate refiftance?

Enthufiafm alone could have furmounted fuch difficulties.   But did it really exift more in the colonies
than in the mother country?

The general opinion in England was, that the parliament had effentially the right of taxing all the regions which conftituted a part of the Britifh empire.
At the commencement of the troubles, there were not
perhaps a hundred individuals who would have called
this authority in queftion.   Neverthelefs, the refufal
of the Americans to acknowledge it, did not fet the
minds of men againft them.   There was no hatred entertained againft them, even after they had taken up
arms to fupport their pretenfions.   As the labours in
the inland parts of the kingdom were not affected, and

as the thunder was only heard at a diftance, every one attended peaceably to his own affairs, or devoted himfelf quietly to his pleafures. All of them expected, without impatience, the end of a fcene, the termination of which did not indeed appear uncertain to them.

The ferment muft at firft have broken out with more violence in the New than in the Old Hemifphere. Hath ever the odious name of tyranny, or the pleafing word of independence, been pronounced to the nations, without raifing emotions in them? But was this ardour kept up? If the imaginations of men had been maintained in their firft ftate of commotion, would it not have been the bufinefs of a rifing authority to attend to the fuppreffion of the excefs of it? But, far from having boldnefs to reftrain it, it was cowardice they had to guard againft. They punifhed defertion with death, and ftained the ftandard of liberty with affaffinations. They refufed to exchange prifoners, for fear of increafing in the troops their inclination to furrender at the firft fummons. They were reduced to the neceffity of erecting tribunals, appointed to profecute their generals or their lieutenants who fhould abandon too lightly the pofts committed to their truft. It is true, an old man of fourfcore years of age, whom they wanted to fend back to his home, exclaimed, *My death may be ufeful; I fhall cover with my body a younger man than I am.* It is true that Putnam faid to a loyalift who was his prifoner, *Return to your commander; and if he fhould afk you how many troops I have, tell him I have enough; that if even he fhould beat them, there will remain enough; and that he will experience, in the end, that I fhall have enough for him, and for the tyrants whom he ferves.* Thefe fentiments were heroic, but rare; and they became lefs common every day.

The intoxication was never general, and indeed could only be temporary. Of all the caufes of energy which have produced fo many revolutions on the globe, none exifted in the North of America. No outrage had been committed either againft religion or

B O O K   the laws.   The blood of martyrs and of citizens had
XVIII.   not flowed upon the fcaffolds.   The morals had received no infult.   The manners and the cuftoms, none
of thofe objects to which the people are fo much attached, had been delivered up to ridicule.   Arbitrary
power had not dragged any inhabitant from the midft
of his family and his friends, to plunge him into the
horrors of a prifon.   Public order had not been fubverted.   The principles of adminiftration had not been
altered ; and the maxims of government had remained always the fame.   The only circumftance was to
know, whether the mother-country had or had not
the right, directly or indirectly, of laying a flight tax
on the colonies ; for the accumulated grievances mentioned in the manifefto arofe only from this firft grie-
vance.   This queftion, which is almoft a metaphyfical
one, was fcarce proper to raife an infurrection among
the multitude, or at leaft to intereft them ftrongly in
a quarrel, for which they faw their lands deprived of
the affiftances neceffary to fertilize them, their harvefts
ravaged, and their fields covered with the dead bodies
of their relations, or ftained with their own blood.   To
thefe calamities, which were occafioned by the royal
troops on the coaft, others were foon added, ftill more
infupportable, in the inland parts of the country.

Whenever the reftleffnefs of the courts of London
and Verfailles had difturbed North America, thofe
two powers had always drawn into their fanguinary
contefts the wandering inhabitants of this part of the
New Hemifphere.   Informed by experience how much
weight thefe hordes of favages could throw into the
fcale, the Englifh and the colonifts refolved equally to
employ them to their mutual deftruction.

Carleton firft endeavoured to put arms into the
hands of thefe barbarians in Canada.   They anfwered his applications with faying, " This is a difpute be-
" tween a father and his children ; it does not become
" us to interfere in this domeftic quarrel."—" But if
" the rebels fhould come to attack this province,
" would you not affift us in repelling them ?"—

"Since the peace, the hatchet of war is buried forty
"fathom deep."—"You could certainly find it, if
"you were to dig for it."—"The handle is rotten,
"and we could make no ufe of it."

The United States were not more fuccefsful. "We
"have heard of the differences that have arifen be-
"tween Old and New England," faid the tribe of the
Oneidas to their deputies. "We will never take a
"part in contefts of fo atrocious a nature. A war
"between brothers is a thing new and unknown in
"thefe regions. Our traditions have not left us any
"inftance of this kind. Extinguifh your extravagant
"hatred; and may a more ferene fky difpel the dark
"cloud that furrounds you."

The Mafphis alone feemed to intereft themfelves
in the fate of the Americans. "Here are fixteen fhil-
"lings for you," faid thefe good favages. "It is all
"we are worth. We intended to buy fome rum with
"it; but we will drink water. We will go to the
"chafe; and if we fhould kill any animals, we will
"fell their fkins, and bring you the money."

But in procefs of time, the very active emiffaries of
Great Britain fucceeded in bringing over to her fide
feveral of the original nations. Her interefts were preferred to thofe of her enemies, becaufe the diftance
had not allowed her fubjects to commit the fame outrages againft the favages as they had received from
their proud neighbours, and becaufe fhe was both able
and inclined to pay more liberally for the fervices fhe
might receive from them. Under her colours thefe
allies, whofe ferocious character knew no reftraint, did
infinitely more mifchief to the colonifts fettled near
the mountains, than fuch of their fellow-citizens who
had the good fortune to be fettled near the borders of
the ocean received from the royal troops.

Thefe calamities fell only upon a more or lefs confiderable number of the Americans; but they were
foon all of them afflicted with an internal misfortune.

The metals, which cover the face of the whole
globe, and reprefent all the objects of commerce, were

never abundant in this part of the New World. The small quantity that was found there even difappeared at the firft breaking out of hoftilities. To thefe figns of univerfal convention were fubftituted others peculiar to thefe diftricts. Paper fupplied the want of money. To give fome kind of dignity to this new pledge, it was furrounded with emblems calculated to recal continually to the minds of the people the greatnefs of their enterprife, the ineftimable value of liberty, and the neceffity of a perfeverance fuperior to all misfortunes. The artifice did not fucceed; and thefe ideal riches were rejected. The more did neceffity oblige them to be multiplied, the more did their difcredit increafe. The congrefs was offended with the infult done to their coin; and they declared traitors to their country all thofe who fhould not receive it as they would have received gold.

Did not the congrefs then know, that authority can no more be exerted over the mind than over opinion? Were they not fenfible, that, in the prefent crifis, every reafonable citizen would be apprehenfive of rifking his fortune? Did they not perceive, that, at the origin of the republic, they indulged themfelves in acts of defpotifm unknown in countries that are even formed to fervitude? Could they conceal from themfelves that they punifhed a want of confidence with the fame punifhment which would fcarce have been merited for revolt and treafon? The congrefs perceived all this, but had no choice of means. Their contemptible and rejected paper was actually thirty times below its original value, when they fabricated more of it. On the 13th September 1779, there was circulating among the public to the amount of 799,744,000 livres [33,322,666l. 13s. 4d.] of it. The ftate was then indebted 188,670,525 livres [7,861,271l. 17s. 6d.], exclufive of the debts peculiar to each province.

The people were not indemnified for a calamity which might be called domeftic, by a free intercourfe with all the other parts of the globe. Great Britain had intercepted their navigation with the Weft Indies, and with all the latitudes which were covered with their ſhips. They then declared to the world, " It is " the Engliſh name which hath rendered us odious; " we ſolemnly abjure it. All men are our brethren. " We are the friends of every nation. All flags may " appear upon our coaſts, and frequent our ports, " without fear of inſult." But this invitation, apparently ſo alluring, was not complied with. The ſtates that were really commercial being appriſed that North America had been obliged to contract debts at the period even of its greateſt proſperity, judiciouſly imagined, that, in its preſent diſtreſs, it would be able to pay very little for what was brought to it. The French alone dared to brave the inconveniencies of this new connection. But by the enlightened vigilance of Admiral Howe, moſt of the ſhips which they fitted out were taken before they arrived to the place of their deſtination, and the reſt at their departure from the American ſhores. Of ſeveral hundred ſhips ſent out from France, no more than twenty-five or thirty returned ; and even theſe were of little or no benefit to their owners.

A number of privations, added to ſo many calamities, might have made the Americans regret their former tranquillity, and inclined them to a reconciliation with England. In vain were the people bound by the faith of oaths, and by the influence of religion, to the new government. In vain had it been endeavoured to convince them of the impoſſibility of negotiating ſafely with a mother-country, in which one parliament could ſubvert what had been regulated by another. In vain had they been threatened with the eternal reſentment of an affronted and vindictive enemy. It was poſſible that theſe diſtant apprehenſions might not counterbalance the weight of the preſent calamities.

Such was the opinion of the Britiſh miniſtry, when they ſent public agents into the New World, who were authoriſed to offer any terms ſhort of independence to thoſe very Americans, from whom, two years

BOOK
XVIII.
before, an unlimited fubmiffion had been required. There is fome probability that this plan of conciliation might have been fuccefsful fome months before. But at the period when the court of London fent to propofe it, it was haughtily rejected, becaufe this ftep appeared only to be the effect of fear and weaknefs. The people were already re-animated; the congrefs, the generals, the troops, the intelligent or bold men who in every colony had affumed the authority, all, in a word, had recovered their former fpirit. This was the effect of a treaty of friendfhip and commerce between the United States and the court of Verfailles, which was figned on the 6th of February 1778.

France acknowledges the independence of the United States. This ftep occafions a war between that crown and the crown of England.

Had the Englifh miniftry reflected, they would have comprehended that the fame delirium which caufed them to attack their colonies, fhould have compelled them inftantly to declare war againft France. The circumfpection which ought always to attend a new reign then prevailed in the councils of this crown. Their finances were then in that ftate of confufion into which they had been plunged by twenty years perfeverance in folly. The ruined ftate of their navy then raifed anxiety in the breaft of every citizen. Spain, already haraffed with her extravagant expedition againft Algiers, was then furrounded with difficulties which would have prevented her from being able to affift her allies. England might, without rafhnefs, have flattered herfelf with fuccefs againft the moft powerful of her enemies, and might have intimidated America by victories obtained in its neighbourhood. The importance it was of to this crown, to deprive its rebellious fubjects of the only fupport they were certain of, would have diminifhed the indignation excited by the violation of the moft folemn treaties.

George III. faw nothing of all this. The clandeftine fuccours which the court of Verfailles ufed to fend to the provinces in arms for the defence of their rights did not open his eyes. The dock-yards of this power were filled with fhip-builders, its arfenals were ftocking with artillery, and there remained no more room

in its magazines for frefh naval ftores. Its harbours BOOK
prefented the moft menacing afpect, and yet this XVIII.
ftrange infatuation ftill continued. To roufe the court
of St. James's from its lethargy, it was neceffary that
Lewis XVI. fhould caufe it to be fignified to them on
the 14th March, that he had acknowledged the independence of the United States.

This declaration was a declaration of war. It was
impoffible that a nation, more accuftomed to give than
to take an affront, fhould patiently fuffer that its fubjects fhould be releafed from their oath of allegiance,
and be raifed with fplendour to the rank of fovereign
powers. All Europe forefaw that two nations, which
had been rivals for fo many centuries, were going to
ftain with blood the waters of the ocean, and engage
again in that terrible conflict in which public profperity can never compenfate private diftrefs. Thofe in
whom ambition had not extinguifhed every fentiment
of benevolence towards their fellow-creatures, previoufly deplored the calamities which were ready to fall
upon the human race in both hemifpheres.

The bloody fcene, however, was not yet begun,
and this delay infpired fome credulous perfons with
the hopes that peace would continue. It was not
known that a fleet had failed from Toulon with directions to attack the Englifh in the North of America.
It was not known that there were orders fent from
London to drive away the French out of the Eaft Indies. Without being initiated in thefe myfteries of
perfidy, which an infidious policy hath made to be
confidered as great ftrokes of ftate, men who were
really enlightened judged that hoftilities were unavoidable, and even near at hand on our own ocean.
This forefeen event was brought about by an engagement between two frigates on the 17th June 1778.

Here our tafk becomes more and more difficult.
Our fole aim is to be ufeful and true. Far from us
be that fpirit of party which fafcinates and difgraces
thofe who lead mankind, or who afpire to inftruct
them. Our wifhes will be for our country, and we

shall pay homage to juftice. In whatever place, and under whatever form, virtue shall prefent herfelf to us, we shall honour her. The diftinction of fociety and of ftates cannot eftrange us from her, and the juft and magnanimous man will everywhere be our fellow-citizen. If in the different events which we review we have the courage to blame what appears to us to deferve it, we do not feek the melancholy and idle fatisfaction of dealing out indifcriminate cenfure. But we addrefs ourfelves to the nations and to pofterity. It is our duty faithfully to tranfmit to them whatever may influence the public felicity. It is our duty to give them the hiftory of the faults that are committed, in order that they may be inftructed to avoid them. Should we dare to betray this noble duty, we fhould perhaps flatter the prefent generation, which is fleeting, and paffeth away; but juftice and truth, which are eternal, would denounce us to future generations, which would read us with contempt, and would never pronounce our name without difdain. In this long career we have undertaken, we will be juft to thofe who ftill exift, as we have been to thofe who are no more. If among men in power there be any who are offended with this liberty, we will not be afraid to fay to them, that we are only the organs of a fupreme tribunal, which is at length erected by reafon upon an immoveable foundation. Every government in Europe muft henceforth dread its decrees. The public opinion, which becomes more and more enlightened, and which is neither ftopped nor intimidated by any thing, is perpetually attentive to nations and to courts. It penetrates into cabinets where policy is fhut up: there it judges the depofitaries of power, their paffions, and their weaknefs, and, by the empire of genius and knowledge, raifes itfelf above the governors of mankind, either to direct or to reftrain them. Woe to thofe who either difdain this tribunal, or fet it at defiance! This apparent boldnefs arifes only from inability. Woe to thofe whofe talents are infufficient to bear its examination! Let them do themfelves juftice.

let them lay down a burden too heavy for their feeble B O O K
hands. They will at leaft no longer compromife them- XVIII.
felves and the States.

France began the war with invaluable advantages.
The place, the time, the circumftances, every thing
fhe had chofen. It was not till after having made
preparations at leifure, till after having brought her
forces to that degree which was proper, that fhe
fhowed herfelf upon the field of battle. She had only to combat an enemy humbled, weakened, and difcouraged by domeftic diffenfions. The favour of the
other nations was on her fide againft thofe imperious
mafters, or, as it was faid, againft thofe tyrants of the
feas.

The events feemed favourable to the wifhes of all
Europe. The French officers, who had former humiliations to efface, exerted themfelves in brilliant actions, the remembrance of which will laft for a long
time. A fkilful theory and an undaunted courage
fupplied any deficiency there might be on the point
of experience. In all the private engagements they
came off with glory, and moft of them terminated to
their advantage. The Britifh fleet was expofed to ftill
greater dangers than the feparate fhips were. It was
fo ill treated, that its total or partial deftruction was
apprehended, if the fleet which had reduced it to this
deplorable ftate off Ufhant had not determined, from
timid orders, from odious intrigues, from the weaknefs
of the admirals, or from all thefe motives combined,
to quit the fea and re-enter firft into port.

In the intoxication of this fuccefs, perhaps unexpected, France feemed to lofe fight of her moft important interefts. Her principal object fhould have
been to intercept the trade of her enemies, to deprive
them of the double ftrength they derived from their
failors and from their riches, and thus to fap the two
foundations of Englifh greatnefs. Nothing was more
eafy to accomplifh by a power long prepared for hoftilities, than to intercept the trading navy, entirely
off its guard, and attended with very feeble convoys.

But this was neglected, and the immenſe riches which
Great Britain expected from all parts of the globe, entered quietly into her harbours, even without the leaſt
loſs.

The trade of France, on the contrary, was haraſſed
in both hemiſpheres, and intercepted everywhere. Her
colonies beheld the ſubſiſtence which they were ex-
pecting, with all the anxiety of want, carried off from
their own coaſt; and the mother-country found itſelf
deprived of fourſcore or a hundred millions [from
3,333,333l. 6s. 8d. to 4,166,666l. 13s. 4d.] almoſt
within her own view. Theſe misfortunes certainly
aroſe from ſome cauſe, which we will endeavour to in-
veſtigate.

The French navy had for a long time been unfortunate, and its numerous calamities were attributed to
the defect of its conſtitution. Several attempts were
made either to modify or to alter the regulations; but
theſe innovations, whether good or bad, were always
rejected with more or leſs viſible diſdain. At length
the admirals dictated themſelves in 1776, an ordinance,
which, by making them abſolute maſters of the harbours, of the arſenals, of the docks, and of the magazines, deſtroyed that mutual ſuperintendence which
Lewis XIV. had thought proper to eſtabliſh between
the officers of the navy and thoſe of adminiſtration.
From that time there was no more order, no more re-
ſponſibility, no more economy in the ports; every
thing there fell into confuſion and diſorder.

The new plan had ſtill a more fatal influence. Till
that period the miniſtry had directed their naval operations in a manner ſuitable to their political plans.
This authority was transferred, without being perceived, perhaps to thoſe who were to carry theſe operations into execution; and they imperceptibly acquired
the tint of their prejudices, which led them to believe
that it was not by heavy and laborious eſcorts of the
ſhips of the nation, or by remaining for a length of
time on difficult cruiſes, in order to ſurpriſe or deſtroy
the veſſels of the enemy, that a reputation was to be

attained; This double duty was therefore either entirely neglected, or very ill fulfilled, on account of the
general opinion prevalent at Breft, that fuch a fervice
had nothing noble in it, and did not lead to any kind
of glory.

It muft be owned, that this prejudice is a very fingular one, and entirely contrary to all the laws of fociety. What can have been the intention of the ftates
in inftituting this military force deftined to traverfe
the feas? Was it only to procure rank to thofe who
commanded or ferved in it? To give them an opportunity to exert a valour ufelefs to any but themfelves?
To ftain another element with blood, with carnage,
and fea-fights? Certainly not. The warlike fleets
are upon the ocean, what fortreffes and ramparts are
for the citizens of towns, and what national armies are
for the provinces expofed to the ravages of the enemy.
There are fome kinds of property attached to a foil;
others are created and tranfported by commerce, and
are, as it were, wandering upon the ocean. Thefe two
fpecies of property required defenders. Warriors, this
is your duty. What fhould we fay, if the land forces
refufed to protect the inhabitants of the cities, or the
hufbandman of the field againft the enemy, or to extinguifh the conflagration which threatens the harveft?
Officers of the navy, you think yourfelves degraded in
protecting and convoying the merchantmen. But if
commerce be deprived of protectors, what will become
of the riches of the ftate, part of which you undoubtedly expect as a reward for your fervices? What will
become, for yourfelves, of the revenues of your lands,
which can only be made fruitful by trade, and by the
circulation of wealth? You think yourfelves degraded. What! degraded in rendering yourfelves ufeful
to your fellow-citizens? What are then all the orders
of the ftate, to whom government hath intrufted fome
portion of the public ftrength, but the protectors and
the defenders of the citizen and his fortune? Your
poft is upon the feas, as that of the magiftrate is upon
the tribunals, that of the land officer and of the foldier

in the camps, that of the monarch upon the throne, where he is only placed upon a more elevated situation, in order that his prospect may be extended to a greater distance, and that he may behold at one view all those who require his protection or his defence. You aspire to glory. Learn that glory is everywhere to be obtained by serving the state. The ancient Romans were likewise undoubtedly attached to glory, and yet the honour of having preserved one single citizen in Rome was preferred to that of having destroyed a multitude of enemies. Do you not perceive, that in saving the trading ships you save the wealth of the state? Yes, your valour is brilliant; it is known to all Europe, as well as to your own country; but what is it to your fellow-citizens that it hath been displayed on a splendid occasion, that it hath taken one of the enemy's ships, or covered the waves of the ocean with wrecks and ruins, if you suffer all the vessels which conveyed the riches of your country to be either taken or destroyed; if, in the very port to which you return victorious, a multitude of desolated families deplore the subversion of their fortune? You will not hear the exclamations of victory on your arrival. All will be silent, and plunged in consternation; and your exploits will serve no other purpose but to swell the accounts of the courts, and to fill those public papers which, being invented to amuse idleness, give glory only for a day, when that glory is not engraved in the hearts of the citizens by the remembrance of some real service done to the country.

The maxims adopted at Portsmouth were very different. There the dignity of commerce was felt and respected. It was considered as a duty, as well as an honour, to defend it; and events decided, which of the two navies had the properest ideas of their functions.

Great Britain had just experienced some very humiliating adversities in the New World, and it was threatened with greater disasters by a still more powerful enemy in the Old one. This alarming situation filled the

minds of all men with miftruft and uncertainty. The
national riches came home fafe, and their enormous
mafs was increafed by thofe of the rival power; public
credit was inftantly revived; expectations were renewed; and this people, who with fatisfaction were looked upon as overcome, recovered and fuftained their
ufual pride.

On the other hand, the French ports were filled
with lamentations. A degrading and ruinous inactivity fucceeded to that activity which gave them fplendour and riches. The indignation of the merchants
communicated itfelf to the whole nation. The firft
moments of fuccefs are the moments of intoxication,
which feem either to conceal or to juftify the faults
committed. But misfortune gives greater feverity to
opinion. The nation then attends more clofely to
thofe by whom they are governed, and demands from
them, with arrogant freedom, an account of the power
and authority that is intrufted to them. The councils
of Lewis XVI. were accufed of derogating from the
majefty of the firft power on the globe, by difavowing,
in the face of the univerfe, the fuccour which they
were inceffantly fending clandeftinely to the Americans. They were accufed of having, either by a mi-
nifterial intrigue, or by the influence of fome obfcure
agents, engaged the ftate in a ruinous war, at a time
when they ought to have been employed in repairing
the fprings of government, in remedying the tedious
diforders of a reign, the latter half of which had been
mean, feeble, divided between depredations and fhame,
between the bafenefs of vice and the convulfions of
defpotifm. They were accufed of having provoked a
rupture by an infidious policy, to have enveloped their
meaning in fpeeches unworthy of France, and to have
employed, with regard to England, the language of a
timorous boldnefs, which feemed to deny the projects
that were formed, and the fentiments they had in their
hearts; a language which can only degrade the perfon
who makes ufe of it, without being able to deceive
him to whom it is addreffed; and which difhonours,

while the difhonour it brings along with it can neither be ufeful to the miniftry nor to the ftate.   How much more noble would it have been to have faid with all the franknefs of dignity : " Englifhmen, you have " abufed your victory. This is the moment to be juft, " or elfe it will be that of revenge. Europe is tired of " bearing with tyrants. She at length refumes her " rights. Henceforth choofe either equality or war." It is thus that Richelieu would have fpoken; that Richelieu, whom every citizen ought indeed to deteft, becaufe he was a fanguinary affaffin, and that in order to become a defpot, he put all his enemies to death with the ax of the executioner; but the nation and the ftate muft revere him as a minifter, becaufe he was the firft who apprized France of her dignity, and afcribed to her in Europe the rank which belonged to her power. It is thus that Lewis XIV. would have fpoken to them, who during forty years fhowed him-felf worthy of the age he lived in, whofe very faults were always mixed with grandeur, and who, even in a ftate of dejection and misfortune, never degraded him-felf or his people. A great character is required to go-vern a great nation. More efpecially, there muft be none of thofe fpirits that are cold and indifferent from levity, for whom abfolute authority is no more than an amufement, who leave great interefts to the effects of chance, and who are more employed in preferving power than in making ufe of it. It is further afked, why men who had all the power of the ftate in their hands, and who had only to command in order to be obeyed, have fuffered themfelves to be foreftalled in all the feas by an enemy whofe conftitution neceffarily produces. delays? Why did they put themfelves, by an inconfiderate treaty, into the fhackles of congrefs, which might itfelf have been kept dependent by plen-tiful and regular fubfidies? Laftly, why did not they fecure the revolution, by keeping conftantly upon the northern coafts of the New World a fquadron to pro-tect the colonies, and at the fame time to make our alliance be refpected? But Europe, whofe eyes are

fixed upon us, beholds a great defign, and no concerted meafures; it beholds in our arfenals and in our
ports immenfe preparations, and no execution; it beholds formidable fleets, and this equipment rendered
almoft ufelefs; it beholds boldnefs and valour in individuals, effeminacy and irrefolution in commanders;
every thing which announces on one hand the awful
power of a great people, and on the other every thing
which announces the weaknefs and delay which arife
from character and from the nature of the views.

It is by this ftriking contraft between our projects
and our meafures, between our means and the fpirit
which animates them, that the Englifh genius, aftonifhed for a moment, hath recovered its vigour; and
it is a problem which Europe cannot folve, whether,
in declaring for America, we have not ourfelves raifed
the ftrength of England.

Such are the complaints which are heard on all fides,
and which we are not afraid of collecting here, and of
laying before the eyes of authority, if it fhould deign
to liften to or to read them.

Laftly, philofophy, whofe firft fentiment is the defire of feeing all governments equitable, and all people
happy, in examining this alliance of a monarchy with
a people who defend their liberty, endeavours to difcover the motive of it. It perceives too clearly that
the happinefs of mankind hath no concern in it. It
imagines, that, if the court of Verfailles had been determined by the love of juftice, they would have mentioned in the firft article of the convention with America, that *all people who are oppreffed have a right to
rife againft their oppreffors.* But this maxim, which
conftitutes one of the laws of England, which a king
of Hungary, upon afcending the throne, ventured to
make one of the conftituent principles of the ftate,
and which Trajan, one of the greateft princes who
ever ruled over the earth, adopted, when in prefence
of the Roman peopled affembled; he faid to the firft
officer of the empire: *I give you up my fword to defend
me while I fhall be juft, and to fight againft me and to*

punish me if I should become a tyrant. This maxim is too foreign to our feeble and corrupt governments, where it is the duty of the people to suffer, and where the oppressed man should be apprehensive of feeling his misfortune, for fear he should be punished for it as a crime.

But it is particularly against Spain that the most bitter complaints are directed. She is censured for her blindness, her irresolution, her delays, sometimes even for her want of fidelity; but all these accusations are groundless.

Some politicians imagined, when they beheld France engaging without necessity in a naval war, that this crown thought itself sufficiently powerful to separate the dominion of Great Britain, without sharing with an ally the honour of this important revolution. We will not examine whether the spirit which prevailed in the cabinet of Versailles authorised this conjecture. It is now known, that this crown, which since the beginning of the troubles had given secret assistance to the Americans, watched the propitious moment for declaring openly in their favour. The event of Saratoga appeared to furnish the most favourable opportunity to propose to his Catholic majesty to join in the common cause. Whether this prince then thought that the liberty of the United States was contrary to his interests; whether the resolution appeared to him to be precipitate, or whether, in a word, other political objects required his whole attention, he refused to accede to this proposal. His character prevented any further solicitations. Since those first attempts he was so little troubled about this great affair, that it was without giving him any previous notice, that the court of Versailles caused it to be signified to that of St. James's, that they had acknowledged the independence of the confederate provinces.

In the meanwhile the land and sea-forces which Spain had employed in the Brazils against the Portuguese were returned. The rich fleet she expected from Mexico had entered into her ports. The treafures which were coming to her from Peru and from her other poffeffions were in fafety. This power was free from any anxiety, and miftrefs of her own operations, when fhe afpired to the glory of introducing peace into both hemifpheres. Her mediation was accepted, both by France, whofe boldnefs had not been followed by thofe happy confequences fhe had expected from it, and by England, who might be apprehenfive of having a new adverfary to contend with.

.Charles III. fupported with dignity the magnanimous part he had undertaken. He declared that arms fhould be laid afide; that each of the belligerent powers fhould be maintained in the poffeffions they might occupy at the period of the convention; that a congrefs fhould be formed, in which the feveral pretenfions fhould be difcuffed; and that no new attack fhould be commenced without the previous notice of a twelvemonth.

This monarch was aware that this arrangement would give to Great Britain the felicity of reconciliation with her colonies, or at leaft would make them purchafe by great advantages for her trade the facrifice of the ports which fhe occupied in the midft of them. Nor was he ignorant of his offending the dignity of the king his nephew, who had engaged to maintain the United States in the entire poffeffion of their territories. But he would be juft; and without fetting afide all perfonal confiderations it is impoffible to be fo.

This plan of conciliation was difpleafing to the court of Verfailles; and the only hope they had was, that it would be rejected at London, as indeed it was. England could not refolve to acknowledge the Americans *ipfo facto* independent, although they were not invited to the conferences that were going to be opened; although France was not allowed to negotiate for them; although their interefts were only to be fupported by a mediator, who was not attached to them by any treaty, and who, perhaps, in fecret, did

BOOK not wiſh them to proſper, and although her refuſal
XVIII. threatened her with an additional enemy.

It is in ſuch a ſituation, when pride elevates the
ſoul above the ſuggeſtions of fear, that nothing appears formidable, except the ſhame of receiving the
law; and that there is no heſitation in chooſing between ruin and diſhonour : it is then that the greatneſs of a nation diſplays itſelf. I acknowledge,· however, that men, accuſtomed to judge of the event,
conſider great and perilous revolutions as acts of he-
roiſm or of folly, according to the good or ill ſucceſs
that hath attended them. If, therefore, I ſhould be
aſked, what name will be given a few years hence to
the firmneſs which the Engliſh ſhowed on this occaſion? I ſhall anſwer, that I know not : as to that which
they deſerve I know very well. I know that the annals of the world rarely preſent to us the auguſt and
majeitic ſpectacle, of a nation which prefers the giving up of its duration to the loſs of its glory.

No ſooner had the Britiſh miniſtry explained themſelves, than the court of Madrid took the part of that
of Verſailles, and conſequently that of the Americans,
in the conteſt. Spain had then ſixty-three veſſels of
the line, and ſix more upon the ſtocks. France had
fourſcore and eight upon the docks. The United States
had but twelve frigates, but a great number of priva-
teers.

To ſo many forces united, England had only ninety-five ſhips of the line to oppoſe, and three-and-twen-
ty upon the ſtocks. The other ſixteen which were
ſeen in her ports were unfit for ſervice, and they had
been converted to the purpoſe of ſhips for receiving
priſoners, or into hoſpital ſhips. Thus inferior in the
inſtruments of war, this power was ſtill more ſo in the
means of employing them upon ſervice. Her domeſtic
diſſenſions contributed ſtill more to render ineffectual
the reſources ſhe had remaining. It is the nature of
governments that are truly free, to be agitated in times
of peace. It is by theſe inteſtine commotions that the

minds of men preserve their energy, and the perpetual remembrance of the rights of the nation. But
in time of war it is necessary that every ferment should
cease, that hatred should be extinguished, and that interests should be blended, and made subservient to each
other. It happened quite otherwise in the British
islands; for the disturbances in them had never been
more violent. Opposite claims were never supported
on any occasion with less moderation. The general
good was insolently disregarded by all factions. Those
houses, in which the most important questions had formerly been discussed, with eloquence, strength, and
dignity, resounded only with the clamours of rage,
gross insults, and altercations as prejudicial as they
were indecent. The few persons who might be called citizens loudly exclaimed for a new Pitt, a minister, who like him had *neither relations nor friends;*
but this extraordinary man did not appear. And indeed it was generally believed that this nation would
fall, notwithstanding the haughtiness of their character, notwithstanding the experience of their admirals,
notwithstanding the boldness of their seamen, and notwithstanding the energy which a free people must acquire in the disturbances they experience.

But the sway of chance is very extensive. Who
knows in favour of which party the elements will declare themselves? A gust of wind snatches away victory, or gives it. A cannon shot disconcerts a whole
army by the death of the general. Signals are either
not well understood, or not obeyed. Experience, courage, and skill, are counteracted by ignorance, by jealousy, by treason, and by the certainty of impunity.
A fog arising, covers both the enemies, and either se-
parates or confounds them. A calm and a storm are
equally favourable or disadvantageous. The forces are
divided by the unequal celerity of the ships. The
opportunity is lost, either by pusillanimity, which post-
pones, or by rashness, which hastens an engagement.
Plans may have been formed with prudence, but they
may remain without effect, by the want of harmony

B O O K in the evolutions for carrying them into execution.
XVIII. An inconfiderate command from court may decide
the misfortune of a day. The difgrace or death of a
minifter alters the projects. Is it poffible that a clofe
union can long fubfift between confederates of fuch
oppofite characters, as the French, who are paffionate, difdainful, and volatile; the Spaniards, who are
flow, haughty, jealous, and cold; and the Americans,
who have conftantly their looks turned towards the
mother-country, and who would rejoice at the difafters of their allies, if they were compatible with their
own independence? Will it be long before thefe nations, whether they act feparately or in concert, reciprocally accufe, complain, and are at variance with
each other? Will not their greateft hope be, that repeated ftrokes of adverfity would only at moft plunge
them again into the humiliating ftate from whence they
wifhed to emerge, and confirm the dominion of the
feas to Great Britain; while one or two confiderable
defeats would for ever remove this ambitious people
from the rank of the firft power of this hemifphere?

Who can therefore decide; who can even forefee
what will be the event? France and Spain united have
the moft powerful means in their favour; England
hath the art of managing her own: France and Spain
have their treafures, England hath a great national
credit. On one hand are the multitude of men, and
the number of troops; on the other, the fuperiority
in the art of conducting fhips, and of fubduing the
fea in engagements. Here there is impetuofity and
valour; there valour and experience. On one hand,
the activity which abfolute monarchy may give to the
meafures; on the other, the vigour and the energy
of liberty. One party is ftimulated by refentment
for loffes, and by a long-continued feries of outrages
they have to avenge; the other, by the recollection
of a recent glory, and by their having the fovereignty of America, as well as that of the ocean, to preferve. The two allied nations have the advantage
which is derived from the union of two immenfe pow-

ers; but at the fame time the inconvenience which
refults from this very union, by the difficulty even of
preferving harmony and concord, either in the plans
or in the difpofal of their forces. England is abandoned to herfelf; but haying nothing but her own
forces to direct, fhe hath the advantage of unity in
her defigns; of a more certain, and perhaps more
fpeedy combination of ideas. She can with greater
facility regulate at one view her plans of attack and
defence.

In order to have an exact idea of things, one ought
alfo to examine the different energy which may be
communicated to the rival nations by a war, which on
one fide is no more in feveral refpects than a war of
kings and minifters; and on the other, a really national war, in which the greatest interefts of England
are concerned, a commerce, which conftitutes her riches;
an empire, and a glory, which compofe her greatnefs.

Finally, if we confider the fpirit of the French nation, in contraft with that of the nation fhe is at war
with, it will be found that the ardour of the French is
perhaps equally ready to be excited and to be extinguifhed; that their hopes are very fanguine at the beginning, and that they defpair of every thing as foon
as they are ftopped by any obftacle; that by their
character they require the enthufiafm of fuccefs, in
order to obtain frefh advantages. The Englifh, on
the contrary, lefs prefumptuous at firft, notwithftanding their natural boldnefs, know how to ftruggle courageoufly, to be elevated in proportion to the increafe
of danger, and to acquire fteadinefs by difgrace: like
the fturdy oak, to which Horace compares the Romans, which, though cut by the ax and mutilated by
iron, revives under the ftrokes which it receives, and
acquires new vigour even from its wounds.

Hiftory informs us, moreover, that few leagues have
ever divided the fpoils of the nation againft which
they had been formed. Athens triumphant over Perfia; Rome faved from Annibal; in modern times,

B O O K Venice, preferved from the famous league of Cam-
XVIII. bray; and even in our days, Pruffia, which by the genius of one fingle man hath held out againft all Europe; all thefe examples authorife us to fufpend our
judgment refpecting the iffue of the prefent war.

What But, let us fuppofe that the houfe of Bourbon fhall
ought to be have obtained all the advantages they may flatter them-
the policy
of the houfe felves with, what conduct ought they to purfue?
of Bourbon,
fhould it be France is, in every point of view, the empire the
victorious. moft ftrongly conftituted of any one the remembrance
of which is preferved in the annals of the world.
Spain, though not to be compared with her, is likewife a ftate of great weight, and her means of profperity are increafing daily, The principal care of
the houfe of Bourbon, then, fhould be, to induce
their neighbours to overlook the advantages which
they derive from nature or from art, or which they
have acquired by events. If they fhould endeavour
to increafe their fuperiority, the alarm would become
general, and people would think themfelves threatened with univerfal flavery. It is perhaps rather extraordinary, that the nations have not thwarted her projects againft England. This fupinenefs muft have
been occafioned by the refentment which the injuftice
and the haughtinefs of that fuperb ifland have excited
in all parts. But hatred is fufpended when intereft is
concerned. It is poffible, Europe may judge the
weakening of Great Britain in the New and in the
Old Hemifphere to be contrary to her own fecurity;
and that, after having enjoyed the fpectacle of the
humiliations and the dangers of that proud and tyrannical power, fhe may at length take up arms in her
defence. Should this happen, the courts of Verfailles
and Madrid would find themfelves difappointed in the
hopes which they had conceived, of acquiring a decided preponderance upon the globe. Thefe confiderations fhould determine them to urge on the attacks, and not to leave time to a provident, or perhaps only a jealous policy, to make frefh plans. Let

them efpecially ftop in time, and let not an immode- B O O K
rate defire of lowering their common enemy blind XVIII.
them with regard to their true interefts.

The United States have openly difcovered the project of drawing all North America into their confederation. Several fteps, and particularly that of foliciting
ing Canada to rebellion, muft have induced an opinion
that it was likewife the defire of France. Spain may
be fufpected of having equally adopted this idea.

The conduct of the provinces which have fhaken
off the yoke of Great Britain is fimple, and fuch as
one would expect. But would not their allies be deficient in forefight, if they had really the fame fyftem?
The New Hemifphere muft one day be detached from
the Old. This great evulfion is prepared in Europe
by the ferment and by the clafh of opinions; by the
overthrow of our rights, which conftituted our courage; by the luxury of our courts, and the mifery of
our country places; by the everlafting hatred there is
between effeminate men who poffefs every thing, and
robuft, and even virtuous men, who have nothing to
lofe but their lives. It is prepared in America, by the
increafe of population, of cultures, of induftry, and of
knowledge. Every thing is tending towards this feparation, both the progrefs of evil in one world, and
the progrefs of good in another.

But can it be fuitable to France and Spain, whofe
poffeffions in the New Hemifphere are an inexhauftible
fource of wealth, can it be fuitable to them to haften
this divifion? Yet this is what would happen, if the
whole northern part of thofe regions were fubject to
the fame laws, or connected by one common intereft.

Scarce would the liberty of this vaft continent be
confirmed, than it would become the afylum of all the
intriguing, feditious, branded, or ruined men, who are
feen amongft us. Neither agriculture, the arts, nor
commerce, would be the refource of refugees of this
character. A lefs laborious and more turbulent life
would be neceffary for them. This turn of mind,
equally averfe from labour and reft, would be difpof

BOOK
XVIII.

ed to conquests; and a passion which is so seducing
would readily subdue the first colonists, diverted from
their ancient labours by a long war. The new people
would have finished their preparations for invasion before the report of them could have reached our climates. They would choose their enemies, their field
of battle, and the moment of victory. Their attacks
would always fall upon defenceless seas, or upon coasts
taken by surprise. In a short time the southern provinces would become the prey of the northern ones,
and would compensate, by the richness of their productions, for the mediocrity of those of the latter.
Perhaps even the possessions of our absolute monarchies
would endeavour to enter into the confederation of
free people, or would detach themselves from Europe,
to belong only to themselves.

The measures which the courts of Madrid and Versailles ought to pursue, if they are at liberty to choose,
is to leave subsisting in the northern part of America
two powers which shall watch over, restrain, and balance each other. Then ages will elapse before England, and the republics formed at her expence will be
united. This reciprocal mistrust will prevent them
from undertaking any thing at a distance; and the
establishment of other nations in the New World will
enjoy that state of tranquillity which hitherto hath
been so much disturbed.

It is even probable that this order of things would
be most suitable to the confederate provinces. Their
respective limits have not been regulated. A great
jealousy prevails between the countries of the North
and those of the South. Political principles vary from
one river to another. Great animosities are observed
to subsist between the citizens of a town and the members of a family. Each of them will be desirous of removing from themselves the oppressive burden of the
public expences and debts. An infinite number of
seeds of division are universally brooding in the heart
of the United States. When once all dangers were
removed, how would it be possible to prevent the

breaking out of so many discontents? How would it be possible to keep attached to the same centre so many deluded and exasperated minds? Let the real friends of America reflect upon this, and they will find, that the only way to prevent disturbances among the people, would be to leave upon their frontiers a powerful rival, always disposed to avail itself of their dissensions.

Peace and security are necessary for monarchies; agitation and a formidable enemy for republics. Rome stood in need of Carthage: and he who destroyed the liberty of the Romans was neither Scylla nor Cæsar; it was the first Cato, when his narrow and stern system of politics deprived Rome of a rival, by kindling in the senate those flames which reduced Carthage to ashes. Venice herself, perhaps, would have lost her government and her laws four hundred years ago, if she had not had at her gates, and almost under her walls, powerful neighbours, who might become her enemies or her masters.

But according to this system, to what degree of fe- What idea must be formed of the thirteen confedera-ted pro-vinces. licity, splendour, and strength, can the confederate provinces attain in process of time?

In this place, to form a proper judgment, let us begin by setting aside that interest which all men, slaves not excepted, have taken in the generous efforts of a nation, which exposed itself to all calamities in order to be free. The name of liberty is so alluring, that all those who fight for it are sure of obtaining our secret wishes in their favour. Their cause is that of the whole human race, and becomes our own. We avenge ourselves of our oppressors, by venting at least freely our hatred against foreign oppressors. At the noise of these chains that are breaking, it seems to us that ours are going to become lighter; and for a few moments we think we breathe a purer air, when we learn that the universe reckons some tyrants less. Besides, these great revolutions of liberty are lessons to despots. They warn them not to reckon upon too

B O O K long a continuance of the people's patience, and upon
XVIII. eternal impunity. So, where fociety and the laws a-
venge themfelves of the crimes of individuals, the good
man hopes that the punifhment of the guilty may prevent the commiffion of frefh crimes. Terror fometimes
fupplies the place of juftice with regard to the robber,
and of confcience with regard to the affaffin. Such
is the fource of the great concern we take in every
war for liberty. Such hath been that with which the
Americans have infpired us. Our imaginations have
been heated in their favour. We have taken a part
in their victories and their defeats. The fpirit of juftice, which delights in compenfating former calamities
by future happinefs, is pleafed with the idea, that this
part of the New World cannot fail to become one of
the moft flourifhing countries on the globe. It is even
fuppofed that Europe may one day find her mafters in
her children. Let us venture to refift the torrent of
opinion, and that of public enthufiafm. Let us not
fuffer ourfelves to be mifled by imagination, which
embellifhes every thing, and by fentiment, which delights in forming illufions, and which realizes every
hope. It is our duty to combat all prejudices, even
thofe which are moft confonant to the wifhes of our
hearts. Above all things, it behoves us to be true,
and not to betray that pure and upright confcience
which prefides over our writings, and dictates our
judgments. At this moment, perhaps, we fhall not
be believed ; but a bold conjecture, which is confirmed at the end of feveral centuries, does more honour
to the hiftorian, than a long feries of facts, the truth
of which cannot be contefted : and I do not write for
my cotemporaries alone, who will only furvive me a
fmall number of years. When a few more revolutions of the fun are paffed, both they and I fhall be
no more. But I deliver up my ideas to pofterity and
to time. It is theirs to judge me.

The fpace occupied by the thirteen republics, between the mountains and the fea, is no more than

fixty-feven fea leagues; but their extent upon the B o o к coaft, in a direct line, is three hundred and forty-five, XVIII. from the river of Sancta Crux to that of Savannah.

The lands in that region are almoft generally bad, or at leaft indifferent.

Scarce any thing but maize grows in the four moft northern colonies. The only refource of the inhabitants is fifhing, the annual produce of which doth not amount to more than 6,000,000 of livres [250,000l.].

Corn is the principal fupport of the provinces of New York, the Jerfeys, and Pennfylvania. But the foil hath degenerated fo rapidly, that an acre, which formerly yielded fixty bufhels of wheat, very feldom produces even twenty at prefent.

Though the lands of Maryland and of Virginia be much fuperior to all the reft, yet they cannot be deemed extremely fertile. The ancient plantations yield no more than one-third of the tobacco which was formerly gathered. It is not poffible to make any new ones; and the planters have been reduced to the neceffity of turning their labours towards other objects.

North Carolina produces fome grain, but of fo inferior a quality, as to be fold in all markets twenty-five or thirty per cent. cheaper than the others.

The foil of South Carolina and of Georgia is perfectly even, as far as fifty miles from the ocean. The exceffive rains which fall there not finding any outlet, form numerous moraffes, where rice is cultivated to the great detriment of the freemen and of the flaves employed in this culture. In the intervening fpaces between thefe large bodies of water fo frequently met with, an inferior kind of indigo grows, which muft be tranfplanted every year. In the elevated part of the country nothing is to be found except barren fands and frightful rocks, interfected at great diftances by pafture grounds of the nature of rufhes.

The Englifh government, convinced that North America would never enrich them by its natural productions, employed the powerful incentive of gratuities, in order to produce in that part of the New

World flax, vines, and filk. The poorneſs of the foil
difconcerted the firſt of theſe views, the defect of the
climate prevented the fuccefs of the fecond, and the
want of hands did not permit the third to be purſued.
The ſociety eſtabliſhed in London for the encouragement of arts was not more fortunate than adminiſtration. Their benefactions did not bring forth any of
the objects which they had propoſed to the activity
and induſtry of thoſe countries.

Great Britain was obliged to be contented with felling every year to the countries we are ſpeaking of to
the amount of about 50,000,000 livres [2,083,333l.
6s. 8d.] of merchandiſe. Thoſe by whom they were
confumed delivered to her excluſively their indigoes,
their iron, their tobacco, and their peltries. They alſo
delivered to her all the money and rough materials
which they had received from the reſt of the globe in
exchange for their grain, their fiſh, their rice, and their
ſalt proviſions.

The balance, however, was always ſo unfavourable
to them, that, at the beginning of the troubles, the colonies were indebted one hundred and twenty, or one
hundred and thirty millions of livres [from 5,000,000l.
to 5,416,666l. 13s. 4d.] to the mother-country; and
they had no ſpecie in circulation.

Notwithſtanding theſe difadvantages, there had been
fuccefſively formed in the midſt of the thirteen provinces a population of two millions nine hundred
eighty-one thouſand fix hundred and ſeventy-eight
perſons, including four hundred thouſand Negroes.
New inhabitants were conſtantly driven there by oppreſſion and intoleration. The unfortunate have been
deprived of this refuge by war; but peace will reſtore
it to them again; and they will reſort there in greater
numbers than ever. Thoſe who ſhall go there with
plans of cultivation, will not have all the ſatisfaction
they may expect, becauſe they will find all the good,
and even the indifferent lands occupied, and that
ſcarce any thing remains to offer them, except barren ſands, unwholefome moraſſes, or ſteep mountains.

The emigrations will be more favourable to manufacturers and to artifts, though perhaps they will gain
nothing by changing their country and their climate.

It cannot be determined without rafhnefs what will
one day be the population of the United States. This
calculation, generally very difficult, becomes impracticable in a region where the lands degenerate very
rapidly, and where reproduction is not in proportion
to the labours and expences beftowed upon them. It
will be a confiderable thing, if ten millions of men can
ever find a certain fubfiftence in thefe provinces, and
even then the exports will be reduced to little or nothing : but internal induftry will fupply the place of
foreign induftry. The country will nearly be able to
fupply its own wants, provided the inhabitants know
how to be happy by economy and in mediocrity.

People of North America, let the example of all
the nations which have preceded you, and efpecially
that of the mother-country, ferve as a leffon to you.
Dread the influence of gold, which, with luxury, introduces corruption of manners and contempt of the
laws. Dread too unequal a repartition of riches, which
indicates a fmall number of wealthy citizens, and a
multitude of citizens plunged in mifery ; from whence
arifes the infolence of the former, and the degradation
of the latter. Keep yourfelves free from the fpirit of
conqueft. The tranquillity of an empire diminifhes in
proportion as it extends itfelf. Have arms to defend
yourfelves, but not to attack. Search for affluence
and health in labour ; for profperity, in the cultivation
of the lands, and in the manufactures of induftry ; for
ftrength, in good manners and in virtue. Encourage
the profperity of the arts and fciences, which diftinguifh the civilized man from the favage. Attend,
above all things, to the education of your children.
Be convinced, that from public fchools come forth
enlightened magiftrates, valiant and well-informed officers, good fathers, good hufbands, good brothers,
good friends, and honeft men. Wherever depravity
of manners is obferved among the youth, the nation is

B O O K upon its decline. Let liberty have a firm and unalter-
XVIII. able bafis in the wifdom of your conftitutions, and let
it be the everlafting cement which connects your provinces together. Eftablifh no legal preference between
the modes of divine worfhip. Superftition is everywhere innocent, where it is neither protected nor perfecuted ; and may your duration, if poffible, be long
as that of the world !

May this wifh be accomplifhed, and confole the
prefent expiring race with the hopes that a better will
fucceed to it ! But waving the confideration of future
times, let us take a view of the refult of three memorable ages. Having feen in the beginning of this work
the ftate of mifery and ignorance in which Europe was
plunged in the infancy of America, let us examine to
what ftate the conqueft of the New World hath led
and advanced thofe that made it. · This was the defign
of a book undertaken with the hopes of being ufeful ;
if the end be anfwered, the author will have difcharged
his duty to the age he lives in, and to fociety.

BOOK XIX.

B O O K WE are advancing in a career, upon which we
XIX. fhould not have entered without knowing the extent
and the difficulties of it, and which we fhould feveral
times have quitted, had we not been fupported by motives which always make us forget the difproportion
between our powers and the experiment. In the event
of a conflagration, we fometimes attempt and accomplifh things which would deprefs our courage, were it
not ftimulated by the danger, and which aftonifh it
when the danger is over. After a battle, either won
or loft, a military man faid at the fight of a mountain
which he had climbed up in order to reach the enemy :
Who would ever have done that, if there had not been
a mufket-fhot to receive ? I was certainly animated
with the fame fentiment when I began this work, and
it muft undoubtedly animate me ftill fince I continue.

We have firſt deſcribed the ſtate of Europe before the diſcovery of the Eaſt and Weſt Indies.

After this we have purſued the uncertain, tyranni-cal, and ſanguinary progreſs of the ſettlements formed in theſe diſtant regions.

It now remains to unfold the influence which the intercourſe eſtabliſhed with the New World has had upon the opinions, government, induſtry, arts, man-ners, and happineſs of the Old. Let us begin by reli-gion.

Had man uninterruptedly enjoyed complete felici- Religion. ty, had the earth ſatisfied of itſelf all the variety of his wants, it may be preſumed that much time would have elapſed before the ſentiment of admiration and grati-tude would have turned towards the Gods, the atten-tion of that being naturally ungrateful. But a barren ſoil did not anſwer to his labours. The torrents rava-ged the fields which he had cultivated. A burning ſky deſtroyed his harveſts. He experienced famine; he became acquainted with diſeaſe; and he endeavour-ed to find out the cauſe of his miſery.

To explain the myſtery of his exiſtence, of his hap-pineſs, and of his misfortune, he invented different ſyſtems equally abſurd. He peopled the univerſe with good and evil ſpirits; and ſuch was the origin of Po-lytheiſm, the moſt ancient and the moſt univerſal of all religions. From Polytheiſm aroſe Manicheiſm, the veſtiges of which will laſt perpetually, whatever may be the progreſs of reaſon. Manicheiſm ſimplified, en-gendered Deiſm; and in the midſt of this diverſity of opinions there aroſe a claſs of men mediators between Heaven and earth.

Then the regions of the earth were covered with al-tars; in one place the hymn of joy reſounded, while in another were heard the complaints of pain; then recourſe was had to prayer and to ſacrifice, the two natural modes of obtaining favour, and of deprecating anger. The harveſt was offered up; the lamb, the goat, and the bull, were ſlain; and the holy ſod was even ſtained with the blood of man.

In the meanwhile the good man was often seen in
adverſity, while the wicked, and even the impious man
proſpered; and then the doctrine of immortality was
ſuggeſted. The ſouls, freed from the body, either circulated among the different beings of nature, or went
into another world to receive the reward of their virtues, or the puniſhment of their crimes. But it is a
problematical circumſtance, whether man became better on this account. It is certain, however, that from
the inſtant of his birth to that of his death, he was tormented with the fear of inviſible powers, and reduced
to a much more wretched ſtate than that which he had
before enjoyed.

Moſt legiſlators have availed themſelves of this pro-
penſity of the mind, to govern the people, and ſtill
more to enſlave them. Some have aſſerted, that they
held from Heaven the right of commanding; and thus
was theocracy or ſacred deſpotiſm eſtabliſhed, the moſt
cruel and the moſt immoral of all legiſlations; that in
which man, proud, malevolent, intereſted and vicious
with impunity, commands man from God; that in
which there is nothing juſt or unjuſt, but what is either
agreeable or diſpleaſing to him, or that Supreme Being with whom he communicates, and whom he cauſes
to ſpeak according to his paſſions, in which it is a
crime to examine his orders, and impiety to oppoſe
them; in which contradictory revelations are ſubſtituted to reaſon and conſcience, which are reduced to ſilence by prodigies or by enormous crimes; in which
the nations, in a word, cannot have any ideas concerning the rights of man, reſpecting what is good and
what is evil, becauſe they ſearch for the foundation of
their privileges and of their duties, only in ſacred writings, the interpretation of which is denied to them.

If this kind of government had a more ſublime origin in Paleſtine, ſtill it was not more exempt than anywhere elſe from the calamities which neceſſarily ariſe
from it.

Chriſtianity ſucceeded the Jewiſh inſtitution. The
ſubjection that Rome, miſtreſs of the world, was under

to the moft favage tyrants; the dreadful miferies, which B O O K
the luxury of a court and the maintenance of armies XIX.
had occafioned throughout this vaft empire under the
reigns of the Neros; the fucceffive irruptions of the
barbarians, who difmembered this great body; the
lofs of provinces, either by revolt or invafion; all
thefe natural evils had already prepared the minds of
men for a new religion, and the changes in politics
muft neceffarily have induced an innovation in the
form of worfhip. In Paganifm, which had exifted for
fo many ages, there remained only the fables to which
it owed its origin, the folly or the vices of its gods, the
avarice of its priefts, and the infamy and licentious
conduct of the kings who fupported them. Then the
people, defpairing to obtain relief from their tyrants
upon earth, had recourfe to Heaven for protection.

Chriftianity appeared, and afforded them comfort,
at the fame time that it taught them to fuffer with patience. While the tyranny and licentioufnefs of princes tended to the deftruction of paganifm as well as to
that of the empire, the fubjects, who had been oppreffed and fpoiled, and who had embraced the new doctrines, were completing its ruin by the examples they
gave of thofe virtues, which always accompany the
zeal of new-made profelytes. But a religion that arofe
in the midft of public calamity muft neceffarily give its
preachers a confiderable influence over the unhappy
perfons who took refuge in it. Thus the power of the
clergy commenced, as it were, with the gofpel.

From the remains of Pagan fuperftitions and philo-
fophic fects, a code of rites and tenets was formed,
which the fimplicity of the primitive Chriftians fanctified with real and affecting piety; but which at the
fame time left the feeds of debates and controverfies,
from whence arofe a variety of paffions difguifed under, and dignified with, the name of zeal. Thefe diffenfions produced fchools, doctors, a tribunal, and a
hierarchy. Chriftianity had begun to be preached by
a fet of fifhermen, deftitute of every knowledge but
that of the gofpel; it was entirely eftablifhed by bi-

BOOK XIX. fhops who formed the church. After this it gained ground by degrees, till at length it attracted the notice of the emperors. Some of thefe tolerated Chriftianity, either from motives of contempt or humanity; others perfecuted it. Perfecution haftened its progrefs, for which toleration had paved the way. Connivance and profcription, clemency and rigour, were all equally advantageous to it. The fenfe of freedom, fo natural to the human mind, induced many perfons to embrace it in its infancy, as it has made others reject it fince it has been eftablifhed. This fpirit of independence, rather adapted to truth than to novelty, would necefſarily have induced a multitude of perfons of all ranks to become converts to Chriftianity, if even the characters it bore had not been calculated to infpire veneration and refpect.

Paganifm, unmafked by philofophy, and brought into difcredit by the fathers of the church, with a fufficient number of temples, but with priefts who were not rich, fank from day to day, and gave way to the new form of worfhip. This penetrated into the hearts of the women by devotion, which is fo naturally allied to tendernefs, and into the minds of children, who are fond of prodigies, and even of the moft rigid morality. Thus it was introduced into courts, where every thing which can become a paffion is certain of finding accefs. A prince, who bathed in the blood of his family, had, as it were, fallen afleep in the arms of impunity; a prince, who had great crimes and great weakneffes to expiate, embraced Chriftianity, which forgave him every thing on account of his zeal, and to which he gave up every thing, in order to be freed from his-remorfe.

Conftantine, inftead of uniting the priefthood to the crown, when he was converted to Chriftianity, as they had been united in the perfons of the Pagan emperors, granted to the clergy fuch a fhare of wealth and authority, and afforded them fo many means of future aggrandizement, that thefe blind conceffions produced an ecclefiaftical defpotifm entirely new.

Profound ignorance was the moſt certain ſupport of this aſcendency over the minds of men. The pontiffs of Rome diffuſed this ignorance, by oppoſing every kind of Pagan erudition. If from time to time ſome efforts were made to diſpel this obſcurity, they were extinguiſhed by capital puniſhments.

While the popes were undeceiving the minds of men reſpecting their authority, even by the abuſe they made of it, knowledge was paſſing on from the Eaſt to the Weſt. As ſoon as the maſter-pieces of antiquity had revived the taſte for uſeful ſtudy, reaſon recovered ſome of the rights which it had loſt. The hiſtory of the church was inveſtigated, and the falſe pretenſions of the court of Rome were diſcovered. Part of Europe ſhook of the yoke. A monk ſet almoſt all Germany, and almoſt the whole North, free from it; a prieſt, ſome provinces of France; and a king, all England, for the ſake of a woman. If other ſovereigns firmly maintained the Catholic religion throughout their poſſeſſions, it was, perhaps, becauſe it was more favourable to that blind and paſſive obedience which they require from their people, and which the popiſh clergy have always preached for their own intereſts.

In the meanwhile, the deſire, on one hand, of preſerving the pontifical authority, and the wiſh of deſtroying it on the other, have produced two oppoſite ſyſtems. The Catholic divines have undertaken, and even ſucceſsfully, to prove that the holy books are not of themſelves the touchſtone of orthodoxy. They have demonſtrated, that, ſince the firſt preaching of the goſpel to our times, the ſcriptures, differently underſtood, had given riſe to the moſt oppoſite, the moſt extravagant, and the moſt impious opinions; and that with this divine word, the moſt contradictory tenets may have been maintained, as long as inward ſentiment hath been the only interpreter of the revelation.

The writers of the reformed religion have ſhown the abſurdity of believing, that one man alone was conſtantly inſpired from Heaven, upon a throne, or in

BOOK XIX. a chair, in which the moſt monſtrous vices have been committed; where diſſolution was ſeated by the ſide of inſpiration; where adultery and concubinage profaned the idols who were inveſted with the character and with the name of ſanctity; where the ſpirit of falſehood and of artifice dictated the pretended oracles of truth. They have demonſtrated, that the church, aſſembled in council, and compoſed of intriguing prelates, under the emperors of the primitive church, of ignorant and debauched ones, in the times of barbariſm and of ambition, and of oſtentatious ones in the ages of ſchiſm; that ſuch a church could not be more enlightened by ſupernatural inſpiration than the vicar of Jeſus himſelf; that the Spirit of God did not more viſibly communicate itſelf to two hundred fathers of the council, than to the holy father himſelf, who was often the moſt profligate of men; that Germans and Spaniards 'without learning, French without morals, and Italians without any virtue, were not ſo well qualified for the ſpirit of revelation, as a ſimple flock of peaſants, who ſincerely ſeek after God by prayer and by labour. In a word, if they have not been able to ſupport their new ſyſtem in the eyes of reaſon, they have at leaſt entirely deſtroyed that of the ancient church.

In the midſt of theſe ruins, philoſophy hath ariſen, and ſaid: If the text of the ſcripture be not ſufficiently clear, preciſe, and authentic, to be the ſole and infallible rule of doctrine and of worſhip; if the tradition of the church, from its firſt inſtitution to the times of Luther and Calvin, hath been corrupted with the manners of prieſts, and of its followers; if the councils have doubted, varied, and decided contradictorily in their aſſemblies; if it be unworthy of the Divinity to communicate its ſpirit and its word to one ſingle man, debauched in his youth, reduced to imbecillity in his old age, ſubject, in a word, to the paſſions, the errors, and the infirmities of man: then, ſay they, there is no firm and ſtable ſupport for the infallibility of the Chriſtian faith; confequently, that religion is not of divine B o o κ inftitution, and God hath not intended that it fhould XIX. be eternal.

This dilemma is very embarraffing. As long as the fenfe of the fcriptures fhall remain open to the contefts it hath ever experienced, and that tradition fhall be as problematical as it hath appeared to be, from the immenfe labours of the clergy of different communions, Chriftianity can have no fupport but from the civil authority, and the power of the magiftrate. The proper force of religion, which fubdues the mind, and reftrains the confcience by conviction, will be wanting to it.

Accordingly, thefe difputes have gradually led the nations which had fhaken off the yoke of an authority, confidered till then as infallible, farther than it had been forefeen. They have almoft generally rejected, from the ancient mode of worfhip, what was contrary to their reafon, and have only preferved a Chriftianity difengaged from all myfteries. Revelation itfelf hath been abandoned in thefe regions, though at a later period, by fome men more bold, or who thought themfelves more enlightened than the multitude. A manner of thinking, fo proud and independent, hath extended itfelf, in procefs of time, to thofe ftates which had remained fubject to Rome. As in thefe countries knowledge had made lefs progrefs, and opinions had been more confined, licentioufnefs in them hath been carried to its utmoft extent. Atheifm, the fyftem either of a difcontented and gloomy fpirit, which fees nothing but confufion in nature, or of a wicked man who dreads future vengeance, or of a fet of philofophers neither gloomy nor wicked, who vainly imagine they find in the properties of eternal matter a fufficient caufe for all the phenomena which excite our admiration.

By an impulfe founded on the nature of religions themfelves, Catholicifm tends inceffantly to Proteftantifm, Proteftantifm to Socinianifm, Socinianifm to Deifm, and Deifm to Scepticifm. Incredulity is become too general, to allow us to hope, with any de-

BOOK gree of foundation, that the ancient tenets can regain
XIX. the afcendant which they enjoyed during fo many
centuries. Let them be always freely followed, by fuch
of their fectators who are attached to them from confcience, by all thofe who find matter of confolation
in them, and by all whom they incite to perform the
duties of a citizen : but let all fects, the principles of
which are not contrary to public order, find in general the fame indulgence. It would be confiftent with
the dignity, as well as with the wifdom of all governments, to have the fame moral code of religion, from
which it fhould not be allowed to deviate, and to give
the reft up to difcuffions, in which the tranquillity of
the world was not concerned. This would be the
fureft way of extinguifhing, infenfibly, the fanaticifm
of the clergy and the enthufiafm of the people.

It is partly to the difcovery of the New World that
we fhall owe that religious toleration which ought to
be, and certainly will be, introduced in the Old.   Perfecution would only haften the downfal of the religions that are now eftablifhed.   Induftry and the
means of information have now prevailed among the
nations, and gained an influence that muft reftore a
certain equilibrium in the moral and civil order of fociety : the human mind is undeceived with regard to
its former fuperftitions.   If we do not avail ourfelves
of the prefent time to re-eftablifh the empire of reafon, it muft neceffarily be given up to new fuperftitions.

Every thing has concurred, for thefe two laft centuries, to extinguifh that furious zeal which ravaged
the globe. The depredations of the Spaniards throughout America have fhown the world to what excefs fanaticifm may be carried.   In eftablifhing their religion by fire and fword through exhaufted and depopulated countries, they have rendered it odious in
Europe ; and their cruelties have contributed to feparate a greater number of Catholics from the church
of Rome, than they have gained converts to Chriftianity among the Indians. The concourfe of perfons

of all sects in North America has necessarily diffused the spirit of toleration into distant countries, and put a stop to religious wars in our climates. The sending of missionaries has delivered us from those turbulent men, who might have inflamed our country, and who are gone to carry the firebrands and swords of the gospel beyond the seas. Navigation and long voyages have insensibly detached a great number of the people from the absurd ideas which superstition inspires. The variety of religious worships, and the difference of nations, has accustomed the most vulgar minds to a sort of indifference for the object that had the greatest influence over their imaginations. Trade carried on between persons of the most opposite sects, has lessened that religious hatred which was the cause of their divisions. It has been found that morality and integrity were not inconsistent with any opinions whatever, and that irregularity of manners and avarice were equally prevalent everywhere; and hence it has been concluded that the manners of men have been regulated by the difference of climate and of government, and by social and national interest.

Since an intercourse has been established between the two hemispheres of this world, our thoughts have been less engaged about that other world, which was the hope of the few and the torment of the many. The diversity and multiplicity of objects industry hath presented to the mind and to the senses, have divided the attachments of men, and weakened the force of every sentiment. The characters of men have been softened, and the spirit of fanaticism, as well as that of chivalry, must necessarily have been extinguished, together with all those striking extravagancies which have prevailed among people who were indolent and averse from labour. The same causes that have produced this revolution in the manners, have yet had a more sudden influence on the nature of government.

Society naturally results from population, and government is a part of the social state. From considering the few wants men have, in proportion to the

Government.

refources nature affords them, the little affiftance and
happinefs they find in a civilized ftate, in comparifon
of the pains and evils they are expofed to in it; their
defire of independence and liberty, common to them
with all other living beings; together with various
other reafons deduced from the conftitutions of human nature; from confidering all thefe circumftances,
it has been doubted whether the focial ftate was fo natural to mankind as it has generally been thought.

Infulated men have generally been compared to feparate fprings. If in the ftate of nature, without.le-
giflation, without government, without chiefs, without magiftrates, without tribunals, and without laws,
one of thefe fprings fhould clafh with another, either
the latter broke the former, or was broken by it, or
they were both of them broken. But when, by collecting and arranging thefe fprings, one of thofe enormous machines, called focieties, had been formed, in
which, being ftretched one againft the other, they act
and re-act with all the violence of their particular
energy, a real ftate of war was artificially created, and
that of war diverfified by an innumerable multitude
of interefts and opinions. The confufion was ftill infinitely greater, when two, three, four, or five of thefe
terrible machines came to fhock each other at the fame
time. It was then, that in the fpace of a few hours,
more fprings were broken and deftroyed, than would
have been in the courfe of twenty centuries, either
before or without this fublime inftitution. Thus it
is that the firft founders of nations are fatirized, under the fuppofition of an ideal and chimerical favage
ftate. Men were never infulated in the manner here
defcribed. They bore within themfelves a germen
of fociability, which was inceffantly tending to unfold
itfelf. Had they been inclined to feparate, they could
not have done it; and fuppofing they could, they
ought not; the defects of their affociation being compenfated by greater advantages.

The weaknefs and long continuance of the infant
ftate of man; the nakednefs of his body, which has

no natural covering like that of other animals; the tendency of his mind to perfection, the neceſſary conſequence of the length of his life; the fondneſs of a mother for her child, which is increaſed by cares and fatigues; who, after ſhe has carried it in the womb for nine months, ſuckles and bears it in her arms for whole years; the reciprocal attachment ariſing from this habitual connection between two beings who relieve and careſs each other; the numerous ſigns of intercourſe in an organization, which, beſide the accents of the voice, common to ſo many animals, adds alſo the language of the fingers, and of geſtures peculiar to the human race; natural events, which in a hundred different ways may bring together, or re-unite wandering and free individuals; accidents and unforeſeen wants, which oblige them to meet for the purpoſes of hunting, fiſhing, or even of defence; in a word, the example of ſo many creatures that live collected together in great numbers, ſuch as amphibious animals and ſea monſters, flights of cranes and other birds, even inſects that are found in columns and ſwarms: all theſe facts and reaſons ſeem to prove, that men are by nature formed for ſociety, and that they are the ſooner diſpoſed to enter into it, becauſe they cannot multiply greatly under the torrid zone, unleſs they be collected into wandering or ſedentary tribes; nor can they diffuſe themſelves much under the other zones, without aſſociating with their fellow-creatures, for the prey and the ſpoils which the neceſſities of food and clothing require.

From the neceſſity of aſſociation, ariſes that of eſtabliſhing laws relative to the ſocial ſtate; that is to ſay, of forming, by a combination of all common and particular inſtincts, one general plan, that ſhall maintain the collective body, and the majority of individuals. For if nature direct man to his fellow-creature, it is undoubtedly by a conſequence of that univerſal attraction which tends to the preſervation and reproduction of the ſpecies. All the propenſities which man brings with him into ſociety, and all the impreſſions

he receives in it, ought to be fubordinate to this firft
impulfe. To live and to propagate being the deftination of every living fpecies, it fhould feem that fociety, if it be one of the firft principles of man, fhould
concur in affifting this double end of nature; and
that inftinct which leads him to the focial ftate fhould
neceffarily direct all moral and political laws, fo as that
they fhould be more durable, and contribute more to
the happinefs of the majority of mankind. If, however, we confider merely the effect, we fhould think
that the principal or fupreme law of all fociety has
been, *to fupport the ruling power*. Whence can arife
this fingular contraft between the end and the means;
between the laws of nature and thofe of politics?

This is a queftion to which it is difficult to give a
proper anfwer, without forming to one's felf juft notions of nature, and of the fucceffion of the feveral
governments; and hiftory fcarce affords us any affiftance refpecting this great object. All the foundations
of the fociety at prefent are loft in the ruins of fome
cataftrophe, fome natural revolution. In all parts we
fee men driven away by fubterraneous fires or by war,
by inundations or by devouring infects, by want or famine; and joining again in fome uninhabited corner
of the world, or difperfing and fpreading themfelves
over places already peopled. Police always arifes from
plunder, and order from anarchy; but in order to obtain fome conclufion which fhall be fatisfactory to reafon, thefe momentary fhocks muft not be attended to,
and nations muft be confidered in a ftationary and tranquil ftate, in which the fingularities of government may
appear without controul.

It hath been faid that there are two worlds, the natural and the moral. The more extenfive the mind
fhall become, and the more experience it fhall acquire,
the more fhall we be convinced that there is but one,
viz. the natural world, which leads every thing, when
it is not oppofed by fortuitous caufes, without which
we fhould conftantly have obferved the fame concatenation in thofe moral events which ftrike us with moft

astonishment, such as the origin of religious ideas, the progress of the human mind, the discovery of truths, the source and the succession of errors, the beginning and the end of prejudices, the formation of societies, and the periodical order of the several governments.

All civilized people have been savages; and all savages, left to their natural impulse, were destined to become civilized. A family was the first society, and the first government was the patriarchal, founded upon attachment, obedience, and respect. The family is extended and divided; opposite interests excite wars between brothers, who disavow each other. One people takes up arms against another. The vanquished become the slaves of the conquerors, who share among themselves their plains, their children, and their wives. The country is governed by a chief, by his lieutenants, and by his soldiers, who represent the free part of the nation, while all the rest is subjected to the atrociousness and to the humiliations of servitude. In this state of anarchy, blinded with jealousy and ferociousness, peace is soon disturbed. These restless men march against and exterminate each other. In process of time there remains only a monarch, or a despot under the monarch. There is a shadow of justice; legislation makes some progress; ideas of property are unfolded; and the name of slave is changed into that of subject. Under the supreme will of a despot, nothing prevails but terror, meanness, flattery, stupidity, and superstition. This intolerable situation ceases, either by the assassination of the tyrant, or by the dissolution of the empire; and democracy is raised upon its ruins. It is then, for the first time, that the sacred name of one's country is heard. It is then that man, bent down to earth, raises his head, and appears in his dignity. Then the annals of the nation are filled with heroic deeds. Then there are fathers, mothers, children, friends, fellow-citizens, public and domestic virtues. Then the empire of the laws is established, soars to its extremest

B O O K height, the fciences arife, and ufeful labours are no
XIX.   longer dergaded.

Unfortunately, this ftate of happinefs is only temporary.   In all parts, revolutions in government fucceed each other with a rapidity fcarce to be followed.   There are few countries which have not experienced them all; and there is not any one which, in
procefs of time, will not fulfil this periodical motion.
They will all, more or lefs frequently, follow a regular circle of misfortunes and profperities, of liberty
and flavery, of morals and corruption, of knowledge
and ignorance, of fplendour and weaknefs; they will
all go through the feveral points of this fatal horizon.
The law of nature, which requires that all focieties
fhould gravitate towards defpotifm and diffolution, that
empires fhould arife and be annihilated, will not be
fufpended for any one of them.   While, like the
needle which indicates the conftant direction of the
winds, they are either advancing or going back, let
us fee by what means Europe is arrived to that ftate
of civilization in which it now exifts.

Waving any further account of the Jewifh government, unlefs juft to obferve, that this fingular nation
hath maintained its character, under all the viciffitudes of its deftiny; that the Jews, conquered, fubdued, difperfed, hated, and defpifed, have ftill remained attached to their nation; that they have carried their annals, and their country with them, into
all climates; that whatever region they inhabit, they
live in expectation of a deliverer, and die with their
looks fixed upon their ancient temple; let us pafs on
to the ftates of Greece.

Thefe were founded by robbers, who deftroyed a
few monfters, and a great number of men, in order to
become kings.   It was there, that during a fhort fpace
of time, at leaft if we date from the heroic ages, and
in a narrow circuit, we have a review of all the fpecies
of governments, of ariftocracy, of democracy, of monarchy, of defpotifm, and of anarchy, which was only
fufpended, without being extinguifhed, by the ap-

proach of the common enemy. There it was that the imminent danger of flavery gave birth and ftability to patriotifm, which leads in its train the origin of all great talents ; fublime inftance of all vices, and of all virtues ; an infinite number of fchools of wifdom, in the midft of debauchery ; and fome models in the fine arts, which in all ages art will always imitate, but will never equal. The Greeks were a frivolous, pleafant, lying, and ungrateful people ; they were the only original people that have exifted, or perhaps will ever exift, upon the face of the earth.

Rome, it is faid, was founded by people who efcaped from the flames of Troy, or was only a retreat for fome banditti from Greece and Italy : but from this fcum of the human race arofe a nation of heroes, the fcourge of all nations, the devourers of themfelves ; a people more aftonifhing than admirable, great by their qualities, and worthy of execration by the ufe they made of them in the times of the republic ; the bafeft and moft corrupt people under their emperors ; a people, of whom one of the moft virtuous men of his age ufed to fay : If the kings be ferocious animals, who devour nations, what kind of beaft muft the Roman people be, who devour kings?

War, which, from all the great nations of Europe together, had formed only the Roman empire, made thefe very Romans, who were fo numerous, become barbarians again. As the difpofitions and manners of the conquering people are generally impreffed upon the conquered, thofe who had been enlightened with the knowledge of Rome at the period when it was diftinguifhed by its learning, now fank again into the darknefs of ftupid and ferocious Scythians. During ages of ignorance, when fuperior ftrength always gave the law, and chance or hunger had compelled the people of the north to invade the fouthern countries, the continual ebb and flow of emigrations prevented laws from being fettled in any place. As foon as a multitude of fmall nations had deftroyed a large one, many chiefs or tyrants divided each vaft monarchy into feve-

BOOK
XIX.
ral fiefs. The people, who gained no advantage by
the government of one, or of feveral men, were always
oppreffed and trampled upon from thefe difmember-
ings of the feudal anarchy. Petty wars were continually kept up between neighbouring towns, inftead
of thofe great wars that now prevail between nations.

In the meanwhile, a continual ferment led the nations to eftablifh themfelves into fome regular and
confiftent form of government. Kings were defirous
of raifing themfelves upon the ruins of thofe individuals, or of thofe powerful bodies of men, by whom
the commotions were kept up; and to effect this, they
had recourfe to the affiftance of the people. They
were civilized, polifhed, and more rational laws were
given them.

Slavery had oppreffed their natural vigour, property
reftored it, and commerce, which prevailed after the
difcovery of the New World, increafed all their powers, by exciting univerfal emulation.

Thefe changes were attended with a revolution of
another kind. The monarchs had not been capable
of aggrandizing their power without diminifhing that
of the clergy, without favouring religious opinions, or
endeavouring to bring them into difcredit. Innova-
tors, who ventured to attack the church, were fupported by the throne. From that time, the human
underftanding was ftrengthened by exerting itfelf a-
gainft the phantoms of imagination, and recovering
the path of nature and of reafon, difcovered the true
principles of government. Luther and Columbus appeared; the whole univerfe trembled; and all Europe
was in commotion: but this ftorm left its horizon clear
for ages to come. The former awakened the underftandings of men, the latter excited their activity.
Since they have laid open all the avenues of induftry
and freedom, moft of the European nations have attended with fome fuccefs to the correction or improvement of legiflation, upon which the felicity of mankind entirely depends. But this fpirit of information
hath not yet reached the Turks.

The Turks were not known in Afia till the beginning of the thirteenth century; at which time the
Tartars, of whom they were a tribe, made frequent
excurfions upon the territories of the eaftern empire,
as the Goths had formerly done in the weftern provinces. It was in 1300 that Ottoman was declared
fultan by his nation, who, living till then upon plunder, or felling their fervice to fome Afiatic prince, had
not yet thought of forming an independent empire.
Ottoman became the chief among thefe barbarians,
as a favage diftinguifhed by his bravery becomes a
chief among his equals; for the Turks at that time
were only a horde fixed in the neighbourhood of a
people who were half civilized.

Under this prince and his fucceffors, the Ottoman
power was daily making frefh progrefs; nothing refifted it. Princes brought up in the midft of camps,
and born captains, armies accuftomed to victory by
continual wars, and better difciplined than thofe of
the Chriftians, repaired the defects of a bad government.

Conftantinople, taken by Mohammed in 1453, became the capital of their empire; and the princes of
Europe, plunged in ignorance and barbarifm, could
only have oppofed an ineffectual dyke to this overflowing torrent, if the firft fucceffors of Mohammed,
at the head of a nation which ftill preferved the manners, the genius, and the difcipline of its founders, had
not been obliged to interrupt their expeditions in Poland, in Hungary, or upon the domains of the republic of Venice, in order to go fometimes into Afia, fometimes into Africa, either againft rebellious fubjects or
turbulent neighbours. Their fortune began to fall off
as foon as their forces were divided. Succeffes lefs rapid and lefs brilliant occafioned their armies to lofe
that confidence which was the foul of their exploits.
The reft of the empire, crufhed under the moft rigorous defpotifm, had not attained to any degree of
fplendour. It had acquired no real ftrength from conquefts, becaufe it had not known how to take advan-

BOOK tage of them by prudent regulations. Deſtroying in
XIX. order to preſerve, the conquerors had acquired nothing. They reigned only over provinces laid waſte,
and over the wrecks of the powers whom they had
ruined.

While a deceitful proſperity was preparing the fall
of the Ottoman empire, a contrary revolution was
taking place in Chriſtendom. The minds of men
were beginning to be enlightened. Principles leſs extravagant were introducing themſelves into Poland.
Feudal government, the fertile ſource of ſo many calamities, and which had laſted for ſo long a time, gave
way in ſeveral ſtates to a more regular form of government. In other ſtates it was gradually altered, either
by laws or by new cuſtoms, with which ſome fortunate circumſtances obliged it to comply. At length a
power was formed in the neighbourhood of the Turks
capable of reſiſting them : I mean the acceſſion of
Ferdinand to the throne of Hungary. This prince,
maſter of the poſſeſſions of the Houſe of Auſtria in
Germany, was beſides certain, from his Imperial crown,
of powerful ſuccours againſt the common enemy.

A military government tends to deſpotiſm ; and reciprocally in every deſpotic government, the military
man diſpoſes ſooner or later of the ſovereign authority. The prince, freed from all kind of law which
might reſtrain his power, doth not fail of abuſing it,
and ſoon commands over none but ſlaves, who take
no kind of concern about his fate. He who oppreſſes
finds no defender, becauſe he deſerves none. His
grandeur is without foundation. His own fears are
awakened from the ſame motives by which he hath
excited terror in others. The uſe he makes of the
militia againſt his ſubjects, teaches this very militia
what they can do againſt himſelf. They try their
ſtrength, they mutiny, and they revolt. The want
of power in the prince makes them inſolent. They
acquire a ſpirit of ſedition, and it is then that they decide of the fate of their maſter and of his miniſters.

Soliman, informed by the internal commotions which

had agitated the empire under the reigns of Bajazet II. B O O K
and Selim II. of the dangers which threatened himself ⁀XIX.
and his fucceffors, thought that he could adopt no better expedient than to enact a law which deprived the
princes of his houfe both of the command of the armies and of the government of the provinces. It was
by burying in the obfcure idlenefs of a feraglio thofe
to whom their birth gave any pretenfions to the empire, that he flattered himfelf he fhould remove from
the Janizaries every pretence of fedition ; but he was
deceived. This bad policy ferved only to increafe
the mifchief of an evil that was perhaps ftill greater.
His fucceffors, corrupted by an effeminate education,
bore without authority the fword which had founded
and had extended the empire. Ignorant princes, who
had frequented none but women, and converfed with
none but eunuchs, were invefted with an unlimited
authority, the moft unparalleled abufe of which completed the hatred and mifery of their fubjects, and
plunged them in an abfolute dependence on the Janizaries, become more avaricious and more untrac-
table than ever. If fometimes, by chance, a fovereign
was raifed to the throne, who was worthy of occupying it, he was driven from it by minifters, enemies of
a mafter who was able to reftrain and examine their
power, and penetrate into their conduct.

Though the Grand Seignior poffeffes vaft domains,
though the fituation of his empire ought to intereft
him in the difputes of the Chriftian princes, he hath
fcarce any influence in the general fyftem of Europe.
This is the effect of the ignorance prevailing among
the miniftry of the Porte, of their prejudices, of the
unvariablenefs of their principles, of the other vices
which flow from defpotifm, and which will perpetuate
their bad policy ; for tyrants dread nothing fo much
as novelty. They imagine that all is right ; and in
fact nothing advances more rapidly towards perfection than defpotifm. The beft princes leave always
a great deal of good to be done by their fucceffors,

while the firſt deſpot ſcarce ever leaves any evil for a
ſecond to do. Beſides, how ſhould a Grand Seignior,
ſunk in the voluptuouſneſs of a ſeraglio, ſuſpect that
the adminiſtration of his dominions is deteſtable ? How
is it poſſible he ſhould not admire the wonderful exactneſs of the ſprings, the prodigious harmony of the
principles, and of the means which all concur to produce that ſingle and ſuper-excellent end, his moſt unlimited power, and the moſt profound ſervitude of his
ſubjects ? None of them are warned by the fate of ſo
many of their predeceſſors, who have been either ſtab-
bed or ſtrangled.

The ſultans have never changed their principles.
The ſcimitar, at Conſtantinople, is ſtill the interpreter
of the Coran. Though the Grand Seignior may not
be ſeen coming in and going out of the ſeraglio, like
the tyrant of Morocco, with a bloody head in his hand,
yet a numerous cohort of ſatellites is engaged to execute theſe horrid murders. The people ſometimes
maſſacred by their ruler, at other times aſſaſſinate the
executioner in their turn ; but, ſatisfied with this temporary vengeance, they think not of providing for their
future ſafety, or for the happineſs of their poſterity.
Eaſtern nations will not be at the trouble of guarding
the public ſafety by laws, which it is a laborious taſk
to form, to ſettle, and to preſerve. If their tyrants
carry their oppreſſions or cruelties too far, the head
of the vizir is demanded, that of the deſpot is ſtricken
off, and thus public tranquillity is reſtored This re-
monſtrance, which ſhould be the privilege of the whole
nation, is only that of the Janizaries. Even the moſt
powerful men in the kingdom have not the leaſt idea
of the right of nations. As perſonal ſafety in Turkey
belongs only to people of a mean and abject condition, the chief families pride themſelves in the very
danger they are expoſed to from the government. A
Baſhaw will tell you, that a man of his rank is not
deſtined, like an obſcure perſon, to finiſh his days
quietly in his bed. One may frequently ſee widows,

whofe hufbands have been juft ftrangled, exulting that B O O K
they have been deftroyed in a manner fuitable to their XIX.
rank.

It is to this pitch of extravagance that men are led,
when tyranny is confecrated by religious ideas, which
fooner or later it muft be. When men ceafe to take
pride in their chains in the eyes of the deity, they
look upon them with contempt, and foon proceed to
break them. If the apotheofis of the tyrants of Rome
had not been a farce, Tiberius would not have been
ftifled, nor would the murders committed by Nero
have been avenged. Oppreffion, authorifed by Heaven, infpires fuch a contempt for life, that it induces
the flave to take pride even in his abject ftate. He is
vain of being become in the eyes of his mafter a being
of fufficient importance, that he fhould not difdain to
put him to death. What difference is there between
man and man? A Roman will kill himfelf for fear of
owing his life to his equal; and the Muffulman will
glory in the fentence of death pronounced againft him
by his mafter. Imagination, which can meafure the
diftance of the earth from the firmament, cannot comprehend this. But what is ftill more furprifing is, that
the affaffination of a defpot, fo profoundly revered, far
from exciting horror, doth not make the leaft impreffion. The man who would have joyfully offered him
his own head a few minutes before, beholds without
emotion his mafter's ftricken off by the fcimitar. His
indifference feems to fay, that, whether the tyrant be
dead or alive, he cannot fail of the honour of being
ftrangled under his fucceffor.

The Ruffians and the Danes do not entertain the
fame prejudices, though fubject to a power equally arbitrary; becaufe thefe two nations have the advantage
of a more tolerable adminiftration, and of fome written
laws. They can venture to think, or even to fay, that
their government is limited; but have never been able
to perfuade any enlightened man of the truth of their
affertion. While the fovereign makes and annuls the
laws, extends or reftrains them, and permits or fufpends

the execution of them at pleafure ; while his paffions are the only rule of his conduct ; while he is the only, the central being to whom every thing tends ; while nothing is either juft or unjuft but what he makes fo ; while his caprice is the law, and his favour the ftandard of public efteem ; if this be not defpotifm, what other kind of government can it poffibly be?

In fuch a ftate of degradation, what are men ? Enflaved as they are, they can fcarce venture to look up to Heaven. They are infenfible of their chains, as well as of the fhame that attends them. The powers of their minds, extinguifhed in the bonds of flavery, have not fufficient energy to difcover the rights infeparable from their exiftence. It may be a matter of doubt ,whether thefe flaves be not as culpable as their tyrants, and whether the fpirit of liberty may not have greater reafon to complain of the arrogance of thofe who invade her rights, than of the weaknefs of thofe who know not how to defend them.

It hath, however, been frequently afferted, that the moft happy form of government would be that of a juft and enlightened defpotic prince. The abfurdity of this is evident ; for it might eafily happen that the will of this abfolute monarch might be in direct oppofition to the will of his fubjects. In that cafe, notwithftanding all his juftice and all his abilities, he would deferve cenfure to deprive them of their rights, even though it were for their own benefit. No man whatfoever is entitled to treat his fellow-creatures like fo many beafts. Beafts may be forced to exchange a bad pafture for a better ; but to ufe fuch compulfion with men, would be an act of tyranny. If they fhould fay that they are very well where they are, or even if they fhould agree in allowing that their fituation is a bad one, but that they choofe to ftay in it, we may endeavour to enlighten them, to undeceive them, and to bring them to jufter notions by the means of perfuafion, but never by thofe of compulfion. The beft of princes, who fhould even have done good againft the general confent of his people, would be culpable

if it were only becaufe he had gone beyond his right. B O O K
He would be culpable not only for the time, but even XIX.
with regard to pofterity; for though he might be juft
and enlightened, yet his fucceffor, without inheriting
either his abilities or his virtues, will certainly inherit
his authority, of which the nation will become the
victim. A firft defpot, juft, fteady, and enlightened,
is a great calamity; a fecond defpot, juft, fteady, and
enlightened, would be a ftill greater one; but a third,
who fhould fucceed with all thefe great qualities,
would be the moft terrible fcourge with which a nation could be afflicted. It is poffible to emerge from
a ftate of flavery into which we may have been plunged by violence, but never from that into which we
have been led by time and juftice. If the lethargy of
the people be the forerunner of the lofs of their liberty, what lethargy can be more mild, more profound,
and more perfidious, than that which hath lafted during three reigns, and which hath been kept up by
acts of kindnefs?

Let not therefore thefe pretended mafters of the
people be allowed even to do good againft the general
confent. Let it be confidered, that the condition of
thofe rulers is exactly the fame as that of the cacique,
who being afked, Whether he had any flaves? anfwered: *Slaves! I know but one flave in all my diftrict,
and that is myfelf.*

It is of fo much importance to prevent the eftablifhment of arbitrary power, and the calamities which are
the infallible confequences of it, that it is impoffible
for the defpot himfelf to remedy thefe great evils.
Should he have been upon the throne for half a century; fhould his adminiftration have been entirely
tranquil; fhould he have had the moft extenfive knowledge; and fhould his zeal for the happinefs of the people not have been one moment flackened; ftill nothing
would be done. The enfranchifement, or, what is the
fame thing under another name, the civilization of an
empire, is a long and difficult work. Before a nation
hath been confirmed, by habit, in a durable attach-

ment for this new order of things, a prince, either from
inability, indolence, prejudice, or jealoufy, from a pre-
dilection for ancient cuftoms, or from a fpirit of tyranny, may annihilate all the good accomplifhed in the
courfe of two or three reigns, or may fuffer it to be ineffectual.   All monuments therefore atteft, that the
civilization of ftates hath been more the effect of circumftances, than of the wifdom of fovereigns.   All
nations have changed from barbarifm to a ftate of civilization ; and from a civilized ftate to barbarifm, till
fome unforefeen caufes have brought them to that level which they never perfectly maintain.

We may, perhaps, be allowed to doubt, whether all
thefe caufes concur with the efforts which are at prefent making towards the civilization of Ruffia.

Is the climate of this region very favourable to civilization, and to population, which is fometimes the
caufe and fometimes the effect of them ?   Doth not
the coldnefs of the climate require the prefervation of
the large forefts, and, confequently, muft not immenfe
fpaces remain uninhabited?   As an exceffive length
of winter fufpends the labours for the fpace of feven
or eight months of the year, doth not the nation, during this time of lethargy, devote itfelf to gaming, to
wine, to debauchery, and to an immoderate ufe of fpirituous liquors?   Can good manners be introduced,
notwithftanding the climate? and is it poffible to civilize a barbarous people without manners?

Doth not the immenfe extent of the empire, which
embraces all kinds of climates, from the coldeft to the
hotteft, oppofe a powerful obftacle to the legiflator?
Could one and the fame code fuit fo many different
regions? and is not the neceffity of having feveral
codes the fame thing as the impoffibility of having only one?   Can any means be conceived of fubjecting
to one fame rule people who do not underftand each
other, who fpeak feventeen or eighteen different languages, and who preferve, from times immemorial, cuftoms and fuperftitions to which they are more attached
than to their exiftence?

As authority weakens, in proportion as the subjects are distant from the centre of dominion, is it possible to be obeyed at a thousand miles distance from the spot from whence the commands are issued? Should any body tell me that the matter is possible by the influence of government, I shall only reply by the speech of one of these indiscreet delegates, who revealed what passed in the mind of all the others: *God is very high; the emperor is at a great distance; and I am master here.*

As the empire is divided into two classes of men, that of the masters and that of the slaves, how can such opposite interests be conciliated? Tyrants will never freely consent to the extinction of servitude; and in order to bring them to this, it would be necessary to ruin or to exterminate them. But supposing this obstacle removed, how is it possible to raise from the degraded state of slavery, to the sentiment and to the dignity of liberty, people who are so entirely strangers to it, as to be either helpless or ferocious, whenever they are released from their fetters? These difficulties will certainly suggest the idea of creating a third order in the state; but by what means is this to be accomplished; and supposing the means discovered, how many ages would it require to obtain any sensible effect from them?

In expectation of the formation of this third class of men, which might, perhaps, be accelerated by colonists invited from the free countries of Europe, it would be necessary that an entire security should be established, both with respect to persons and to property; and could such a security be established in a country where the tribunals are occupied by the lords alone; where these species of magistrates reciprocally favour each other; where there can be no prosecution against them, or against their creatures, from which either the natives or the foreigners can expect that the injuries they have received should be redressed; and where venality pronounces the sentence in every kind of contest? We shall ask, whether there can be any civili-

zation without juſtice, and whether it be poſſible to
eſtabliſh juſtice in ſuch an empire?

The towns are diſtributed over an immenſe territory.
There are no roads, and thoſe which might be conſtructed would be ſoon ſpoiled by the climate. Accordingly, deſolation is univerſal, when a damp winter puts a ſtop to every communication. Let us travel
over all the countries of the earth, and wherever we
ſhall find no facility of trading from a city to a town,
and from a village to a hamlet, we may pronounce the
people to be barbarians; and we ſhall only be deceived reſpecting the degree of barbariſm. In this ſtate of
things, the greateſt happineſs that could happen to a
country of an enormous extent would be to be diſ-
membered by ſome great revolution, and to be divided into ſeveral petty ſovereignties, contiguous to each
other, where the order introduced into ſome of them
would be diffuſed through the reſt. If it be very difficult to govern properly a large civilized empire, muſt
it not be more ſo to civilize a vaſt and barbarous empire?

Toleration, it is true, ſubſiſts at Peterſburgh, and
almoſt in an unlimited degree. Judaiſm alone is excluded, becauſe it hath been thought that its ſectators
were either too crafty, or too deceitful in trade, to expoſe to their ſnares a people who had not experience
enough to preſerve themſelves from them. This toleration in the capital would be a great ſtep towards civilization, if in the reſt of the empire the people did
not remain immerſed in the moſt groſs ſuperſtitions;
and if theſe ſuperſtitions were not fomented by a numerous clergy, plunged in debauchery and ignorance,
without being the leſs revered. How can a ſtate be
civilized without the interference of prieſts, who are
neceſſarily prejudicial, if not uſeful?

The high opinion that, according to the example of
the Chineſe, the Ruſſians have of themſelves, is another obſtacle to reformation. They truly conſider
themſelves as the moſt ſenſible people upon the earth,
and are confirmed in this abſurd vanity by thoſe among

them who have visited the rest of Europe. These tra- B O O K
vellers bring back, or feign to bring back, into their
country, the prejudice of their own superiority, and
enrich it only with the vices which they have acquired
in the divers regions where chance hath conducted
them. Accordingly, a foreign observer, who had gone
over the greatest part of the empire, used to say, that
the Ruffian was rotten before he had been ripe.

We might extend ourselves more upon the difficulties which nature and customs obstinately oppose to
the civilization of Ruffia. Let us examine the means
which have been contrived to succeed in it.

Catherine hath undoubtedly been very well convinced, that liberty was the only source of public happiness: and yet, hath she really abdicated despotic authority? In reading attentively her instructions to the
deputies of the empire, apparently intrusted with the
formation of the laws, is any thing more found in
them than the desire of altering denominations, and of
being called monarch, instead of autocratrix? of calling her people subjects, instead of slaves? Will the
Ruffians, blind as they are, take the name, instead of
the thing, for any length of time? and will their character be elevated, by this farce, to that great degree
of energy with which it was proposed to inspire them?

A sovereign, however great his genius may be, seldom makes alterations of any consequence by himself,
and still more unfrequently gives them any degree of
stability. He stands in need of assistance, and Ruffia
can offer no other than that of fighting. Its soldiers
are hardy, sober, indefatigable. Slavery, which hath
inspired them with a contempt of life, hath united with
superstition, which hath inspired them with contempt
of death. They are persuaded, that, whatever crimes
they may have committed, their soul will ascend to
heaven from the field of battle. But military men, if
they defend the provinces, do not civilize them. In
vain do we seek for statesmen about the person of Catherine. What she hath done of herself may be asto-

BOOK nifhing; but who can be fubftituted to her, when fhe
XIX. fhall be no more?

This princefs hath founded houfes, in which young
people of both fexes are brought up with the fentiment
of liberty. This will undoubtedly produce a different
race from the prefent. But are thefe eftablifhments
founded upon a folid bafis? Are they fuftained by
themfelves, or by the fuccours which are inceffantly
lavifhed upon them? If the prefent reign hath feen
the origin of them, will not the fucceeding reign fee
them annihilated? Are they very agreeable to the
great, who perceive the deftination of them? Will
not the climate, which difpofes of every thing, prevail
at length over good principles? Will corruption fpare
thofe young people who are loft in the immenfity of
the empire, and who are affailed on all fides by bad
morals?

There are a great number of academies of all kinds
in the capital; and if thefe be filled by foreigners, will
not thefe eftablifhments be ufelefs and ruinous, in a
country where the learned are not underftood, and
where there is no employment for artifts? In order
that talents and knowledge might thrive, it would be
neceffary, that, being offsprings of the foil, they fhould
be the effect of a fuperabundant population. When
will this population arrive to the proper degree of increafe, in a country where the flave, to confole himfelf
for the wretchednefs of his condition, may indeed produce as many children as he can, but will care very
little about preferving them?

All thofe who are admitted and brought up in the
hofpital recently eftablifhed for foundlings, are for ever
emancipated from flavery. Their defcendants will not
fubmit to the yoke again; and as in Spain there are
old or new Chriftians, fo in Ruffia there will be old and
new freemen. But the effect of this innovation can
only be proportioned to its continuance: and can we
reckon upon the duration of any eftablifhment, in a
country where the fucceffion to the empire is not yet

inviolably confirmed, and where the inconftancy which is natural to an enflaved people brings on frequent and fudden revolutions? If the authors of thefe confpiracies do not form a body, as in Turkey, if they be a fet of infulated individuals, they are foon affembled together, by a fecret ferment and by a common hatred.

During the laft war, a fund was created for the ufe of all the members of the empire, even of flaves. By this idea of found and deep policy, the government acquired a capital, of which it ftood in great need; and it fheltered, as much as poffible, the vaffals from the vexations of their tyrants. It is in the nature of things, that the confidence with which this paper money hath been received fhould change, and be annulled. It doth not belong to a defpot to obtain credit; and if fome fingular events have procured it to him, it is a neceffary confequence, that fucceeding events will make him lofe it.

Such are the difficulties which have appeared to us to counteraÄ the civilization of the Ruffian empire. If Catherine II. fhould fucceed in furmounting them, we fhall have made the moft magnificent eulogium of her courage and her genius; and perhaps the beft apology, if fhe fhould fail in this great defign.

Sweden is fituated between Ruffia and Denmark. Let us examine the hiftory of its conftitution, and endeavour, if poffible, to find out the nature of it.

Nations that are poor are almoft neceffarily warlike; becaufe their very poverty, the burden of which they conftantly feel, infpires them fooner or later with a defire of freeing themfelves from it; and this defire, in procefs of time, becomes the general fpirit of the nation, and the fpring of the government.

It only requires a fucceffion of fovereigns, fortunate in war, to change fuddenly the government of fuch a country, from the ftate of a mild monarchy, to that of the moft abfolute defpotifm. The monarch, proud of his triumph, thinks he will be fuffered to do whatever he choofes, begins to acknowledge no law but his will; and his foldiers, whom he hath led fo often to

BOOK
XIX.

victory, ready to ferve him in all things, and againſt all men, become, by their attachment to the prince, the terror of their fellow-citizens. The people, on the other hand, dare not refuſe the chains, when offered to them by him, who, to the authority of his rank, joins that which he holds from their admiration and gratitude.

The yoke impoſed by a monarch who has conquered the enemies of the ſtate is certainly burdenſome; but the ſubjects dare not ſhake it off. It even grows heavier under ſucceſſors, who have not the ſame claim to the indulgence of the people. Whenever any conſiderable reverſe of fortune takes place, the deſpot will be left to their mercy. Then the people, irritated by their long ſufferings, ſeldom fail to avail themſelves of the opportunity of recovering their rights. But as they have neither views nor plans, they quickly paſs from ſlavery to anarchy. In the midſt of this general confuſion, one exclamation only is heard, and that is, Liberty. But, as they know not how to ſecure to themſelves this ineſtimable benefit, the nation becomes immediately divided into various factions, which are guided by different intereſts.

If there be one among theſe factions that deſpairs of prevailing over the others, that faction ſeparates itſelf from the reſt, unmindful of the general good; and being more anxious to prejudice its rivals than to ſerve its country, it ſides with the ſovereign. From that moment there are but two parties in the ſtate, diſtinguiſhed by two different names, which, whatever they be, never mean any thing more than royaliſts and anti-royaliſts. This is the period of great commotions and conſpiracies.

The neighbouring powers then act the ſame part they have ever acted at all times, and in all countries, upon ſimilar occaſions. They foment jealouſies between the people and their prince; they ſuggeſt to the ſubjects every poſſible method of debaſing, degrading, and annihilating the ſovereignty; they corrupt even thoſe who are neareſt the throne; they occaſion some form of administration to be adopted, prejudicial

both to the whole body of the nation, which it impoverishes under pretence of exerting itself for their liberty, and injurious to the sovereign, whose prerogative it reduces to nothing.

The monarch then meets with as many authorities opposed to his, as there are ranks in the state. His will is then nothing, without their concurrence. Assemblies must then be holden, proposals made, and affairs of the least importance debated. Tutors are assigned to him, as to a pupil in his non-age; and those tutors are persons whom he may always expect to find ill-intentioned towards him.

But what is then the state of the nation? The neighbouring powers have now, by their influence, thrown every thing into confusion; they have overturned the state, or seduced all the members of it by bribery or intrigues. There is now but one party in the kingdom, and that is the party which espouses the interest of the foreign powers. The members of the factions are all dissemblers. Attachment to the king is an hypocrisy, and aversion for monarchy another. They are two different masks to conceal ambition and avarice. The whole nation is now entirely composed of infamous and venal men.

It is not difficult to conceive what must happen after this. The foreign powers that had corrupted the nation must be deceived in their expectations. They did not perceive that they carried matters too far; that, perhaps, they acted a part quite contrary to that which a deeper policy would have suggested; that they were destroying the power of the nation, while they meant only to restrain that of the sovereign, which might one day exert itself with all its force, and meet with no resistance capable of checking it; and that this unexpected effect might be brought about in an instant, and by one man.

That instant is come; that man hath appeared; and all these base creatures of adverse powers have prostrated themselves before him. He told these men, who

BOOK thought themfelves all-powerful, that they were no-
XIX. thing. He told them, I am your mafter; and they
declared unanimoufly that he was. He told them,
thefe are the conditions to which I would have you
fubmit; and they anfwered, we agree to them. Scarce
one diffenting voice was heard among them. It is impoffible for any man to know what will be the confequence of this revolution. If the king will avail himfelf of thefe circumftances, Sweden will never have
been governed by a more abfolute monarch. If he be
prudent; if he underftand that an unlimited fovereign
can have no fubjects, becaufe he can have no perfons
under him poffeffed of property; and that authority
can only be exerted over thofe who have fome kind of
property; the nation may, perhaps, recover its original character. Whatever may be his defigns or his
inclinations, Sweden cannot poffibly be more unhappy than fhe was before.

Poland, which has none but flaves within, and therefore deferves to meet with none but oppreffors without,
ftill preferves, however, the fhadow and the name of
liberty. This kingdom is, at prefent, no better than
all the European ftates were ten centuries ago, fubject
to a powerful ariftocracy, which elects a king, in order
to make him fubfervient to its will. Each nobleman,
by virtue of his feudal tenure, which he preferves with
his fword, as his anceftors acquired it, holds a perfonal
and hereditary authority over his vaffals. The feudal
government prevails there in all the force of its primitive inftitution. It is an empire compofed of as many
ftates as there are lands. All the laws are fettled there,
and all refolutions taken, not by the majority, but by
the unanimity of the fuffrages. Upon falfe notions of
right and perfection, it has been fuppofed that a law
was only juft when it was adopted by unanimous confent; becaufe it has undoubtedly been thought, that
what was right would both be perceived and put in
practice by all; two things that are impoffible in a national affembly. But can we even afcribe fuch pure
intentions to a fet of tyrants? For this conftitution,

which boasts the title of a republic, and profanes it, is only a league of petty tyrants against the people. In this country, every one has the power to restrain, and no one the power to act. Here the will of each individual may be in opposition to the general one; and here only a fool, a wicked man, and a madman, is sure to prevail over a whole nation.

In this state of anarchy, there is a perpetual struggle between the great and the monarch. The former torment the chief of the state by their avidity, their ambition, and their mistrust; they irritate him against liberty, and compel him to have recourse to intrigue. The prince, on his part, divides in order to command, seduces in order to defend himself, and opposes artifice to artifice in order to maintain himself. The factions are inflamed, discord throws every thing into confusion, and the provinces are delivered up to fire, to sword, and to devastation. If the confederacy should prevail, he who should have governed the nation is expelled from the throne, or reduced to the most ignominious dependence. If it should be subdued, the sovereign reigns only over carcases. Whatever may happen, the fate of the multitude experiences no fortunate revolution. Such of these unhappy people who have escaped from famine and carnage, continue to bear the chains with which they were crushed.

If we go over these vast regions, what shall we see in them? The regal dignity, with the title of a republic; the pomp of the throne, with the inability of insuring obedience; the extravagant love of independence, with all the meanness of slavery; liberty, with cupidity; laws, with anarchy; the most excessive luxury, with the greatest indigence; a fertile soil, with fallow lands; a taste for all the arts, without any one of them. Such are the enormous contrasts Poland will exhibit.

It will be found exposed to every danger. The weakest of its enemies may enter with impunity, and without precaution, upon its territory, levy contributions, destroy the towns, ravage the country places,

B O O K and maffacre or carry off the inhabitants. Deftitute
XIX. of troops, of fortreffes, of artillery, of ammunition, of
money, of generals, and totally ignorant of military
principles, what defence could it think of making?
With a fufficient population, with fufficient genius and
refources to appear of fome confequence, Poland is become the opprobrium and the fport of nations.

If turbulent and enterprifing neighbours had not
yet invaded its poffeffions ; if they had been fatisfied
with laying it wafte, with dictating to it, and with giving it kings ; it is becaufe they were continually mif-
truftful of each other, but particular circumftances
have united them. It was referved for our days to fee
this ftate torn in pieces by three powerful rivals, who
have appropriated to themfelves thofe provinces that
were moft fuitable to them, while no power of Europe
hath exerted itfelf to prevent this invafion. It is in the
midft of the fecurity of peace, without rights, without
pretenfions, without grievances, and without a fhadow
of juftice, that the revolution hath been accomplifhed
by the terrible principle of force, which is, unfortunately, the beft argument of kings. How great Po-
niatowfki would have appeared, if, when he faw the
preparatives for this divifion, he had prefented himfelf in the midft of the diet, and there abdicating the
marks of his dignity, had proudly faid to his nobles
affembled, " It is your choice that hath raifed me to
" the throne. If you repent of it, I refign the royal
" dignity. The crown which you have placed upon
" my head, let it devolve to any one whom you fhall
" think more worthy of it than me : name him, and
" I will withdraw. But if you perfift in your former
" oaths, let us fight together to fave our country, or
" let us perifh along with it." I appeal to the dividing powers, whether fo generous a ftep would not have
faved Poland from ruin, and its prince from the difgrace of having been its laft fovereign. But fate hath
determined the matter otherwife. May this crime of
ambition turn out to the advantage of mankind ; and
by prudently recurring to the found principles of good

policy, may the usurpers break the chains of the most B O O K laborious part of their new subjects! These people, XIX. become less unhappy, will be more intelligent, more active, more affectionate, and more faithful.

In a monarchy, the forces and wills of every individual are at the disposal of one single man; in the government of Germany, each separate state constitutes a body. This is, perhaps, the nation that resembles most what it formerly was. The ancient Germans, divided into colonies by immense forests, had no occasion for a very refined legislation. But in proportion as their descendants have multiplied and come nearer each other, art has kept up in this country what nature had established, the separation of the people and their political union. The small states that compose this confederate republic preserve the character of the first families. Each particular government is not always parental, or the rulers of the nations are not always mild and humane. But still reason and liberty, which unite the chiefs to each other, soften the severity of their dispositions and the rigour of their authority: a prince in Germany cannot be a tyrant with the same security as in large monarchies.

The Germans, who are rather warriors than a warlike people, because they are rather proficients in the art of war than addicted to it from inclination, have been conquered but once; and it was Charlemagne who conquered, but could not reduce them to subjection. They obeyed the man, who, by talents superior to the age he lived in, had subdued and enlightened its barbarism; but they shook off the yoke of his successors. They preserved, however, the title of emperor to their chief; but it was merely a name, since, in fact, the power resided almost entirely in the barons who possessed the lands. The people, who in all countries have unfortunately always been enslaved, spoiled, and kept in a state of misery and ignorance, each the effect of the other, reaped no advantage from the legislation. This subverted that social equality which does not tend to reduce all conditions and estates to

BOOK
XIX.
the fame degree, but to a more general diffufion of property; and upon its ruins was formed the feudal government, the characteriftic of which is anarchy. Every nobleman lived in a total independence, and each people under the moft abfolute tyranny. This was the unavoidable confequence of a government where the crown was elective. In thofe ftates where it was hereditary, the people had at leaft a bulwark and a permanent refuge againft oppreffion. The regal authority could not extend itfelf, without alleviating for fome time the fate of the vaffals, by diminifhing the power of the nobles.

But in Germany, where the nobles took advantage of each interregnum to invade and to reftrain the rights of the Imperial power, the government could not but degenerate. Superior force decided every difpute between thofe who could appeal to the fword. Countries and people were only the caufes or the objects of war between the proprietors. Crimes were the fupport of injuftice. Rapine, murder, and conflagrations, not only became frequent, but even lawful. Superftition, which had confecrated tyranny, was compelled to reftrain it. The church, which afforded an afylum to banditti of every kind, eftablifhed a truce between them. The protection of faints was implored to efcape the fury of the nobles. The afhes of the dead were only fufficient to awe the ferocioufnefs of thefe people; fo alarming are the terrors of the grave, even to men of cruel and favage difpofitions.

When the minds of men, kept in conftant alarm, were difpofed to tranquillity through fear, policy, which avails itfelf equally of reafon and the paffions, of ignorance and underftanding, to rule over mankind, attempted to reform the government. On the one hand, feveral inhabitants in the countries were enfranchifed; and on the other, exemptions were granted in favour of the cities. A number of men in all parts were made free. The emperors, who, to fecure their election even among ignorant and ferocious princes, were obliged to difcover fome abilities and

fome virtues, prepared the way for the improvement
of the legiflation.

Maximilian improved the means of happinefs which
time and particular events had concurred to produce
in his age. He put an end to the anarchy of the
great. In France and Spain, they had been made
fubject to regal authority ; in Germany, the emperors
made them fubmit to the authority of the laws. For
the fake of the public tranquillity, every prince is a-
menable to juftice. It is true, that thefe laws eftablifhed among princes, who may be confidered as
lions, do not fave the people, who may be compared
to lambs : they are ftill at the mercy of their rulers,
who are only bound one towards another. But as
public tranquillity cannot be violated, nor war commenced, without the prince who is the caufe of it being fubject to the penalties of a tribunal that is always
open, and fupported by all the forces of the empire,
the people are lefs expofed to thofe fudden irruptions,
and unforefeen hoftilities, which, threatening the property of the fovereigns, continually endangered the
lives and fafety of the fubjects.

Why fhould not Europe be one day entirely fubject
to the fame form of government ? Why fhould there
not be the ban of Europe, as there is the ban of the
empire ? Why fhould not the princes compofing fuch
a tribunal, the authority of which fhould be confented
to by all, and maintained unanimoufly againft any one
refractory member, realize the beautiful vifionary fyftem of the Abbé St. Pierre ? Why fhould not the
complaints of the fubjects be carried to this tribunal,
as well as the complaints of one fovereign againft another ? Then would wifdom reign upon the earth.

While this perpetual peace, which hath been fo long
wifhed for, and which is ftill at fuch a diftance, is expected, war, which formerly eftablifhed right, is now
fubject to conditions that moderate its fury. The
claims of humanity are heard even in the midft of carnage. Thus Europe is indebted to Germany for the
improvement of the legiflation in all ftates ; regulari-

ty and forms even in the revenge of nations; a certain
equity even in the abufe of power; moderation in the
midft of victory; a check to the ambition of all potentates; in a word, frefh obftacles to war, and frefh
encouragements to peace.

This happy conftitution of the German empire has
improved with the progrefs of reafon ever fince the
reign of Maximilian. Neverthelefs, the Germans themfelves complain, that, although they form a national
body, diftinguifhed by the fame name, fpeaking the
fame language, living under the fame chief, enjoying
the fame privileges, and connected by the fame interefts, yet their empire has not the advantage of that
tranquillity, that power and confideration, which it
ought to have.

The caufes of this misfortune are obvious. The firft
is the obfcurity of the laws. The writings upon the
jus publicum of Germany are numberlefs; and there
are but few Germans who are verfed in the conftitution of their country. All the members of the empire now fend their reprefentatives to the national affembly, whereas they formerly fat there themfelves.
The military turn, which is become univerfal, has pre-
cluded all application to bufinefs, fuppreffed every generous fentiment of patriotifm, and all attachment to
fellow-citizens. There is not one of the princes who
has not fettled his court too magnificently for his income, and who does not authorife the moft flagrant
oppreffions to fupport this ridiculous pomp. In fhort,
nothing contributes to the decay of the empire fo
much as the too extenfive dominion of fome of its
princes. The fovereigns, become too powerful, feparate their private intereft from the general good. This
reciprocal difunion among the ftates, is the reafon that,
in dangers which are common to all, each province is
left to itfelf. It is obliged to fubmit to that prince,
whoever he may be, whofe power is fuperior; and thus
the Germanic conftitution degenerates infenfibly into
flavery or tyranny.

Great Britain was but little known before the Romans had carried their arms there. After these proud B O O K conquerors had forsaken it, as well as the other pro- XIX. vinces distant from their dominion, in order to defend the centre of their empire against the barbarians, it became the prey of the inhabitants of the Baltic Sea. The natives of the country were massacred; and upon their remains several sovereignties were founded, which were in time united into one. The principles by which the Anglo-Saxons were guided have never been handed down to us; but we know, that, like all the northern nations, they had a king and a body of nobility.

William subdued the southern part of the island, which even at that time was called England, and established a feudal government in it, but very different from that which was seen in the rest of Europe. In other parts, government was nothing but a labyrinth without an issue, a perpetual anarchy, and the right of the strongest. This terrible conqueror established it upon a more respectable, a more regular, and a more permanent footing, referving to himself exclusively the right of hunting and of war, the power of levying taxes, the advantage of having a court of justice, where civil or criminal causes of all the orders of the state were ultimately adjudged by him and by the great officers of his crown, whom he appointed or dismissed at pleasure.

As long as the tyrant lived, the conquered people, and the foreigners whom he had employed to subdue them, submitted to this harsh yoke, as it were, almost unanimously, and without murmuring openly. Afterwards, both the one and the other, being accustomed to a more moderate authority, endeavoured to recover some of their primitive rights. Despotism was so firmly established, as to render it impossible to subvert it, without the most complete unanimity. Accordingly, a league was formed, in which all the citizens without distinction, either of noblemen or of peasants, of inhabitants of towns or of the country, united their resentments and their interests. This universal confederacy

B O O K foftened a little the deftiny of the nation under the
XIX. reigns of the two firft Henrys ; but it was not till during that of John that it truly recovered its liberty.
Fortunately this turbulent, cruel, ignorant, and diffipated monarch, was compelled, by force of arms, to
grant that famous charter, which abolifhed the moft
oppreffive of the feudal laws, and fecured to the vaffals, refpecting their lords, the fame rights as were
confirmed to the lords in regard to kings ; which put
all perfons, and every fpecies of property, under the
protection of peers and of juries, and which, even in
favour of the vaffals, diminifhed the oppreffion of
flavery.

This arrangement fufpended for a fhort time the
jealoufy fubfifting between the barons and the princes,
without extinguifhing entirely the fource of it.   The
wars began again, and the people availed themfelves
of the idea they had given of their ftrength and courage during thefe commotions, in order to gain ad-
miffion into parliament under Edward I.   Their deputies, it is true, had at firft no more than the rights
of reprefentation in this affembly ; but this fuccefs
was the prelude to other advantages, and accordingly
the commons foon determined the fubfidies, and made
part of the legiflation ; they even foon acquired the
prerogative of impeaching and bringing to judgment
thofe minifters who had abufed the authority they were
intrufted with.

The nation had gradually reduced the power of the
chiefs to what it ought to be, when it became engaged in long and obftinate wars againft France, and
when the pretenfions of the Houfes of York and Lancafter made all England a fcene of carnage and of
defolation.   During thefe dreadful commotions the
din of arms alone was heard.   The laws were filent,
and they did not even recover the leaft part of their
force when the ftorms were appeafed.   Tyranny was
exerted with fo many atrocious acts, that citizens of
all ranks gave up every idea of general liberty in order to attend only to their perfonal fafety.   This cruel

despotism lasted more than a century. Elizabeth herself, whose administration might, in several respects,
serve as a model, always conducted herself according
to principles entirely arbitrary.

James I. apparently recalled to the minds of the
people those rights which they seemed to have forgotten ; less wise than his predecessors, who had contented themselves with tacitly enjoying unlimited power, and, as it were, under the veil of mystery, this
prince, deceived by the name of monarchy, encouraged in his illusion by his courtiers and his clergy,
openly avowed his pretensions with a degree of blind
simplicity, of which there had been no example. The
doctrine of passive obedience, issued from the throne,
and taught in the churches, diffused universal alarm.

At this period, liberty, that idol of elevated minds,
which renders them ferocious in a savage state and
haughty in a civilized one, liberty, which had reigned in the breasts of the English at a time even when
they were but imperfectly acquainted with its advantages, inflamed the minds of all men. In the reign
of this first of the Stuarts, however, it was only a perpetual struggle between the prerogatives of the crown
and the privileges of the citizens. Opposition appeared under another aspect in the reign of the obstinate
successor of this weak despot. Arms became the sole
arbiter of these great concerns, and the nation show-
ed, that in combating formerly for the choice of their
tyrants, they had paved the way for destroying them,
punishing, and expelling them at another time.

To put an end to the spirit of revenge and mistrust,
which would have been perpetuated between the king
and the people as long as the Stuarts had occupied
the throne, the English chose from a foreign race, a
prince who was obliged to accept at last of that social compact of which all hereditary monarchs affect
to be ignorant. William III. received the crown on
certain conditions, and contented himself with an authority established upon the same basis as the rights of
the people. Since a parliamentary claim is become

the fole foundation of royalty, the conventions have
not been infringed.

The government is formed between abfolute monarchy, which is tyranny; democracy, which tends
to anarchy; and ariftocracy, which, fluctuating between one and the other, falls into the errors of both.
The mixt government of the Englifh, combining the
advantages of thefe three powers, which mutually obferve, moderate, affift, and check each other, tends
from its very principles to the national good. Thefe
feveral fprings, by their action and reaction, form an
equilibrium from which liberty arifes. This conftitution, of which there is no inftance among the ancients, and which ought to ferve as a model to all
people, whofe geographical pofition will admit of it,
will laft for a long time, becaufe at its origin, which
is ufually the work of commotions, of manners, and
of tranfient opinions, it became the work of reafon
and experience.

The firft fortunate fingularity in the conftitution of
Great Britain, is to have a king. Moft of the republican ftates known in hiftory, had formerly annual
chiefs. This continual change of magiftrates proved
an inexhauftible fource of intrigues and confufion,
and kept up a continual commotion in the minds of
men. By creating one very great citizen England
hath prevented the rifing up of many. By this ftroke
of wifdom thofe diffenfions have been prevented, which
in all popular affociations have induced the ruin of liberty, and the real enjoyment of this firft of bleffings
before it had been loft.

The royal authority in England is not only for life,
but is alfo hereditary. At firft fight, nothing appears
more advantageous for a nation than the right of
choofing its mafters. An inexhauftible fource of talents and virtues feems to fpring from this brilliant prerogative. This would indeed be the cafe, if the crown
were neceffarily to devolve to the citizen moft worthy
to wear it. But this is a chimerical idea, difproved by
the experience of all people and of all ages. A throne

hath always appeared to the eyes of ambition, of too
great a value to be the appurtenance of merit alone.
Thofe who afpire to it have always had recourfe to intrigue, to corruption and to force. Their competition hath excited at every vacancy a civil war, the
greateft of political calamities, and the perfon who hath
obtained the preference over his competitors, hath
been nothing more during the courfe of his reign but
the tyrant of the people, or the flave of thofe to whom
he owed his elevation. The Britons are therefore to
be commended for having averted from themfelves
thefe calamities, by putting the reins of government
into the hands of a family that had merited and obtained their confidence.

It was proper to fecure to the chief of the ftate a
revenue fufficient to fupport the dignity of his rank.
Accordingly, at his acceffion to the throne, an annual
fubfidy is granted to him for his own life, fit for a
great king, and worthy of an opulent nation. But
this conceffion is not to be made till after a ftrick
examination of the ftate of public affairs; after the
abufes which might have introduced themfelves in
preceding reigns have been reformed, and after the
conftitution hath been brought back to its true principles. By this management England hath obtained
an advantage which all free governments had endeavoured to procure to themfelves, that is to fay, a periodical reformation.

To affign to the monarch that kind of authority
beft calculated for the good of the people, was not
fo eafy a matter. All hiftories atteft, that wherever
the executive power hath been divided, the minds of
men have always been agitated with endlefs hatred
and jealoufies, and that a fanguinary conteft hath always tended to the ruin of the laws and to the eftablifhment of the ftrongeft power. This confideration
determined the Englifh to confer on the king alone
this fpecies of power, which is nothing when it is divided; fince there is then neither that harmony, nor

BOOK
XIX.

that fecrecy, nor that difpatch, which can alone impart energy to it.

From this great prerogative neceffarily follows the
difpofal of the forces of the republic. The abufes of
them would have been difficult in times when the militia were but feldom affembled, and only for a few
months, and when therefore they had no time to lofe
that attachment they owed to their country. But
fince all the princes of Europe have contracted the
ruinous habit of maintaining, even in time of peace,
a ftanding army of mercenary troops, and fince the
fafety of Great Britain hath required that fhe fhould
conform to this fatal cuftom, the danger is become
greater, and it has been neceffary to increafe the precautions. The nation alone hath the power of affembling the troops ; fhe never fettles them for more than
a year, and the taxes eftablifhed for the payment of
them have only the fame duration. So that if this
mode of defence, which circumftances have induced
to think neceffary, fhould threaten liberty, it would
never be long before the troubles would be put an end
to.

A ftill firmer fupport to the Englifh liberty, is the
divifion of the legiflative power. Whereyer the monarch can eftablifh or abolifh laws at pleafure there is
no government ; the prince is a defpot, and the people are flaves. If the legiflative power be divided, a
well-regulated conftitution will fcarce ever be corrupted, and that only for a fhort time. From the fear of
being fufpected of ignorance or corruption, neither of
the parties would venture to make dangerous propofals,
and if either of them fhould, it would difgrace itfelf to
no purpofe. In this arrangement of things, the greateft inconvenience that can happen, is that a good law
fhould be rejected, or that it fhould not be adopted fo
foon as the greateft poffible good might require. The
portion of the legiflative power which the people have
recovered, is infured to them by the exclufive regulation they have of the taxes. Every ftate hath both cuf-
tomary and contingent wants. Neither the one nor the

other can be provided for any otherwife than by taxes, B O O K
and in Great Britain the fovereign cannot exact one. XIX.
He can only addrefs himfelf to the Commons, who
order what they think moft fuitable to the national intereft, and who, after having regulated the taxes, have
an account given to them of the ufe they have been
put to.

It is not the multitude who exercife thefe ineftimable prerogatives, which their courage and their perfeverance have procured to them. This order of things,
which may be proper for feeble affociations, would neceffarily have fubverted every thing in a great ftate.
Reprefentatives, chofen by the people themfelves, and
whofe deftiny is connected with theirs, reflect, fpeak,
and act for them. As it was poffible, however, that,
either from indolence, weaknefs, or corruption, thefe
reprefentatives might fail in the moft auguft and the
moft important of duties, the remedy of this great
evil hath been found in the right of election. As foon
as the time of the commiffion expires, the electors are
affembled. They grant their confidence again to thofe
who have fhown themfelves worthy of it, and they reject with difdain thofe who have betrayed it. As a
difcernment of this kind is not above the abilities of
common men, becaufe it depends upon facts, which
are ufually very fimple, thofe diforders are thus terminated which did not derive their fource from the effects of government, but from the particular difpofitions of thofe who directed its operations.

Neverthelefs, there might refult from this divifion of
power between the king and the people a continual
ftruggle, which, in procefs of time, might have brought
on either a republic or flavery. To prevent this inconvenience, an intermediate body hath been eftablifhed, which muft be equally apprehenfive of both thefe
revolutions. This is the order of the nobility, deftined to lean to the fide which might become the weak-
eft, and thus ever to maintain the equilibrium. The
conftitution, indeed, hath not given them the fame
degree of authority as to the Commons; but the fplen-

B O O K dour of hereditary dignity, the privileges of a seat in
XIX. the House of Peers, belonging to themselves and without election, together with some other prerogatives of
honour, have been contrived to substitute as much as
possible to what they wanted in real strength.

But if, notwithstanding so many precautions, it should
at length happen, that some ambitious and enterprising
monarch should wish to reign without his parliament,
or to compel them to agree to his arbitrary decisions,
the only resource remaining to the nation would be
resistance.

It was upon a system of passive obedience, of divine right, and of power not to be dissolved, that the
regal authority was formerly supported. These absurd and fatal prejudices had subdued all Europe,
when, in 1688, the English precipitated from the
throne a superstitious, persecuting, and despotic prince.
Then it was understood, that the people did not belong to their chiefs; then the necessity of an equitable government among mankind was incontestibly
established; then were the foundations of societies
settled; then the legitimate right of defence, the last
resource of nations that are oppressed, was incontro-
vertibly fixed. At this memorable period, the doctrine of resistance, which had till then been only one
act of violence opposed to other acts of violence, was
avowed in England by the law itself.

But how is it possible to render this great principle
useful and efficient? Will a single citizen, left to his
own strength, ever venture to strive against the power,
always formidable, of those who govern? Will he not
necessarily be crushed by their intrigues, or by their
oppression? This would undoubtedly be the case, were
it not for the indefinite liberty of the press. By this
fortunate expedient, the actions of the depositaries of
authority become public. Any vexations or outrages
that have been committed over the most obscure individual, are soon brought to light. His cause becomes the cause of all; and the oppressors are punished, or satisfaction is only offered for the injury, accord-

ing to the nature of the offence, or the difpofition of the people.

This defcription of the Britifh Conftitution, made without art, muft have convinced all perfons of a proper way of thinking, that there hath never been a conftitution fo well regulated upon the face of the globe. We fhall be confirmed in this opinion, when we confider that the moft important affairs have always been publicly canvaffed in the fenate of the nation, without any real mifchief having ever refulted from it. Other powers think they ftand in need of the veil of myftery, to cover their operations. Secrecy appears to them effential to their prefervation, or to their profperity. They endeavour to conceal their fituation, their projects, and their alliancies, from their enemies, from their rivals, and even from their friends. The quality of being impenetrable, is the greateft praife they think they can beftow upon a ftatefman. In England, the internal, as well as external, proceedings of government, are all open, all expofed to the face of day. How noble and confident it is, in a nation, to admit the univerfe to its deliberations! How honeft, and advantageous it is, to admit all the citizens to them! Never hath Europe been told, in a more energetic manner: *We do not fear thee.* Never hath it been faid, with more confidence and juftice, to any nation: *Try us, and fee whether we be not faithful depofitaries of your interefts, of your glory, and of your happinefs.* The empire is conftituted with fufficient ftrength, to refift the fhocks which are infeparable from fuch a cuftom, and to give this advantage to neighbours who may not be favourably inclined.

But is this government a perfect one? Certainly not; becaufe there is not, neither can there be, any thing perfect in this world. In a matter fo complicated, how is it poffible to forefee and to obviate every thing? Perhaps, in order that the chief of the nation fhould be as dependent upon the will of the people, as would be fuitable to their fecurity, liberty, and happinefs, it

B O O K would be neceffary that this chief fhould have no
XIX. property out of his kingdom. Otherwife the good
of one country happening to clafh with that of the
other, the interefts of the precarious fovereignty will
often be facrificed to thofe of the hereditary fovereignty; otherwife, the enemies of the ftate will have
two powerful means of molefting it; fometimes by
intimidating the king of Great Britain, by threats addreffed to the elector of Hanover; fometimes by engaging the king in fatal wars, which they will prolong
at pleafure; fometimes by compelling the elector to
put an end to thefe hoftilities by a fhameful peace.
Will the nation meanly abandon the king in quarrels
that are foreign to them? and if they fhould interfere,
will it not be at their expence, at the lofs of their revenues and of their population? Who knows whether
the danger of the foreign fovereign will not render
him bafe, and even treacherous, to the national fovereign? In this cafe, the Britifh nation could do nothing better than to fay to their fovereign : *Either refign your fovereignty or your electorate ; abdicate the dominions you hold from your anceftors, if you mean to keep
thofe you hold from us.*

A conftitution, in which the legiflative and executive power are feparate, bears within itfelf the feeds of
perpetual conteft. It is impoffible that peace fhould
reign between two oppofite political bodies. Prerogative muft endeavour to extend itfelf, and prefs upon
liberty, and *vice verfa*.

Whatever admiration we may have for a government, if it can only preferve itfelf by the fame means
by which it had been eftablifhed; if its future hiftory
muft exhibit the fame fcenes as the paft, fuch as rebellion, civil wars, deftruction of the people, the affaffination or expulfion of kings, a ftate of perpetual
alarms and commotions, who would wifh for a government upon fuch conditions? If peace, both within and without, be the object of adminiftration, what
fhall we think of an order of things that is incompatible with it?

Would it not be to be wished, that the number of representatives should be proportioned to the value of property, and to the exact ratio of patriotism? Is it not absurd that a poor hamlet, or a wretched village, should depute as many or more members to the assembly of the Commons, as the most opulent city or district? What interest can these men take in the public felicity, which they scarce partake of? What facility will not bad ministers find in their indigence to bribe them; and to obtain, by money, that majority they stand in need of. O, shame! The rich man purchases the suffrages of his constituents, to obtain the honour of representing them; and the court buys the vote of the representative, in order to govern with more despotic sway. Would not a prudent nation endeavour to prevent both the one and the other of these corruptions? Is it not surprising that this hath not been done upon the day, when a representative had the impudence to make his constituents wait in his antichamber, and afterwards to say to them: *I know not what you want, but I will only act as I think proper; I have bought you very dear, and I am resolved to sell you as dear as I can:* Or even upon that day, when the minister boasted of having in his pocket-book the rates of every man's probity in England?

Is there nothing to object against the effort of these three powers, acting perpetually one upon the other, and tending incessantly to an equilibrium which they will never obtain? This struggle, is it not somewhat similar to a continual anarchy? Doth it not endanger commotions, in which, from one moment to another, the blood of the citizens may be spilt, without our being able to foresee whether the advantage will remain on the side of tyranny or on that of liberty? And if all circumstances be well weighed, would not a nation less independent and more quiet be happy?

These defects, and others added to them, will they not one day bring on the decline of the government? This is a circumstance we cannot decide; but we are

BOOK
XIX.

convinced it would be a great misfortune for the nations, since they all owe to it a milder destiny than that which they before enjoyed. The example of a free, rich, magnanimous, and happy people, in the midst of Europe, hath engaged the attention of all men. The principles from which many benefits have been derived, have been adopted, discussed, and presented to the monarchs, and to their delegates; who, to avoid being accused of tyranny, have been obliged to adopt them, with more or less modification. The ancient maxims would soon be revived, if there did not exist, as it were, in the midst of us, a perpetual tribunal, which demonstrated the depravity and absurdity of them.

But, if the enjoyments of luxury should happen totally to pervert the morals of the nation; if the love of pleasure should soften the courage of the commanders and officers of the fleets and armies; if the intoxication of temporary successes, if vain ideas of false greatness, should excite the nation to enterprises above their strength; if they should be deceived in the choice of their enemies, or their allies; if they should lose their colonies, either by making them too extensive, or by laying restraints upon them; if their love of patriotism be not exalted to the love of humanity; they will, sooner or later, be enslaved, and return to that kind of insignificancy from whence they emerged only through torrents of blood, and through the calamities of two ages of fanaticism and war. They will become like other nations whom they despise, and Europe will not be able to show the universe one nation in which she can venture to pride herself. Despotism, which always oppresses most heavily minds that are subdued and degraded, will alone rise superior, amidst the ruin of arts, of morals, of reason, and of liberty.

The history of the United Provinces is replete with very singular events. Their combination arose from despair, and almost all Europe encouraged their establishment. They had but just triumphed over the long and powerful efforts of the court of Spain to reduce them to fubjection, when they were obliged to try their ftrength againft the Britons, and difconcerted the fchemes of France. They afterwards gave a king to England, and deprived Spain of the provinces fhe pof-feffed in Italy and the Low Countries, to give them to Auftria. Since that period, Holland has been difguft-ed of fuch a fyftem of politics, as would engage her in war; fhe attends folely to the prefervation of her con-ftitution, but, perhaps, not with fufficient zeal, care, and integrity.

The conftitution of Holland, though previoufly mo-delled on a plan that was the refult of reflection, is not lefs defective than thofe which have been formed by chance. One of its principal defects is, that the fove-reignty is too much divided.

It is a miftake to fuppofe that the authority refides in the States General fixed at the Hague. The fact is, that the power of the members who compofe this af-fembly confifts only in deciding upon matters of form, or police. In alliances, peace, war, new taxes, or any other important matter, each of the deputies muft re-ceive the orders of his province; which is itfelf obli-ged to obtain the confent of the cities. The confe-quence of this complicated order of things is, that the refolutions, which would require the greateft fecrecy and celerity, are neceffarily tardy and public.

It feems, that in an union contracted between this number of ftates, independent of each other, and con-nected only by their common intereft, each of them ought to have had an influence proportioned to its ex-tent, to its population, and to its riches: but this for-tunate bafis, which enlightened reafon ought to have founded, is not adopted by the confederate body. The province which bears more than half of the pub-lic expences hath no more votes than that which con-tributes only one hundredth part of them; and in that province, a petty town, uninhabited and unknown, hath legally the fame weight as this unparalleled city,

the activity and industry of which are a subject of astonishment and of jealousy to all nations.

The unanimity of the towns and provinces, which
is required for all important resolutions, is not a measure of more judicious policy. If the most considerable members of the republic should resolve to act
without the concurrence of the less important branches,
this would be a manifest infringement of the principles
of the union; and if they should lay a great stress upon obtaining their suffrages, they will not succeed without much solicitation or concessions. Whichever of
these two expedients have been adopted, when the
parties have differed, the harmony of the United States
hath usually been disturbed, and frequently in a violent and permanent manner.

The imperfections of such a constitution did not, in
all probability, escape the Prince of Orange, the founder of this republic. If this great man permitted that
they should serve as a basis to the government which
was establishing, it was undoubtedly in hopes that they
would render the election of a Stadtholder necessary,
and that this supreme magistrate would always be
chosen in his family. This view of a profound ambition hath not always been attended with success; and
this singular magistracy, which united to the absolute
disposal of the land and sea forces several other important prerogatives, hath been twice abolished.

At these periods, which are remarkable in the history of a state, unparalleled in the annals of the Old and
of the New World, great changes have been produced. The authors of the revolution have boldly divided all the authority among themselves. An intolerable tyranny hath been everywhere established, with
more or less effrontery. Under pretence that the general assemblies were tumultuous, fatiguing, and dangerous, the people have no longer been called in to
elect the depositaries of the public authority. The
burgomasters have chosen their sheriffs, and have seized upon the finances, of which they gave no account,
but to their equals or constituents. The senators have

arrogated to themfelves the right of completing their own body. Thus the magiftracy hath been confined to a few families, who have affumed an almoft exclufive right of deputation to the States General. Each province and each town have been at the difpofal of a fmall number of citizens, who, dividing the rights and the fpoils of the people, have had the art of eluding their complaints, or of preventing the effects of any extraordinary difcontent. The government is become almoft ariftocratic. Had the reformation been extended only to what was defective in the conftitution, the Houfe of Orange might have apprehended that they fhould no more be reinftated in that degree of fplendour from which they had fallen. A lefs difinterefted conduct hath occafioned the reftoration of the ftadtholderfhip; and it hath been made hereditary, even in the female line.

But will this dignity become in time an inftrument of oppreffion? Enlightened men do not think it poffible. Rome, fay they, is always quoted as an example to all our free ftates, that have no circumftance in common with it. If the dictator became the oppreffor of that republic, it was in confequence of its having oppreffed all other nations; it was becaufe its power, having been originally founded by war, muft neceffarily be deftroyed by it; and becaufe a nation compofed of foldiers could not efcape the defpotifm of a military government. However improbable it may appear, it is yet certain, that the Roman republic fubmitted to the yoke, becaufe it paid no taxes. The conquered people were the only tributaries to the treafury. The public revenues, therefore, neceffarily remaining the fame after the revolution as before, property did not appear to be attacked; and the citizen thought he fhould be ftill free enough, while he had the difpofal of his own.

Holland, on the contrary, will maintain its liberty, becaufe it is fubject to very confiderable taxes. The Dutch cannot preferve their country without great expences. The fenfe of their independence alone excites

an induſtry proportionable to the load of their contributions, and to the patience neceſſary to ſupport the
burden of them. If to the enormous expences of the
ſtate it were neceſſary to add thoſe which the pomp of
a court requires; if the prince were to employ in maintaining the agents of tyranny what ought to be be-
ſtowed on the foundations of a land obtained, as it
were, from the ſea, he would ſoon drive the people to
deſpair.

The inhabitant of Holland, placed upon a mountain, and who obſerves at a diſtance the ſea riſing eighteen or twenty feet above the level of the lands, and
daſhing its waves againſt the dykes he has raiſed, con-
ſiders within himſelf, that ſooner or later this boiſterous
element will get the better of him. He diſdains ſo
precarious a dwelling; and his houſe, made either of
wood or ſtone at Amſterdam, is no longer looked upon
as ſuch: it is his ſhip that is his aſylum; and by degrees he acquires an indifference and manners conformable to this idea. The water is to him what the vici-
nity of volcanos is to other people.

If to theſe natural cauſes of the decay of a patriotic
ſpirit were joined the loſs of liberty, the Dutch would
quit a country that cannot be cultivated but by men
who are free; and theſe people, ſo devoted to trade,
would carry their ſpirit of commerce, together with
their riches, to ſome other part of the globe. Their
iſlands in Aſia, their factories in Africa, their colonies
in America, and all the ports in Europe, would afford
them an aſylum. What ſtadtholder, what prince, revered by ſuch a people, would wiſh, or dare, to become
their tyrant?

A ſenſeleſs, ambitious man, or a ferocious warrior,
might poſſibly attempt it. But among thoſe who are
deſtined to govern the nation, are ſuch men rarely to
be found. Every thing ſeems to conſpire in exciting
the greateſt apprehenſions in the republic upon this
important point. There are ſcarce any natives on
board their fleets, except a few officers. Their armies
are compoſed of, recruited, and commanded by fo-

reigners, devoted to a chief, who, according to their ideas, can never arm them againſt people to whom they are attached by no tie. The fortreſſes of the ſtate are all governed by generals who acknowledge no other laws beſide thoſe of the prince. Courtiers degraded in their characters, overwhelmed with debts, deſtitute of virtue, and intereſted in the ſubverſion of the eſtabliſhed order, are perpetually raiſed to the moſt important poſts. It is by favour, that a ſet of commanders, devoid of ſhame and of ability, have been placed, and are maintained in the colonies; men who, either from motives of gratitude or of cupidity, are inclined to accompliſh the ſlavery of thoſe diſtant regions.

Againſt ſo many dangers, of what avail can be the general lethargy, the thirſt of riches, the taſte for luxury, which begins to inſinuate itſelf, the ſpirit of trade, and the perpetual condeſcenſions ſhown for an hereditary authority? According to every probability, the United Provinces, without effuſion of blood, and without commotion, muſt inſenſibly fall under the yoke of a monarchy. As the ſpirit of deſpotiſm, or the deſire of meeting with no oppoſition to our wiſhes, is inherent in the mind of every man in a greater or leſs degree, ſome ſtadtholder may ariſe, and perhaps ſoon, who, regardleſs of the fatal conſequences of his enterpriſe, will enſlave the nation. It concerns the Dutch attentively to conſider theſe obſervations.

The Roman empire was ſhaking on all ſides, when the Germans entered into Gaul, under the guidance of a chief whom they had choſen themſelves, and to whom they were rather companions than ſubjects. This was not an army, the ambition of which was limited to the ſeizing of ſome fortified places; it was the irruption of a people in ſearch of a ſettlement. As they attacked none but ſlaves, diſſatisfied with their fate, or maſters enervated by the luxuries of a long peace, they met with no very obſtinate reſiſtance. The conquerors appropriated to themſelves the lands which fuited them, and feparated foon after, in order to enjoy their fortune in peace.

The divifion was not the work of blind chance. The poffeffions were fettled by the general affembly, and they were enjoyed under its authority. They were granted at firft for no more than one year; but this period was gradually prolonged, and was at laft extended to the life of the poffeffor. Matters were carried ftill further, when the fprings of government became entirely relaxed; and under the feeble defcendants of Charlemagne, hereditary poffeffion was almoft generally eftablifhed. This ufurpation was confecrated by a folemn convention, at the acceffion of Hugo Capet to the throne; and at that period the feudal tenure, that moft deftructive of all rights, prevailed in all its force.

France was then no more than an affemblage of petty fovereignties, fituated near each other, but without having any connection. In this ftate of anarchy, the lords, entirely independent of the apparent chief of the nation, oppreffed their fubjects, or their flaves, at pleafure. If the monarch interefted himfelf in the fate of thefe unhappy people, they declared war againft him; and if thefe people themfelves fometimes ventured to appeal to the rights of mankind, the confequence was, that the chains with which they were crufhed became ftill more oppreffive.

In the meanwhile, the extinction of fome powerful houfes, together with various treaties and conquefts, were fucceffively adding to the royal domain territories of greater or lefs extent. This acquifition of feveral provinces gave to the crown a mafs of power, which imparted to it fome degree of energy. A perpetual conteft between the kings and the nobles, an alternate fuperiority of the power of one fingle perfon, or of feveral; fuch was the kind of anarchy that lafted, almoft without interruption, till about the middle of the fifteenth century.

The character of the French was then changed by

a train of events which had altered the form of go- vernment. The war which the Englifh, in conjunction with, or under the direction of, the Normans, had inceffantly carried on againft France for two or three hundred years paft, fpread a general alarm, and occafioned great ravages. The triumphs of the enemy, the tyranny of the great, all confpired to make the nation wifh that the prince might be invefted with power fufficient to expel foreigners out of the kingdom, and to keep the nobles in fubjection. While princes, diftinguifhed by their wifdom and bravery, were endeavouring to accomplifh this great work, a new generation arofe. Every individual, when the general alarm was paft, thought himfelf happy enough in the privileges his anceftors had enjoyed. They neglected to trace the fource of the power of kings, which was derived from the nation; and Lewis XI. having few obftacles to furmount, became more powerful than his predeceffors.

Before his time, the hiftory of France prefents us with an account of a variety of ftates, fometimes divided and fometimes united. Since that prince's reign, it is the hiftory of a great monarchy. The power of feveral tyrants is centered in one perfon. The people are not more free; but the conftitution is different. Peace is enjoyed with greater fecurity within, and war carried on with more vigour without.

Civil wars, which tend to make a free people become flaves, and to reftore liberty to a nation that is already enflaved, have had no other effect in France than that of humbling the great, without exalting the people. The minifters, who will always be the creatures of the prince, while the general fenfe of the nation has no influence in affairs of government, have fold their fellow-citizens to their mafter; and as the people, who were poffeffed of nothing, could not be lofers by this fervitude, the kings have found it the more eafy to carry their defigns into execution, efpecially as they were always concealed under pretence of political advantage, and even of alleviating the burden of the people. The jealoufy excited by a great inequality of conditions and fortunes, hath favoured every fcheme that tended to aggrandize the regal authority. The princes have had the art to engage the attention of the people, fometimes by wars abroad, fometimes by religious difputes at home ; to fuffer the minds of men to be divided by opinions, and their hearts by different interefts ; to excite and keep up jealoufies between the feveral ranks of the ftate ; to flatter alternately each party with an appearance of favour, and to fatisfy the natural envy of the people by the depreffion of them all. The multitude, reduced to poverty, and become the objects of contempt, having feen all-powerful bodies brought low one after another, have at leaft loved in their monarch the enemy of their enemies.

The nation, though by inadvertency it has loft the privilege of governing itfelf, has not, however, fubmitted to all the outrages of defpotifm. This arifes from the lofs of its liberty not having been the effect of a tumultuous and fudden revolution, but gradually brought about in a fucceffion of feveral ages. The national character which hath always influenced the princes as well as the court, if it were only by means of the women, hath eftablifhed a fort of balance of power ; and thus it is that polite manners having tempered the exertion of force, and foftened the oppofition that might be made to it, have prevented thofe fudden and violent commotions, from whence refults either monarchical tyranny or popular liberty.

Inconfiftence, as natural to the minds of a gay and lively people as it is to children, hath fortunately prevailed over the fyftems of fome defpotic minifters. Kings have been too fond of pleafure, and too converfant with the real fource of it, not to be induced frequently to lay afide the iron fceptre, which would have terrified the people, and prevented them from indulging in thofe frivolous amufements to which they were addicted. The fpirit of intrigue, which hath ever prevailed among them, fince the nobles have been invited to court, hath occafioned continual removals of ftatefmen, and confequently fubverted all their pro-jects. As the change in government has been imperceptibly brought about, the fubjects have preferved a kind of dignity, which the monarch himfelf feemed to refpect, confidering it as the fource or confequence of his own. He has continued the fupreme legiflator for a long time, without being either willing or able to abufe his whole power. Kept in awe by the bare idea only of the fundamental laws of the nation he governed, he has frequently been afraid to act contrary to the principles of them. He has been fenfible that the people had right to oppofe to him. In a word, there has been no tyrant, even at a time when there was no liberty.

Such, and ftill more arbitrary, have been the governments of Spain and Portugal, of Naples and Piedmont, and of the feveral fmall principalities of Italy. The people of the fouth, whether from inactivity of mind or weaknefs of body, feem to be born for defpotifm. The Spaniards, though they are extremely proud, and the Italians, notwithftanding all the powers of genius they poffefs, have loft all their rights, and every idea of liberty. Wherever the monarchy is unlimited, it is impoffible to afcertain, with any degree of precifion, what the form of government is, fince that varies, not only with the character of each fovereign, but even at every period of the fame prince's life. Thefe ftates have written laws and cuftoms, and focieties that enjoy certain privileges; but when the legiflator can fubvert the laws and tribunals of juftice; when his authority is founded only on fuperior ftrength, and when he calls upon God with a view to infpire his fubjects with fear, inftead of imitating him in order to become an object of affection; when the original right of fociety, the unalienable right of property among citizens, when national conventions and the engagements of the prince are in vain appealed to; in a word, when the government is arbitrary, there

B O O K is no longer any ftate; the nation is no more than the
XIX. landed property of one fingle individual.

In fuch countries, no ftatefmen will ever be formed.
Far from its being a duty to be acquainted with public affairs, it is rather criminal and dangerous to have
any knowledge of the adminiftration. The favour of
the court, the choice of the prince, fupply the place
of talents. Talents, it is true, have their ufe ; and are
fometimes of ufe to ferve the defigns of others, but never to command. In thefe countries, the people fubmit to the government their fuperiors impofe, provided only they are indulged in their natural indolence.
There is only one fyftem of legiflation in thefe delightful regions of Europe that merits our attention, which
is the republic of Venice. Three great phenomena
make this ftate remarkable ; thefe are, its firft foundation, its power at the time of the crufades, and its prefent form of adminiftration.

A great, magnificent, and rich city, impregnable,
though without walls or fortifications, rules over fe-
venty-two iflands. They are not rocks and mountains raifed by time in the midft of a vaft fea, but rather a plain, parcelled out and cut into channels by
the ftagnations of a fmall gulf, upon the flope of a low
land. Thefe iflands, feparated by canals, are at prefent joined by bridges. They have been formed by
the ravages of the fea, and the ravages of war have
occafioned them to be peopled towards the middle of
the fifth century. The inhabitants of Italy, flying
from Attila, fought an afylum on the fea.

The Venetian Lagunes at firft neither made a part
of the fame city, nor of the fame republic. United
by one general commercial intereft, or rather by the
neceffity of defending themfelves, they were, however,
divided into as many feparate governments as iflands,
each fubjed to its refpective tribune.

From the plurality of chiefs contentions arofe, and
the public good was confequently facrificed. Thefe
people, therefore, in order to conftitute one body,

chose a prince, who, under the title of Duke or Doge, enjoyed for a confiderable time all the rights of fo-vereignty, of which he only now retains the figns. Thefe Doges were elected by the people till 1173 : at that period the nobles arrogated to themfelves the ex-clufive privilege of appointing the chief of the repub-lic ; they feized upon the authority, and formed an ariftocracy.

Thofe political writers who have given the prefe-rence to this kind of government, have faid, with fome fhow of reafon, that all focieties, in whatever way they may have been formed, have been governed in this manner. If in democratic ftates the people were to fettle their adminiftration themfelves, they would ne-ceffarily fall into extravagances ; and they are there-fore obliged, for their own prefervation, to fubmit to a fenate, more or lefs numerous. If in monarchies kings pretended to fee every thing with their own eyes, and to do every thing themfelves, nothing would either be feen or done ; and it hath therefore been ne-ceffary to have recourfe to councils, to preferve em-pires from a ftagnation, more fatal, perhaps, than a ftate of action ill conducted. Every thing, therefore, may be traced to the authority of many, and of a fmall number ; every thing is conducted according to the principles of ariftocracy.

But in the monarchical form of government, com-mand is not fettled in one clafs of citizens, and obedi-ence in the reft ; the road to honours and to employ-ments is open to every one who hath the neceffary ta-lents to obtain them ; the nobles are not every thing, and the people nothing. Subftitute ariftocracy to this form of government, and we fhall find nothing but flavery and defpotifm.

Venice, in its origin, tempered as much as poffible the defects of this odious and unjuft government. The feveral branches of power were diftributed and balan-ced with remarkable accuracy. Prudent and fevere laws were enacted, to fupprefs and ftrike awe into the ambition of the nobles. The great reigned without diſturbance, and with a kind of equality, as the ſtars ſhine in the firmament amidſt the ſilence of the night. They were obliged outwardly to conform to the cuſtoms of the ſeveral orders of the republic, in order that the diſtinction between patricians and plebeians might become leſs odious. The hope even of ſharing, in proceſs of time, the rights of ſovereignty, was extended to thoſe who from rank were excluded from it, if by their ſervices and their induſtry they ſhould one day acquire conſideration and riches.

This was the only regular form of government then exiſting in Europe. Such an advantage raiſed the Venetians to great opulence, enabled them to keep armies in their pay, and imparted to them that knowledge which made them a political people, before any of the reſt were. They reigned over the ſeas ; they had a manifeſt preponderance in the continent ; they formed or diſſipated leagues, according as it ſuited their intereſt.

When the commerce of the republic was ruined by the diſcovery of the New World, and of the paſſage to India by the Cape of Good Hope, it was deprived of every advantage which had given it grandeur, ſtrength, and courage. To thoſe illuſions, which in ſome meaſure conſole the ſubjects for the loſs of their liberty, were ſubſtituted the ſeduction of voluptuouſneſs, pleaſures, and effeminacy. The great grew corrupt as well as the people, the women as well as the men, the prieſts as well as the laymen, and licentiouſneſs knew no bounds. Venice became the country upon the earth where there were fewer factitious vices and virtues.

In proportion as the minds, the diſpoſitions, and the power of man became enervated within, it was a neceſſary conſequence that leſs vigour and leſs exertion ſhould ſhow itſelf without. Accordingly the republic fell into the moſt puſillanimous circumſpection. They aſſumed and added ſtill more to the national character of Italy, which is jealouſy and miſtruſt. With one half of the treaſures and care which it hath coſt them to

maintain that neutrality they have obferved for two B O O K
centuries paft, they would perhaps have freed them- XIX.
felves for ever from the dangers to which their very
precautions have expofed them.

The republic doth not appear to be in a ftate of
tranquillity, notwithftanding all the cares that have
been taken for its fecurity. Its anxiety is manifefted
by the principles of its government, which become
conftantly more fevere by the extreme horror of every
thing that is in the leaft elevated ; by the averfion
which it fhows for reafon, the ufe of which it confiders
as a crime ; by the myfterious and dark veils with
which it conceals its operations ; by the precaution
which it conftantly takes to place foreign commanders at the head of its feeble troops, and to appoint infpectors over them ; by the forbidding, indifcriminately, all thofe who are its fubjects, to go and inure themfelves to war in the field of battle ; by its informers ;
by all the refinements of infidious policy ; and by various other means which difcover continual apprehenfions and alarms. It feems to place its chief confidence in an inquifitor, who is continually prying a-
bout amongft individuals, with the axe raifed over the
head of any one who fhall venture to difturb public
order by his actions or by his difcourfes.

Every thing, however, is not cenfurable in Venice.
The impoft which fupplies the treafury with 25,000,000
of livres [1,041,666l. 13s. 4d.], hath neither increafed
nor diminifhed fince the year 1707. Every method is
taken to conceal from the citizens the idea of their
flavery, and to make them eafy and cheerful. The
form of worfhip is replete with ceremonies. There
are no great feftivals without public fpectacles and
mufic. One may fay and do what one choofes at Venice, if one does not fpeak in public either of politics
or of religion. A Chriftian orator preaching before
the chiefs of the republic, imagined that he ought to
begin his difcourfe with an eulogium of the government ; immediately a fatellite was difpatched to take
him out of his pulpit ; and being the next day fum-

B O O K
XIX.

moned to appear before the tribunal of the ſtate inquiſitors, he was told, *What need have we of your enco-
miums? Be more cautious.* They were well aware that
an adminiſtration is ſoon cenſured in every place where
it is allowed to be extolled. The ſtate inquiſitors do
not retain their functions longer than eighteen months.
They are choſen from among the moſt moderate perſons, and the leaſt act of injuſtice is followed by their
depoſition. They addreſs all men in the familiar mode
of the ſecond perſon, and would even adopt it in ſpeaking to the doge. Any perſon who is ſummoned before
them is obliged to appear without delay. A ſecretary
of ſtate was not excuſed by alleging the neceſſity of
finiſhing his diſpatches. It is true that the doors are
ſhut while cauſes are trying; but theſe cauſes of alarm
to foreigners are the real protection of the people, and
the counterpoiſe to the tyranny of the ariſtocratic body. About ſix years ago it was deliberated in council
whether this formidable tribunal ſhould not be abo-
liſhed; and immediately the moſt wealthy citizens
were preparing to withdraw themſelves; and a neighbouring king foretold that Venice would not exiſt ten
years longer after the ſuppreſſion of this magiſtracy.
Accordingly, were it not for the terror with which it
inſpires the citizens, they would be inceſſantly expoſed to vexations from a number of patricians who lau-
guiſh in indigence. After ſome violent conteſts, the
inquiſition was confirmed by a majority of votes, and
the four perſons who had moved the debate were puniſhed only by aſſigning to them honourable employments, which kept them at a diſtance from the republic.

During the carnival, monks and prieſts go to the
public diverſions in maſks. It is well known, that a
degraded eccleſiaſtic can have no influence. A patrician, who is become either monk or prieſt, is no more
than a common citizen. The horror of executions is
kept up by the unfrequency of them. The people
are perſuaded that the devils are flying about the gibbet to ſeize upon the ſouls of the perſons executed. A

capuchin friar once thought of faying, that *of a hun-* B O O K
dred drowned perfons no one would be faved, and that of XIX.
a hundred perfons executed on the gallows not one would
be damned. As it was of confequence to the Venetians that one fhould not fear being drowned, but
that one fhould fear being hanged, the preacher had
orders to teach the contrary, notwithftanding the authority of St. Auftin.

If the naval forces of the Venetians are commanded by a patrician alone, it is only fince the celebrated Morofini, admiral of their fleet at the expedition
of the Peloponnefus, told them, that it had been in
his power to ftarve them. If the land forces can
only be commanded by a foreign general, it is from
the juft apprehenfion, that a citizen might take advantage of the affection of the foldiers to become the
tyrant of his country.

There are a multitude of magiftrates placed at the
head of different affairs, which muft accelerate the
difpatch of them. The doge may folicit and obtain
favours, but he cannot grant any. There are pre-
fervers of the laws, to whom the new regulations propofed by the fenate to the council are referred. They
examine them and make their reports to the council,
who decide accordingly. The council therefore reprefents the republic, the fenate the legiflative body
fubordinate to the council, and the ftate inquifitor is
a kind of tribune to protect the people.

An inquifitor is not, in my opinion, a very tremen-
dous perfon, fince it is poffible to punifh him when
he becomes infolent. There is no fuch thing to be
found in France as a fheriff's officer, who would venture to deliver a fummons to a magiftrate of a fuperior order. At Venice a legal proceeding may be carried on againft either a patrician or an inquifitor. Their
goods may be fold, their perfons feized, and they may
be thrown into prifon.

The Venetian miniftry have obfcure agents in all
the courts, by whom they are informed of the character of the men in favour, and the means of fedu-

cing them; they support themselves by their cunning. There is another republic which derives its strength, and supports itself by its form and its courage, and that is Switzerland.

The Switzers, known in antiquity by the name of Helvetians, were, as the Gauls and the Britons, only to be subdued by Cæsar, who was the greatest of the Romans, if he had been more attached to his country. They were united to Germany, as a Roman province, under the reign of Honorius. Revolutions, which are frequent and easily accomplished in such a country as the Alps, divided colonies, that were separated by large lakes or great mountains, into several baronies. The most considerable of these occupied by the House of Austria, in process of time seized upon all the rest. Conquest introduced slavery, oppression excited the people to revolt, and thus liberty arose from an unbounded exertion of tyranny.

There are now thirteen cantons of robust peasants, who defend almost all the kings of Europe, and fear none; who are better acquainted with their real interests than any other nation; and who constitute the most sensible people in all modern political states. These thirteen cantons compose among themselves, not a republic as the seven provinces of Holland, nor a simple confederacy as the Germanic body, but rather a league, a natural association of so many independent republics. Each canton has its respective sovereignty, its alliancies, and its treaties separate. The general diet cannot make laws or regulations for either of them.

The three most ancient cantons are immediately connected with each of the others. It is from this union of convenience, not of constitution, that if one of the thirteen cantons were attacked, all the rest would march to its assistance. But there is no common alliance between the whole body and each particular canton. Thus the branches of a tree are united among themselves, without having an immediate connection with the common trunk.

The union of the Switzers was, however, indiſſo-
luble till the beginning of the 16th century; when
religion, which ought to be the bond of peace and
charity, diſunited them. The reformation cauſed a
ſeparation of the Helvetic body, and the ſtate was divided by the church. All public affairs are tranſact-
ed in the ſeparate and particular diets of the Catholic
and Proteſtant parties. The general diets are aſſembled
only to preſerve the appearance of union. Notwithſtanding this ſource of diſcord, Switzerland has enjoyed
peace much more than any ſtate in Europe.

Under the Auſtrian government, oppreſſion and the
raiſing of troops impeded population. After the revolution, there was too great an increaſe of the number of people in proportion to the barrenneſs of the
land. The Helvetic body could not be enlarged without endangering its ſafety, unleſs it made ſome excur-
ſions abroad. The inhabitants of theſe mountains,
as the torrents that pour down from them, were to
ſpread themſelves in the plains that border upon the
Alps. Theſe people would have deſtroyed each other,
had they remained ſequeſtered among themſelves. But
ignorance of the arts, the want of materials for manufactures, and the deficiency of money, prevented the
importation of foreign merchandiſe, and excluded them
from the means of procuring the comforts of life, and
of encouraging induſtry. They drew even from their
increaſe of numbers, a method of ſubſiſting and acquiring riches, a ſource and an object of trade.

The duke of Milan, maſter of a rich country open
on every ſide to invaſion, and not eaſily defended, was
in want of ſoldiers. The Switzers, who were his moſt
powerful neighbours, muſt neceſſarily become his enemies, if they were not his allies, or rather his protectors. A kind of traffic was therefore ſet on foot between theſe people and the Milaneſe, in which men
were bartered for riches. The nation engaged troops
ſucceſſively in the ſervice of France, of the emperor,
of the pope, of the duke of Savoy, and all the potentates of Italy. They ſold their blood to the moſt di-

B O O K ſtant powers, and to the nations moſt in enmity with
XIX. each other; to Holland, to Spain, and to Portugal;
as if theſe mountains were nothing more than a repo-
ſitory of arms and ſoldiers, open to every one who
wanted to purchaſe the means of carrying on war.

Each canton treats with that power which offers the
moſt advantageous terms. The ſubjects of the country are at liberty to engage in war at a diſtance, with
an allied nation. The Hollander is, by the conſtitution of his country, a citizen of the world; the Swit-
zer, by the ſame circumſtance, a deſtroyer of Europe.
The profits of Holland are in proportion to the degree of cultivation, and the conſumption of merchandiſe; the proſperity of Switzerland increaſes in proportion to the number of battles that are fought, and
the ſlaughter that attends them.

It is by war, that calamity inſeparable from mankind, whether in a ſtate of civilization or not, that the
republics of the Helvetic body are obliged to live and
ſubſiſt. It is by this that they preſerve a number of
inhabitants within their country proportioned to the
extent and fertility of their lands, without forcing any
of the ſprings of government, or reſtraining the inclinations of any individual. It is by the traffic of troops
with the powers at war with each other, that Switzerland has not been under the neceſſity of making ſud-
den emigrations, which are the cauſe of invaſions, and
of attempting conqueſts, which would have occaſioned the loſs of its liberty, as it cauſed the ſubverſion of
all the republics of Greece.

As far as human foreſight can penetrate into futurity, the ſtate of theſe people muſt be more permanent
than that of all other nations, if differences in their
form of worſhip do not become fatal to them. From
the top of their barren mountains, they behold, groaning under the oppreſſion of tyranny, whole nations
which nature hath placed in more plentiful countries,
while they enjoy in peace the fruits of their labour,
of their frugality, of their moderation, and of all
the virtues that attend upon liberty. If it were poſ-

fible that habit could blunt their fenfibility for fo BOOK
mild a deftiny, it would be inceffantly revived in them XIX.
by that multitude of travellers who refort there to enjoy the fight of that felicity which is not to be feen
elfewhere. Undoubtedly, the love of riches hath
fomewhat altered that amiable fimplicity of manners,
in fuch of the cantons where the arts and commerce
have made any confiderable progrefs; but the features
of their primitive character are not entirely effaced,
and they ftill retain a kind of happinefs unknown to
other men. Can it be apprehended that a nation may
grow tired of fuch an exiftence?

The weight of taxes cannot alter the advantages of
this deftiny. Thefe fcourges of the human race are
unknown in moft of the cantons, and in the reft they
amount to little or nothing. In fome places only, a
dangerous abufe hath been introduced. Adminiftrators,
known under the title of bailiffs, take upon themfelves
to impofe in their own jurifdiction arbitrary fines, which
they make ufe of for their own private benefit. This
extravagance of the feudal laws cannot laft, and every
veftige will foon be loft of fo odious a cuftom, which
in procefs of time would affect the public felicity.

The nation will never be difturbed by its propenfities, which naturally lead it to order, tranquillity, and
harmony. If any turbulent or dangerous characters
are to be found there, who may be fond of factions
and tumults, they mix in foreign wars to endeavour to
gratify this reftlefs difpofition.

It is not poffible that the feveral cantons fhould attempt reciprocally to fubdue each other. Thofe in
which democracy is eftablifhed, are too feeble to conceive fo unreafonable a project; and in the others, the
patricians and plebeians will never unite their wifhes
and their exertions for an aggrandizement, the confequences of which might become fatal to one of the
orders.

The tranquillity of the Helvetic body is ftill lefs in
danger from their neighbours than from their citizens.
As in the difputes between crowned heads, the Swifs

obferve a very impartial neutrality, and as they never
become guarantees of any engagement, they are not
known to have any enemies. If any power fhould
think it had a caufe of complaint againft them, it
would ftifle its refentment from the well-grounded apprehenfion of mifcarrying in its projects of revenge
againft a country entirely military, and which reckons
as many foldiers as men. If even it were certain of
conquering them, they would never be attacked, becaufe the blindeft and moft violent policy doth not exterminate a people to take poffeffion of nothing but
rocks. Such are the motives which induce us to believe in the ftability of the republic of Switzerland.

It now remains that we fpeak of the ecclefiaftical
government. If the foundation of Chriftianity prefents us with a fcene that aftonifhes the mind, the hiftory of the revolutions in the government of the
church is not lefs furprifing. What an enormous difference is there between St. Peter, a poor fifherman,
on the borders of the lake of Genezareth, and fervant
of the fervants of God; and fome of his proud fucceffors, their brows girt with the triple crown, mafters
of Rome, and of a great part of Italy, and calling
themfelves the Kings of the Kings of the earth! Let
us trace things up to their origin; and let us take a
rapid view of the fplendour and of the corruption of
the church. Let us fee what its government is become in the fpace of eighteen centuries; and let prefent and future fovereigns learn what they are to expect from the priefthood, the fole principle of which
is to render the authority of the magiftrates fubordinate to the divine authority, of which it is the depofitary.

In an obfcure village of Judea, and in the houfe
of a poor carpenter, there arofe a man of auftere morals. His candour was difgufted with the hypocrify
of the priefts of his time. He had difcovered the vanity of legal ceremonies, and the vice of expiations;
at thirty years of age this virtuous perfon quitted his
employment, and began to preach his opinions. The

multitude, from the villages and country places, flocked around him, liftened to him, and followed him.
He affociated to himfelf a fmall number of difciples,
ignorant and weak men, taken from the loweft conditions of life. He wandered for fome time about the
capital, and at length ventured to appear there. One
of his own difciples betrayed him, and the other denied him. He was taken up, accufed of blafphemy,
and crucified between two thieves. After his death his
difciples appeared in the public places, and in the
great cities, at Antioch, at Alexandria, and at Rome.
They announced, both to barbarous and civilized people, at Athens and at Corinth, the refurrection of their
Mafter; and the belief of their doctrine, which feemed fo contrary to reafon, was univerfally adopted. In
all parts corrupt men embraced a fyftem of morality,
auftere in its principles and unfociable in its councils.
Perfecution arofe; and the preachers, together with
their converts, were imprifoned, fcourged, and put to
death. The more blood is fpilt, the more doth the
fect extend itfelf. In lefs than three centuries, the
temples of idolatry are fubverted or abandoned; and
notwithftanding the hatred, herefies, fchifms, and fanguinary quarrels, which have torn Chriftianity fince
its origin, even down to our latter times; yet there
are fcarce any altars remaining, except fuch as are
raifed to the man God, who died upon a crofs.

It was no difficult matter to demonftrate to the Pagans the abfurdity of their worfhip; and in all general, as well as particular difputes, if we can prove
that our adverfary is in the wrong, he immediately con-
cludes that we are in the right. Providence, which
tends to the accomplifhment of its defigns by all forts
of means, intended that this mode of reafoning fhould
lead men into the way of falvation. The founder of
Chriftianity did not arrogate to himfelf any authority, either over the partners of his miffion, or over his
followers, or over his fellow-citizens. He refpected the
authority of Cæfar. When he faved the life of an
adulterous woman, he took care not to attack the law

BOOK which condemned her to death. He referred two bro-
XIX. thers, who were at variance concerning the division
of an inheritance, to the civil tribunal. When persecuted, he suffered persecution. In the midst of intolerant persons, he recommended toleration. *You
shall not*, said he to his disciples, *command fire to come
down from heaven upon the head of the unbeliever ; you
shall shake off the very dust from your feet, and you shall
retire :* Fastened to a cross, his head crowned with
thorns, his side pierced with a spear, he said to God :
Father, forgive them, for they know not what they do. To
instruct and to baptize the nations, was the object of
the mission of the apostles ; to employ persuasion and
not violence ; to go about in the same manner God
had sent his Son, such were the means employed for
the purpose. Priesthood hath in no time conformed
itself to such maxims ; and yet religion hath not been
the less prosperous.

In proportion as the new doctrine gained ground, a
kind of hierarchy was instituted among its ministers,
consisting of bishops, priests, acolytes, and sacristans,
or porters. The object of the administration itself, included doctrine, discipline, and morals. To confer
sacred orders, was the first act of the jurisdiction of
the church. To set persons free, or to bind them, and
to appoint a spiritual and voluntary expiation for offences, was the second. To excommunicate the rebellious sinner, or the heretic, was the third ; and the
fourth, which is common to every association, was to
institute rules of discipline. These rules, at first kept
secret, and which were chiefly on the administration
of the sacraments, were made public, assemblies or
councils were holden. The bishops were the representatives of the apostles ; the rest of the clergy were
subordinate to them. Nothing was decided without
the concurrence of the faithful ; so that this was a true
democracy. Civil matters were referred to the ar-
bitration of the bishops. The Christians were blamed
for having law-suits ; and still more for exposing themselves to be brought before the magistrate. It is pro-

bable that property was in common, and that the bifhop difpofed of it at pleafure.

Hitherto every thing was conducted without the interference of the fecular power. But under Aurelian,
the Chriftians applied to the emperor for juftice againft
Paul of Samofata. Conftantine banifhed Arius, and
condemned his writings to the flames; Theodofius
perfecuted Neftorius; and thefe innovations fixed the
period of the fecond ftate of ecclefiaftical jurifdiction:
when it had now deviated from its primitive fimplicity, and was become a mixture of fpiritual power
and coercive authority. The faithful, already extremely numerous, in the fecond century, were diftributed in different churches fubject to the fame adminiftration. Among thefe churches, there were fome
more or lefs confiderable; fecular authority interfered
in the election of bifhops, and the confufion between
thefe two powers increafed. There were fome poor
and fome rich among them, and this was the firft origin
of the ambition of the clergy. There were indigent
believers among them all; and the bifhops became
the difpenfers of the alms: and this is the moft ancient fource of the corruption of the church.

What a rapid progrefs hath ecclefiaftical authority
made fince the end of the third century! Proceedings
are carried on before the bifhops; and they become
the arbiters in civil matters. The judicial fentence of
the bifhop admits of no appeal; and the execution of
it is referred to the magiftrates. The trial of a prieft
cannot be carried out of the province. A diftinction
arifes between civil and ecclefiaftical crimes, and this
gives birth to the privilege of the clergy. The appeal
to the fovereign is allowed, if it fhould happen that
the fentence of the bifhop fhould be invalidated at the
tribunal of the magiftrates. Long before thefe conceffions, the bifhops had obtained the infpection over
the police and the morals; they took cognizance of
proftitutions, foundlings, guardianfhips, lunatics, and
minors; they vifited the prifons; they folicited the en-
largement of the prifoners; they denounced the negli-

gent judges to the fovereign; they interfered with the
difpofal of the public money, with the conftruction and
repairing of the great roads, and other edifices. Thus
it is, that, under pretence of affifting each other, the
two authorities were blended, and paved the way for
the diffenfions which were one day to arife between
them.   Such was in the firft centuries, in the profpe-
rous days of the church, the third ftate of its government, HALF CIVIL, HALF ECCLESIASTICAL, to which, at
prefent, we fcarcely know what name to give.   Was
it from the weaknefs of the emperors, from their fear,
from intrigue, or from fanctity of manners, that the
chiefs of Chriftianity conciliated to themfelves fo many important prerogatives?   At that time religious
terror had peopled the deferts with anchorets, more
than feventy-fix thoufand of whom were reckoned:
this was a nurfery of deacons, priefts, and bifhops.

Conftantine transferred the feat of empire to Byzan-
tium.   Rome was no more its capital.   The Barbarians, who had taken it more than once, and ravaged
it, were converted.   It was the fate of Chriftianity,
which had conquered the gods of the Capitol, to fubdue the deftroyers of the throne of the Cæfars; but in
changing their religion, thefe chiefs of hordes did not
change their manners.   What ftrange kind of Chriftians were Clovis and his fucceffors! exclaims the author of the hiftory of the church.   Notwithftanding
the analogy between the ecclefiaftical and the feudal
government, it would be an illufion to make one the
model of the other.   Literature was no longer cultivated; and the priefts employed the little knowledge
they had preferved, in forging titles, and in fabricat-
ing legends.   The harmony between the two powers
was difturbed.   The origin and the riches of the bifhops attached the Romans, who neither had, nor
could have, any thing but contempt and averfion for
their new mafters; fome of whom were Pagans, others
Heretics, and all of them ferocious.   No man ever
doubted of the donation of Conftantine; and that of
Pepin was confirmed by Charlemagne.   The grandeur

of the bishops of Rome increased under Lewis the Debonnaire, and under Otho. They arrogated that sovereignty which their benefactors had reserved for
themselves. Like other potentates, they founded their
claim upon prescription. The church was already infested with pernicious maxims; and the opinion, that
the bishop of Rome might depose kings, was universally adopted. Different causes afterwards concurred
in establishing the supremacy of this see over the rest.
The prince of the apostles had been the first bishop of
Rome. Rome was the centre of union between all
the other churches, the indigence of which she relieved. She had been the capital of the world; and the
Christians were not so numerous anywhere else. The
title of pope was a title common to all bishops, over
whom the bishop of Rome did not obtain the superiority till the end of the eleventh century. At that
time ecclesiastical government tended not only to MO-
NARCHY, but had even advanced towards UNIVERSAL
MONARCHY.

Towards the end of the eighth century, the famous
decretals of Isidorus of Seville appeared. The pope
announced himself to be infallible. He withdrew himself from his former submission to the councils. He
held in his hand two swords; one the emblem of his
spiritual, the other of his temporal power. Discipline
was no more. The priests were the slaves of the pope,
and kings were his vassals. He required tributes from
them; he abolished the ancient judges, and appointed
new ones. He created primates. The clergy were
exempted from all civil jurisdiction; and Gratian the
monk, by his decree, completed the mischief occasioned by the decretals. The clergy employed themselves
in augmenting their income by every possible mode.
The possession of their estates was declared immutable
and sacred. Men were terrified with temporal as well
as spiritual threats. Tithes were exacted. A traffic
was made of relics; and pilgrimages were encouraged.
This completed the destruction of morality, and the
last stroke was thus given to the discipline of the

B O O K church. A criminal life was expiated by a wandering
XIX. one. Events were conftrued into the judgments of
God; and decifions by water, by fire, or by the deftiny of the faints, were adopted. The folly of judiciary aftrology was added to fuperftitious opinions. Such was the ftate of the Weftern church: AN ABSOLUTE DESPOTISM, with all its atrocious characters.

The Eaftern church experienced alfo its calamities. The Grecian empire had been difmembered by the Arabian Muffulmen, by modern Scythians, by the Bulgarians, and by the Ruffians. Thefe laft were not amended by being wafhed with the waters of baptifm. Mohammedifm deprived Chriftianity of part of its followers, and threw the reft into flavery. In the Weft, the Barbarians, converted to Chriftianity, had carried their manners along with them into the church. In the Eaft, the Greeks had become depraved by their commercial intercourfe with a race of men perfectly fimilar. Neverthelefs, literature feemed to revive under the learned and vicious Photius. While the clergy of the Eaft were ftriving againft ignorance, our clergy in the Weft became hunters and warriors, and were poffeffed of lordfhips fubject to military fervice. Bifhops and monks marched under ftandards, maffacred, and were maffacred. The privileges of their domains had engaged them in public affairs. They wandered about with the ambulatory courts; they affifted at the national affemblies, which were become parliaments or councils; and this was the period of entire confufion between the two powers. Then it was that the bifhops pretended openly to be the judges of fovereigns; that Vamba was compelled to do penance, invefted with a monk's habit, and depofed; that the right of reigning was contefted to Lewis the Debonnaire; that the popes interfered in the quarrels between nations, not as mediators, but as defpots; that Adrian II. forbade Charles the Bald to invade the ftates of his nephew Clotaire; and that Gregory IX. wrote to St. Lewis in thefe terms: *We have condemned Frederick II. who called himfelf Emperor, and have de-*

poſed him; and we have elected in his ſtead Count Ro-
bert, your brother.

But if the clergy encroached upon the rights of the temporal power, the lay lords appointed and inſtalled prieſts, without the participation of the biſhops; regular benefices were given to ſeculars, and the convents were pillaged. Neither incontinence nor ſimony excited any ſhame. Biſhopricks were ſold; abbeys purchaſed; prieſts had either a wife or a concubine; the public temples were forſaken; and this diſorder brought on the abuſe and contempt of cenſures, which were poured forth againſt kings, and againſt their ſubjects; and torrents of blood were ſhed in all countries. The church and the empire were then in a ſtate of ANARCHY. Pilgrimages were preludes to the cruſades, or the expiation for crimes and aſſaſſinations. Eccleſiaſtics of all orders, believers of all ranks, inliſted themſelves. Perſons loaded with debts were diſpenſed from paying them; malefactors eſcaped the purſuit of the laws; corrupt monks broke through the reſtraints of their ſolitude; diſſolute huſbands forſook their wives. Courtezans exerciſed their infamous trade at the foot of the ſepulchre of their God, and near to the tent of their ſovereign. But it was impoſſible to carry on this expedition, and the ſucceeding ones, without funds. An impoſt was levied, and this gave riſe to the claims of the pope upon all the eſtates of the church; to the inſtitution of a multitude of military orders; to the alternative given to the vanquiſhed, of ſlavery or of embracing Chriſtianity, of death or of baptiſm: and to conſole the reader for ſo many calamities, this circumſtance occaſioned the increaſe of navigation and commerce, which enriched Venice, Genoa, Piſa, and Florence; the decline of the feudal government, by the diſorder in the fortunes of the noblemen, and the habit of the ſea, which, perhaps, paved the way from afar for the diſcovery of the New World. But I have not the courage to purſue any further the account of the diſorders, and of the exorbitant increaſe of papal authority. Under Innocent III. there was no

B O O K more than one tribunal in the world, and that was at
XIX. Rome; there was but one master, and he was at Rome,
from whence he reigned over Europe by his legates.
The ecclesiastical hierarchy extended itself one step
further, by the creation of cardinals. Nothing was
now wanting to the despot but Janizaries, whom he
acquired by creating a multitude of monastic orders.
Rome, formerly the mistress of the world by arms, became so by opinion. But why did the popes, who were
all-powerful over the minds of men, forget to maintain
the terrors of their spiritual thunder, by directing it
only against ambitious or unjust sovereigns? Who
knows whether this kind of tribunal, so much wished
for, to which crowned heads might be summoned,
would not have existed to this day in Rome; and whether the threats of one common father, supported by
general superstition, might not have put an end to every military contest?

The papal militia, composed of monks, who were
laborious and austere in their origin, became corrupted. The bishops, tired out with the enterprises of the
legates, of the secular magistrates, and of the monks,
over their jurisdiction, encroached, on their parts, upon
the secular jurisdiction, with a degree of boldness of
which it is difficult to form an idea. If the clergy
could have determined to erect gibbets, perhaps we
should at present be under a government entirely sa-
cerdotal. It is the maxim, that *the church abhors the
effusion of blood*, which has preserved us from it. There
were schools in France and in Italy; and those at Paris were famous towards the eleventh century. The
number of colleges was increased; and, nevertheless,
this state of the church, which we have described without malice or exaggeration, was continued in all Christian countries, from the ninth to the fourteenth century, an interval of four or five hundred years. The
emperors have lost Italy, and the popes have acquired
a great temporal power. No one hath yet raised himself against their spiritual power. The interests of this
sovereign are embraced by all the Italians. The dig-

BOOK
XIX.

nity of epifcopacy is eclipfed by that of cardinal, and
the fecular clergy were always ruled by the regular
clergy. Venice alone hath known and defended its
rights. The irruption of the Moors in Spain hath
thrown Chriftianity there into an abject ftate, from
which it hath fcarce emerged for thefe two laft centuries; and even down to our days, the inquifition difplays it under the moft hideous afpect:—the inquifition, a terrible tribunal, a tribunal infulting to the fpirit of Jefus Chrift; a tribunal, which ought to be detefted by fovereigns, by bifhops, by magiftrates, and
by fubjects: by fovereigns, whom it ventures to threaten, and whom it hath fometimes cruelly perfecuted;
by bifhops, whofe jurifdiction it annihilates; by the
magiftrates, whofe legitimate authority it ufurps; by
the fubjects, whom it keeps in continual terror, whom
it reduces to filence, and condemns to ftupidity, from
the danger that attends their acquiring inftruction,
their reading, their writing, and their fpeaking: a tribunal which hath only owed its inftitution, and which
only owes its continuance, in thofe regions where it is
ftill maintained, to a facrilegious policy, jealous of per-
petuating prejudices and prerogatives, which could not
have been difcuffed, without being difpelled.

Before the fchifm of Henry VIII. England was fubject to the pope, even in temporal concerns. London
fhook off the yoke of Rome; but this reformation was
lefs the effect of reafon than of paffion. Germany hath
been a continual fcene of violence on both fides; and
fince the time of Luther, the Catholics and Schifma-
tics have fhown themfelves equally enthufiafts in that
country, the former for papal tyranny, the latter for
independence. Chriftianity was eftablifhed in Poland,
with all the claims of papal authority. In France the
temporal power was confidered as fubordinate to the
fpiritual power. According to the fentiment of the
favourers of the Tramontane opinions, this kingdom,
as well as all the kingdoms of the earth, was fubject to
the church of Rome; its princes might be excommu-
nicated, and its fubjects freed from the oath of alle-

BOOK
XIX.

giance. But the papal coloffus was fhaken; and even fince the fourteenth century it approached the inftant of its downfal. Then literature was revived; the ancient languages were cultivated; the firft Hebrew grammar was printed, and the Royal College was founded. Towards the middle of the fifteenth century, the art of printing was invented. A multitude of writings of all kinds were drawn out of the duft of monaftic libraries, to be diffufed among the people. The vulgar tongue was improved, and tranflations were made. The fovereign, and individuals, collected great libraries. The decrees of the councils, the fathers, and the holy fcriptures, were read. The canon law was attended to, and the hiftory of the church was inveftigated. The fpirit of criticifm arofe, and the apocryphal books were detected; while infpired writings were reftored to their original purity. The eyes of the fovereigns and of the clergy were opened, and they were enlightened by religious difputes. The origin of immunities, exemptions, and privileges, was traced; and the futility of them was demonftrated. Ancient times were fearched into, and their difcipline compared to modern cuftoms. The hierarchy of the church refumed its influence, and the two powers withdrew into their refpective limits. The decifions of the church refumed their efficacy; and if papal tyranny hath not been extinguifhed in France, it is at leaft confined within very narrow bounds. In 1681, the clergy of that kingdom decided, that temporal power was independent of fpiritual power, and that the pope was fubject to the canons of the church. If the miffion of the prieft be of divine right; if it belonged to him to fet men free, and to enclofe them in bonds; can he not excommunicate the impenitent finner, or the heretic, whether he be a fovereign or a private man? According to our principles, this is a power that cannot be denied to him: but prudent men perceived, in this violent proceeding, fuch mifchievous confequences, that they have declared it was fcarce ever to be referred to. Doth excommunication involve the de-

pofition of the fovereign, and difengage the fubjects
from their oath of allegiance? It would be high-trea-
fon to fuppofe it. Hence we fee, that the ecclefiaftical government, at leaft, in France, hath paffed on,
from the *tyranny of anarchy, to a kind of moderate ariftocracy.*

But if I might be allowed to explain myfelf upon a
matter fo important, I fhould venture to fay, that neither in England, nor in the countries of Germany, of
the United Provinces, and of the North, the true principles have been traced. Had they been better known,
how much blood and how many troubles would they
have fpared, the blood of Pagans, Heretics, and Chriftians, fince the firft origin of natural forms of worfhip
to the prefent day; and how much would they fpare
in future, if the rulers of the earth were prudent and
fteady enough to conform to them?

It appears to me, that the ftate is not made for religion, but religion for the ftate: this is the firft principle.

The general intereft is the univerfal rule that ought
to prevail in a ftate: this is the fecond principle.

The people, or the fovereign authority, depofitary
of theirs, have alone the right to judge of the conformity of any inftitution whatever with the general intereft: this is the third principle.

Thefe three principles appear to me inconteftibly
evident; and the propofitions that follow are no more
than corollaries deduced from them.

It therefore belongs to this authority, and to this
authority alone, to examine the tenets and the difcipline of religion: the tenets, in order to afcertain,
whether, being contrary to common fenfe, they will
not expofe the public tranquillity to commotions, fo
much the more dangerous, as the ideas of future happinefs will be complicated with zeal for the glory of
God, and with fubmiffion to truths, which will be confidered as revealed: the difcipline, to obferve whether
it doth not clafh with the prevailing manners, extinguifh the fpirit of patriotifm, damp the ardour of cou-

rage, occasion an aversion for industry, for marriage,
and for public affairs; whether it be not injurious to
population, and to the social state; whether it doth
not inspire fanaticism, and a spirit of intoleration;
whether it doth not sow the seeds of division between
the relations of the same family, between families of
the same city, between the cities of the same kingdom,
and between the several kingdoms of the earth; whether it doth not diminish the respect due to the sovereign and the magistrates; and whether it doth not
inculcate maxims so austere as to occasion melancholy,
or practices which lead on to extravagance.

This authority, and this authority alone, can therefore proscribe the established mode of worship, adopt
a new one, or even abolish every form of worship, if
it should find it convenient. The general form of government being always settled at the first minute of its
adoption, how is it possible that religion should give
the law by its antiquity?

The state hath the supremacy in every thing. The
distinction between a temporal and a spiritual power is
a palpable absurdity; and there neither can, nor ought
to be, any more than one sole and single jurisdiction,
wherever it belongs, to public utility alone, to order,
or to defend.

For every offence whatever there should be but one
tribunal; for every guilty person but one prison; for
every illegal action but one law. Every contrary claim
is injurious to the equality of the citizens; every possession is an usurpation of the claimant, at the expence
of the common interest.

There should be no other councils than the assembly of the ministers of the sovereign. When the administrators are assembled, the church is assembled.
When the state has pronounced, the church has nothing more to say.

There should be no other canons, except the edicts
of the princes, and the decrees of the courts of judi-
cature.

What is a common offence, and a privileged offence,

where there is but one law, and one public matter, B O O K between the citizens? XIX.

Immunities, and other exclusive privileges, are so many acts of injustice, exercised against the other ranks of society that are deprived of them.

A bishop, a priest, or a member of the clerical body, may quit his country, if he chooses it; but then he is nothing. It belongs to the state to watch over his conduct, to appoint and to remove him.

If we understand by a benefice, any thing more than the salary every citizen ought to reap from his labour, this is an abuse which requires a speedy reformation. The man who doth nothing hath no right to eat.

And wherefore should not the priest acquire, enrich himself, enjoy, sell, buy, and make his will, as another citizen?

Let him be chaste, docile, humble, and even indigent; let him not be fond of women, let him be of a meek disposition, and let him prefer bread and water to all the conveniencies of life; but let him be forbidden to bind himself to these observances by vows. The vow of chastity is repugnant to nature and injurious to population; the vow of poverty is only that of a foolish or of an idle man; the vow of obedience to any other than to the ruling power, and to the law, is that of a slave or of a rebel.

If there existed, therefore, in any district of a country, sixty thousand citizens bound by such vows, what could the sovereign do better, than to repair to the spot, with a sufficient number of satellites, armed with whips, and to say to them, Go forth, ye lazy wretches, go forth; go to the fields, to agriculture, to the manufactures, to the militia?

Charity is the common duty of all those whose property exceeds their absolute wants.

The relief of old men, and of indigent and old persons is the duty of the state they have served.

Let there be no other apostles but the legislator and the magistrates.

Let there be no sacred writings, except those which they shall acknowledge as such.

Let there be no divine right but the good of the republic.

I could extend these consequences to many other objects; but I stop here, protesting, that if in what I have said there should be any thing contrary to the good order of a well-regulated society, and to the felicity of the citizens, I retract; although I can scarce persuade myself that the nations can become enlightened, and not be sensible one day of the truth of my principles. As for the rest, I forewarn my readers that I have spoken only of the external forms of religion. With respect to internal religion, man is only accountable for it to God. It is a secret between man and him, who hath taken him out of nothing, and can plunge him into it again.

If we now take a review of what has been said, we shall find that all the governments of Europe are comprehended under some of the forms we have been describing, and are differently modelled according to the local situation, the degree of population, the extent of territory, the influence of opinions and occupations, and the external connections and viciffitudes of events that act upon the system of the body politic, as the impreffion of furrounding fluids does upon natural bodies.

We are not to imagine, as it is often afferted, that all governments nearly resemble each other, and that the only difference between them confifts in the character of those who govern. This maxim may, perhaps, be true in absolute governments, among such nations as have no principles of liberty. These take the turn the prince gives them; they are haughty, proud, and courageous, under a monarch who is active and fond of glory; indolent and stupid under a superftitious king; full of hopes and fears under a young prince; of weaknefs and corruption under an old despot; or rather alternately confident and weak, under the feveral minifters who are raifed by intrigue. B O O K In fuch ftates, government affumes the character of $\underset{\smile}{\text{XIX.}}$ the adminiftration; but in free ftates it is juft the re-verfe.

Whatever may be faid of the nature and fprings of the different fyftems of government to which men are fubject, the art of legiflation being that which ought to be the moft perfect, is alfo the moft proper to em-ploy men of the firft genius. The fcience of govern-ment does not contain abftracted truths, or rather it has not one fingle principle which does not extend to all the branches of adminiftration.

The ftate is a very complicated machine, which cannot be wound up or fet in motion without a tho-rough knowledge of all its component parts. If any one of the parts be too much ftraitened or relaxed, the whole muft be in diforder. Every project that may be beneficial to a certain number of citizens, or in critical times, may become fatal to the whole na-tion, and prejudicial for a long continuance. If we deftroy or change the nature of any great body, thofe convulfive motions, which are called ftrokes of ftate, will difturb the whole nation, which may, perhaps, feel the effects of them for ages to come. All inno-vations ought to be brought about infenfibly; they fhould arife from neceffity, be the refult, as it were, of the public clamour, or at leaft agree with the gene-ral wifhes. To abolifh old cuftoms, or to introduce new ones on a fudden, tends only to increafe that which is bad, and to prevent the effect of that which is good. To act without confulting the will of the ge-nerality, without collecting, as it were, the majority of votes in the public opinion, is to alienate the hearts and minds of men, and to bring every thing into dif-credit, even what is honeft and good.

It would be a defirable thing in Europe, that the fovereigns, convinced of the neceffity of improving the fcience of government, fhould imitate a cuftom eftablifhed in China. In this empire, the minifters are diftinguifhed into two claffes, the *thinkers* and the *fign-*

BOOK *ers.* While the latter are employed in the arrange-
XIX. ment and difpatch of public affairs, the firft attend only to the forming of projeds, or to the examination
of fuch as are prefented to them.   According to the
admirers of the Chinefe government, this is the fource
of all thofe judicious regulations, which eftablifh in
thofe regions the moft enlightened fyftems of legiflation, together with the moft prudent adminiftration.
All Afia is fubjed to a defpotic government; but in
Turkey and Perfia, it is a defpotifm of opinion by
means of religion ; in China, it is the defpotifm of the
laws by the influence of reafon. Among the Moham-
medans, they believe in the divine authority of the
prince ; among the Chinefe, they believe in natural
authority, founded upon the law of reafon. But in
thefe empires it is convidion that influences the will.

In the happy ftate of policy and knowledge to which
Europe hath attained, it is plain that this convidion
of the mind, which produces a free, eafy, and general
obedience, can proceed from nothing but a certain
evidence of the utility of the laws. If the governments will not pay *thinkers,* who may, perhaps, become
fufpicious or corrupt as foon as they are mercenary, let
them, at leaft, allow men of fuperior underftandings to
watch in fome meafure over the public good.   Every
writer of genius is born a magiftrate of his country ;
and he ought to enlighten it as much as it is in his
power. His abilities give him a right to do it. Whether he be an obfcure or a diftinguifhed citizen, whatever be his rank or birth, his mind, which is always
noble, derives its claims from his talents. His tribunal
is the whole nation ; his judge is the public, not the
defpot who does not hear him, nor the minifter who
will not attend to him.

All thefe truths have, doubtlefs, their boundaries ;
but it is always more dangerous to fupprefs the freedom of thought, than to leave it to its bent or impetuofity.   Reafon and truth triumph over thofe daring
and violent minds, which are roufed only by reftraint,
and irritated only by perfecution. Kings and mini-

fters, love your people, love mankind, and ye will be B O O K
happy. Ye will then have no reafon to fear men of XIX.
free fentiments or unfatisfied minds, nor the revolt of
bad men. The revolt of the heart is much more dangerous; for virtue, when foured, and roufed into indignation, is guilty of the moft atrocious acts. Cato
and Brutus were both virtuous : they were reduced
to the alternative of choofing between two great e-
normities, fuicide, or the death of Cæfar.

Remember that the interefts of government and
thofe of the nation are the fame. Whoever attempts
to feparate them, is unacquainted with their true nature, and will only injure them.

Authority divides this great intereft, when the wills
of individuals are fubftituted to the eftablifhed order.
The laws, and thofe alone, ought to have the fway.
This univerfal rule is not a yoke for the citizens, but
a power which protects them, and a watchfulnefs
which infures their tranquillity. They think themfelves free ; and this opinion, which conftitutes their
happinefs, determines their fubmiffion. If the arbitrary caprices of a turbulent and enterprifing admini-
ftrator fhould fubvert this fortunate fyftem, the people, who from habit, prejudice, or felf-love, are generally inclined to confider the government under which
they live as the beft of all poffible governments, are
deprived of this illufion, to which nothing can be fubftituted.

Authority divides this great intereft, when it obftinately perfeveres in any error into which it hath fall-
en. Let it not be blinded by a foolifh pride, and it
will perceive that thofe changes, which bring it back
to what is true and good, far from weakening its
fprings, will ftrengthen them. To be undeceived with
refpect to a dangerous miftake, is not to contradict
one's felf; it is not to difplay to the people the inconftancy of government ; it is to demonftrate to them its
wifdom and its uprightnefs. If their refpect were to
diminifh, it would be for that power which would ne-

BOOK ver know its miftakes, or would always juftify them,
XIX. and not for thofe who would avow and correct them.

Authority divides this great intereft, when it facrifices the tranquillity, eafe, and blood of the people, to
the terrible and tranfient brilliancy of warlike exploits.
It is in vain that we endeavour to juftify thefe deftructive propenfities by ftatues and by infcriptions. Thefe
monuments of arrogance and flattery will one day be
deftroyed by time or overthrown by hatred. The
memory of that prince only will be refpected, who
fhall have preferred peace, which muft have infured
happinefs to his fubjects, to victories, which would
have been only for himfelf; who fhall have confidered the empire as his family; who fhall have made no
other-ufe of his power, than for the advantage of thofe
who had intrufted him with it. His name and his character will be univerfally cherifhed. Fathers will inform pofterity of the happinefs which they enjoyed.
Their children will repeat it to their defcendants; and
this delightful remembrance will be preferved from
one age to another, and will be perpetuated in each
family, and to the remoteft centuries.

Authority divides this great intereft, when the perfon in whofe hands the reins of government have been
placed, by birth or election, fuffers them to be guided
at pleafure by blind chance; when he prefers a mean
repofe to the dignity and the importance of the functions with which he is intrufted. His inaction is criminal and infamous. The indulgence with which his
faults might have been treated, will be juftly denied
to his indolence. This feverity will be the more lawful, as his character will have determined him to choofe
for fubftitutes the firft ambitious men who may offer,
and thefe almoft neceffarily men of no capacity. If
even he had the fingular good fortune of making a
good choice, he would ftill be unpardonable, becaufe
it is not allowable to impofe our duties upon others.
He will die without having lived. His name will be
forgotten, or, if remembered, it will only be as the

names of thofe fluggard kings, the years of whofe reign hiftory hath with reafon difdained to count.

Authority divides this great intereft, when the pofts which determine the public tranquillity are intrufted to vile or corrupt men of intrigue; when favour fhall obtain the rewards due to fervices; when the powerful fprings, which infure the grandeur and the duration of empires, are deftroyed. All emulation is extinct. The enlightened and laborious citizens either conceal themfelves, or retire. The wicked and the audacious fhow themfelves infolently, and profper. Every thing is directed and determined by prefumption, by intereft, and by the moft difordinate paffions. Juftice is difregarded, virtue is degraded, and propriety, which might in fome meafure be a fubftitute to it, is confidered as an old prejudice or a ridiculous cuftom. Difcouragement within and opprobrium without, thefe are all that remain to a nation formerly powerful and refpected.

There may fometimes be people diffatisfied under a good government; but where there are many that are unhappy, without any kind of public profperity, then it is that the government is vicious in its nature.

Mankind are juft as we would have them to be; it is the mode of government which gives them a good or an evil propenfity.

A ftate ought to have one object only in view; and that is, public felicity. Every ftate has a particular manner of promoting this end; which may be confidered as its fpirit, its principle, to which every thing elfe is fubordinate.

A nation can have no induftry for the arts, nor courage for war, without a confidence in, and an attachment to, the government. But when the principle of fear hath broken every other fpring of the foul, a nation then becomes of no confequence, the prince is expofed to a thoufand enterprifes from without, and a thoufand dangers from within. Defpifed by his neighbours, and abhorred by his fubjects, he muft be in perpetual fear for the fafety of his kingdom, as well

BOOK as for that of his own life. It is a happiness for a na-
XIX. tion that commerce, arts, and sciences, should flourish
within it. It is even a happiness for those who govern,
when they are not inclined to exert acts of tyranny.
Upright minds are very easily led; but none have a
greater aversion for violence and slavery. Let good
monarchs be blessed with enlightened people, and let
tyrants have none but brutes to reign over.

Military power is both the cause and the destruction
of despotism; which in its infant state may be compared to a lion that conceals his talons in order to let
them grow. In its full vigour, it may be considered
as a madman who tears his body to pieces with his
arms. In its advanced age, it is like Saturn, who, after having devoured his children, is shamefully mutilated by his own race.

Government may be divided into legislation and
policy. Legislation relates to the internal management of the state, and policy to the external direction
of it.

Policy. Savage nations, which are addicted to hunting, have
rather a policy than a legislation. Governed among
themselves by manners and example, the only conventions or laws they have are between one nation
and another. Treaties of peace or alliance constitute
their only code of legislation.

Such were nearly the societies of ancient times.
Separated by deserts, without any communication of
trade or voyages, they had only a present and immediate interest to settle. All their negotiations consisted in putting an end to a war by fixing the boundaries of a state. As it was necessary to persuade a nation, and not bribe a court by the mistresses or favourites of a prince, eloquent men were employed for this
purpose; and the names of orator and ambassador
were synonymous.

In the middle ages, when every thing, even justice
itself, was decided by force; when the Gothic government divided by separate interests all those petty states
which owed their existence to its constitution; nego-

tiations had but little influence over a wild and recluse people, who knew no right but that of war, no treaties but for truces or ransoms.

During this long period of ignorance and barbarism, policy was entirely confined to the court of Rome. It had arisen from the artifices which had founded the papal government. As the pontiffs, by the laws of religion and the system of the hierarchy, influenced a very numerous clergy, whose proselytes extended perpetually in all the Christian states, the correspondence kept up with the bishops, established early at Rome a centre of communication for all the different churches or nations. All rights were subordinate to a religion which exercised an absolute authority over the mind of every individual; it had a share in almost every transaction, either as the motive or the means; and the popes, by the Italian agents they had placed in all the prelacies of the Christian state, were constantly informed of every commotion, and availed themselves of every event. They had the highest interest in this; that of attaining universal monarchy. The barbarism of the times in which this project was conceived, does not lessen its greatness and sublimity. How daring was the attempt, to subdue, without troops, nations that were always in arms! What art to make even the weakness of the clergy respectable and sacred! What skill to agitate, to shake thrones one after the other, in order to keep them all in subjection! So deep, so extensive a design could only be carried into execution, by being concealed; and therefore was inconsistent with an hereditary monarchy; in which the passions of kings, and the intrigues of ministers, are the cause of so much instability in affairs. This project, and the general rule of conduct it requires, could not be formed but in an elective government, in which the chief is always chosen from a body animated with the same spirit, and guided by the same maxims; in which an aristocratic court rather governs the prince, than suffers itself to be governed by him.

While Iialian policy was engaged in examining all
the states of Europe, and availing itself of every opportunity to aggrandize and confirm the power of the
church, each fovereign faw with indifference the revolutions that were taking place without. Moft of
them were too much engaged in eftablifhing their
authority in their own dominions, in difputing the
branches of power with the feveral bodies which were
in poffeffion of them, or which were ftriving againft
the natural bent that monarchy has to defpotifm :
they were not fufficiently mafters of their own inheritance, to interfere in the difputes of their neighbours.

The fifteenth century changed the order of things.
When the princes had collected their forces, they were
inclined to bring them to action, and try their refpective ftrength. Till that time, the nations had only carried on war with each other upon their feveral frontiers. The feafon of the campaign was loft
in affembling troops, which every baron always raifed very flowly. There were then only fkirmifhes between fmall parties, not any regular battles between different armies. When a prince, either by alliances or
inheritance, had acquired poffeffions in different ftates,
the interefts were confounded, and contentions arofe
among the people. It was neceffary to fend regular
troops in the pay of the monarch, to defend at a diftance territories that did not belong to the ftate. The
crown of England no longer held provinces in the
midft of France ; but that of Spain acquired fome
rights in Germany, and that of France laid fome claims
in Italy. From that time all Europe was in a perpetual alternate ftate of war and negotiation.

The ambition, talents, and rivalfhip of Charles V.
and Francis I. gave rife to the prefent fyftem of modern politics. Before thefe two kings, France and
Spain had difputed the kingdom of Naples, in the
name of the houfes of Arragon and Anjou. Their
diffenfions had excited a ferment throughout all Italy,
and the republic of Venice was the chief caufe of

that inteftine commotion that was excited againft two foreign powers. The Germans took a part in thefe difturbances, either as auxiliaries, or as being interefted in them. The emperor and the pope were concerned in them with almoft all Chriftendom. But Francis I. and Charles V. engaged in their fate, the views, the anxiety, the deftiny of all Europe. All the powers feemed to be divided between two rival houfes, in order to weaken alternately the moft powerful. Fortune favoured the talents, the force, and the artifice of Charles V. More ambitious and lefs voluptuous than Francis I., his character turned the fcale, and Europe for a time inclined to his fide, but did not continue always to favour the fame intereft.

Philip II. who had all the fpirit of intrigue, but not the military virtues of his father, inherited his projects and ambitious views, and found the times favourable to his aggrandizement. He exhaufted his kingdom of men and fhips, and even of money, though he was in poffeffion of the mines of the New World ; and left behind him a more extenfive monarchy, but Spain itfelf in a much weaker ftate than it had been under his father.

His fon imagined he fhould again make all Europe dependent, by an alliance with that branch of his houfe which reigned in Germany. Philip II. had through negligence relinquifhed this political idea : Philip III. refumed it. But in other refpects he followed the erroneous, narrow, fuperftitious, and pedantic principles of his predeceffor. Within the ftate, there was much formality, but no order and no economy. The church was perpetually encroaching upon the ftate. The inquifition, that horrid monfter, which conceals its head in the heavens and its feet in the infernal regions, ftruck at the root of population, which at the fame time fuffered confiderably from war and the colonies. In the external operations of the ftate, there were ftill the fame ambitious views, and lefs fkilful meafures. Rafh and precipitate

in his enterprifes, flow and obftinate in the execution
of them, Philip III. had all thofe defects which are
prejudicial to each other, and occafion every project
to mifcarry. He deftroyed the fmall degree of life
and vigour the monarchy yet retained. Richelieu a-
vailed himfelf of the weaknefs of Spain, and the foibles
of the king whom he ruled over, to fill that period
with his intrigues, and caufe his name to defcend to
pofterity. Germany and Spain were in fome manner
connected to each other by the houfe of Auftria : to
this league, he oppofed that of France with Sweden,
to counteract the effect of the former. This fyftem
would naturally have taken place in his times, if it
had not been the work of his genius. Guftavus A-
dolphus by his conquefts enflaved all the north. All
Europe concurred in lowering the pride of the houfe
of Auftria ; and the peace of the Pyrenees turned the
fcale againft Spain in favour of France.

Charles V. had been accufed of aiming at univerfal
monarchy ; and Lewis XIV. was taxed with the fame
ambition. But neither of them ever conceived fo high
and fo rafh a project. They were both of them paf-
fionately defirous of extending their empire, by the
aggrandizement of their families. This ambition is
equally natural to princes of common abilities, who
are born without any talents, as it is to monarchs of
fuperior underftanding, who have no virtues or moral
qualifications. But neither Charles V. nor Lewis XIV.
had that kind of fpirit of refolution, that impufe of
the foul to brave every thing, which conftitutes heroic conquerors : they bore no refemblance in any
particular to Alexander. Neverthelefs ufeful alarms
were taken and fpread abroad. Such alarms cannot
be too foon conceived, nor too foon diffufed, when
there arife any powers that are formidable to their
neighbours. It is chiefly among nations, and with refpect to kings, that fear produces fafety.

When Lewis XIV. began to reflect on his own fituation, perhaps he might be furprifed at feeing himfelf more powerful than he thought he was. His great-

nefs was partly owing to the little harmony that fubfifted betweed the forces and the defigns of his enemies. Europe had, indeed, felt the neceffity of a general union, but had not difcovered the means of forming it. In treating with this monarch, proud of fuccefs, and vain from the applaufe he had received, it
was thought a confiderable advantage if every thing
was not given up. In a word, the infults of France,
which increafed with her victories; the natural turn of
her intrigues to fpread diffenfion everywhere, in order
to reign alone; her contempt for the faith of treaties;
the haughty and authoritative tone fhe ufurped, turned the general envy fhe had excited into deteftation,
and raifed univerfal alarms. Even thofe princes, who
had feen without umbrage, or favoured the increafe of
her power, felt the neceffity of repairing this error in
politics, and of combining and raifing among themfelves a body of forces fuperior to thofe of France,
in order to prevent her tyrannizing over the nations.

Leagues were, therefore, formed, which were for a
long time ineffectual. One man alone was found capable to animate and conduct them. Warmed with
that public fpirit, which only great and virtuous fouls
can poffefs, it was a prince, though born in a republic, who, for the general caufe of Europe, was inflamed with that love of liberty, fo natural to upright
minds. He turned his ambition towards the greateft
object and moft worthy of the time in which he lived. His own intereft never warped him from that of
the public. With a courage peculiar to himfelf he
knew how to defy thofe very misfortunes which he
forefaw; depending lefs for fuccefs upon his military
abilities, than, waiting for a favourable turn of affairs,
from his patience and political activity. Such was
the fituation of affairs when the fucceffion to the throne
of Spain fet all Europe in flames.

Since the empire of the Perfians and that of the
Romans, ambition had never been tempted by fo rich
a fpoil. The prince, who might have united this
crown to his own, would naturally have rifen to that

B O O K univerfal monarchy, the idea of which raifed a gene-
XIX.   ral alarm.   It was therefore neceffary to prevent this
empire from becoming the poffeffion of a power already formidable, and to keep the balance equal between the Houfes of Auftria and Bourbon, which had
the only hereditary right to the throne.

Men well verfed in the knowledge of the manners
and affairs of Spain, have afferted, if we may believe
Bolingbroke, that had it not been for the hoftilities,
which were then excited by England and Holland, we
fhould have feen Philip V. as good a Spaniard as his
predeceffors, and that the French miniftry would then
have had no influence over the Spanifh adminiftration;
but that the war raifed againft the Spaniards for the
fake of giving them a ruler, obliged them to have recourfe to the fleets and armies of a ftate that was a-
lone capable of affifting them in fixing upon fuch a
king as they wanted.   This juft idea, the refult of
deep reflection, has been confirmed by the experience
of half a century.   The turn of the Spaniards has
never been able to coincide with the tafte of the
French.   Spain, from the character of her inhabitants, feems rather to belong to Africa than to Europe.

The train of events, however, anfwered to the general wifhes.   The armies and the councils of the
quadruple alliance gained an equal fuperiority over
the common enemy.   Inftead of thofe languid and
unfortunate campaigns which had tried the patience
of the prince of Orange, but not difcouraged him,
all the operations of the confederates were fuccefsful.
France, in her turn, humbled and defeated on every
fide, was upon the brink of ruin, when fhe was reftored by the death of the emperor.

It was then perceived, that if the archduke Charles,
crowned with the imperial diadem, and fucceeding to
all the dominions of the Houfe of Auftria, fhould join
Spain and the Weft Indies to this vaft inheritance, he
would be in poffeffion of that fame exorbitant power,
which the Houfe of Bourbon had been deprived of by

the war. But the enemies of France still persisted in their design of dethroning Philip V. without thinking of the person that was to succeed him; while true politicians, notwithstanding their triumphs, grew tired of a war, the very success of which always became an evil, when it could no longer do any good. B O O K XIX.

This difference of opinions raised dissensions among the allies, which prevented them from reaping all those advantages from the peace of Utrecht, they might reasonably have expected from their success. The best means that could be devised to protect the provinces of the allies, were to lay open the frontiers of France. Lewis XIV. had employed forty years in fortifying them, and his neighbours had suffered him quietly to raise these bulwarks which kept them in continual awe. It was necessary to demolish them: for every strong power that puts itself in a posture of defence, intends to form an attack. Philip remained upon the throne of Spain; and the fortifications were left standing in Flanders, and on the borders of the Rhine.

Since this period, no opportunity hath offered to rectify the mistake committed at the peace of Utrecht. France hath always maintained its superiority on the continent; but chance hath often diminished its influence. The scales of the political balance will never be perfectly even, nor accurate enough to determine the degrees of power with exact precision. Perhaps, even this balance of power may be nothing more than a chimera. It can be only fixed by treaties, and these have no validity, when they are only made between absolute monarchs, and not between nations. These acts must be permanent when made by the people themselves, because the object of them is their peace and safety, which are their greatest advantages: but a despot always sacrifices his subjects to his anxiety, and his engagements to his ambition.

But it is not war alone that determines the superiority of nations, as it hath been hitherto imagined; since during the last half-century commerce hath had

BOOK a much greater influence in it. While the powers of
XIX. the continent divided Europe into unequal portions,
which policy, by means of leagues, treaties, and alliances, always preferved in a certain equilibrium; a
maritime people formed as it were a new fyftem, and
by their induftry made the land fubject to the fea;
as nature herfelf has done by her laws. They formed, or brought to perfection, that extenfive commerce,
which is founded on an excellent fyftem of agriculture, flourifhing manufactures, and the richeft poffeffions of the four quarters of the world. This is the
kind of univerfal monarchy that Europe ought to
wreft from England, in reftoring to each maritime
ftate that freedom and that power it hath a right to
have upon the element that furrounds it. This is a
fyftem of public good founded upon natural equity,
and in this cafe juftice is the voice of general intereft. The people cannot be too much warned to refume all their powers, and to employ the refources offered them by the climate and the foil they inhabit,
to acquire that national and diftinct independence in
which they were born.

If all Europe were fufficiently enlightened, and each
nation were acquainted with its rights and its real advantages, neither the continent nor the ocean would
mutually give laws to each other; but a reciprocal influence would be eftablifhed between the continental
and maritime people, a balance of induftry and power, which would induce a mutual intercourfe for the
general benefit. Each nation would fow and reap
upon its proper element. The feveral ftates would
enjoy the fame liberty of exportation and importation
that fhould fubfift between the provinces of the fame
empire.

There is a great error that prevails in modern politics, which is, that every ftate fhould endeavour to
weaken its enemies as much as poffible. But no nation can feek the ruin of another ftate, without paving the way for, and haftening its own flavery. There
are certainly moments in which fortune at once throws

into the way of a people a great increafe of power; B O O K
but fuch fudden elevations are not lafting. It is fome- XIX.
times better to fupport rivals, than to opprefs them.
Sparta refufed to enflave Athens, and Rome repented
of having deftroyed Carthage.

Thefe noble and generous fentiments would prevent policy from the neceffity of committing many
crimes and afferting many falfehoods; policy, which
for thefe two or three centuries paft hath had more
important and more various objects to attend to. The
influence of policy was formerly much limited, it feldom extended beyond the frontiers of the feveral nations. Its fphere hath been fingularly enlarged in proportion as the nations moft diftant from each other
have formed connections among themfelves. It hath
particularly received an immenfe increafe fince the
time, when by difcoveries, either fortunate or unfortunate, all the parts of the univerfe have been rendered fubordinate to thofe which we inhabit.

As the operations of policy were multiplied in proportion to the extent which it acquired, every power
thought it neceffary for their interefts to fix agents in
foreign courts, who had formerly been employed there
but for a very fhort time. The habit of treating inceffantly gave birth to maxims unknown before that
period. Delays and artifices were fubftituted to the
franknefs and celerity of tranfient negotiations. The
powers founded and ftudied each other, and reciprocal
attempts were made to tire out or to furprife all parties. Secrets which had been found impenetrable were
purchafed with gold, and bribery completed what intrigue had begun.

It appeared neceffary to furnifh a continual fupply
of matter to quiet that fpirit of anxiety with which the
minds of all the ambaffadors had been impreffed. Policy, like that infidious infect that weaves its web in
darknefs, hath ftretched forth its net in the midft of
Europe, and faftened it, as it were, to every court.
One fingle thread cannot be touched without drawing
all the reft. The moft petty fovereign hath fome fe-

cret intereſt in the treaties between the greater powers.
Two petty princes of Germany cannot exchange a fief,
or a domain, without being thwarted or ſeconded by
the courts of Vienna, Verſailles, or London. Negotiations muſt be carried on in all the cabinets for years
together for every the moſt trifling change in the diſ-
poſition of the land. The blood of the people is the
only thing that is not bargained for. War is determined upon in a day or two; the ſettling of peace is
protracted during ſeveral years. This ſlowneſs in negotiations, which proceeds from the nature of affairs,
is alſo increaſed by the character of the negotiators.

Theſe are generally ignorant perſons, who are treating with ſome men of knowledge and abilities. The
chancellor Oxenſtiern ordered his ſon to prepare himſelf to go to Weſtphalia, where the troubles of the empire were to be pacified. *But*, ſaid the young man,
*I have not attended to any previous ſtudies neceſſary for
this important commiſſion. I will prepare you for it*, replied the father. A fortnight after, Oxenſtiern, who
had not ſpoken upon the ſubject to his ſon, ſaid to him,
*My ſon, you muſt ſet out to-morrow.—But, ſir, you had
promiſed to inſtruct me, and you have not done it. Go,
nevertheleſs*, replied the experienced miniſter, ſhrug-
ging up his ſhoulders, *and you will ſee by what kind of
men the world is governed.* There are, perhaps, two or
three wiſe and judicious councils in Europe. The reſt
are in the poſſeſſion of intriguing men, raiſed to the
management of affairs by the paſſions and ſhameful
pleaſures of a prince and his miſtreſſes. A man is advanced to a ſhare in the adminiſtration, without any
knowledge of the ſubject; he adopts the firſt ſyſtem
that is offered to his caprice, purſues it without under-
ſtanding it, and, with a degree of obſtinacy proportionate to his ignorance, he changes the whole plan of
his predeceſſors, in order to introduce his own ſyſtem
of adminiſtration, which he will never be able to ſupport. Richelieu's firſt declaration, when he became
miniſter, was, *the council hath altered its plan.* This
ſaying, which was once found to be a good one, in the

mouth of one single man, has, perhaps, been repeated, B O O K
or thought of, by every one of Richelieu's succeffors. XIX.
All men engaged in public affairs have the vanity not
only to proportion the parade of their expence, of their
manner, and of their air, to the importance of their
office, but even to raife the opinion they have of their
own underftanding, in proportion to the influence of
their authority.

When a nation is great and powerful, what fhould
its governors be? The court and the people will anfwer this queftion, but in a very different manner.
The minifters fee nothing in their office but the extent
of their rights; the people the extent only of their duties. The ideas of the latter are juft; for the duties
and rights arifing from each mode of government
ought to be regulated by the wants and defires of each
nation. But this principle of the law of nature is not
applicable to the focial ftate. As focieties, whatever
be their origin, are almoft all of them fubject to the
authority of one fingle man, political meafures are dependent on the character of the prince.

If the king be a weak and irrefolute man, his government will change as his minifters, and his politics
will vary with his government. He will alternately
have minifters that are ignorant or enlightened, fteady
or fickle, deceitful or fincere, harfh or humane, inclined to war or peace; fuch, in a word, as the variety of
intrigues will produce them. Such a ftate will have
no regular fyftem of politics; and all other governments will not be able to maintain any permanent defigns and meafures with it. The fyftem of politics
muft then vary with the day, or the moment; that is,
with the humour of the prince. Under a weak and
unfteady reign, none but temporary interefts ought to
prevail, and connections fubordinate to the inftability
of the miniftry.

The reciprocal jealoufy prevailing between the depofitaries of the royal authority is another caufe of this
inftability. One man, againft the teftimony of his

B O O K conscience and of his knowledge, counteracts, from a
XIX. motive of mean jealousy, a useful measure, the honour
of which would belong to his rival. The next day the
same infamous part is adopted by the latter. The sovereign alternately grants what he had refused, or re-
fuses what he had granted. The negotiator will easily
perceive which of his ministers he has least consulted,
but it is impossible for him to foresee what his last refolution will be. In this embarrassment to whom shall
we have recourse? To bribery and to the women, if
he be sent into a country governed by a man. To
bribery and to the men, if he be sent into a country
governed by a woman. He must lay aside the character of the ambassador or of the envoy, in order to
assume that of the corrupter, the only one by which
he can succeed. It is gold which he must substitute to
the most profound policy. But if by some chance, of
which perhaps there is scarce any example, gold should
fail of its effect, the only resource he has remaining is
to solicit to be recalled.

But the fate of nations and political interests are very different in republican governments. As the authority there resides in the collective body of the people, there are certain principles and some public interests attended to in every negotiation. In this case,
the permanency of a system is not to be confined to
the duration of the ministry, or to the life of one single man. The general spirit that exists and perpetuates itself in the nation is the only rule of every negotiation. Not but that a powerful citizen, or an eloquent demagogue, may sometimes lead a popular government into a political mistake; but this is easily recovered. Faults, in these instances, may be considered
equally with successes as lessons of instruction. Great
events, and not men, produce remarkable periods in
the history of republics. It is in vain to attempt to
surprise a free people by artifice or intrigues, into a
treaty of peace or alliance. Their maxims will always
make them return to their lasting interests, and all en-

gagements will give way to the fupreme law. In thefe B o o k governments, it is the fafety of the people that does XIX. every thing, while in others it is the will of the ruler.

This contraft of political principles has rendered every popular government fufpicious or odious to all abfolute monarchs. They have dreaded the influence of a republican fpirit upon their own fubjects, the weight of whofe chains they are every day increafing. A kind of fecret confpiracy may therefore be perceived between all monarchies, to deftroy, or infenfibly to fap, the foundations of all free ftates. But liberty will arife from the midft of oppreffion. It already exifts in every breaft; public writings will contribute to inftil it into the minds of all enlightened men, and tyranny into the hearts of the people. All men will, at length, be fenfible, and this period is at no great diftance, that liberty is the firft gift of Heaven, as it is the firft fource of virtue. The inftruments of defpotifm will become its deftroyers; and the enemies of humanity, thofe who feem armed at prefent merely to oppofe it, will exert themfelves in its defence.

In this place I was intending to fpeak of war, or that War. rage which, being kindled by injuftice, ambition, and revenge, affembles, under two adverfe commanders, a multitude of armed men, impels them againft each other, drenches the earth with their blood, ftrews it with dead bodies, and prepares nourifhment for the animals that come after them, but who are lefs ferocious than they.

But I have fuddenly poftponed my intention, by afking of myfelf what peace is, and whether it exifts anywhere? Upon the fpot where I now am, in the centre of my own city, a multitude of interefts oppofite to mine confine me, and I repel them. If I pafs the limits of that fpace which I call my own country, I am confidered with an anxious eye; I am accofted, and afked who I am, from whence I came, and where I am going? At length I obtain a bed, and am preparing to take fome reft, when a fudden clamour compels me to depart. If I remain, I am profcribed; and

the next day the houfe which had given me refuge
fhall be fet on fire, and thofe who have treated me as
a fellow-citizen fhall be murdered by affaffins who
fpeak my own language. Should curiofity, or a thirft
of knowledge, induce me to vifit another country; if
I take fome pains to examine it, I am immediately
fufpected, and a fpy is commiffioned to watch me.
Should I have the misfortune to worfhip God in my
own way, which happens not to be that of the country
I am vifiting, I am furrounded by priefts and executioners. I then make my efcape, exclaiming, with
grief: Peace, then, that bleffing fo earneftly wifhed
for, exifts not in any place.

The good man, however, hath his dreams; and I
will acknowledge, that being witnefs to the progrefs of
knowledge, which hath fhaken fo many prejudices,
and introduced fo much foftnefs in our manners, I
have thought that it was impoffible the infernal art of
war fhould be perpetuated, but that it would fink into
oblivion. The people who have brought it to perfection will become accurfed; and the moment when
thefe formidable inftruments of death fhall be generally demolifhed cannot be far diftant. The univerfe
will at length execrate thofe odious conquerors, who
have rather chofen to be the terror of their neighbours
than the fathers of their fubjects, and to invade provinces rather than to gain the affections of men; who
have chofen that the cries of grief fhould be the only
hymn accompanying their victories; who have raifed
up melancholy monuments, deftined to immortalize
their rage and their vanity, in the countries which
they had fpoiled, in the cities they had reduced to
afhes, and over the carcafes which their fwords had
heaped on each other; conquerors, who have had no
other wifh than that the hiftory of their reign fhould
contain only the remembrance of the calamities they
had occafioned. Mankind will no longer be deceived
refpecting the objects of their admiration. They will
no longer, with abject infatuation, proftrate themfelves
before thofe who trampled them under their feet. Ca-

iamities will be confidered in their proper light; and the nocturnal labours and talents of great artifts will no longer be proftituted to the commemoration of brilliant crimes. Princes themfelves will partake of the wifdom of their age. The voice of philofophy will revive in their minds fentiments which have long lain dormant, and will infpire them with horror, and a contempt for fanguinary glory. They will be confirmed in thefe ideas by the minifters of religion ; who, availing themfelves of the facred privilege of their functions, will drag them before the tribunal of the Great Judge, where they will be obliged to anfwer for the thoufands of unfortunate perfons facrificed to their hatred or caprice. If it were refolved in the decrees of Heaven, that fovereigns fhould perfevere in their frenzy, thofe numberlefs hordes of affaffins who are kept in pay would throw away their arms. Filled with a juft horror for their deteftable employment, and with profound indignation againft the cruel abufe which was made of their ftrength and of their courage, they would leave their extravagant defpots to fettle their quarrels themfelves.

But this illufion did not laft long. I was foon perfuaded that the difputes between kings would never end, any more than their paffions, and that they could only be decided by the fword. I thought that it would be impoffible ever to difguft of the horrors of war a people, who, notwithftanding all forts of cruelties and devaftations were committed around them without fcruple and without remorfe, upon the fcene of difcord, ftill found, while fitting quietly by their fire-fide, that there were not fieges, battles, or cataftrophes enough to fatisfy their curiofity and amufe their vacant hours. I thought, that there was nothing either reafonable or humane to be expected from a fet of fubaltern butchers, who, far from giving themfelves up to defpair, from tearing their hair, from detefting themfelves, and from fhedding rivers of tears at the fight of a vaft plain filled with fcattered members, were, on the contrary, able to go over it with an air of triumph, bathing their feet in the blood of their friends and of their enemies, walking over their carcafes, and mixing fongs of mirth with the plaintive accents of expiring men. It feemed to me, as if I heard the fpeech of one of thofe tygers, who, blending flattery with ferocioufnefs, faid to a monarch, feized with a confternation at the fight of a field of battle covered with torn limbs and dead bodies, fcarcely cold: *Sir, it is not us, but thofe, who are too happy:* and thus prevented the tears from falling from the eyes of a young prince; tears, which he ought rather to have prompted him to fhed, by faying to him: " Behold, and confider the " effects of thy ambition, of thy folly, of thy rage, and " of ours; and feel the drops of blood trickling down " thy cheeks, which fall from the laurels with which " we have crowned thee." Thefe diftreffing reflections plunged me into melancholy; fo that it was fome time before I could refume the thread of my ideas, and go on with my fubject.

War has exifted at all times and in all countries; but the art of war is only to be found in certain ages of the world, and among certain people. The Greeks inftituted it, and conquered all the powers of Afia. The Romans improved it, and fubdued the world. Thefe two nations, worthy to command all others, as their genius and virtue were the caufes of their profperity, owed this fuperiority to their infantry, in which every fingle man exerts his whole ftrength. The Grecian phalanx and the Roman legions were everywhere victorious.

When indolence had introduced a fuperior number of cavalry into the armies of the ancients, Rome loft fome of its glory and fuccefs. Notwithftanding the exact difcipline of its troops, it could no longer refift thofe barbarous nations that fought on foot.

Thefe men, however, little better than favages, who, with arms only, and thofe powers nature had taught them the ufe of, had fubdued the moft extenfive and the moft civilized empire of the univerfe, foon changed their infantry into cavalry. This was properly called the line of battle, or the army. All the nobility, who were the fole poffeffors of lands and of privileges, thofe ufual attendants of victory, chofe to ride on horfeback; while the enflaved multitude were left on foot, almoft without arms, and were fcarce holden in any degree of eftimation.

In times when the gentleman was diftinguifhed by his horfe; when the man himfelf was of little confequence, and every idea of importance was attached to the knight; when wars confifted in fmall incurfions, and campaigns lafted but a day; when fuccefs depended upon the quicknefs of marches; then the fate of armies was determined by cavalry. During the thirteenth and fourteenth centuries, there were fcarce any other troops in Europe. The dexterity and ftrength of men was no longer fhown in wreftling, at the ceftus, in the exercife of arms, and of all the mufcles of the body; but in tournaments, in managing a horfe, and in throwing the lance at full fpeed. This fpecies of war, better calculated for wandering Tartars, than for fixed and fedentary focieties, was one of the defects of the feudal government. A race of conquerors, whofe rights were to be determined by their fwords, whofe merit and glory were in their arms, whofe fole occupation was hunting, could fcarce avoid riding on horfeback, with all that parade and fpirit of authority which muft neceffarily arife from a rude and uncultivated underftanding. But what could troops of heavy-armed cavalry avail in the attack and defence of caftles and towns, fortified by walls or by furrounding waters?

To this imperfection of the military art, muft be afcribed the duration of war for feveral ages, without intermiffion, between France and England. War continued inceffantly for want of a fufficient number of men. Whole months were required to collect, to arm, to bring into the field troops that were only to continue there a few weeks. Kings could not affemble more than a certain number of vaffals, and thofe at ftated times. The lords had only a right to call under

BOOK their banners fome of their tenants, upon ftipulated
XIX. terms. The time that ought to have been employed
in carrying on war was loft in forms and regulations,
in the fame manner as courts of juftice confume thofe
eftates they are to determine. At length the French,
tired with being conftantly obliged to repulfe the Englifh, like the horfe that implored the affiftance of man
againft the ftag, fuffered the yoke and burden to be
impofed upon them, which they bear to this day.
Kings raifed and maintained at their own expence a
conftant body of troops. Charles VII. after having
expelled the Englifh by the affiftance of mercenary
troops, when he difbanded his army, kept nine thoufand horfe and fixteen thoufand infantry.

This was the origin of the abafement of the nobility
and the elevation of monarchy, of the political liberty
of the nation without, and its civil flavery within. The
people were delivered from feudal tyranny, only to
fall, fome time or other, under the defpotifm of kings.
So much does human nature feem born for flavery! It
became neceffary to raife a fund for the payment of an
army; and the taxes were arbitrary, and unlimited as
the number of foldiers, who were diftributed in the
different parts of the kingdom, under a pretence of
guarding the frontiers againft the enemy; but in reality to reftrain and opprefs the fubject. The officers,
commanders, and governors, were tools of government always armed againft the nation itfelf. They,
as well as their foldiers, no longer confidered themfelves as citizens of the ftate, folely devoted to the defence of the property and rights of the people. They
acknowledged no longer any perfon in the kingdom
except the king, in whofe name they were ready to
maffacre their fathers and brothers. In fhort, the body of troops raifed by the nation was nothing more
than a royal army.

The difcovery of gun-powder, which required confiderable expence and great preparation, forges, magazines, and arfenals, made arms more than ever dependent on kings, and determined the advantage that in-

fantry hath over cavalry. The latter prefented the flank of the man and horfe to the former. A horfe-man difmounted was either loft or good for nothing; and a horfe without a leader occafioned confufion and diforder among the ranks. The havock which the artillery and fire-arms made in fquadrons, was more difficult to repair than it was in battalions. In a word, men could be bought and difciplined at a lefs expence than horfes; and this made it eafy for kings to procure foldiers.

Thus the innovation of Charles VII. fatal to his fubjects, at leaft in futurity, became from his example prejudicial to the liberty of all the people of Europe. Every nation was obliged to keep itfelf upon the defence againft a nation always in arms. The right fyftem of politics, if there were any politics at a time when arts, literature, and commerce had not yet opened a communication among people, fhould have been, for the princes to have jointly attacked that particular power that had put itfelf into a ftate of continual war. But inftead of compelling it to fubmit to peace, they took up arms themfelves. This contagion fpread itfelf the quicker, as it appeared the fole remedy againft the danger of an invafion, the only guarantee of the fecurity of the nations.

There was, however, a general want of the knowledge neceffary to difcipline a body of infantry, the importance of which began to be perceived. The manner of fighting which the Switzers had employed againft the Burgundians, had rendered them as celebrated as formidable. With heavy fwords and long halberds, they had always overcome the horfes and men of the feudal army. As their ranks were impenetrable, and as they marched in clofe columns, they overthrew all that attacked and all that oppofed them. Every power was then defirous of procuring fome Swifs foldiers. But the Switzers, fenfible of the need there was of their affiftance, and fetting the purchafe of it at too high a rate, it became neceffary to refolve not

to employ them, and to form in all parts a national
infantry, in order not to depend upon thefe auxiliary
troops.

The Germans firſt adopted a diſcipline that required
only ſtrength of body, and ſubordination. As their
country abounded in men and horſes, they almoſt ri-
valled the reputation of the Swiſs infantry, without
loſing the advantage of their own cavalry.

The French, more lively, adopted, with greater difficulty, and more ſlowly, a kind of military ſyſtem that
laid a reſtraint upon all their motions, and ſeemed rather to require perſeverance than impetuoſity. But
the taſte for imitation and novelty prevailed among
this light people over that vanity which is fond of its
own cuſtoms.

The Spaniards, notwithſtanding the pride they have
been reproached with, improved the military art of the
Switzers, by bringing to greater perfection the diſcipline of that warlike people. They formed an infantry which became alternately the terror and admiration of Europe.

In proportion as the infantry increaſed, the cuſtom
and ſervice of the feudal militia ceaſed in all parts, and
war became more general. The conſtitution of each
nation had for ages paſt ſcarce allowed the different
people to wage war and maſſacre one another beyond
the barriers of their own ſtates. War was carried on
upon the frontiers only between the neighbouring
powers. When France and Spain had carried their
arms to the moſt remote extremities of Italy, it was
no longer poſſible to call together the ban and arriere
ban of the nations, becauſe it was not in fact the people who made war againſt each other, but the kings
with their troops, for the honour of themſelves or their
families, without any regard to the good of their ſubjects. Not that the princes did not endeavour to intereſt the national pride of the people in their quarrels; but this was done merely to weaken, or totally
to ſubdue that ſpirit of independence, which was ſtill

ftruggling among fome fets of men, againft that abfolute authority which the princes had gradually affumed.

All Europe was in commotion. The Germans
marched into Italy, the Italians into Germany, the
French into both thefe countries. The Turks befieged Naples and Nice, and the Spaniards were at
the fame time difperfed in Africa, in Hungary, in Italy, in Germany, in France, and in the Low Countries.
All thefe people, inured and practifed in arms, acquired great fkill in the art of fighting and deftroying each
other with infallible regularity and precifion.

It was religion that caufed the Germans to contend
with the Germans, the French with the French, but
which more particularly excited Flanders againft Spain.
It was on the fens of Holland that all the rage of a bi-
goted and defpotic king fell, of a fuperftitious and fanguinary prince, of the two Philips, and of the duke of
Alva. It was in the Low Countries that a republic
arofe from the perfecution of tyranny and the flames
of the inquifition. When freedom had broken her
chains, and found an afylum in the ocean, fhe raifed
her bulwarks upon the continent. The Dutch firft
invented the art of fortifying places; fo much do genius and invention belong to free minds. Their example was generally followed. Extenfive ftates had
only occafion to fortify their frontiers. Germany and
Italy, divided among a number of princes, were crowded with ftrong citadels from one end to the other.
When we travel through thefe countries, we meet
every evening with gates fhut and draw-bridges at the
entrance of the towns.

While Naffau, who had taken up arms to fecure the
independence of his country, was renewing the fcience
of fortification, the paffion for glory ftimulated Guftavus Adolphus to inveftigate, according to the maxims
of the ancients, the principles of the military fcience
of the field, which were almoft entirely loft. He had
the honour to difcover, to apply, and to diffufe them;
but, if the moft experienced judges may be credited,

B O O K
XIX.
he did not introduce into thofe principles the modifications which the difference of men's minds, of conftitutions, and of arms, would have required. The perfons trained up under him, great captains as they were,
could not venture to be more bold or more enlightened than himfelf; and this timid circumfpection prevented the alterations and improvements which might
have been made. Cohorn and Vauban alone inftructed Europe in the art of defending, but efpecially in
that of attacking places. It happened, by one of thofe
contradictions which are fometimes obferved among
nations, as well as among individuals, that the French,
notwithftanding their ardent and impetuous difpofition, appeared more expert in fieges than any other
nation; and that they feemed to acquire at the foot
of the walls that patience and coolnefs, in which they
are moft commonly deficient in all other military operations.

The king of Pruffia appeared, and with him a new
order of things was introduced. Without fuffering
himfelf to be fwayed by the authority of thofe who
had gone before him, this prince created a fyftem of
tactics almoft entirely new. He demonftrated, that
troops, however numerous, might be difciplined and
manœuvred; that the motions of the greateft armies
were not fubject to calculations more complicated and
lefs certain than thofe of the moft feeble corps; and
that the fame fprings by which one battalion was put
in motion, when properly managed, and put together
by a great commander, might fet a hundred thoufand
men in motion. His genius fuggefted to him many
fcientific details, of which no man had previoufly entertained the leaft idea; and by giving, in a manner,
the advantage to the legs over the arms, he introduced into his evolutions, and into his marches, a celerity, which is become neceffary, and almoft decifive,
fince armies have been unfortunately fo much multiplied, and fince they have been obliged to occupy a
very extenfive front.

This prince, who, fince Alexander, hath not had his

equal in hiftory, for extent and variety of talents ; who, B O O K
without having been himfelf formed by Greeks, hath   XIX.
been able to form Lacedemonians ; this monarch, in a
word, who hath deferved beyond all others that his
name fhould be recorded in his age, and who will have
the glory, fince it is one, of having carried the art of
war to a degree of perfection, from which, fortunately,
it cannot but degenerate.   Frederic hath feen all Europe adopt his inftitutions with enthufiafm.   In imitation of the Roman people, who, by inftructing themfelves at the fchool of their enemies, learnt the art of
refifting, of vanquifhing, and of enflaving them, the
modern nations have endeavoured to follow the example of a neighbour, formidable by his military capacity, and who might become dangerous by his fuccefs.   But have they accomplifhed their defign ? Some
external parts of his difcipline have undoubtedly been
imitated ; but let us be allowed to doubt whether his
great principles have been perfectly underftood, thoroughly inveftigated, and properly combined.

But even if this fublime and terrible doctrine were
become common among the powers, would it be e-
qually ufeful to them all?   The Pruffians never lofe
fight of it one moment.   They are ignorant of the intrigues of courts, the luxuries of cities, and the idlenefs
of a country life.   Their colours are their roofs, warlike fongs their amufements, the recital of their firft
exploits their converfation, and frefh laurels their only hope.   Eternally under arms, eternally in exercife,
they have perpetually before them the image, and almoft the reality, of a prudent and obftinate war, whether they be collected together in camps, or difperfed
in garrifons.

Military men of all countries, draw the contraft between this defcription and that of your education, of
your laws, and of your manners, and compare yourfelves to fuch men, if you can.   I will allow that the
found of the trumpet may roufe you from your lethargy, from balls, from public amufements ; and that,
from the arms of your miftreffes, you may rufh with

eagerness into danger. But will a transient ardour supply the place of that vigilance, of that activity, of that
application, and of that foresight, which can alone determine the operations of a war or of a campaign?
Will a body, enervated by effeminate habits, resist the
horrors of famine, the rigour of seasons, and the diversity of climates? Will a mind, ruled by the taste for
pleasure, bend itself to regular, profound, and serious
reflections? In a heart replete with various and frivolous objects, will not one of them be found which may
be incompatible with courage? On the borders of the
Po, of the Rhine, and of the Danube, in the midst of
those destructions and ravages which always attend
upon his steps, will not the Frenchman, covered with
dust, his strength exhausted, and destitute of every
thing, turn his sorrowful eyes towards the smiling borders of the Loire or of the Seine? Will he not sigh after those ingenious diversions, those tender connections,
those charming societies, and after those voluptuous
delights of every kind which he hath left there, and
which await him at his return? Imbued with the absurd and unfortunate prejudice, that war, which is a
profession for other nations, is only a rank or condition of life to him, will he not quit the camp as soon
as he shall think he can do it without exposing his reputation too openly? If example, or circumstances, do
not allow him to follow his inclination, will he not exhaust in a few months the income of ten years, to
change a foraging party into a party of pleasure, or to
display his luxury at the head of the trenches? The
dislike of his duties, and his indifference for public affairs, will they not expose him to the ridicule of an
enemy, who may have different principles and a different rule of conduct?

It is not to the king of Prussia, but to Lewis XIV.
that we must attribute that prodigious number of
troops, which presents us with the idea of war, even
in the midst of peace. By keeping always numerous
armies on foot, that proud monarch obliged his neighbours or his enemies, to exert efforts nearly similar,

The contagion spread itself even among the princes who were too weak to raise disturbances, and too poor to keep them up. They sold the blood of their legions to the greater powers; and the number of soldiers was gradually raised in Europe to two millions.

The barbarous ages are spoken of with horror; and yet war was then only a period of violence and of commotions, but at present it is almost a natural state. Most governments are either military, or become so; even the improvement in our discipline is a proof of it. The security we enjoy in our fields, the tranquillity that prevails in our cities, whether troops are passing through, or are quartered in them; the police which reigns around the camps, and in garrisoned towns, proclaim indeed that arms are under some kind of controul, but at the same time indicate that every thing is subject to their power.

Fortunately, the hostilities of our days do not resemble those of former times. At those distant periods, the conquered provinces were laid waste, the towns subdued were reduced to ashes, the vanquished citizens were either put to death, or reduced to servitude. At present, war is much less cruel. When the battle is at an end, no more atrocious acts are committed; the prisoners are taken care of; the cities are no more destroyed, nor the countries ravaged. The contributions exacted from a subdued people scarce amount to as much as they paid for taxes before their misfortunes; and when they are restored by peace to their former masters, no alteration appears in their situation. When treaties insure their submission to the conqueror, they enjoy the same advantages as all the other subjects, and sometimes even several very important prerogatives. Accordingly, the nations, even those which are the least enlightened, show very little concern for these dissensions between princes; they consider those quarrels as disputes between one government and another; and they would behold these events with total indifference, were they not obliged to pay the mercenaries employed to support the ambition, the turbulence, or the caprices of a tyrannical mafter.

Thefe mercenaries are very ill paid. They coft the nation four or five times lefs than the meaneft mechanic. They receive no more than what is abfolutely neceffary to keep them from ftarving. Notwithftanding this, the troops, the generals, the fortified places, the artillery, and the inftruments of war, have been multiplied to fuch a degree, that the maintenance of them hath driven the people to defpair. In order to provide for thefe expences, it hath been neceffary to overburden all the claffes of fociety, which, preffing one upon another, muft crufh the loweft and the moft ufeful of them, that of the hufbandman. The increafe of taxes, and the difficulty of collecting them, deftroy, through want or diftrefs, thofe very families which are the parents and nurferies of the armies.

If an univerfal oppreffion be the firft inconvenience arifing from the increafe of foldiers, their idlenefs is a fecond. Let them be inceffantly employed, but not to excefs, as foon as the din of war fhall no longer be heard, and their morals will be lefs diffolute, lefs contagious; the ftrength neceffary to bear the fatigues of their profeffion will always be preferved, and their health will feldom be affected; they will no more be confumed by hunger, tedium, or affliction; defertions and quarrels will no more be common among them, and they may ftill be ufeful to fociety after the time of their fervice fhall be expired. For a moderate increafe of their pay, they will cheerfully make the roads over which they are to march; they will level the mountains they are to climb up; they will fortify the towns they are to defend; they will dig the canals from whence they are to derive their fubfiftence; they will improve the ports in which they are to embark; they will deliver the people from the moft cruel and the moft ignominious of all vexations, the labours of vaffalage. After having expiated, by ufeful labours, the misfortune of being devoted, by their condition,

to defolate the earth, and to maffacre the inhabitants, B O O K
they will perhaps ceafe to be detefted ; they will per- XIX.
haps one day attain the honour of being confidered in
the light of citizens.

The Romans were acquainted with thefe truths, and
had made them the bafis of their conduct. How is it
come to pafs that we, who were formerly the flaves,
and who are become at prefent the difciples of thefe
mafters of the world, have deviated fo much from this
important object of their principles ? It is becaufe Europe hath believed, and doth ftill believe, that men
who are deftined to handle arms, and to gather laurels,
would be degraded by ufing inftruments which are
only in the hands of the loweft clafs of the people.
How long will this abfurd prejudice, formed in barbarous times, fubfift ? How long fhall we ftill remain in
the twelfth century ?

A third inconvenience arifing from the increafe of
foldiers, is a decreafe of courage. Few men are born
fit for war. If we except Lacedæmon and Rome,
where women who were citizens, and free, brought
forth foldiers ; where children were lulled to fleep by,
and awakened with the found of trumpets and fongs
of war ; where education rendered men unnatural, and
made them beings of a different fpecies : all other nations have only had a few brave men among them.
And, indeed, the lefs troops are raifed, the better will
they be. In the earlier ages of our anceftors, who
were lefs civilized, but ftronger than we are, armies
were much lefs numerous than ours, but engagements
were more decifive. It was neceffary to be a noble or
a rich man to ferve in the army, which was looked upon both as an honour and a privilege. None but vo-
lunteers entered into the fervice. All their engagements ended with the campaign ; and any man who
difliked the art of war was at liberty to withdraw. Befides, there was then more of that ardour, and of that
pride of fentiment, which conftitutes true courage. At
prefent, what glory is there in ferving under abfolute
commanders, who judge of men by their fize, eftimate

them by their pay, enlift them by force or by ſtrata-
gem, and keep or difcharge them without their confent, as they have taken them? What honour is there
in afpiring to the command of armies under the bane-
ful influence of courts, where every thing is given or
taken away without reafon; where men without merit are raifed, and others, though innocent, are degraded by mere caprice; where the department of
war is intrufted to a favourite, who hath not diftinguifhed himfelf upon any occafion, and to whom the
art of war is unknown both in theory and practice;
where a favourite miftrefs marks with patches, upon
a map fpread out upon her toilet, the rout which the
army is to take; or where it is neceffary to fend to folicit permiffion at court before a battle can be given;
a fatal delay, during which time the enemy may have
changed his pofition, and the moment of victory be
loft; where a general, without the confent of the
prince, hath fometimes been commanded, under pain
of difgrace, to fuffer himfelf to be beaten; where
jealoufy, hatred, and a variety of other motives equally deteftable, fruftrate the hopes of a fortunate campaign; where, either through negligence or inability,
camps are fuffered to want provifions, forage, or ammunition; where the perfon who is to obey, to march, or
to ftop, to execute the motions concerted, betrays his
commander, and fets difcipline at defiance, without
endangering his life? Accordingly, except in rifing
empires, or in the inftant of a crifis, the greater number there are of foldiers in the ftate, the more is the
nation weakened; and in proportion as a ftate is en-
feebled, the number of its foldiers is increafed.

A fourth inconvenience is, that the increafe of foldiers tends to defpotifm. A number of troops, towns
well fortified, magazines and arfenals, may prevent invafions; but while they preferve a people from the irruptions of a conqueror, they do not fecure them from
the encroachments of a defpotic prince. Such a number of foldiers ferve only to keep thofe who are already flaves in chains. The tyrant then prevails, and

makes every thing conform to his will, as every thing is fubfervient to his power. By the force of arms a-lone, he fets the opinions of men at defiance, and con-trouls their will. By the affiftance of foldiers he le-vies taxes; and by thefe he raifes foldiers. He ima-gines that his authority is fhown and exercifed, by deftroying what he hath formed; but his exertions are vain and fruitlefs. He is perpetually renewing his forces, without being ever able to recover the national ftrength. In vain do his foldiers keep his people in continual war; if his fubjects tremble at his troops, his troops in re-turn will fly from the enemy. But in thefe circum-ftances, the lofs of a battle is that of a kingdom. The minds of all men being alienated, they voluntarily fubmit to a foreign yoke; becaufe, under the domi-nion of a conqueror, hope is ftill left; while, under that of a defpot, nothing remains but fear. When the progrefs of the military government hath intro-duced defpotifm, then the nation exifts no more. The foldiery foon becomes infolent and detefted. Barren-nefs, occafioned by wretchednefs and debauchery, is the caufe of the extinction of families. A fpirit of difcord and hatred prevails among all orders of men, who are either corrupted or difgraced. Societies be-tray, fell, and plunder each other, and give themfelves up, one after another, to the fcourges of the tyrant, who plunders, oppreffes, deftroys, and annihilates them all. Such is the end of that art of war, which paves the way for a military government. Let us now con-fider what influence the navy has.

The ancients have tranfmitted to us almoft all thofe Navy. arts that have been revived with the reftoration of let-ters; but we have furpaffed them in the military ma-nagement of the navy. Tyre and Sidon, Carthage and Rome, fcarce knew any fea but the Mediterra-nean; to fail through which it was only neceffary to have rafts, galleys, and men to row them. Sea en-gagements might then be bloody; but it required no great fkill to conftruct and equip the fleets. To pafs from Europe into Africa, it was only neceffary to

B O O K be fupplied with boats, which may be called flat bot-
   XIX.   tomed ones, which tranfmitted Carthaginians or Romans,
⌣‿⌣‿ the only people almoft who were engaged in fea-fights.
Commerce was, fortunately, a greater object of attention to the Athenians, and the republics of Afia, than
victories at fea.

After thefe famous nations had abandoned both the
land and the fea to plunderers and to pirates, the navy
remained, during twelve centuries, equally neglected
with all the other arts.   Thofe fwarms of barbarians,
who over-ran and totally deftroyed Rome in its declining ftate, came from the Baltic upon rafts or ca-
noes, to ravage and plunder our fea-coafts, without
going far from the continent.   Thefe were not voyages, but defcents upon the coaft, that were continually renewed.   The Danes and Normans were not
armed for a cruize, and fcarce knew how to fight but
upon land.

At length, chance or the Chinefe fupplied the Europeans with the compafs, and this was the caufe of
the difcovery of America.   The needle, which taught
failors to know how far they were diftant from the
north, or how near they approached to it, emboldened them to attempt longer voyages, and to lofe fight
of land for whole months together.   Geometry and
aftronomy taught them how to compute the progrefs of the conftellations, to determine the longitude
by them, and to judge pretty nearly how far they
were advancing to the eaft and weft.   Even at that
time, the height and the diftance of veffels from the
coaft might always have been known.   Though the
knowledge of the longitude be much more inaccurate
than that of the latitude, yet they both foon occafioned fuch improvement to be made in navigation, as to
give rife to the art of carrying on war by fea.   The
firft effay, however, of this art was made between
galleys that were in poffeffion of the Mediterranean.
The moft celebrated engagement of the modern navy
was that of Lepanto, which was fought two centuries
ago, between two hundred and five Chriftians, and two

hundred and fixty Turkifh galleys. This prodigious armament was entirely conftructed in Italy; a country from which almoft every invention of art has been derived, though not preferved in it. But at that time, its trade, its population, were double what they are at prefent. Befides, thofe galleys were neither fo long nor fo large as thofe of our times, as we may judge from fome of the old carcafes that are ftill preferved in the arfenal of Venice. The number of rowers amounted to one hundred and fifty, and the troops did not exceed fourfcore men in one galley. At prefent, Venice hath more beautiful galleys, and lefs influence, upon that fea which the doge marries, and which other powers frequent and trade upon.

Galleys, indeed, were proper for criminals; but ftronger veffels were required for foldiers. The art of conftructing fhips improved with that of navigation. Philip II. king of all Spain, and of the Eaft and Weft Indies, employed all the docks of Spain and Portugal, of Naples and Sicily, which he then poffeffed, in conftructing fhips of an extraordinary fize and ftrength; and his fleet affumed the title of the Invincible Armada. It confifted of one hundred and thirty fhips, near one hundred of which were the largeft that had yet been feen on the ocean. Twenty fmall fhips followed this fleet, and failed or fought under its protection. The pride of the Spaniards, in the fixteenth century, hath dwelt very much upon, and exaggerated the pompous defcription of this formidable armament. But a circumftance which diffufed terror and admiration two centuries ago, would now ferve only to excite laughter. The largeft of thofe fhips would be no more than a third-rate in our fquadrons. They were fo heavily armed, and fo ill managed, that they could fcarce move, or fail near the wind, nor board another veffel, nor could the fhip be properly worked in tempeftuous weather. The failors were as awkward as the fhips were heavy, and the pilots almoft as ignorant as the failors.

The Englifh, who were already acquainted with the

weakneſs and little ſkill of their enemies at ſea, concluded that inexperience would occaſion their defeat.
They carefully avoided boarding theſe unwieldy machines, and burned a part of them. Some of theſe
enormous galleons were taken, others diſabled. A
ſtorm aroſe, in which moſt of the ſhips loſt their an-
chors, and were abandoned by their crews to the fury
of the waves, and caſt away, ſome upon the weſtern
coaſts of Scotland, others upon the coaſts of Ireland.
Scarce one half of this invincible fleet was able to
return to Spain, where the damages it had ſuffered,
joined to the terror of the ſailors, ſpread a general
conſternation, from which Spain has never recovered.
The Spaniards were for ever depreſſed by the loſs of an
armament that had coſt three years preparation, and
upon which all the forces and revenues of the kingdom had been almoſt exhauſted.

The deſtruction of the Spaniſh navy occaſioned the
dominion of the ſea to paſs into the hands of the
Dutch. The pride of their former tyrants could not
be more ſignally puniſhed than by the proſperity of
a people, forced by oppreſſion to break the yoke of
regal authority. When this republic began to emerge
from its fens, the reſt of Europe was embroiled in civil wars by the ſpirit of fanaticiſm. Perſecution drove
men into Holland from all other ſtates. The inquiſition which the Houſe of Auſtria wiſhed to extend
over all parts of its dominions; the perſecution which
Henry II. raiſed in France; the emiſſaries of Rome,
who were ſupported in England by Mary; every thing,
in a word, concurred to people Holland with an immenſe number of refugees. This country had neither lands nor harveſt for their ſubſiſtence. They
were obliged to ſeek it by ſea throughout the whole
univerſe. Almoſt all the commerce of Europe was
engroſſed by Liſbon, Cadiz, and Antwerp, under one
ſovereign, whoſe power and ambition rendered him a
general object of hatred and envy. The new republicans having eſcaped his tyranny, and being excited
by reſentment and neceſſity, became pirates, and form-

ed a navy at the expence of the Spaniards and Por- B O O K
tuguefe, whom they held in utter averfion. France XIX.
and England, who, in the progrefs of this rifing republic, only perceived the humiliation of the Houfe
of Auftria, affifted Holland in preferving the conquefts
and fpoils fhe had made, the value of which fhe was yet
unacquainted with. Thus the Dutch fecured to themfelves eftablifhments wherever they chofe to direct their
forces; fixed themfelves in thefe acquifitions before the
jealoufy of other nations could be excited, and imperceptibly made themfelves mafters of all commerce by
their induftry, and of all the feas by the ftrength of
their fquadrons.

The domeftic troubles in England were for a while
favourable to this profperity, which had been fo filently acquired in remote countries. But at length Cromwell excited in his country an emulation for commerce,
fo natural to the inhabitants of an ifland. To fhare
the empire of the feas with the Englifh, was, in fact,
to give it up to them; and the Dutch were determined to maintain it. Inftead of forming an alliance with
England, they courageoufly refolved upon war. They
carried it on for a long time with unequal force; and
this perfeverance againft misfortune preferved to them,
at leaft, an honourable rivalfhip. Superiority in the
conftruction and form of the fhips often gave the victory to their enemies; but the vanquifhed never met
with any decifive loffes.

In the meanwhile, thefe long and dreadful combats
had exhaufted, or at leaft diminifhed, the ftrength of
the two nations, when Lewis XIV. willing to avail
himfelf of their mutual weaknefs, afpired to the empire of the fea. When this prince firft affumed the
reins of government, he found only eight or nine veffels in his harbours, and thofe very much decayed;
neither were they fhips of the firft or fecond rate.
Richelieu had perceived the neceffity of raifing a pier
before Rochelle, but not of forming a navy; the idea
of which muft, however, have been conceived by Henry IV. and his friend Sully. But it was referved to

the moſt brilliant age of the French nation to give birth to every improvement at once. Lewis, who conceived, at leaſt, all the ideas of grandeur he did not himſelf ſuggeſt, inſpired his ſubjects with the ſame paſſion which prevailed in him. Five ports were opened to the military navy. Docks and arſenals, equally convenient and magnificent, were conſtructed. The art of ſhip-building, ſtill very imperfect everywhere, was eſtabliſhed upon more certain principles. A ſet of naval regulations much ſuperior to thoſe of the other nations, and which they have ſince adopted, obtained the ſanction of the laws. Seamen emerged from the midſt of the ocean, as it were, already formed. In leſs than twenty years the harbours of the kingdom reckoned one hundred ſhips of the line.

The French navy firſt exerted its power againſt the people of Barbary, who were beaten. It afterwards obtained ſome advantages over the Spaniards. It then engaged the fleets of England and Holland, ſometimes ſeparately and ſometimes combined, and generally obtained the honour and advantage of the victory. The firſt memorable defeat the French navy experienced was in 1692, when with forty ſhips they attacked ninety Engliſh and Dutch ſhips oppoſite La Hogue, in order to give the Engliſh a king they rejected, and who was not himſelf very deſirous of the title. The moſt numerous fleet obtained the victory. James the Second felt an involuntary pleaſure at the triumph of the people who expelled him; as if at this inſtant the blind love of his country had prevailed within him, over his ambition for the throne. Since that day the naval powers of France have been upon the decline, and it was impoſſible that they ſhould not be.

Lewis XIV. accuſtomed to carry on his enterpriſes with more haughtineſs than method, more ambitious of appearing powerful than of being really ſo, had begun by completing the higher parts of his military navy before he had ſettled its foundation. The only ſolid baſis which could have been given to it would have been an extenſive commercial navy, carried on with activity; and there was not even the fhadow of fuch a thing exifting in the kingdom. The trade with the Eaft Indies was ftill in its infancy. The Dutch had appropriated to themfelves the fmall quantity of commodities which the American iflands then produced. The French had not yet thought of giving to the great fifheries that degree of extenfion of which they were fufceptible. There were no French veffels admitted in the northern harbours, and the fouthern very feldom faw any. The ftate had even given up its coafting trade to foreigners. Was it not therefore unavoidable, that this coloffus fhould be overturned, and the illufion diffipated upon the firft remarkable check which this proud difplay of power fhould receive?

From that period England acquired a fuperiority, which hath raifed her to the greateft profperity. A people, who are at prefent the moft confiderable power at fea, eafily perfuade themfelves that they have always holden that empire. Sometimes they trace their maritime power to the era of Julius Cæfar; fometimes they affert that they have ruled over the ocean, at leaft, fince the ninth century. Perhaps, fome day or other, the Corficans, who are at prefent a nation of little confequence, when they are become a maritime people, will record in their annals that they have always ruled over the Mediterranean. Such is the vanity of man, which muft endeavour to aggrandize itfelf in paft as well as future ages. Truth alone, which exifts before all nations, and furvives them all, informs us, that there hath been no navy in Europe from the Chriftian era till the 10th century. The Englifh themfelves had no need of it, while they remained in puffeffion of Normandy and of the coafts of France.

When Henry VIII. was defirous of equipping a fleet, he was obliged to hire veffels from Hamburgh, Lubeck, and Dantzic; but efpecially from Genoa and Venice, in which ftates it was only known how to build and conduct a fleet; which fupplied failors and admirals; and which gave to Europe a Columbus, an Americus, a Cabot, and a Verezani; thofe wonderful

men, who by their discoveries have added so much to
the extent of the globe.   Elizabeth was in want of a
naval force against Spain, and permitted her subjects
to fit out ships to act against the enemies of the state.
This permission formed sailors for the service.   The
queen herself went to see a ship that had been round
the world; on board of which she embraced Drake,
at the time she knighted him.   She left forty-two men
of war to her successors.   James and Charles the First
added some ships to the naval forces they had received
from the throne; but the commanders of this navy
were chosen from the nobility, who, satisfied with this
mark of distinction, left the labours to the pilots; so
that the art of navigation received no improvements.

There were few noblemen in the party that dethroned the Stuarts.   Ships of the line were at that time
given to captains of inferior birth, but of uncommon
skill in navigation.   They improved, and rendered the
English navy illustrious.

When Charles II. reascended the throne, the kingdom was possessed of six and fifty ships.   The navy increased under his reign to the number of eighty-three,
fifty-eight of which were ships of the line.   Nevertheless, towards the latter days of this prince, it began to
decline again.   But his brother, James II. restored it
to its former lustre, and raised it even to a greater degree of splendour.   Being himself high-admiral before
he came to the throne, he had invented the art of re-
gulating the manœuvres of the fleet, by the signals of
the flag.   Happy, if he had better understood the art
of governing a free people!   When the prince of
Orange, his son-in-law, became possessed of his crown,
the English navy consisted of one hundred and sixty-
three vessels of all sizes, armed with seven thousand
pieces of cannon, and equipped with forty-two thousand men.   This force was doubled during the war
that was carried on for the Spanish succession.   It hath
since so considerably increased, that the English think
they are able alone to balance, by their maritime forces, the navy of the whole universe.   England is now

at fea what Rome formerly was upon land, when fhe
began to decline.

The Englifh nation confiders its navy as the bulwark
of its fafety, and the fource of its riches. On this they
found all their hopes in times of peace as well as war.
They therefore raife a fleet more willingly, and with
greater expedition than a battalion. They fpare no
expence, and exert every political art to acquire fea-
men.

The foundations of this power were laid in the middle of the laft century by the famous act of navigation,
which fecured to the Englifh all the productions of
their vaft empire, and which promifed them a great
fhare in thofe of other regions. This law feemed to
advife all people to think only of themfelves. This
leffon, however, hath been of no ufe hitherto; and no
government hath made it the rule of their conduct.
It is poffible that the eyes of men may foon be opened; but Great Britain will however have enjoyed, during the fpace of more than a century, the fruits of its
forefight; and will perhaps have acquired, during that
long interval, fufficient ftrength to perpetuate her advantages. It may readily be fuppofed that fhe is inclined to employ all poffible means to prevent the ex-
plofion of that mine which time is gradually and flowly digging under the foundation of her fortune, and to
declare war againft the firft people who fhall attempt
to blow it up. Her formidable fleets impatiently expect the fignal of hoftilities. Their activity and their
vigilance are redoubled, fince it hath been decided
that the prizes were to belong entirely to the officers
and the crews of the victorious fhip, fince the ftate
hath granted a gratuity of one hundred and thirty-two
livres ten fols [5l. 10s. 5d.] to every perfon who fhould
board, take, or fink, any of the enemy's fhips. This
allurement of gain will be increafed, if it be neceffary,
by other rewards. Will the nations which are fo habitually divided by their interefts and by their jealoufies confent together to fupprefs this boldnefs; and if

BOOK one of them fhould undertake it feparately, will it
XIX. fucceed in this terrible conflict?

The navy is a new fpecies of power, which hath given the univerfe in fome meafure to Europe. This part of the globe, though fo limited, hath acquired by its fquadrons an abfolute empire over the reft, which are much more extenfive. It hath feized upon thofe regions that were fuitable to it, and hath placed under its dependence the inhabitants and productions of all countries. A fuperiority fo advantageous will laft for ever, unlefs fome event, which it is impoffible to fore-fee, fhould d fguft our defcendants of an element in which fhipwrecks are fo frequent. As long as they fhall have any fleets remaining, they will pave the way for revolutions, they will draw along with them the deftinies of nations, and they will be the levers of the world.

But it is not only to the extremities of the world, or in barbarous regions, that fhips have carried terror, and dictated laws. Their influence hath been fenfibly felt even in the midft of ourfelves, and hath difturbed the ancient fyftems of things. A new kind of equili-brium hath been formed, and the balance of power hath been transferred from the continent to the mari-time nations. In proportion as the nature of their forces brought them nearer to all countries bordering upon the ocean and its feveral gulfs, fo they have had it in their power to do good or mifchief to the greater number of ftates; confequently they muft have had more allies, more confideration, and more influence. Thefe advantages have been evident to the govern-ments which, by their fituation, were at hand to fhare them; and there is fcarce any one which hath not ex-erted greater or lefs efforts to fucceed in it.

Since nature hath decided that men muft be in per-petual agitation upon our planet, and that they fhould continually difturb it with their inquietude, it is a for-tunate circumftance for modern times, that the forces of the fea fhould make a diverfion from thofe of the land. A power which hath coafts to protect will not eafily encroach upon the territories of its neighbours. It would require immenfe preparations, innumerable troops, arfenals of all kinds, and a double fupply of means and of refources to execute its project of conqueft. Since Europe hath employed its forces on the fea, it enjoys greater fecurity than before. Its wars are perhaps as frequent and as bloody, but it is lefs ravaged and lefs weakened by them. The operations are carried on with greater harmony and with more regular plans; and there are lefs of thofe great effects which derange all fyftems. There are greater efforts, and lefs fhocks. All the paffions are turned towards one certain general good, one grand political aim, towards a happy employment of all the natural and moral powers, which is commerce.

The importance to which the navy has arifen will lead, in procefs of time, every thing which has a greater or lefs diftant affinity to it, to the degree of perfection it is fufceptible of: till the middle of the laft century an uncertain routine was followed in the conftruction of fhips. *One knows not what the fea requires,* was ftill a common proverb. At this period geometry carried its attention to this art, which was becoming every day more interefting, and applied to it fome of its principles. Since that, its attention has been more ferioufly engaged, and always with fuccefs. Matters, however, are ftill far from being brought to demonftration; for there is ftill great variety in the dimenfions adopted in the different docks.

In proportion as the navy became a fcience, it became a neceffary object of ftudy to thofe who engaged in this profeffion. They were made to underftand, though very flowly, that thofe commanders who had general ideas, founded upon mathematical rules, would have a great fuperiority over officers, who, having nothing but habit to lead them, could only judge of the things they had to do from their analogy to thofe which they had already feen. Schools were opened

on all fides, where young men were inftructed in naval
tactics, and in other knowledge of equal importance.

This was fomething, but it was not all. In a profeffion where the difpofition of the fea and of the cur-
rents, the motion of the fhips, the ftrength and variety
of the winds, the frequent accidents from fire, the ordinary breaking of the fails and ropes, and many other
circumftances, infinitely multiply the plans; where,
in the midft of the noife of cannon, and of the greateft
dangers, one muft inftantly take a refolution which
fhall determine at once either victory or defeat; where
the evolutions muft be fo rapid, that they feem rather
to be the effect of fentiment than the refult of reflection: in fuch a profeffion, the moft learned theory
cannot be fufficient. Deprived of that certain and
fpeedy effect of fight which practice, and that the moft
conftant, can only give, it would lofe in reflection the
time for action. Experience muft therefore complete
the feaman, whofe education hath been begun by the
ftudy of the exact fciences. In procefs of time, this
union of theory with practice muft prevail in every
place where there are navigators, but nowhere more
fpeedily than in an ifland, becaufe arts are fooner
brought to perfection, wherever they are of indifpenfable neceffity.

For the fame reafon, in an ifland there will be better failors, and more of them; but will they be treated with that juftice and humanity which is due to
them?   Let us fuppofe that one of them, who hath
fortunately efcaped from the devouring heats of the
line, from the horror of ftorms, and from the intemperature of climates, returns from a voyage of feveral
years, and from the extremities of the globe. His
wife expects him with impatience; his children are
anxious to fee a father whofe name hath been repeated
to them a multitude of times; he himfelf fooths his
anxiety by the pleafing hope that he fhall foon fee
again what is moft dear to him in the world, and an-
ticipates by his wifhes the delightful moment when his

heart will be comforted in the tender embraces of his family. All at once, at the approach of the fhore, within fight of his country, he is forcibly taken out of the fhip in which he had braved the fury of the waves in order to enrich his fellow-citizens, and is put, by a fet of infamous fatellites, on board of a fleet, where thirty or forty thoufand of his brave companions are to fhare his misfortunes, till the end of hoftilities. In vain do their tears flow, in vain do they appeal to the laws; their deftiny is irrevocably fixed. This is a feeble image of the atrocioufnefs of the Englifh mode of preffing.

In our abfolute governments another mode is adopted; perhaps, in fact, as cruel, though apparently more moderate. The failor is there inlifted, and for life. He is employed or difbanded at pleafure; his pay is regulated by caprice, which alfo fixes the period when he fhall receive it. Both in time of peace, as in time of war, he hath never any will of his own, but is always under the rod of a fubaltern defpot, moft commonly unjuft, cruel, and interefted. The greateft difference I can obferve between thefe two modes is, that the former is only a temporary fervitude, the latter is a flavery which hath no end.

Neverthelefs, we fhall find fome apologifts, and perhaps fome admirers, of thefe inhuman cuftoms. It will be faid, that, in a ftate of fociety, the wills of individuals muft always be fubject to the general will; and that their convenience muft always be facrificed to the public good. Such hath been the practice of all nations and of all ages. It is upon this bafis alone that all inftitutions, ill or well planned, have been founded. They will never deviate from this central point, without haftening the inevitable period of their ruin.

Undoubtedly the republic muft be ferved, and that by the citizens: but, is it not juft that every one fhould contribute to this fervice, according to his means? In order to preferve to the poffeffor of millions, often unjuft, the entire enjoyment of his fortune and of his delights, muft the unfortunate failor be obliged to facri-

fice two-thirds of his falary, the wants of his family,
and the moft valuable of his property, his liberty?
Would not the country be ferved with more zeal,
with more vigour and underftanding, by men who
fhould voluntarily devote to it all the natural and moral powers they have acquired, or exercifed, upon all
the feas, than by flaves, who are necelfarily and inceffantly employed in attending to the breaking of
their chains? Improperly will the adminiftrators of
empires allege, in juftification of their atrocious conduct, that thefe navigators would refufe to employ
their hands, and exert their courage in engagements,
if they were not dragged to them againft their inclinations. Every circumftance confirms that their moft
favourite object would be to follow their profeffions;
and it is demonftrated, that even if they had any diflike to it, ftill their neceffities, which are ever renewed
would compel them to attend to it.

But wherefore fhould we not declare, that governments are as well convinced as thofe who cenfure them,
of the injuftice they commit towards their failors? but
they choofe rather to erect tyranny into a principle,
than to own that it is impoffible for them to be juft.
In the prefent ftate of things, all of them, and more
efpecially fome, have raifed their naval forces beyond
what their circumftances would allow. Their pride
hath not yet fuffered them to defcend from that exaggerated grandeur with which they had intoxicated
both themfelves and their neighbours. The time will
come, however, and it cannot be very diftant, when it
will be neceffary to proportion armaments to the refources of an exhaufted treafury. This will be a fortunate epocha for Europe, if it fhould follow fo bright
an example. That part of the world which poffeffes
at prefent three hundred and ninety-two fhips of the
line, and four times that number of fhips of war of an
inferior order, will derive great advantages from this
revolution. The ocean will then be ploughed with
fewer fleets, and thofe will confift of a lefs number of
fhips. The mercantile navy will be enriched from the

military navy; and commerce will acquire a greater B O O K
degree of extenfion throughout the whole univerfe. XIX.

Commerce produces nothing of itfelf; for it is not Commerce.
of a plaftic nature. Its bufinefs confifts in exchanges.
By its operations, a town, a province, a nation, a part
of the globe, are difencumbered of what is ufelefs to
them, and receive what they are in want of. It is
perpetually engaged in fupplying the refpective wants
of men. Its knowledge, its funds, and its labours, are
all devoted to this honourable and neceffary office. Its
influence could not exift without the arts and without
cultivation: but thefe would be very infignificant without its influence. By pervading the earth, by croffing
the feas, by raifing the obftacles which oppofed themfelves to the intercourfe of nations, by extending the
fphere of wants and the thirft of enjoyments, it multiplies labour, it encourages induftry, and becomes, in
fome meafure, the moving principle of the world.

The Phœnicians were the firft merchants of whom
hiftory hath preferved the remembrance. Situated on
the borders of the fea on the confines of Afia and
Africa, to receive and difpenfe all the riches of the ancient world, they founded their colonies, and built
their cities, with no other view but that of commerce.
At Tyre, they were the mafters of the Mediterranean;
at Carthage, they laid the foundations of a republic
that traded, by the ocean, upon the richeft of the European coafts.

The Greeks fucceeded the Phœnicians, as the Romans did the Carthaginians and the Greeks: they held
the dominion of the fea as well as of the land; but
they carried on no other kind of commerce, except
that of conveying into Italy, for their own ufe, all the
riches of Africa, Afia, and the conquered world. When
Rome had invaded the whole world, and had loft all
her acquifitions, commerce returned, as it were, to its
original fource towards the Eaft. There it was eftablifhed, while the Barbarians overran Europe. The
empire was divided; the din of arms, and the art of
war, remained in the Weft; Italy, however, preferved

its communication with the Levant, where all the treafures of India were circulated.

The Crufades exhaufted in Afia all the rage of zeal
and ambition, of war and fanaticifm, with which the
Europeans were poffeffed; but they were the caufe of
introducing into Europe a tafte for Afiatic luxury, and
redeemed, by giving rife to fome degree of traffic and
induftry, the blood and the lives they had coft. Three
centuries, taken up in wars and voyages to the Eaft,
gave to the reftlefs fpirit of Europe a recruit it ftood
in need of, that it might not perifh by a kind of internal confumption : they prepared the way for that exertion of genius and activity, which fince arofe, and
difplayed itfelf in the conqueft and trade of the Eaft
Indies, and of America.

The Portuguefe attempted, by degrees, and with
circumfpection, to double the African coaft. It was
not till after fourfcore years of labours and of war, and
after having made themfelves mafters of all the weftern
coaft of that vaft region, that they ventured to double
the Cape of Good Hope. The honour of clearing this
formidable barrier was referved to Vafco de Gama, in
1497, who at length reached the coaft of Malabar,
where all the treafures of the moft fertile countries of
Afia were to be circulated. This was the fcene on
which the Portuguefe difplayed all their conquefts.

While this nation made itfelf mafter of the articles
of trade, the Spaniards feized upon that which purchafes them, the mines of gold and filver. Thefe metals became not only a ftandard to regulate the value,
but alfo the object of commerce. In this double ufe
they foon engroffed all the reft. All nations were in
want of them to facilitate the exchange of their commodities, and obtain the conveniencies they ftood in
need of. The luxury and the circulation of money in
the fouth of Europe, changed the nature as well as the
direction of commerce, at the fame time that it extended its bounds.

In the meanwhile, the two nations that had fubdued the Eaft and Weft Indies, neglected arts and

agriculture. They imagined every thing was to be
obtained by gold, without confidering that it is labour
alone that procures it : they were convinced, though
late, and at their own expence, that the induftry which
they loft was more valuable than the riches they acquired; and the Dutch taught them this fevere leffon.

The Spaniards and the Portuguefe, though poffeffed
of all the gold in the world, remained or became poor;
the Dutch prefently acquired riches, without either
lands or mines. As foon as thefe intrepid republicans
had taken refuge in the midft of the feas, with Liberty
their tutelary divinity, they perceived that their moraffes would never be any thing more than the feat of
their habitation, and that they fhould be obliged to
feek refources and fubfiftence elfewhere. They caft
their eyes over the globe, and faid to themfelves,
" The whole world is our domain ; we will enjoy it
" by navigation and commerce. The revolutions
" which fhall happen upon this immenfe and perpe-
" tually agitated fcene, will never be concealed from
" our knowledge. Indolence and activity, flavery
" and independence, barbarifm and civilization, opu-
" lence and poverty, culture and induftry, purchafes
" and fales, the vices and the virtues of men, we will
" turn them all to our advantage. We will encourage
" the labours of the nations, or we will impede their
" profperity ; we will urge them on to war, or we will
" endeavour to reftore tranquillity among them, as it
" may be moft fuitable to our own interefts."

Till that period, Flanders had been the centre of
communication between the north and the fouth of
Europe. The United Provinces of Holland, which
had detached themfelves from it in order to belong
only to themfelves, took its place, and became, in
their turn, the ftaple of all the powers which had more
or lefs exchanges to make.

The ambition of the new republic was limited to
this firft advantage. After having drawn into its ports
the productions of other countries, its navigators went
themfelves in queft of them. Holland foon became

an immenſe magazine, where all the productions of
the ſeveral climates were collected ; and this union of
ſo many important objects increaſed continually, in
proportion as the wants of the people were multiplied,
with the means of ſatisfying them. One merchandiſe
attracted another. The commodities of the Old World
invited thoſe of the New. One purchaſer brought another ; and the treaſures already acquired became a certain method of acquiring more.

Every circumſtance was favourable to the riſe and
progreſs of the commerce of this republic. Its poſition
on the borders of the ſea, at the mouths of ſeveral great
rivers ; its proximity to the moſt fertile or beſt cultivated lands of Europe ; its natural connections with
England and Germany, which defended it againſt
France ; the little extent and fertility of its own ſoil,
which obliged the inhabitants to become fiſhermen,
ſailors, brokers, bankers, carriers, and commiſſaries ;
in a word, to endeavour to live by induſtry for want
of territory. Moral cauſes contributed, with thoſe of
the climate and the ſoil, to eſtabliſh and advance its
proſperity. The liberty of its government, which
opened an aſylum to all ſtrangers diſſatisfied with
their own ; the freedom of its religion, which permitted a public and quiet profeſſion of all other modes of
worſhip ; that is to ſay, the agreement of the voice of
nature with that of conſcience, of intereſts with duty ;
in a word, that toleration, that univerſal religion of all
equitable and enlightened minds, friends to heaven
and earth ; to God, as to their father ; to men, as to
their brethren. Finally, this commercial republic
found out the ſecret of availing itſelf of all events, and
of making even the calamities and vices of other nations concur in advancing its felicity. It turned to its
own advantage the civil wars which fanaticiſm had
raiſed among people of a reſtleſs ſpirit, or which pa-
triotiſm had excited among a free people ; it profited
by the indolence and ignorance which bigotry ſupported among two nations who were under the influence of the imagination.

This spirit of industry in Holland, with which was intermixed a considerable share of that political art which sows the seeds of jealousy and discord among the nations, at length excited the attention of other powers. The English were the first to perceive that traffic might be carried on without the interposition of the Dutch. England, where the encroachments of despotism had given birth to liberty, because they were antecedent to corruption and effeminacy, was desirous of obtaining riches by labour, which is their antidote. The English first considered commerce as the proper science and support of an enlightened, powerful, and even a virtuous people. They considered it rather as an improvement of industry than an acquisition of enjoyments; rather as an encouragement and a source of activity in favour of population, than as a promoter of luxury and magnificence, for the purpose of parade. Invited to trade by their situation, this became the spirit of their government and the means of their ambition. All their schemes tended to this great object. In other monarchies, trade is carried on by the people; in this happy constitution by the state, or the whole nation: she carries it on indeed with a constant desire of dominion, which implies that of enslaving other people, but by means, at least, which constitute the happiness of the world before it is subdued. By war, the conqueror is little happier than the conquered, because injuries and massacres are their mutual object; but by commerce, the conquering people necessarily introduce industry into the country, which they would not have subdued if it had been already industrious, or in which they would not maintain themselves, if they had not brought industry in along with them. Upon these principles England had founded her commerce and her empire, and mutually and alternately extended one by the other.

The French, situated under as favourable a sky, and upon as happy a soil, have, for a long time, flattered themselves with the idea that they had much to give to other nations, without being under a necessity of asking scarce any return. But Colbert was sensible that in the ferment Europe was in at that time, there would be an evident advantage for the culture and productions of a country that should employ those of the whole world. He opened manufactures for all the arts, the woollens, silks, dyes, embroideries, the gold and silver stuffs; all acquired, in the establishments the operations of which he directed, a degree of perfection, which the other manufactures could not attain. To increase the utility of these arts, it was necessary to possess the materials for them. The culture of them was encouraged according to the diversity of climates and territory. Some of them were required even of the provinces of the kingdom, and the rest from the colonies which chance had given it in the New World, as well as from all the navigators who had for a century past infested the seas with their robberies. The nation must then necessarily have made a double profit upon the materials and the workmanship of the manufactures. The French pursued, for a long time, this precarious and temporary object of commerce, with an activity and spirit of emulation which must have made them greatly surpass their rivals; and they still enjoy that superiority over other nations in all those arts of luxury and ornament which procure riches to industry.

The natural volatility of the national character, and its propensity to trifling pursuits, hath brought treasures to the state, by the taste that has fortunately prevailed for its fashions. Like to that light and delicate sex, which teaches and inspires us with a taste for dress, the French reign in all courts, and in all regions, respecting every thing that concerns ornament or magnificence; and their art of pleasing is one of the mysterious sources of their fortune and power. Other nations have subdued the world by those simple and rustic manners, which constitute the virtues that are fit for war; to them it was given to reign over it by their vices. Their empire will continue, till being degraded and enslaved by their masters, by exertions

of authority equally arbitrary and unlimited, they will B O O K
become contemptible in their own eyes. Then they XIX.
will lofe, with their confidence in themfelves, that induftry, which is one of the fources of their opulence
and of the fprings of their activity.

Germany, which hath only a few ports, and thofe
bad ones, hath been obliged to behold, with an indifferent or a jealous eye, its ambitious neighbours enriching themfelves with the fpoils of the fea, and of
the Eaft and the Weft Indies. Its induftry hath been
reftrained even upon its frontiers, which were perpetually ravaged by deftructive wars, and as far as into
the interior part of its provinces, by the nature of its
conftitution, which is fingularly complicated. A great
deal of time, extenfive knowledge, and confiderable
efforts, would be requifite, to eftablifh a commerce of
any importance in a region where every thing feemed
unfavourable to it. This period, however, is now at
hand. Flax and hemp are already induftrioufly cultivated, and appear under agreeable forms. Wool and
cotton are wrought with fkill; and other manufactures
are begun or improved. If, as the laborious and fteady
character of the inhabitants induces us to hope, the
empire fhould ever attain to the advantage of paying,
with its own productions and manufactures, for thofe
which it is obliged to provide itfelf with from other
nations, and to preferve within itfelf the metals which
are extracted from its mines, it will foon become one
of the moft opulent countries of Europe.

It would be abfurd to announce fo brilliant a deftiny to the northern nations, although commerce hath
alfo begun to meliorate their condition. The iron of
their rude climate, which formerly ferved only for
their mutual deftruction, hath been turned to ufes beneficial to mankind; and part of that which they ufed
to deliver in its rough ftate, is never fold at prefent
till after it hath been wrought. They have found a
mart for their naval ftores at a higher price than they
were formerly fold for, before navigation had acquired
that prodigious extenfion which aftonifhes us. If fome

of thefe people indolently wait for purchafers in their harbours, others carry out their productions themfelves into foreign ports; and this activity extends their ideas, their tranfactions, and their advantages.

This new principle of the moral world hath infinuated itfelf by degrees, till it is become, as it were, neceffary to the formation and exiftence of political bodies. The tafte for luxury and conveniencies hath produced the love of labour, which at prefent conftitutes the chief ftrength of a ftate. The fedentary occupations of the mechanic arts indeed render men more liable to be affected by the injuries of the feafons, lefs fit to be expofed to the open air, which is the firft nutritive principle of life. But ftill it is better that the human race fhould be enervated under the roofs of the workfhops, than inured to hardfhips under tents; becaufe war deftroys, while commerce, on the contrary, gives new life to every thing. By this ufeful revolution in manners, the general maxims of politics have altered the face of Europe. It is no longer a people immerfed in poverty that becomes formidable to a rich nation. Power is at prefent an attendant on riches, becaufe they are no longer the fruit of conqueft, but the produce of conftant labour, and of a life fpent in perpetual employment. Gold and filver corrupt only thofe indolent minds which indulge in the delights of luxury, upon that ftage of intrigue and meannefs, that is called greatnefs. But thefe metals employ the hands and arms of the people; they excite a fpirit of agriculture in the fields, of navigation in the maritime cities, and in the centre of the ftate they lead to the manufacturing of arms, clothing, furniture, and the conftruction of buildings. A fpirit of emulation exifts between man and nature: they are perpetually improving each other. The people are formed and fafhioned by the arts they profefs. If there be fome occupations which foften and degrade the human race, there are others by which it is hardened and repaired. If it be true that art renders them unnatural, they do not, at leaft, propagate in order to deftroy themfelves, as among the barbarous nations in heroic times. It is certainly an eafy, as well as a captivating fubject, to defcribe the Romans with the fingle art of war fub-duing all the other arts, all other nations indolent or commercial, civilized or favage ; breaking or defpifing the vafes of Corinth ; more happy with their gods made of clay, than with the golden ftatues of their worthlefs emperors. But it is a more pleafing, and perhaps a nobler fight, to behold all Europe peopled with laborious nations, who are continually failing round the globe, in order to cultivate and render it fit for mankind ; to fee them animate, by the enlivening breath of induftry, all the regenerating powers of na-ture ; feek in the abyfs of the ocean, and in the bowels of rocks, for new means of fubfiftence, or new enjoy-ments ; ftir and raife up the earth with all the mecha-nic powers invented by genius ; eftablifh between the two hemifpheres, by the happy improvements in the art of navigation, a communication of flying bridges, as it were, that re-unite one continent to the other ; purfue all the tracks of the fun, overcome its annual barriers, and pafs from the tropics to the poles upon the wings of the wind ; in a word, to fee them open all the ftreams of population and pleafure, in order to pour them upon the face of the earth through a thou-fand channels. It is then, perhaps, that the Divinity contemplates his work with fatisfaction, and does not repent himfelf of having made man.

Such is the image of commerce ; let us now ad-mire the genius of the merchant. The fame under-ftanding that Newton had to calculate the motion of the ftars, the merchant exerts in tracing the progrefs of the commercial people that fertilize the earth. His problems are the more difficult to refolve, as the cir-cumftances of them are not taken from the immu-table laws of nature, as the fyftems of the geometri-cian are ; but depend upon the caprices of men, and the uncertainty of a thoufand complicated events. That accurate fpirit of combination that Cromwell and Richelieu muft have had, the one to deftroy, the

other to eſtabliſh deſpotic government, the merchant
alſo poſſeſſes and carries it further: for he takes in
both worlds at one view, and directs his operations upon an infinite variety of relative conſiderations, which
it is ſeldom given to the ſtateſman, or even to the
philoſopher, to comprehend and eſtimate. Nothing
muſt eſcape him; he muſt foreſee the influence of
the ſeaſons upon the plenty, the ſcarcity, and the
quality of proviſions; upon the departure or return
of his ſhips; the influence of political affairs upon
thoſe of commerce; the changes which war or peace
muſt neceſſarily occaſion in the prices and demands for
merchandiſe, in the quantity and choice of proviſions,
in the ſtate of the cities and ports of the whole world;
he muſt know the conſequences that an alliance of
the two northern nations may have under the torrid
zone; the progreſs, either towards aggrandizement or
decay, of the ſeveral trading companies; the effect
that the fall of any European power in India may
have over Africa and America; the ſtagnation that
may be produced in certain countries by the blocking
up of ſome channels of induſtry; the reciprocal connection there is between moſt branches of trade, and
the mutual aſſiſtances they lend by the temporary injuries they ſeem to inflict upon each other; he muſt
know the proper time to begin and when to ſtop in
every new undertaking; in a word, he muſt be acquainted with the art of making all other nations tri-
butary to his own, and of increaſing his own fortune
by increaſing the proſperity of his country; or rather
he muſt know how to enrich himſelf by extending
the general proſperity of mankind. Such are the objects that the profeſſion of the merchant engages him
to attend to: and ſtill this is not the whole extent of
them.

Commerce is a ſcience which requires the knowledge of men ſtill more than of things. Its difficulties ariſe leſs from the multiplicity of its tranſactions
than from the avidity of thoſe who are engaged in
them. It is therefore neceſſary to treat with them

apparently as if we were convinced of their good
faith, and at the fame time to take as many precautions as if they were deftitute of every principle.

Almoft all men are honeft out of their of own profeffion ; but there are few who, in the exercife of it,
conform to the rules of fcrupulous probity. This
vice, which prevails from the higheft to the loweft
ranks, arifes from the great number of malverfations
introduced by time and excufed by cuftom. Perfonal intereft and general habit conceal the crime and
the meannefs of fuch proceedings. *I do no more*, it is
faid, *than what others do*, and thus we accuftom ourfelves to commit actions which our confcience foon
ceafes to reproach us with.

Thefe kinds of fraud do not appear fo in the eyes
of thofe who indulge themfelves in them. As they
are common to all profeffions, do they not reciprocally expiate each other? I take out of the purfe of
thofe who deal with me, what thofe whom I have
dealt with have taken too much out of mine. Will
it be required, that a merchant, a workman, or any
individual whatever, fhould fuffer the tacit and fecret
oppreffions of all thofe to whom his daily wants o-
blige him to addrefs himfelf, without ever feeking his
indemnity from any one of them? Since every thing
is compenfated by general injuftice, all will be as well
as if the moft rigid juftice prevailed.

But can there be any kind of compenfation in thefe
rapines of detail exercifed by one clafs of citizens over
all the reft, or in thofe exercifed by the latter over the
former? Are all profeffions in equal want of each o-
ther? Several of them, which are expofed to frauds
inceffantly renewed, do they not moftly want opportunities of impofing in their turn? Do not circumftances make an alteration from one day to another in
the proportion there is between thefe impofitions?
Thefe obfervations will perhaps appear too trifling ;
let us therefore be allowed to dwell upon one more
important reflection. Will any wife man think it to
be a matter of indifference that iniquity fhould be

practifed with impunity, and almoft with univerfal confent, in all ftates ; that the body of a nation fhould be corrupt, and to a degree of corruption that knows neither reftraint nor bounds ; and that there is a material difference between a theft which hath the fanction of cuftom and is daily repeated, and any other poffible act of injuftice ?

The evil muft, however, be thought irremediable, at leaft with refpect to retail trades, fince the only fyftem of morality applicable to thofe who follow them is comprifed in thefe maxims : " Endeavour not to be " difhonoured in your profeffion. If you fell dearer " than other people, keep up at leaft the reputation of " felling better merchandife. Gain as much as you " can ; and efpecially avoid the having of two prices " for your goods. Make your fortune as fpeedily as " you can. If you fhould not be ill-fpoken of, and " fhould not forfeit your character, all is well." Honefter principles might be fubftituted to thefe ; but it would be in vain. The trifling daily profits, thofe niggardly favings which conftitute effential refources in fome profeffions, lower and degrade the foul, and extinguifh in it all fenfe of dignity, and nothing truly laudable can be either recommended to, or expected from a fpecies of men who have arrived to fuch a pitch of degradation.

It is not the fame thing with thofe whofe fpeculations embrace all the countries of the earth, whofe complicated operations connect the moft diftant nations, and by whofe means the whole univerfe becomes one fingle family. Thefe men may have a noble idea of their profeffion, and it is almoft unneceffary to fay to moft of them, Be honeft in your dealings ; becaufe difhonefty, while it would be prejudicial to yourfelves, would alfo be injurious to your fellow-citizens, and afperfe the character of your nation.

Do not abufe your credit ; that is to fay, in cafe of any unexpected misfortune, let your own funds be able to replace thofe you have obtained from the confidence which your correfpondents have repofed in your knowledge, your talents, and your probity. In the midſt of the ſubverſion of your fortunes, ſhow yourſelves ſimilar to thoſe great trees which the thunder hath thrown down, but which ſtill preſerve all their appearance of majeſty.

You will miſtruſt yourſelves ſo much the more, as you are almoſt always the only judges of your own probity.

I know very well that you will be always reſpected by the multitude as long as you are wealthy; but how will you appear in your own eyes? If you have no regard for your own eſteem, heap up gold upon gold and be happy, if it be poſſible for a man deſtitute of morals to be ſo.

You muſt undoubtedly have retained, as you ought, ſome religious principles. Remember, therefore, that a time will come when your conſcience will reproach you for riches diſhoneſtly acquired, and which you muſt reſtore, unleſs, like madmen, you ſet at defiance a Judge who is ready to call you to a rigid account of them.

Serve all nations; but whatever advantage may be offered to you from ſpeculation, give it up, if it ſhould be injurious to your own country.

Let your word be ſacred. Be ruined if it be neceſſary, rather than break it; and ſhow that honour is more precious to you than gold.

Do not embrace too many objects at once. Whatever ſtrength of mind you may have, or however extenſive your genius may be, remember that the common day of the labouring man conſiſts of little more than ſix hours, and that all affairs which may require a longer day, would be neceſſarily intruſted to your ſubaltern aſſiſtants. A chaos would ſoon be formed around you, in diſſipating of which you might find yourſelf plunged from the ſummit of proſperity, where you imagine yourſelf to be, to the bottomleſs pit of misfortune.

I ſhall never ceaſe to recommend order to you: without it, every thing becomes uncertain. Nothing

is done, or every thing is ill and haſtily done. Neglect renders all undertakings equally ruinous.

Although there be perhaps not one government honeſt enough to induce an individual to aſſiſt it with his
credit, neverthelefs I advife you to run the chance of
it : but let not this aſſiſtance exceed your own fortune.
You may injure yourſelf for your country, but none
but yourſelf. The love of one's country muſt be ſubordinate to the laws of honour and of juſtice.

Never put yourſelf under the neceſſity of diſplay-
ing your ſorrows and your deſpair to a court, who will
coolly allege to you the public neceſſity, and will make
you the ſhameful offer of a ſafe conduct. It is in you
that the foreigners and the citizens have placed their
confidence, and not in the miniſtry of a nation. It is
in your hands that they have depoſited their funds, and
nothing can ſcreen you from their reproaches and from
thoſe of your conſcience, if you have one.

You will be exceedingly prudent if you form no o-
ther enterpriſes, except thoſe which may miſcarry,
without affecting your family or diſturbing your own
repoſe.

Be neither puſillanimous nor raſh. Puſillanimity
would keep you in a ſtate of mediocrity ; raſhneſs
might deprive you in one day of the fruit of ſeveral
years labour.

There is no compariſon to be made between fortune and credit. Fortune without credit is of little
conſequence. Credit without fortune is unlimited. As
long as credit remains, ruin is not completed ; but the
leaſt ſhock to your credit may be followed by the
worſt of cataſtrophes. I have known an inſtance in
which, at the end of twenty years, it had not yet
bee forgotten, that an opulent company had ſtopped
payment for the ſpace of four-and-twenty hours.

The credit of a merchant is recovered with ſtill
greater difficulty than the honour of a woman : nothing but a kind of miracle can put a ſtop to an alarm
which ſpreads itſelf inſtantaneouſly from one hemiſphere of the globe to the other.

The merchant ought not to be lefs jealous of his credit, than the military man of his honour.

If you have any elevation of mind, you will rather choofe to ferve your fellow citizens with lefs advantage, than foreigners at a lefs rifk, with lefs trouble, and with more profit.

Prefer an honeft to a more lucrative fpeculation.

It hath been faid, that the merchant, the banker, and the factor, being citizens of the world by profeffion, were not citizens of any particular country. Let fuch injurious difcourfe no longer be holden againft you.

If, when you quit trade, you fhould only enjoy among your fellow-citizens that degree of confideration granted to confiderable riches, you will not have acquired every thing which you might have obtained from commerce.

The contempt of riches is perhaps incompatible with the fpirit of commerce : but woe be to thofe in whom that fpirit fhould exclude all fentiments of honour.

I have raifed an altar in my heart to four claffes of citizens : to the philofopher, who fearches after truth, who enlightens the nations, and who preaches, by his example, virtue to men ; to the magiftrate, who knows how to maintain an equal balance of juftice ; to the military man who defends his country ; and to the honeft merchant, who enriches and honours it. The hufbandman, by whom we are fed, will excufe me for having forgotten him.

If the merchant doth not confider himfelf among this diftinguifhed rank of citizens, he doth not hold himfelf in fufficient eftimation. He forgets, that in his morning's work a few ftrokes of his pen put the four quarters of the world in motion for their mutual happinefs.

Suffer not yourfelves to indulge any bafe jealoufy for the profperity of another. If you thwart his operations without any motive, you are a bad man ; and if you happen to difcover his operations, and appropriate them to yourfelf, you will have robbed him.

BOOK
XIX.

The influence of gold is as fatal to individuals as to nations. If you do not take care, you will be intoxicated with it. You will be defirous of heaping wealth upon wealth, and you will become either avaricious or prodigal. If you be avaricious, you will be rigid, and the fentiment of commiferation and benevolence will be extinguifhed within you. If you be prodigal, after having wafted the prime of your life in acquiring riches, you will be reduced to indigence by extravagant expences; and if you fhould efcape this misfortune, you will not efcape contempt.

Open fometimes your purfe to the unfortunate and induftrious man.

If you wifh to be honoured during your life, and after your death, confecrate a part of your fortune to fome monument of public utility. Woe to your heirs, if they be difpleafed at this expence.

Remember, that when a man dies who hath nothing but his wealth to boaft of, he is no lofs to fociety.

Thefe maxims, which we have allowed ourfelves to recal to the memory of man, have always been, and will always be true. If it fhould happen that they fhould appear problematical to fome of thofe perfons whofe actions they are intended to regulate, the public authority muft be blamed for it. The rapacious and fervile treafury encourage in all parts private injuftice, by the general acts of injuftice they are feen to commit. They opprefs commerce with the numberlefs impofts they lay upon it; they degrade the merchant, by the injurious fufpicions which they are inceffantly throwing out againft his probity; they render, in fome meafure, fraud neceffary, by the fatal invention of monopolies.

Monopoly is the exclufive privilege of one citizen, over all others, to buy or to fell. At this definition every fenfible man will ftart, and fay: Among citizens, all equals, all ferving fociety, all contributing to its expences, in proportion to their means, how is it poffible that one of them fhould have a right, of which another is legally deprived? What matter, then, is this,

fo facred in its nature, that any man whatever cannot
acquire it, if he be in want of it ; or difpofe of it, if
it fhould belong to him?

If any one could pretend to this privilege, it would
undoubtedly be the fovereign.   Neverthelefs, he cannot do it, for he is nothing more than the firft of the
citizens.   The body of the nation may gratify him
with it ; but then it is only an act of deference, and
not the confequence of a prerogative, which would
neceffarily be tyrannical.   If, therefore, the fovereign
cannot arrogate it to himfelf, much lefs can he confer
it upon another.   We cannot give away what is not
our legitimate property.

But if, contrary to the nature of things, there fhould
exift a people, having fome pretenfions to liberty, and
where the chief hath neverthelefs arrogated to himfelf,
or conferred a monopoly on another, what hath been
the confequence of this infringement of general rights?
Rebellion undoubtedly.   No ; it ought to have been,
although it has not.   The reafon of this is, that a fociety is an affemblage of men, employed in different
functions, having different interefts, jealous, pufillanimous, preferring the peaceable enjoyment of what
is left them, to the having recourfe to arms in the
defence of what is taken from them ; living by the
fide of each other, and preffing upon each other,
without any concurrence of inclination : it is becaufe
this unanimity, fo ufeful, if even it fhould fubfift a-
mong them, would neither give them the courage nor
the ftrength they are in want of, and confequently
neither the hope of conquering, nor the refolution of
perifhing : it is, becaufe they would fee for themfelves
an imminent danger in a fruitlefs attempt, while in
fuccefs they would fee only advantages for their defcendants, whom they have lefs regard for than they
have for themfelves.—Sometimes, however, this circumftance hath happened.—Yes, but it was brought
about by the enthufiafm of fanaticifm.

But in whatever country monopoly may have taken
place, it hath produced nothing but devaftation.   Ex-

clufive privileges have ruined the Old and the New
World.   There is no infant colony in the New Hemifphere which hath not been either weakened or deftroyed by it.   In our hemifphere, there is no flourifhing country the fplendour of which it hath not extinguifhed ;   no enterprife, however brilliant, which it
hath not obfcured ;   no circumftance, more or lefs flattering, which it hath not turned to the general detriment.

But by what fatality hath all this happened?   It
was not a fatality, but a neceffity.   It hath been done,
becaufe it was neceffary it fhould be done, and for
this reafon :   becaufe the poffeffor of a privilege, however powerful he may be, can never have either the
credit or the refources of a whole nation :   becaufe his
monopoly not being able to laft for ever, he avails
himfelf of it as faft as he can, fees nothing but the prefent moment, and every thing which is beyond the
term of his exclufive privilege is nothing to him ;   he
choofes rather to be lefs rich without waiting, than
more rich by waiting.   By an inftinct natural to man,
whofe enjoyments are founded upon injuftice, tyranny, and vexation, he is perpetually in dread of the
fuppreffion of a privilege fatal to all.   This has happened, becaufe his intereft is all to himfelf, and the intereft of the nation is nothing to him :   it is becaufe,
for a fmall and momentary advantage, but for a certain one, he fcruples not to do a great and permanent
mifchief :   it is becaufe the exclufive privilege, when it
comes to the fpot where it is to be exercifed, introduces along with it the train of all perfecutions :   it is becaufe, by the folly, the vague extent, or the extenfion
of the terms of his grant, and by the power of him
who hath either granted or protects it, he becomes
mafter of all, interferes with every thing ;   he reftrains
and deftroys every thing ;   he will annihilate a branch
of induftry ufeful to all, in order to compel another
branch, prejudicial to all but himfelf ;   he will pretend
to command the foil, as he hath commanded the labours, and the ground muft ceafe producing what is

proper to it, in order to produce only what is suitable B O O K
to the monopoly, or to become barren; for he will XIX.
prefer barrenness to a fertility which interferes with
him, and scarcity which he does not feel, to plenty
which might diminish his profits: it is because, according to the nature of the thing of which he hath got the
exclusive trade, if it be an article of primary necessity,
he will starve at once a whole country, or leave it quite
bare; if it be not an article of primary necessity, he
will soon be able, by indirect means, to make it one,
and he will still starve, and leave quite bare the country, which he will easily deprive of the means of acquiring this article: it is because it is almost possible
for him, who is the sole vender, to make himself, by
contrivances as artful and deep as they are atrocious,
the only buyer; and that then he will put at pleasure
the article he sells at a very exorbitant price, and that
which the people are obliged to sell to him at a very
low one. Then it is, that the seller, being disgusted
of a branch of industry, of a culture and of a labour
which doth not bring him the equivalent of his expences, every thing goes to ruin, and the nation falls into
misery.

The term of the exclusive privilege expires, and the
possessor of it retires opulent; but the opulence of a
single man, raised upon the ruin of the multitude, is a
great evil; and, therefore, why hath it not been ob-
viated? Wherefore is it not opposed? From the prejudice, as *cruel* as it is *absurd*, that it is a matter of indifference to the state, whether wealth be in the purse
of one man, or of another; whether it be confined to
one man, or distributed among several. *Absurd*, because in all cases, and especially in those of great necessity, the sovereign addresses himself to the nation;
that is, to a great number of men, who possess scarce
any thing, and whose ruin is completed by the little
that is taken from them; and to a very small number
of men, who possess a great deal, and who give a little, or indeed who never give in proportion to what
they possess; and whose contribution, if even it were

upon a level with their wealth, would never yield the
hundredth part of what might have been obtained,
without exaction and without murmur, from a numerous fet of people in eafy circumftances. *Cruel*, becaufe, with equal advantages, it would be an act of
inhumanity to compel the multitude to want and to
fuffer.

But is the exclufive privilege gratuitoufly granted?
Sometimes; and it is then a mark of acknowledgment
either for great fervices, or for a long train of mean
fervilities, or the refult of the intrigues of a feries of
fubalterns, bought and fold; one extremity of which
feries comes from the loweft claffes of fociety, while
the other is contiguous to the throne; and that is what
is called protection. When fold, it is never for its full
value, and that for feveral reafons. It is impoffible
that the price paid for it can compenfate for the ravages it occafions. Its value cannot yet be known,
neither by the chief of the nation, who knows nothing,
nor by his reprefentative, who is often as ill informed,
befide that he is fometimes a traitor to his mafter and
to his country; nor even by the purchafer himfelf,
who always calculates his acquifition by the rate of its
leaft produce. In a word, thefe fhameful bargains being moftly made in times of crifis, the adminiftration
accepts a fum little proportioned to the value of the
thing, but advanced in the moment of urgent neceffity, or, what is more common, of urgent caprice.

Laftly, let us examine what is the refult of thefe
monopolies repeated, and of the difafters which attend
them; the ruin of the ftate, and the contempt of public faith. After thefe acts of infidelity, which cannot
be mentioned without exciting a blufh, the nation is
plunged into defolation. In the midft of feveral millions of unfortunate wretches, there arifes the proud
head of fome extortioners, gorged with riches, and infulting over the mifery of all. The empire, enervated,
totters for fome time on the borders of the abyfs into
which it falls, amongft the acclamations of contempt
and ridicule from its neighbours; unlefs Heaven fhould

raife up a faviour in its favour, whom it always expects, but who doth not always arrive, or who is foon difguft-ed by the general perfecution he experiences from thofe villains of whom he is the terror.

The obftacles with which the feveral governments clog the trade which their fubjects either carry on, or ought to carry on, among themfelves, are ftill much more multiplied in that trade which is carried on between one ftate and the reft. This jealoufy of the powers, which is almoft of modern date, might be taken for a fecret confpiracy to ruin each other, without advantage to any one of them.

Thofe who govern the people exert the fame fkill in guarding againft the induftry of the nations, as in preferving themfelves from the artifices of the intriguing men by whom they are furrounded. Acts of violence and reciprocal enmity univerfally prevail in all parts. Some ignorant, mean, and corrupt men, have filled Europe, and the whole world, with a multitude of unbearable reftraints, which have been more and more extended. Centinels and obftacles are placed in every part of the fea and of the land. The traveller enjoys no repofe, the merchant no property; both are equally expofed to all the fnares of an infidious legiflation, that gives rife to crimes by its prohibitions, and to penalties by crimes. Men become culpable without knowing it, or without defign; are arrefted, plundered, and taxed, without having any thing to reproach themfelves with. Such is the ftate of commerce in time of peace. But what fhall we fay of commercial wars?

It is natural enough for a people, pent up in the icy regions of the north, to dig out iron from the bowels of the earth that refufes them fubfiftence, and to reap the harveft of another nation by force of arms: hunger, which is reftrained by no laws, cannot violate any, and feems to plead an excufe for thefe hoftilities. Men muft neceffarily live by plunder, when they have no corn. But when a nation enjoys the privilege of an extenfive commerce, and can fupply feveral other ftates

from its fuperfluity, what motive can induce it to declare war againft other induftrious nations, to obftruct
their navigation and their labours; in a word, to forbid them to live, on pain of death? Why does it arrogate to itfelf an exclufive branch of trade, a right of
fifhing and of navigation, as if it were a matter of property, and as if the fea were to be divided into acres
as well as the land? The motives of fuch wars are
eafily difcovered: we know that the jealoufy of commerce is nothing more than a jealoufy of power. But
have any people a right to obftruct a work they cannot execute themfelves, and to condemn another nation to indolence, becaufe they themfelves choofe to
be entirely given up to it?

How unnatural and contradictory an expreffion is a
war of commerce! Commerce is the fource and
means of fubfiftence; war of deftruction. Commerce
may, poffibly, give rife to war, and continue it; but
war puts a ftop to every branch of commerce. Whatever advantage one nation may derive from another in
trade becomes a motive of induftry and emulation to
both: in war, on the contrary, the injury affects both;
for plunder, fire, and fword, can neither improve lands
nor enrich mankind. The wars of commerce are fo
much the more fatal, as by the prefent fuperiority of
the maritime powers over thofe of the continent, and
of Europe over the three other parts of the world, the
conflagration becomes general; and that the diffenfions of two maritime powers excite the fpirit of difcord among all their allies, and occafion inactivity even
among the neutral powers.

Coafts and feas ftained with blood, and covered with
dead bodies; the horrors of war extending from pole
to pole, between Africa, Afia, and America, as well
throughout the fea that feparates us from the New
World, as throughout the vaft extent of the Pacific
Ocean: fuch has been the fpectacle exhibited in the
two laft wars, in which all the powers of Europe have
been alternately fhaken, or have diftinguifhed themfelves by fome remarkable exertion. In the mean-

while, the earth was depopulated, and commerce did
not supply the losses it had sustained; the lands were
exhausted by taxes, and the channels of navigation did
not assist the progress of agriculture. The loans of the
state previously ruined the fortunes of the citizens by
usurious profits, the forerunners of bankruptcy. Even
those powers that were victorious, oppressed by the
conquests they had made, and having acquired a greater extent of land than they could keep or cultivate,
were involved in the ruin of their enemies. The neutral powers, who were desirous of enriching themselves
in peace, in the midst of this commotion, were exposed,
and tamely submitted to insults more disgraceful than
the defeats of an open war.

The spirit of discord had been transferred from the
sovereigns to the people. The citizens of the several
states took up arms reciprocally to plunder each other.
Nothing was seen but merchantmen changed into pri-
vateers: those by whom they were commanded were
not urged by necessity to follow this employment;
some of them had fortunes, and the others might have
received advantageous salaries from all sides. An inordinate passion for plunder was the only stimulus they
had to this depravity. When they met with a peaceful merchantman, they were seized with a ferocious
joy, which manifested itself in the most lively tran-
sports: they were cruel, and homicides. An enemy
more fortunate, stronger, or bolder, might, in their
turn, deprive them of their prey, their liberty, and
their life. But the aspect of a danger so common did
not diminish either their avarice or their rage. This
species of frenzy was not new. It had been known in
the most distant ages, and had been perpetuated from
one century to another. Man, at all times, though
not urged by the unconquerable stimulus of hunger,
hath sought to devour man. The calamity, however,
which we here deplore, had never arisen to that pitch
at which we have seen it. The activity of piracy hath
increased in proportion as the seas have furnished it

with more means to satisfy its avidity and its turbulent
spirit.

Will nations, then, never be convinced of the neceffity of putting an end to thefe acts of barbarifm?
Would not a reftraint which fhould check their progrefs prove a circumftance of evident utility? Wherefore muft the productions of the two worlds be either
fwallowed up in the abyfs of the ocean, together with
the veffels which convey them; or become the prey
of the vices and debauchery of a few vagabonds, deftitute of morals and of principles? Will this infatuation continue much longer, or will the adminiftrators
of empires at length open their eyes to the light?
Should they one day be made acquainted with their
true interefts, with the effential interefts of the focieties at the head of which they are placed, they will
not limit their policy to the clearing of the feas from
pirates, but they will extend it fo far, as to leave a
free intercourfe to the connections fubfifting between
their refpective fubjects, during thofe murderous and
deftructive hoftilities which frequently harafs and ravage the globe.

They are fortunately paft thofe deplorable times,
when the nations fought for their mutual annihilation.
The troubles which at prefent divide Europe have not
fo fatal an aim. It is feldom that any other object is
propofed, than the reparation of fome injuftice, or the
maintenance of a certain equilibrium between empires.
The belligerent powers will undoubtedly endeavour
to annoy and to weaken each other as much as poffible: but if none of them could do more mifchief than
they fuffered, would it not be generally ufeful to put
a ftop to thefe calamities? This is what conftantly
happens, when war fufpends the operations of commerce.

Then one ftate rejects the productions and the induftry of the adverfe ftate, which, in its turn, rejects
her productions and her induftry. This is, on both
fides, a diminution of labour, of profit, and of enjoy-

ments. The interference of neutral powers, in thofe B O O K circumftances, is not fo favourable as we are perhaps XIX. accuftomed to confider it. Befide that their agency muft neceffarily be very expenfive, they endeavour to raife themfelves upon the ruin of thofe whom they feem to ferve. Whatever their foil and their manufactures can furnifh is fubftituted, as much as poffible, to the productions of the foil and manufactures of the armed powers, which frequently do not recover at the peace what the hoftilities had made them lofe. It will therefore be always confiftent with the interefts of the nations which make war againft each other, to continue, without reftraint, the exchanges they carried on before their diffenfions.

All truths hold by each other. Let this truth, the importance of which we have eftablifhed, direct the conduct of governments; and we fhall foon fee thofe innumerable barriers, which, even in times of the moft profound tranquillity, feparate the nations, whatever may be the affinities which nature or chance hath created between them, will exift no more.

The moft fanguinary difputes were formerly no more than tranfient explofions, after which, each people repofed upon their arms, either defeated or triumphant. Peace, at that time, was peace; but, at prefent, it is nothing more than a tacit war. Every ftate rejects foreign productions, either by prohibitions, or by reftraints often equivalent to prohibitions. Every ftate refufes its own, upon fuch equitable terms which might make them be fought after, or extend their confumption. The defire of mutually annoying each other is extended from one pole to the other. In vain hath nature regulated, that, under her wife laws, every country fhould be opulent, powerful, and happy, from the wealth, the power, and the felicity of the reft. They have, unanimoufly as it were, difturbed this plan of univerfal benevolence, to the detriment of them all. Their ambition hath led them to infulate themfelves; and this folitary fituation hath made them defirous of an exclufive profperity. Evil for evil hath then been returned. Artifices have been oppofed to artifices, profcriptions to profcriptions, and fraud to fraud. Nations have become enervated, in attempting to enervate the rival powers; and it was impoffible that it fhould be otherwife. The conneciions of commerce are all very clofe. One of its branches cannot experience any oppofition, without the others being fenfible of it. Commerce connects people and fortunes together, and eftablifhes the intercourfe of exchanges. It is one entire whole, the feveral parts of which attract, fupport, and balance each other. It refembles the human body, all the parts of which are affected, when one of them doth not fulfil the functions that were deftined to it.

Would you wifh to put an end to the calamities which ill contrived plans have brought upon the whole earth, you muft pull down the fatal walls with which they have encompaffed themfelves. You muft reftore that happy fraternity which conftituted the delight of the firft ages. Let the people, in whatever country fate may have placed them, to whatever government they may be fubject, whatever religion they may profefs, communicate as freely with each other, as the inhabitants of a hamlet with thofe of a neighbouring one; with thofe of the moft contiguous town, and with all thofe of the fame empire; that is to fay, free from duties, formalities, or predilections.

Then, but not before, the earth will be filled with productions, and thofe of an exquifite quality. The frenzy of impofitions and prohibitions hath reduced each ftate to cultivate commodities, which its foil and its climate rejected, and which were never either of good quality, or plentiful. The labours will be directed to another channel. When the earth can fatisfy its wants in a more pleafant way, and at a cheaper rate, it will turn all its activity to objects for which nature had deftined it; and which being fuch as they fhould be, will find an advantageous mart in thofe places even where an enlightened fyftem of economy fhall have determined the people to reject them.

Then, but not before, all nations will attain to that B O O K
degree of prosperity, to which they are allowed to a- XIX.
spire : they will enjoy both their own riches, and the
riches of other nations.   The people who had till then
had some success in trade, have hitherto imagined that
that their neighbours could only make their own trade
flourish at the expence of theirs.   This presumption
had made them behold with an anxious and suspicious
eye the efforts that were made to improve their situation ; and had excited them to interrupt, by the manœuvres of an active and unjust cupidity, labours the
consequences of which they dreaded.   They will alter their conduct, when they shall have understood,
that the natural and moral order of things is subverted by the present state of them ; that the idleness of
one country is hurtful to all the rest, either because it
condemns them to more labour, or because it deprives
them of some enjoyments ; that foreign industry, far
from confining theirs, will extend it ; that the more
benefits shall be multiplied around them, the more
easy it will be for them to extend their conveniences
and their exchanges ; that their harvests and their manufactures must necessarily fall to ruin, if the marts,
and their returns, are to be deficient ; that states, as
well as individuals, have a visible interest, habitually,
to sell at the highest price possible, and to purchase
at the highest price possible ; and that this double advantage can be found only in the greatest possible
competition, and in the greatest affluence, between
the sellers and the purchasers.   This is the interest of
every government, and it is therefore the interest of all
of them.

Let it not be said, that, in the system of a general
and illimited liberty, some people would acquire a
too determined ascendant over the rest.   The new
plans will not deprive any state of its soil or of its genius.   Whatever advantages each may have had in
times of prohibition, it will preserve under the guidance of better principles.   Its utility will even in-

creafe confiderably, becaufe its neighbours, enjoying more wealth, will more and more extend its confumptions.

If there exifted a country which might be allowed to have fome diflike to the abolition of the prohibitive government, it undoubtedly would be that which improvident nature hath condemned to an eternal poverty. Accuftomed to reject, by fumptuary laws, the delights of more fortunate countries, they might be apprehenfive that a communication entirely free, with them, might fubvert their maxims, corrupt their morals, and pave the way for their ruin. Thefe alarms would be ill-founded. Except, perhaps, a few moments of illufion, every nation would regulate their wants by their abilities.

Happy, then, and infinitely happy, will be that power, which fhall be the firft to difencumber itfelf of the reftraints, the taxes, and the prohibitions, which in all parts opprefs and ftop the progrefs of commerce. Attracted by the liberty, the facility, the fafety, and the multiplicity of exchanges; the fhips, the productions, the commodities, and the merchants of all countries, will crowd into their ports. The caufes of fo fplendid a profperity will foon be underftood; and the nations, renouncing their ancient errors and their deftructive prejudices, will haften to adopt principles fo fertile in favourable events. The revolution will become general. Clouds will be difpelled in all parts; a ferene fky will fhine over the face of the whole globe, and nature will refume the reins of the world. Then, or never, will that univerfal peace arife, which a warlike but humane monarch did not think to be a chimerical idea. If fo defirable and fo little expected a benefit fhould not iffue from this new order of things, from this great unfolding of reafon, at leaft the general felicity of men will be eftablifhed upon a more folid bafis.

Agriculture,

Commerce, which naturally arifes from agriculture, returns to it by its bent and by its circulation. Thus

it is that the rivers return to the fea, which has produced them, by the exhalations of its waters into vapours, and by the fall of thofe vapours into waters.
The flow of gold brought by the circulation and confumption of the fruits of the earth, returns, at length,
into the fields, there to produce all the neceffaries of
life and the materials of commerce. If the lands be
not cultivated, all commerce is precarious; becaufe it
is deprived of its original fupplies, which are the productions of nature. Nations that are only maritime,
or commercial, enjoy, it is true, the fruits of commerce;
but the tree of it belongs to thofe people who cultivate it. Agriculture is therefore the firft and real
opulence of a ftate.

Thefe benefits were not enjoyed in the infancy of
the world. The firft inhabitants of the globe relied
only upon chance, and upon their dexterity, for procuring to themfelves an uncertain fubfiftence. They
wandered from one region to another. Inceffantly
abforbed in the ideas of want or fear, they reciprocally fled from, or deftroyed, each other. The earth
was ftirred up, and the miferies of a vagabond life
were alleviated. In proportion as agriculture was
extended, mankind were multiplied with the means
of fubfiftence. Nations, and even great ones, were
formed. Some of them difdained the fource of their
profperity, and were punifhed for that fenfelefs pride by
invafions. Upon the ruins of vaft monarchies, funk
in lethargy, by the neglect of ufeful labours, new ftates
arofe; which having, in their turn, contracted the habit of trufting the care of their fubfiftence to their flaves,
were not able to refift the nations ftimulated either by
indigence or barbarifm.

Such was the fate of Rome. Proud of the fpoils
of the univerfe, fhe held in contempt the rural occupations of her founders, and of her moft illuftrious citizens. Her country-places were filled with delightful retreats. She fubfifted only upon foreign contributions. The people, corrupted by perpetual profufions, abandoned the labours of tillage. All the ufe-

BOOK XIX.
ful or honourable places were purchafed with abundant diftributions of corn. Hunger gave the law in
the comitia. All the orders of the republic were no
longer governed by any thing but hunger and amufement. Then the empire fell to ruin, deftroyed rather
by its internal vices, than by the barbarians who tore
it to pieces.

The contempt which the Romans had for agriculture, in the intoxication of thofe conquefts which had
given them the whole world without their cultivating
it, was perpetuated. It was adopted by thofe favage
hordes, who, deftroying by the fword, a power which
was eftablifhed by it, left to the vaffals the clearing of
the lands, of which they referved to themfelves the
fruits and the property. Even in the age fubfequent
to the difcovery of the Eaft and Weft Indies, this truth
was unattended to; whether in Europe the people
were too much engaged in wars of ambition or religion to confider it; or whether the conquefts made by
Portugal and Spain beyond the feas, having brought
us treafures without labour, we contented ourfelves
with enjoying them by encouraging luxury and the
arts, before any method had been thought of to fecure thefe riches.

But the time came, when plunder ceafed, having
no object on which it could be exercifed. When the
conquered lands in the New World, after having been
much contefted for, were divided, it became neceffary
to cultivate them, and to fupport the colonifts who
fettled there. As thefe were natives of Europe, they
cultivated for that country fuch productions as it did
not furnifh, and required in return fuch provifions as
cuftom had made natural to them. In proportion as
the colonies were peopled, and as the number of failors and manufacturers increafed with the increafe of
productions, the lands muft neceffarily furnifh a greater quantity of fubfiftence for the increafe of population, and an augmentation of indigenous commodities,
for foreign articles of exchange and confumption. The
laborious employment of navigation, and the fpoiling

of provisions in the transport, causing a greater loss of materials and produce, it became necessary to cultivate the earth with the greatest care and assiduity, in order to render it more fruitful. The consumption of American commodities, far from lessening that of European productions, served only to increase and extend it upon all the seas, in all the ports, and in all the cities where commerce and industry prevailed. Thus the people who were the most commercial necessarily became, at the same time, the greatest promoters of agriculture.

England first conceived the idea of this new system. She established and encouraged it by honours and premiums proposed to the planters. A medal was stricken, and presented to the duke of Bedford, with the following inscription: *For having planted Oak*. Triptolemus and Ceres were adored in antiquity only from similar motives; and yet temples and altars are still erected to indolent monks. The God of nature will not suffer that mankind should perish. He hath implanted in all noble and generous minds, in the hearts of all people and of enlightened monarchs, this idea, that labour is the first duty of man, and that the most important of all labours is that of cultivating the land. The reward that attends agriculture, the satisfying of our wants, is the best encomium that can be made of it. *If I had a subject who could produce two blades of corn instead of one*, said a monarch, *I should prefer him to all the men of political genius in the state*. How much is it to be lamented, that such a king and such an opinion are merely the fiction of Swift's brain? But a nation that can produce such writers must necessarily confirm the truth of this sublime idea; and accordingly we find that England doubled the produce of its cultivation.

Europe had this great example for more than half a century under her eyes, without its making a sufficient impression upon her to induce her to follow it. The French, who, under the administration of three cardinals, had scarce been allowed to turn their thoughts to

public affairs, ventured at length, in 1750, to write on
ſubjects of importance and general utility. The undertaking of An Univerſal Dictionary of Arts and Sciences brought every great object to view, and exerciſed the thoughts of every man of genius and of knowledge. Monteſquieu wrote The Spirit of Laws, and
the boundaries of genius were extended. Natural Hiſtory was written by a French Pliny, who ſurpaſſed
Greece and Rome in the knowledge and deſcription
of nature. This hiſtory, bold and ſublime as its ſubject, warmed the imagination of every reader, and
powerfully excited them to ſuch inquiries as a nation
cannot relinquiſh without returning into a ſtate of
barbariſm. It was then that a great number of ſubjects became ſenſible of the real wants of their country. Government itſelf ſeemed to perceive that all
kinds of riches originated from the earth. They granted ſome encouragement to agriculture, but without
having the courage to remove the obſtacles which prevented its improvement.

The French huſbandman doth not yet enjoy the
happineſs of being taxed only in proportion to his
abilities. Arbitrary impoſts ſtill moleſt and ruin him.
Jealous or rapacious neighbours have it always in their
power to exerciſe either their cupidity or their revenge
againſt him. A barbarous collector, a haughty lord,
an arrogant and authoriſed monopoliſt, a man raiſed
to fortune, and who is a greater deſpot than all the
reſt, may humiliate, beat, and plunder him ; they may
deprive him, in a word, of all the rights of mankind,
of property, of ſafety, and of liberty. Degraded by
this kind of abject ſtate, his clothes, his manners, his
language, become an object of deriſion for all the o-
ther claſſes of ſociety ; and authority often gives a
ſanction by its conduct to this exceſs of extravagance.

I have heard that ſtupid and ferocious ſtateſman,
and the indignation which he excited in me almoſt
prompts me to name him, and to give up his memory
to the execration of all honeſt and ſenſible men ; I
have heard him ſay, that the labours of the field were

fo hard, that, if the cultivator were allowed to acquire fome eafe in his circumftances, he would forfake his plough, and leave the lands untilled. His advice was therefore to perpetuate labour by mifery, and to condemn to eternal indigence the man, without the fweat of whofe brow he muft have been ftarved to death. He ordered that the oxen fhould be fattened, while he curtailed the fubfiftence of the hufbandman. He governed a province, and yet he did not conceive that it was the impoffibility of acquiring a fmall degree of eafe, and not the danger of fatigue, which difgufted the hufbandman of his condition. He did not know that the ftate into which men are anxious to enter, is that which they hope to quit by the acquifition of riches ; and that however hard may be the daily labours of agriculture, it will neverthelefs find more votaries in proportion as the reward of its labours fhall be more certain and more abundant. He had not noticed, that in the towns there were a multitude of employments, which, although they fhortened the lives of thofe who were engaged in them, yet this did not deter others from following them. He did not know, that, in fome countries of vaft extent, there were miners who voluntarily devoted themfelves to deftruction in the bowels of the earth, and that even before they were thirty years of age, upon condition of reaping from this facrifice clothes and provifions for their wives and children. It had never fuggefted itfelf to him, that, in all profeffions, that fort of eafe in circumftances, which admits of calling in affiftance, alleviates the fatigue of them ; and that inhumanly to exclude the peafant from the clafs of proprietors, was to put a ftop to the progrefs of the firft of the arts, which could not become flourifhing, as long as the perfon who tilled the earth was obliged to till it for another. This ftatefman had never compared with his own immenfe vineyards that fmall portion of vines belonging to his vine-dreffer, nor known the difference there is between the foil cultivated for one's felf and that which is cultivated for others.

Fortunately for France, all the agents of government have not had such destructive prejudices; and more fortunately still, the obstacles which impeded the improvement of the lands and of agriculture in that country have been often overcome. Germany, and after that the northern climates, have been attracted by the taste of the age, which sensible men had turned towards these great objects. These vast regions have at length understood that the most extensive countries were of no value, if they were not rendered useful by a perseverance in labour; that the clearing of a soil extended it; and that territories the least favoured by nature might become fertile by prudent and skilful expenditures bestowed upon them. A multiplicity and a variety of productions have been the reward of so judicious a proceeding. Nations, who have been in want of the necessaries of life, have been enabled to furnish provisions even to the southern parts of Europe.

But how is it possible that men, situated upon so rich a territory, should have wanted foreign assistance to subsist? The great excellence of the territory hath been perhaps the true reason of this. In the countries which were not so favourably treated by nature, it hath been necessary that the cultivator should have considerable funds, that he should condemn himself to assiduous watchings, in order to acquire from the bosom of an ungrateful or rebellious soil harvests moderately plentiful. Under a more fortunate sky, it was only necessary for him, as it were, to scratch the earth; and this advantage hath plunged him into misery and indolence. The climate hath still increased his misfortunes, which have been completed by religious institutions.

The Sabbath, considering it even only under a political point of view, is an admirable institution. It was proper to give a stated day of rest to mankind, that they might have time to recover themselves, to lift up their eyes to heaven, to enjoy life with reflection, to meditate upon past events, to reason upon present transactions, and in some measure to form plans for the future. But by multiplying those days of inactivity, hath not that which was established for the advantage of individuals and of societies, been converted into a calamity for them? Would not a soil, which should be ploughed three hundred days in the year by strong men and vigorous animals, yield double the produce of that which should only be worked one hundred and fifty days in the year? What strange infatuation! Torrents of blood have been shed an infinite number of times to prevent the dismembering of a territory, or to increase its extent; and yet the powers intrusted with the maintenance and happiness of empires, have patiently suffered that a priest, sometimes even a foreign priest, should invade successively one third of this territory, by the proportional diminution of labour, which alone could fertilize it. This inconceivable disorder hath ceased in several states, but it continues in the south of Europe. This is one of the greatest obstacles to the increase of its subsistence and of its population. The importance of agriculture begins, however, to be perceived: even Spain hath exerted herself; and for want of inhabitants, who would employ themselves in the labours of the field, she hath at last invited foreigners to till her uncultivated provinces.

Notwithstanding this almost universal emulation, it must be acknowledged that agriculture hath not made the same progress as the other arts. Since the revival of letters, the genius of men hath measured the earth, calculated the motion of the stars, and weighed the air. It hath penetrated through the darkness which concealed from it the natural and moral system of the world. By investigating nature, it hath discovered an infinite number of secrets, with which all the sciences have enriched themselves. Its empire hath extended itself over a multitude of objects necessary to the happiness of mankind. In this ferment of men's minds, experimental philosophy, which had but very imperfectly enlightened ancient philosophy, hath too seldom

turned its obfervations towards the important part of
the vegetable fyftem. The different qualities of the
foil, the number of which is fo various, are ftill unknown, as well as the kind of foil which is the beft
adapted to every production; the quantity and the
quality of the feeds which it is proper to fow in them;
the feafons moft propitious for ploughing, fowing, and
reaping them; and the fpecies of manure fit to increafe
their fertility. No better information is procured concerning the moft advantageous manner of multiplying
flocks, of breeding and of feeding them, and of improving their fleece. No greater light hath been
thrown upon the cultivation of trees. We have fcarce
any but imperfect notions concerning all thefe articles
of primary neceffity, fuch as have been tranfmitted to
us by a blind routine, or by practice followed with little reflection. Europe would be ftill lefs advanced in
this knowledge, were it not for the obfervations of a
few Englifh writers, who have fucceeded in eradicat-
ing fome prejudices, and in introducing feveral excellent methods. This zeal for the firft of arts hath been
communicated to the cultivators of their nation. Fair-
child, one of them, hath carried his enthufiafm fo far,
as to order that the dignity of his profeffion fhould be
annually celebrated by a public difcourfe. His will
was complied with for the firft time in 1760, in St.
Leonard's church in London; and this ufeful ceremony hath never been omitted fince that period.

It is a fact fomewhat remarkable, though it might
naturally be expected, that men fhould have returned
to the exercife of agriculture, the firft of the arts, only after they had fucceffively tried the reft. It is the
common progreffion of the human mind not to regain
the right path till after it hath exhaufted itfelf in pur-
fuing falfe tracks. It is always advancing; and as it
relinquifhed agriculture to purfue commerce and the
enjoyments of luxury, it foon traverfed over the different arts of life, and returned at laft to agriculture,
which is the fource and foundation of all the reft, and
to which it devoted its whole attention, from the fame

motives of interest that had made it quit it before.
Thus the eager and inquisitive man, who voluntarily
banishes himself from his own country in his youth,
wearied with his constant excursions, returns at last to
live and die in his native land.

Every thing, indeed, depends upon, and arises from,
the cultivation of land. It forms the internal strength
of states, and occasions riches to circulate into them
from without. Every power which comes from any
other source is artificial and precarious, either considered in a natural or moral light. Industry and commerce, which do not directly affect the agriculture of
a country, are in the power of foreign nations, who
may either dispute these advantages through competition, or deprive the country of them through envy.
This may be effected either by establishing the same
branch of industry among themselves, or by suppress-
ing the exportation of their own unwrought materials,
or the exportation of those materials when manufactured. But a country well cultivated occasions an increase of population, and riches are the natural consequence of that increase. This is not the teeth which
the dragon sows to bring forth soldiers to destroy each
other; it is the milk of Juno, which peoples the heavens with an innumerable multitude of stars.

The government, therefore, should rather be attentive to the support of the country places than of great
cities. The first may be considered as parents and
nurseries always fruitful, the others only as daughters
which are often ungrateful and barren. The cities can
scarce subsist but from the superfluous part of the population and produce of the countries. Even the fortified places and ports of trade, which seem to be connected with the whole world by their ships, which dif-
fuse more riches than they possess, do not, however,
attract all the treasures they dispense, but by means
of the produce of the countries that surround them.
The tree must, therefore, be watered at its root. The
cities will only be flourishing in proportion as the fields
are fruitful.

But this fertility depends ftill lefs upon the foil than upon the inhabitants. Some countries, though fitr-^t-ed under a climate the moft favourable to agriculture, produce lefs than others inferior to them in every re-fpect, becaufe the efforts of nature are impeded in a thoufand ways by the form of their government. In all parts where the people are attached to the country by property, by the fecurity of their funds and reve-nues, the lands will flourifh ; in all parts where privi-leges are not confined to the cities, and labour to the countries, every proprietor will be fond of the inheri-tance of his anceftors, will increafe and embellifh it by affiduous cultivation, and his children will be multi-plied in proportion to his means, and thefe be increaf-ed in proportion to his children.

It is, therefore, the intereft of government to favour the hufbandman, in preference to all the indolent claffes of fociety. Nobility is but an odious diftinction, when it is not founded upon fervices of real and evident uti-lity to the ftate ; fuch as the defence of the nation a-gainft the encroachments of conqueft, and againft the enterprifes of defpotifm. The nobles furnifh only a precarious, and oftentimes fatal affiftance ; when, after having led an effeminate and licentious life in the ci-ties, they can only afford a weak defence for their country upon her fleets and in her armies, and after-wards return to court, to folicit, as a reward for their bafenefs, places and honours, which are revolting and burdenfome to the nation. The clergy are a fet of men ufelefs, at leaft, to the earth, even when they are employed in prayer. But when, with fcandalous mo-rals, they preach a doctrine which is rendered doubly incredible and impracticable from their ignorance and from their example ; when, after having difgraced, dif-credited, and overturned religion, by a variety of a-bufes, of fophifms, of injuftices and ufurpations, they wifh to fupport it by perfecution ; then this privileged, indolent, and turbulent clafs of men, become the moft dreadful enemies of the ftate and of the nation. The only good and refpectable part of them that remains, is that portion of the clergy who are moſt deſpiſed and moſt burdened with duty, and who, being ſituated among the lower claſs of people in the country, labour, edify, adviſe, comfort, and relieve a multitude of unhappy men.

The huſbandmen deſerve to be preferred by government even to the manufacturers, and the profeſſors of either the mechanical or liberal arts. To encourage and to protect the arts of luxury, and at the ſame time neglect the cultivation of the land, that ſource of induſtry to which they owe their exiſtence and ſupport, is to forget the order of the ſeveral relations between nature and ſociety. To favour the arts, and to neglect agriculture, is the ſame thing as to remove the baſis of a pyramid, in order to finiſh the top. The mechanical arts engage a ſufficient number of hands by the allurement of the riches they procure, by the comforts they ſupply the workmen with, by the eaſe, pleaſures, and conveniencies, that ariſe in cities where the ſeveral branches of induſtry unite. It is the life of the huſbandman that ſtands in need of encouragement for the hard labours it is expoſed to, and of indemnification for the loſſes and vexations it ſuſtains. The huſbandman is placed at a diſtance from every object that can either excite his ambition or gratify his curioſity. He lives in a ſtate of ſeparation from the diſtinctions and pleaſures of ſociety. He cannot give his children a polite education, without ſending them at a diſtance from him, nor place them in ſuch a ſituation as may enable them to diſtinguiſh and advance themſelves by the fortune they may acquire. He does not enjoy the ſacrifices he makes for them, while they are educated at a diſtance from him. In a word, he undergoes all the fatigues that are incident to man, without enjoying his pleaſures, unleſs ſupported by the paternal care of government. Every thing is burdenſome and humiliating to him, even the taxes, the very name of which ſometimes makes his condition more wretched than any other.

Men are naturally attached to the liberal arts by

BOOK the bent of their talents, which makes this attachment
XIX. grow up into a kind of paffion ; and likewife by the
confideration they reflect on thofe who diftinguifh
themfelves in the purfuit of them. It is not poffible
to admire the works of genius, without efteeming and
careffing the perfons endowed with that valuable gift
of nature. But the man devoted to the labours of
hufbandry, if he cannot enjoy in quiet what he poffeffes, and what he gathers ; if he be incapable of improving the benefits of his condition, becaufe the
fweets of it are taken from him ; if the military fervice, if vaffalage and taxes are to deprive him of his
child, his cattle, and his corn, nothing remains for him
but to imprecate both the fky and the land that torment him, and to abandon his fields and his country.

A wife government cannot, therefore, refufe to pay
its principal attention to agriculture, without endangering its very exiftence : the moft ready and effectual
means of affifting it, is to favour the multiplication of
every kind of production, by the moft free and general circulation.

An unreftrained liberty in the exchange of commodities renders a people at the fame time commercial
and attentive to agriculture ; it extends the views of
the farmer towards trade, and thofe of the merchant
towards cultivation. It connects them to each other
by fuch relations as are regular and conftant. All
men belong equally to the villages and to the cities,
and there is a reciprocal communication maintained
between the provinces. The circulation of commodities brings on in reality the golden age, in which
ftreams of milk and honey are faid to have flowed
through the plains. All the lands are cultivated ; the
meadows are favourable to tillage by the cattle they
feed ; the growth of corn promotes that of vines, by
furnifhing a conftant and certain fubfiftence to him
who neither fows nor reaps, but plants, prunes, and
gathers.

Let us now confider the effects of a contrary fyftem,
and attempt to regulate agriculture, and the circula-

tion of its produce, by particular laws; and let us observe what calamities will enſue. Power will not only be deſirous of obſerving and being informed of every action, but will even want to aſſume every important act to itſelf, in conſequence of which nothing will ſucceed. Men will be led like their cattle, or tranſported like their corn; they will be collected and diſperſed at the will of a tyrant, to be ſlaughtered in war, or periſh upon fleets, or in different colonies. That which conſtitutes the life of a ſtate will become its deſtruction. Neither the lands nor the people will proſper, and the ſtates will tend quickly to their diſſolution; that is, to that ſeparation which is always preceded by the maſſacre of the people, as well as their tyrants. What will then become of manufactures?

Agriculture gives birth to the arts, when it is carried to that degree of plenty, which gives men leiſure to invent, and procure themſelves the conveniencies of life; and when it has occaſioned a population ſufficiently numerous to be employed in other labours beſide thoſe of the land, then a people muſt neceſſarily become either ſoldiers, navigators, or manufacturers. As ſoon as war has changed the rude and ſavage manners of a laborious people; as ſoon as it has nearly circumſcribed the extent of their empire; thoſe men who were before engaged in the exerciſe of arms muſt then apply themſelves to the management of the oar, the ropes, the ſciſſars, or the ſhuttle; in a word, of all the inſtruments of commerce and induſtry; for the land, which ſupported ſuch a number of men without the aſſiſtance of their own labour, does not any more ſtand in need of it. As the arts ever have a country of their own, their peculiar place of refuge, where they are carried on and flouriſh in tranquillity, it is eaſier to repair thither in ſearch of them, than to wait at home till they ſhall have grown up, and advanced with the tardy progreſſion of ages, and the favour of chance, which preſides over the diſcoveries of genius. Thus every nation of Europe that has had any induſtry, has borrowed the moſt conſiderable ſhare

Manufactures.

B O O K of the arts from Afia. There invention feems to have
XIX. been coeval with mankind.

The beauty and fertility of thofe climates have always produced a moft numerous race of people, as
well as abundance of fruits of all kinds. There laws
and arts, the offspring of genius and tranquillity, have
arifen from the ftability of empires ; and luxury, the
fource of every enjoyment that attends induftry, has
fprung out of the richnefs of the foil. India, China,
Perfia, and Egypt, were in poffeffion not only of all
the treafures of nature, but alfo of the moft brilliant
inventions of art. War in thefe countries hath often
deftroyed every monument of genius, but they rife a-
gain out of their own ruins, as well as mankind. Not
unlike thofe laborious fwarms we fee perifh in their
hives by the wintry blaft of the north, and which re-
produce themfelves in fpring, retaining ftill the fame
love of toil and order ; there are certain Afiatic nations which have ftill preferved the arts of luxury with
the materials that fupply them, notwithftanding the
invafions and conquefts of the Tartars.

It was in a country fucceffively fubdued by the Scythians, Romans, and Saracens, that the nations of Europe, which not even Chriftianity nor time could civilize, recovered the arts and fciences, without endeavouring to difcover them. The Crufades exhaufted
the fanatic zeal of thofe who engaged in them, and
changed their barbarous manners at Conftantinople.
It was by journeying to vifit the tomb of their Savi-
our, who was born in a manger, and died on a crofs,
that they acquired a tafte for magnificence, pomp, and
wealth. By them the Afiatic grandeur was introduced into the courts of Europe. Italy, the feat from
whence religion fpread her empire over other countries, was the fiift to adopt a fpecies of induftry that
was of benefit to her temples, the ceremonies of her
worfhip, and thofe proceffions which ferve to keep up
devotion by means of the fenfes, when once it has engaged the heart. Chriftian Rome, after having borrowed her rites from the eaftern nations, was ftill to

draw from thence the wealth by which they are supported.

Venice, whofe galleys were ranged under the ban-
ner of liberty, could not fail of being induftrious. The
people of Italy eftablifhed manufactures, and were a
long time in poffeffion of all the arts, even when the
conqueft of the Eaft and Weft Indies had caufed the
treafures of the whole world to circulate in Europe.
Flanders derived her manual arts from Italy; England obtained thofe fhe eftablifhed from Flanders;
and France borrowed the general induftry of all countries. Of the Englifh fhe purchafed her ftocking-
looms, which work ten times as faft as the needle.
The number of hands unoccupied from the introduc-
tion of the loom, were employed in making of lace,
which was taken from the Flemings. Paris furpaffed
Perfia in her carpets, and Flanders in her tapeftry, in
the elegance of her patterns, and the beauty of her
dyes; and excelled Venice in the tranfparency and fize
of her mirrors. France learned to difpenfe with part
of the filks fhe received from Italy, and with Englifh
broad cloths. Germany, together with her iron and
copper mines, has always preferved the fuperiority
fhe had acquired in melting, tempering, and working up thofe metals. But the art of giving the polifh
and fafhion to every article that can be concerned in
the ornaments of luxury and the conveniencies of life,
feems to belong peculiarly to the French; whether it
be that, from the vanity of pleafing others, they find
the means of fucceeding by all the outward appearances of brilliant fhow; or that in reality grace and
eafe are the conftant attendants of a people naturally
lively and gay, and who by inftinct are in poffeffion of
tafte.

Every people given to agriculture ought to have arts
to employ their materials, and fhould multiply their
productions to maintain their artifts. Were they acquainted only with the labours of the field, their induftry muft be confined in its caufe, its means, and
its effects. Having but few wants and defires, they

BOOK
XIX.

would exert themselves but little, employ fewer hands, and work less time. Their cultivation would neither be extended nor improved. Should such a people be possessed of more arts than materials, they must be indebted to strangers, who would ruin their manufactures, by sinking the price of their articles of luxury, and raising the value of their subsistence. But when a people, engaged in agriculture, join industry to property, the culture of their produce to the art of working it up, they have then within themselves every thing necessary for their existence and preservation, every source of greatness and prosperity. Such a people is endued with a power of accomplishing every thing they wish, and stimulated with a desire of acquiring every thing that is possible.

Nothing is more favourable to liberty than the arts; it may be said to be their element, and that they are, in their nature, citizens of the world. An able artist may work in every country, because he works for the world in general. Genius and abilities every where avoid slavery, while soldiers find it in all parts. When, through the want of toleration in the clergy, the Protestants were driven out of France, they opened to themselves a refuge in every civilized state in Europe: but priests, banished from their own country, have found no asylum any where; not even in Italy, the parent of monachism and intoleration.

The arts multiply the means of acquiring riches, and contribute, by a greater distribution of wealth, to a more equitable repartition of property. Thus is prevented that excessive inequality among men, the unhappy consequence of oppression, tyranny, an lethargic state of a whole people.

How many objects of instruction and admiration doth not the most enlightened man find in manufactures and workshops! To study the productions of nature is undoubtedly beautiful; but is it not more interesting to know the different means made use of by the arts, either to alleviate the misfortunes, or to increase the enjoyments of life? Should we be in

search of genius, let us go into the workshops, and
there we shall find it under a thousand different forms.
If one man alone had been the inventor of the manufacture for figured stuffs, he would have displayed
more intelligence than Leibnitz or Newton : and I
may venture to say, that there is no problem in the
mathematical principles of the latter, more difficult to
be solved, than that of weaving a thread by the assistance of a machine. Is it not a shameful thing to
see the objects which surround us viewing themselves
in a glass, while they are unacquainted with the manner in which glass is melted ; or clothing themselves
in velvet to keep out the cold, while they know not
how it is manufactured ? Let men who are well informed, go and assist with their knowledge the wretched artisan, condemned blindly to follow the routine
he has been used to, and they may be certain of being
indemnified by the secrets he will impart to them.
The torch of industry serves to enlighten at once a
vast horizon. No art is single : the greater part of
them have their forms, modes, instruments, and elements, that are peculiar to them. The mechanics
themselves have contributed prodigiously to extend the
study of mathematics. Every branch of the genea-
logical tree of science has unfolded itself with the progress of the arts, as well liberal as manual. Mines,
mills, the manufacture and dying of cloth, have enlarged the sphere of philosophy and natural history.
Luxury has given rise to the art of enjoyment, which
is entirely dependent on the liberal arts. As soon as
architecture admits of ornaments without, it brings
with it decorations for the inside of our houses ; while
sculpture and painting are at the same time employed in the embellishment and adorning of the edifice.
The art of design is applied to our dress and furniture.
The pencil, ever fertile in new designs, is varying without end its sketches and shades on our stuffs and our
porcelain. The powers of genius are exerted in com-
posing at leisure master-pieces of poetry and eloquence,
or those happy systems of policy and philosophy, which

reftore to the people their natural rights, and to fovereigns all their glory, which confifts in reigning over
the heart and the mind, over the opinion and will of
their fubjects, by the means of reafon and equity.

Then it is that the arts produce that fpirit of fociety
which conftitutes the happinefs of civil life ; which
gives relaxation to the more ferious occupations, by
entertainments, fhows, concerts, converfations, in fhort,
by every fpecies of agreeable amufement. Eafe gives
to every virtuous enjoyment an air of liberty, which
connects and mingles the feveral ranks of men. Employment adds a value or a charm to the pleafures that
are its recompence. Every citizen depending upon
the produce of his induftry for fubfiftence, has leifure
for all the agreeable or toilfome occupations of life, as
well as that repofe of mind which leads on to the fweets
of fleep. Many, indeed, fall victims to avarice, but ftill
lefs than to war or fuperftition, the continual fcourges
of an idle people.

After the cultivation of the land, the encouragement of the arts and fciences is the next object that
deferves the attention of man. At prefent, both ferve
to conftitute the ftrength of civilized governments.
If the arts have tended to weaken mankind, then the
weaker people muft have prevailed over the ftrong ;
for the balance of Europe is in the hands of thofe nations which are in poffeffion of the arts.

Since manufactures have prevailed in Europe, the
human heart, as well as the mind, have changed their
bent and difpofition. The defire of wealth has arifen
in all parts from the love of pleafure. We no longer
fee any people fatisfied with being poor becaufe poverty is no longer the bulwark of liberty. We are obliged, indeed, to confefs, that the arts in this world fupply the place of virtues. Induftry may give birth to
vices ; but it banifhes, however, thofe of idlenefs, which
are infinitely more dangerous. As information gradually difpels every fpecies of fanaticifm, while men
are employed in the gratifications of luxury, they do
not deftroy one another through fuperftition. At leaft,

human blood is never fpilt without fome appearance of interest; and war, probably, deftroys only thofe violent and turbulent men, who in every ftate are born to be enemies to, and difturbers of all order, without any other talent, any other propenfity, than that of doing mifchief. The arts reftrain that fpirit of diffenfion, by fubjecting man to ftated and daily employments. They beftow on every rank of life the means and the hopes of enjoyment, and give even the meaneft a kind of eftimation and importance, by the advantage that refults from them. A workman at forty has been of more real value to the ftate than a whole family of vaffals who were employed in tillage under the old feudal fyftem. An opulent manufacture brings more benefit into a village, than twenty caftles of ancient barons, whether hunters or warriors, ever conferred on their province.

If it be a fact, that in the prefent ftate of things, the people who are the moft induftrious ought to be the moft happy and the moft powerful, either becaufe in wars that are unavoidable they furnifh of themfelves, or purchafe by their wealth, more foldiers, more ammunition, more forces, both for fea or land fervice; or that having a greater intereft in maintaining peace, they avoid contefts, or terminate them by negotiation; or that, in cafe of a defeat, they the more readily repair their loffes by the effect of labour; or that they are bleffed with a milder and more enlightened government, notwithftanding the means of corruption and flavery that tyranny is fupplied with, by the effeminacy which luxury produces; in a word, if the arts really civilize nations, a ftate ought to neglect no opportunity of making manufactures flourifh.

Thefe opportunities depend on the climate, which, as Polybius fays, forms the character, complexion, and manners of nations. The moft temperate climate muft neceffarily be the moft favourable to that kind of induftry which requires lefs exertion. If the climate be too hot, it is inconfiftent with the eftablifhment of manufactures, which require the concurrence of feveral

B O O K XIX.

perfons together to carry on the fame work; and it excludes all thofe arts which employ furnaces or ftrong
lights.   If the climate prove too cold, it is not proper
for thofe arts which can only be carried on in the open
air.   At too great or too fmall a diftance from the
equator, man is unfit for feveral labours, which feem
peculiarly adapted to a mild temperature.   In vain did
Peter the Great fearch among the beft-regulated ftates
for all fuch arts as were beft calculated to civilize his
people: during a period of fifty years, not one of thefe
principles of civilization has been able to flourifh a-
mong the frozen regions of Ruffia.   All artifts are
ftrangers in that land; and if they endeavour to refide
there, their talents and their works foon die with them.
When Lewis XIV. in his old age (as if that were the
time of life for profcriptions) perfecuted the Proteftants, in vain did they introduce their arts and trades
among the people who received them; they were no
longer able to work in the fame manner as they had
done in France.   Though they were equally active
and laborious, the arts they had introduced were loft,
or they declined, from not having the advantage of
the fame climate and heat to animate them.

To the favourable difpofition of climate, for the encouragement of manufactures, fhould be added the advantage of the political fituation of the ftate.   When
it is of fuch extent as to have nothing to fear or want
in point of fecurity; when it is in the neighbourhood
of the fea for the landing of its materials, and the exportation of its manufactures; when it is fituated between powers that have iron mines to employ its induftry, and others that have mines of gold to reward
it; when it has nations on each fide, with ports and
roads open on every fide; fuch a ftate will have all the
external advantages neceffary to excite a people to o-
pen a variety of manufactures.

But one advantage ftill more effential is fertility of
foil.   If cultivation fhould require too many hands,
there will be a want of labourers, or the manufacturers
will employ fo many hands, that there will not be men

enough to cultivate the fields; and this muft occafion B O O K
a dearnefs of provifions, which, while it raifes the price   XIX.
of workmanfhip, will alfo diminifh the number of
trades.

Where fertility of foil is wanting, manufactures require, at leaft, as few men to be employed as poffible.
A nation that fhould expend much on its mere fubfiftence, would abforb the whole profits of its induftry.
When the gratifications of luxury are greater or more
expenfive than the means of fupplying them, the fource
from which they are derived is loft, and they can no
longer be fupported. If the workman will feed and
clothe himfelf like the manufacturer who employs him,
the manufacture is foon ruined. The degree of frugality that republican nations adhere to from motives
of virtue, the manufacturer ought to obferve from
views of parfimony. This may be the reafon, perhaps,
that the arts, even thofe of luxury, are more adapted
to republics than monarchies; for, under monarchical
inftitutions, poverty is not always the fharpeft fpur
with the people to induftry. Labour, proceeding from
hunger, is narrow and confined, like the appetite it
fprings from; but the work that arifes from ambition
fpreads and increafes as naturally as the vice itfelf.

National character has confiderable influence over
the progrefs of the arts of luxury and ornament. Some
people are fitted for invention by that levity which naturally inclines them to novelty. The fame nation is
fitted for the arts, by their vanity, which inclines them
to the ornament of drefs. Another nation, lefs lively,
has lefs tafte for trivial matters, and is not fond of
changing fafhions. Being of a more ferious turn, thefe
people are more inclined to indulge in exceffes of the
table, and in drinking, which relieves them from all
anxiety and apprehenfion. Of thefe nations, the one
muft fucceed better than its rival in the arts of decoration, and muft have the preference over it among all
the other nations which are fond of the fame arts.

The advantages which manufactures derive from nature are further feconded by the form of government.

While induſtry is favourable to national liberty, that
in return ſhould aſſiſt induſtry.   Excluſive privileges
are enemies to commerce and the arts, which are to
be encouraged only by competition.   Even the rights
of apprenticeſhip, and the value ſet on corporations,
are a kind of monopoly.   The ſtate is prejudiced by
that ſort of privilege which favours incorporated trades;
that is to ſay, petty communities are protected at the
expence of the greater body.   By taking from the
lower claſs of the people the liberty of chooſing the
profeſſion that ſuits them, every profeſſion is filled
with bad workmen.   Such as require greater talents
are exerciſed by thoſe who are the moſt wealthy; the
meaner, and leſs expenſive, fall often to the ſhare of
men born to excel in ſome ſuperior art.   As both are
engaged in a profeſſion for which they have no taſte,
they neglect their work, and prejudice the art: the
firſt, becauſe they have no abilities; the latter, becauſe they are convinced that their abilities are ſuperior to it.   But if we remove the impediment of corporate bodies, we ſhall produce a competition in the
workmen, and conſequently the work will increaſe, as
well as be more perfect.

It may be a queſtion, whether it be beneficial to
collect manufactures in large towns, or to diſperſe them
over the country.   This point is determined by facts.
The arts of primary neceſſity have remained where
they were firſt produced, in thoſe places which have
furniſhed the materials for them.   Forges are in the
neighbourhood of the mine, and linen near the flax.
But the complicated arts of induſtry and luxury cannot be carried on in the country.   If we diſperſe over
a large extent of territory all the arts which are combined in watch and clock-making, we ſhall ruin Geneva, with all the works that ſupport it.   If we diſperſe
among the different provinces of France the ſixty
thouſand workmen who are employed in the ſtuff manufactory of Lyons, we ſhall annihilate taſte, which is
kept up only by the competition of a great number
of rivals, who are conſtantly employed in endeavour-

ing to furpafs each other. The perfection of ftuffs re- B O O K XIX.
quires their being made in a town, where fine dyes
may at once be united with beautiful patterns, and
the art of working up woollens and filks with that of
making gold and filver lace. If there be wanting
eighteen hands to make a pin, through how many manual arts, and artificers, muft a laced coat, or an em-
broidered waiftcoat, pafs? How fhall we be able to
find, amidft an interior central province, the immenfe
apparatus of arts that contribute to the furnifhing of a
palace, or the entertainments of a court? Thofe arts,
therefore, that are moft fimple and unconnected with
others, muft be confined to the country; and fuch
clothes as are fit for the lower clafs of people muft be
made in the provinces. We muft eftablifh between
the capital and the other towns a reciprocal dependence of wants and conveniences, of materials and
works; but ftill nothing muft be done by authority
or compulfion; workmen muft be left to act for themfelves. Let there be freedom of traffic and freedom of
induftry, and manufactures will profper, population
will increafe.

Has the world been more peopled at one time than Population.
another? This is not to be afcertained from hiftory,
on account of the deficiency of hiftorians in one half
of the globe that has been inhabited, and becaufe one
half of what is related by hiftorians is fabulous. Who
has ever taken, or could at any time take, an account
of the inhabitants of the earth? She was, it is faid,
more fruitful in earlier times. But when was the period of this golden age? Was it when a dry fand arofe
from the bed of the fea, purged itfelf in the rays of
the fun, and caufed the flime to produce vegetables,
animals, and human creatures? But the whole furface
of the earth muft alternately have been covered by
the ocean. The earth has then always had, like the
individuals of every fpecies, an infant ftate, a ftate of
weaknefs and fterility, before fhe arrived at the age of
fertility. All countries have been for a long time buried under water, lying uncultivated beneath fands

B O O K and moraffes, wild and overgrown with bufhes and fo-
XIX. refts, till the human fpecies, being thrown by accident
on thefe deferts and folitudes, has cleared, altered, and
peopled the land. But as all the caufes of population
are fubordinate to thofe natural laws which govern
the univerfe, as well as to the influences of foil and at-
mofphere, which are fubject to a number of calamities, it muft ever have varied with thofe periods of nature that have been either adverfe or favourable to the
increafe of mankind. However, as the lot of every
fpecies feems in a manner to depend on its faculties,
the hiftory of the progrefs and improvement of human
induftry muft therefore, in general, fupply us with the
hiftory of the population of the earth. On this ground
of calculation, it is at leaft doubtful, whether the world
was formerly better inhabited and more peopled than
it is at prefent.

Let us leave Afia under the vail of that antiquity
which reports it to us ever covered with innumerable
nations, and fwarms of people fo prodigious, that (notwithftanding the fertility of a foil which ftands in need
but of one ray of the fun to enable it to produce all
forts of fruit) men did but juft arife, and fucceed one
another with the utmoft rapidity, and were deftroyed
either by famine, peftilence, or war. Let us confider
with more attention the population of Europe, which
feems to have taken the place of Afia, by conferring
upon art all the powers of nature.

In order to determine whether our continent was,
in former ages, more inhabited than at prefent, it would
be neceffary to know whether public fecurity was better eftablifhed at that time, whether the arts were in
a more flourifhing condition, and whether the land was
better cultivated. This is what we muft inveftigate.

Firft, in thefe diftant periods, the political inftitutions were very defective. Thofe ill-regulated governments were agitated with continual factions. The civil wars which fprang from thefe divifions were frequent and cruel. It often happened that one half of
the people were maffacred by the other half. Thofe

citizens who had efcaped the fword of the conqueror took refuge upon an unfavourable territory. From that afylum they did every poffible mifchief to an implacable enemy, till a new revolution enabled them to take memorable and complete vengeance for the calamities which they had endured.

The arts had not more vigour than the laws. Commerce was fo limited, as to be reduced to the exchange of a fmall number of productions peculiar to fome territories and to fome climates. The manufactures were fo little varied, that both the fexes were equally obliged to clothe themfelves with a woollen ftuff, which even was but feldom dyed. All the branches of induftry were fo little advanced, that there did not exift a fingle city which was indebted to them for its increafe or its profperity. This was the effect and the caufe of the general contempt in which thefe feveral occupations were holden.

It was difficult for commodities to find a certain and advantageous vent, in regions where the arts were in a languid ftate. Accordingly, agriculture felt the effects of this want of confumption. It is a certain proof, that moft of thefe fine countries remained untilled, becaufe the climate was evidently more rude than it hath fince been. If immenfe forefts had not deprived the countries of the influence of the beneficent planet which animates every thing, would our anceftors have had more to fuffer from the rigour of the feafon than ourfelves?

Thefe facts, which cannot reafonably be called in queftion, demonftrate that the number of men was then very much limited in Europe; and that, excepting one or two countries, which may have fallen off from their ancient population, all the reft had only a few inhabitants.

What were thofe multitudes of people which Cæfar reckoned in Gaul, but a fet of favage nations, more formidable in name than number? Were all thofe Britons, who were fubdued in their ifland by two Roman legions, much more numerous than the Corficans at prefent? Muft not the North have been ftill lefs peopled? Regions where the fun fcarce appears above the horizon; where the courfe of the waters is fufpended for eight months in the year; where heaps of fnow cover, for the fame fpace of time, a foil frequently barren; where trees are rooted up by the winds; where the corn, the plants, and the fprings, every thing which contributes to the fupport of life, is in a ftate of annihilation; where the bodies of all men are afflicted with pain; where reft, more fatal than the moft exceffive fatigues, is followed by the moft dreadful calamities; where the arms of children are ftiffened, while they are ftretching them up to their mothers; and where their tears are converted to icicles on their cheeks; where nature .... Such regions could only have been inhabited at fome late period, and then only by fome unfortunate people, flying from flavery or tyranny. They have never multiplied under fo intemperate a fky. Over the face of the whole globe, numerous focieties have always left behind them fome durable monuments or ruins, but in the North there are abfolutely no remains which bear the impreffion of human power or induftry.

The conqueft of the fineft part of Europe, in the fpace of three or four centuries, by the inhabitants of the moft northern nations, feems at firft fight to argue againft what we have been faying. But let us confider, that thefe were the people of a territory ten times as large, who poffeffed themfelves of a country inhabited at prefent by three or four nations only; and that it was not owing to the number of her conquerors, but to the revolt of her fubjects, that the Roman empire was deftroyed and reduced to fubjection. In this aftonifhing revolution, we may readily admit that the victorious nations did not amount to one twentieth part of thofe that were conquered; becaufe the former made their attacks with half their numbers of effective men, and the latter employed no more than the hundredth part of their inhabitants in their defence. But a people, who engage entirely in their own de-

fence and fupport, are more powerful than ten armies BOOK
raifed by kings and princes.

Befides, thofe long and bloody wars, with the accounts of which ancient hiftory is replete, are deftructive of that exceffive population they feem to prove.
If, on the one hand, the Romans endeavoured to fupply the loffes their armies fuftained in confequence of
the victories they obtained, that defire of conqueft to
which they were devoted, deftroyed at leaft other nations; for as foon as the Romans had fubdued any
people, they incorporated them into their own armies,
and exhaufted their ftrength as much by recruits, as
by the tribute they impofed upon them. It is well
known with what rage wars were carried on by the
ancients; that often in a fiege, the whole town was
laid in afhes; men, women, and children, perifhed in
the flames, rather than fall under the dominion of the
conqueror; that in affaults, every inhabitant was put
to the fword; that in regular engagements, it was
thought more defireable to die fword in hand, than to
be led in triumph, and be condemned to perpetual flavery. Were not thefe barbarous cuftoms of war injurious to population? If, as we muft allow, fome unhappy men were preferved to be the victims of flavery,
this was but of little fervice to the increafe of mankind, as it eftablifhed in a ftate an extreme inequality
of conditions among beings by nature equal. If the
divifion of focieties into fmall colonies or ftates, were
adapted to multiply families by the partition of lands;
it likewife more frequently occafioned contefts among
the nations; and as thefe fmall ftates touched one another, as it were, in an infinite number of points, in
order to defend them, every inhabitant was obliged to
take up arms. Large bodies are not eafily put into
motion on account of their bulk; fmall ones are in
perpetual motion, which entirely deftroys them.

If war were deftructive of population in ancient
times, peace was not always able to promote and reftore it. Formerly all nations were ruled by defpotic

or ariftocratic power, and thefe two forms of government are by no means favourable to the increafe of the human fpecies. The free cities of Greece were fubject to laws fo complicated, that there were continual diffenfions among the citizens. Even the inferior clafs of people, who had no right of voting, obtained a fuperiority in the public affemblies, where a man of talents, by the power of eloquence, might put fo many men into commotion. Befides, in thefe ftates, population tended to be confined to the city, in conjunction with ambition, power, riches, and, in fhort, all the effects and fprings of liberty. Not but that the lands under the democratical ftates muft have been well cultivated and well peopled. But the democracies were few ; and as they were all ambitious, and could only aggrandize themfelves by war, if we except Athens, whofe commerce, indeed, was alfo owing to the fuperiority of its arms, the earth could not long flourifh and increafe in population. In a word, Greece and Italy were at leaft the only countries better peopled than they are at prefent.

Except in Greece, which repelled, reftrained, and fubdued Afia ; in Carthage, which appeared for a moment on the borders of Africa, and foon ·declined to its former ftate ; and in Rome, which brought into fubjection and deftroyed the known world ; where do we find fuch a degree of population, as will bear any comparifon with what a traveller meets with every day on every fea-coaft, along all the great rivers, and on the roads leading to capital cities ? What vaft forefts are turned to tillage ? What harvefts are waving in the place of reeds that covered marfhy grounds ? What numbers of civilized people who fubfift on dried fifh and falted provifions ?

Notwithftanding this, there hath arifen, for fome years paft, an almoft general exclamation refpecting the depopulation of all ftates. We think we can difcover the caufe of thefe ftrange exclamations. Men preffing, as it were, one upon the other, have left be-

hind them fome regions lefs inhabited; and the different diftribution of mankind hath been taken for a diminution of the human race.

During a long feries of ages empires were divided
into fo many fovereignties, as there were private noblemen in them. Then thefe fubjects, or the flaves
of thefe petty defpots, were fixed, and that for ever,
upon the territory where they were born. At the a-
bolition of the feudal fyftem, when there remained no
more than one mafter, one king, and one court, all
men crowded to that fpot, from whence favours,
riches, and honour flowed. Such was the origin of
thofe proud capitals, where the people have been fucceffively heaped one upon another, and which are gradually become, in a manner, the general affembly of
each nation.

Other cities, lefs extenfive, but ftill very confiderable, have alfo been raifed in each province, in proportion as the fupreme authority hath been confirmed. They have been formed by the tribunals, public
bufinefs, and the arts, and they have been conftantly
more and more increafed, by the tafte for the conveniencies and pleafures of fociety.

Thefe new eftablifhments could not be formed but
at the expence of the country places. Accordingly,
there are fcarce any inhabitants remaining there, except fuch as were neceffary for the tilling of the lands,
and for the employments that are infeparable from it.
The productions have not felt the effect of this revolution; they are even become more abundant, more
varied, and more agreeable, becaufe more of them have
been fought after, and better paid; becaufe the methods and the inftruments have acquired a degree of
fimplicity and of improvement they had not formerly; and becaufe the cultivators, encouraged in a variety of ways, have become more active and more intelligent.

In the police, in the morals, and in the politics, of
the moderns, we may difcern many caufes of propagation that did not exift among the ancients; but at

the fame time, we obferve likewife fome impediments
which may prevent or diminifh among us that fort of
progrefs, which, in our fpecies, fhould be moft conducive to its being raifed to the greateft degree of perfection : for population will never be very confiderable, unlefs men are more numerous and more happy.

Population depends, in a great meafure, on the diftribution of landed property. Families are multiplied
in the fame manner as poffeffions ; and when thefe are
too large, they are always injurious to population from
their inordinate extent. A man of confiderable property, working only for himfelf, fets apart one half of
his lands for his income, and the other for his pleafures. All he appropriates to hunting, is a double lofs
in point of cultivation ; for he breeds animals on the
land that fhould be appropriated to men, inftead of
fubfifting men on the land which is appropriated to
animals. Wood is neceffary in a country for edifices
and fuel ; but is there any occafion for fo many avenues in a park, or for parterres and kitchen-gardens,
of fuch extent as belong to a large eftate? In this cafe,
does luxury, which in its magnificence contributes to
the fupport of the arts, prove as favourable to the increafe of mankind as it might by employing the land
to better purpofes? Too many large eftates, therefore,
and too few fmall ones, this is the firft impediment to
population.

The next obftacle is the unalienable domains of the
clergy. When fo much property remains for ever in
the fame hands, how fhall population flourifh, while it
entirely depends upon the improvement of lands by
the increafe of fhares among different proprietors?
What intereft has the incumbent to increafe the value
of an eftate he is not to tranfmit to any fucceffor, to
fow or plant for a pofterity not derived from himfelf?
Far from diminifhing his income to improve his lands,
will he not rather impair the eftate, in order to increafe
the rents which he is to enjoy only for life?

The entails of eftates in great families are not lefs
prejudicial to the propagation of mankind. They lef-

fen at once both the nobility and the other ranks of people. As the right of primogeniture among the great facrifices the younger children to the intereft of the elder branch, in the fame manner entails deftroy feveral families for the fake of a fingle one. Almoft all entailed eftates are ill cultivated, on account of the negligence of a proprietor who is not attached to a poffeffion he is not to difpofe of, which has been ced- ed to him only with regret, and which is already given to his fucceffors, whom he cannot confider as his heirs, becaufe they are not named by him. The right of primogeniture and of entail is therefore a law, one may fay, made on purpofe to defeat the increafe of population in any ftate.

From thefe obftacles to population, produced by the defect of legiflation, there arifes a third, which is the poverty of the people. Wherever the farmers have not the property of the ground-rent, their life is miferable, and their condition precarious. Not being certain of their fubfiftence, which depends on their health, having but fmall reliance on their ftrength, which is not at their own difpofal, and weary of their exiftence, they are afraid of breeding a race of wretch- ed beings. It is an error to imagine that plenty of children are produced in the country, where there die as many, if not more, than are born every year. The toil of the father and the milk of the mother are loft to them and their children; for they will never attain to the flower of their age, or to that period of matu- rity, which, by its fervices, will recompence all the pains that have been beftowed upon their education. With a fmall portion of land, the mother might bring up her child, and cultivate her own little garden, while the father, by his labour abroad, might add to the con- veniencies of his family. Thefe three beings, without property, languifh upon the little that one of them gains, or the child perifhes.

What a variety of evils arife from a faulty or defec- tive legiflation! Vices and calamities are infinite in their effects; they mutually affift each other in fpread-

ing general deſtruction, and ariſe from one another,
till they are both exhauſted. The indigence of the
country produces an increaſe of troops, a burden ruinous in its nature, deſtructive of men in time of war,
and of land in time of peace. It is certain that the
military deſtroy the fields, which they do not cultivate
themſelves ; becauſe every ſoldier deprives the ſtate of
a huſbandman, and burdens it with an idle or uſeleſs
conſumer. He defends the country in time of peace,
merely from a pernicious ſyſtem, which, under the pre-
text of defence, makes all nations aggreſſors. If all
governments would, as they eaſily might, let thoſe
men, whom they devote to the army, be employed in
the labours of huſbandry, the number of huſbandmen
and artiſans throughout Europe would in a ſhort time
be conſiderably increaſed. All the powers of human
induſtry would be exerted in improving the advantages
of nature, and in ſurmounting every obſtacle to improvement ; every thing would concur in promoting
life, not in ſpreading deſtruction.

The deſerts of Ruſſia would be cleared, and the
plains of Poland not laid waſte. The vaſt dominions
of the Turks would be cultivated, and the bleſſings of
their prophet would be extended over an immenſe population. Egypt, Syria, and Paleſtine, would again
become what they were in the times of the Phœnicians, in the days of their ſhepherd kings, and of the
Jews, who enjoyed happineſs and peace under their
judges. The parched mountains of Sierra Morena
would be rendered fertile, the heaths of Aquitaine
would be cleared of inſects, and be covered with people.

But general good is merely the deluſive dream of
benevolent men. This brings to my remembrance
the virtuous prelate of Cambray, and the good Abbé
of St. Pierre. Their works are compoſed with a deſign to make deſerts inhabited, not indeed with her-
mits, who fly from the vices and misfortunes of the
world, but with happy families, who would proclaim
the glory of God upon earth, as the ſtars declare it in

the firmament. Their writings abound with focial views and fentiments of humanity, and may be confidered as truly infpired ; for humanity is the gift of Heaven. Kings will infure the attachment of their people, in proportion as they themfelves are attached to fuch men.

It is fcarce neceffary to obferve, that one of the means to favour population, is to fupprefs the celibacy of the regular and fecular clergy. Monaftic inftitutions have a reference to two eras remarkable in the hiftory of the world. About the year 700 of Rome, Jefus Chrift was the founder of a new religion in the Eaft ; and the fubverfion of Paganifm was foon attended with that of the Roman empire itfelf. Two or three hundred years after the death of Chrift, Egypt and Paleftine were filled with monks. About the year 700 of the Chriftian era, Mohammed appeared, and eftablifhed a new religion in the Eaft ; and Chriftianity was transferred to Europe, where it fixed. Three or four hundred years afterwards, there arofe multitudes of religious orders. At the time of the birth of Chrift, the books of David, and thofe of the Sybil, foretold the deftruction of the world, a deluge, or rather an univerfal conflagration, and general judgment : and all people, opprefied by the dominion of the Romans wifhed for and believed in a general diffolution. A thoufand years after the Chriftian era, the books of David, and thofe of the Sybil, ftill announced the laft judgment : and feveral penitents, as ferocious and wild in their extravagant piety as in their vices, fold all their poffeffions to go to conquer and die upon the tomb of their Redeemer. The nations groaning under the tyranny of the feudal government, wifhed for, and ftill believed in, the end of the world.

While one part of the Chriftian world, impreffed with terror, went to perifh in the crufades, another part were burying themfelves in cloifters. This was the origin of the monaftic life in Europe. Opinion gave rife to monks, and it will be the caufe of their deftruction. The eftates they poffeffed they will leave behind them for the ufe and increafe of fociety; and all thofe hours, that are loft in praying without devotion, will be confecrated to their primitive intention, which is labour. The clergy are to remember, that, in the facred fcriptures, God fays to man, in a ftate of innocence, Increafe and multiply; to man, in a fallen ftate, Till the earth, and work for thy fubfiftence. If the duties of the priefthood feem yet to allow the prieft to incumber himfelf with the care of a family and an eftate, the duties of fociety more ftrongly forbid celibacy. If the monks, in earlier times, cleared the deferts they inhabited, they now contribute to depopulate the towns where their number is very great: if the clergy has fubfifted on the alms of the people, they in their turn reduce the people to beggary. Among the idle claffes of fociety, the moft prejudicial is that which, from its very principles, muft tend to promote a general fpirit of indolence among men; make them wafte at the altar, as well the work of the bees, as the falary of the workmen; which burns in day-time the candles that ought to be referved for the night, and makes men lofe in the church that time they owe to the care of their families; which engages men to afk of Heaven the fubfiftence that the ground only can give, or produce in return for their toil.

There is ftill another caufe of the depopulation of fome ftates, which is, that want of toleration which perfecutes and profcribes every religion but that of the prince on the throne. This is a fpecies of oppreffion and tyranny peculiar to modern politics, to extend its influence even over men's thoughts and confciences: a barbarous piety, which, for the fake of exterior forms of worfhip, extinguifhes, in fome degree, the very idea of the exiftence of God, by deftroying multitudes of his worfhippers: it is an impiety ftill more barbarous, that, on account of things fo indifferent as religious ceremonies muft appear, deftroys the life of man, and impedes the population of ftates, which fhould be confidered as points of the utmoft importance. For neither the number nor the allegiance of fubjects is increafed by exacting oaths contra- ry to confcience, by forcing into fecret perjury thofe who are engaged in the marriage ties, or in the different profeffions of a citizen. Unity in religion is proper only when it is naturally eftablifhed by conviction. When once that is at an end, a general liberty, if granted, would be the means of reftoring tranquillity and peace of mind. When no diftinction is made, but this liberty is fully and equally extended to every citizen, it can never difturb the peace of families.

Next to the celibacy of the clergy and of the military, the former of which arifes from profeffion, the latter from cuftom, there is a third, derived from convenience, and introduced by luxury : I mean that of life annuitants. Here we may admire the chain of caufes. At the fame time that commerce favours population by the means of induftry both by land and fea, by all the objects and operations of navigation, and by the feveral arts of cultivation and manufactures, it alfo decreafes it by reafon of all thofe vices which luxury introduces. When riches have gained a general afcendant over the minds of men, then opinions and manners alter by the intermixture of ranks. The arts and the talents of pleafing corrupt fociety while they polifh it. When the intercourfe between the fexes becomes frequent, they mutually feduce each other, and the weaker induce the ftronger to adopt the frivolous turn for drefs and amufement. The women become children, and the men effeminate. Entertainments are the fole topic of their converfation, and the object of their occupation. The manly and robuft exercifes, by which the youth were trained up to difcipline, and prepared for the moft important and dangerous profeffions, give place to the love of public fhows, where every paffion that can render a nation effeminate is caught, as long as there is no appearance of a patriotic fpirit among them. Indolence prevails among all perfons of eafy circumftances, and labour diminifhes among that clafs of men deftined to be employed in it. The variety of arts multiplies fafhions,

B O O K and thefe increafe our expences; articles of luxury be-
XIX.   come neceffary ; what is fuperfluous is looked upon as
needful ; and people in general are better dreffed, but
do not live fo well ; and purchafe clothes at the expence of the neceffaries of life. The lower clafs of
men become debauched before they are fenfible of
the paffion of love ; and, marrying later, have fewer
or weaker children. The tradefman feeks a fortune,
not a wife; and he prematurely lofes both the one
and the other, in the exceffes of libertinifm. The rich,
whether married or not, are continually feducing women of every rank, or debauching girls of low condition. The difficulty of fupporting the charges of marriage, and the readinefs of finding the joys of it without bearing any of its difagreeable inconveniencies,
tends to increafe the number of unmarried people in
every clafs of life. The man who renounces the hope
of being the father of a family, confumes his patrimony, and in concert with the ftate, which increafes
his income, by borrowing money from him at a ruinous intereft, he lavifhes upon one generation the fupport of many; he extinguifhes his own pofterity, as
well as that of the women by whom he is rewarded,
and that of the girls who are paid by him. Every
kind of proftitution prevails at the fame time. Honour and duty are forfeited in every rank ; the ruin of
the women is but the forerunner of that of the men.

The nation that is inclined to gallantry, or rather to
libertinifm, foon lofes its power and credit in other
countries, and is ruined at home. There is no longer
any nobility, no longer any body of men to defend
their own or the people's rights ; for everywhere divifion and felf-intereft prevail. No one wifhes to be
ruined alone. The love of riches becomes the general
object of attraction. The honeft man is apprehenfive
of lofing his fortune, and the man of no honour is intent upon making his : the one retires from the world,
the other fets himfelf up to fale ; and thus the ftate is
loft. Such is the conftant progrefs of commerce in a
monarchical government. What its effects are in a

republic we know from ancient hiftory. But ftill it is
neceffary at this period to excite men to commerce,
becaufe the prefent fituation of Europe is favourable
to it, and commerce itfelf promotes population.

But it will be afked, whether a great degree of population be ufeful in promoting the happinefs of mankind. This is an idle queftion. In fact, the point is
not to multiply men, in order to make them happy;
but it is fufficient to make them happy, that they
fhould multiply. All the means which concur in the
profperity of any ftate, tend of themfelves to the propagation of its people. A legiflator defirous of an increafe of people, merely to have a great number of
foldiers and of fubjects, only for the purpofe of fubduing his neighbours, would be a monfter, and an enemy
to the human race, fince his plans of political increafe
would be folely directed to the deftruction of others.
A legiflator, on the contrary, who, like Solon, fhould
form a republic, whofe multitudes might people the
defert coafts of the fea; or who, like Penn, fhould
make laws for the cultivation of his colony, and forbid war; fuch a legiflator would undoubtedly be confidered as a god on earth. Even though his name
fhould not be immortalized, he would live in happinefs, and die contented, efpecially if he could be certain of leaving behind him laws of fuch wifdom, as to
free the people for ever from the vexation of taxes.

It is to be prefumed, from what we know of the
ftate of the favages, that the advantage of not being
confined by the reftraints of our ridiculous clothing,
the unwholefome inclofure of fuperb edifices, and the
complicated tyranny of our cuftoms, laws, and manners, is not a compenfation for a precarious life, for
contufions received, and perpetual combats engaged
for a portion of a foreft, for a cavern, a bow, an arrow,
a fruit, a fifh, a bird, a quadruped, the fkin of a beaft,
or the poffeffion of a woman. Let mifanthropy exaggerate at pleafure the vices of our cities, it will not
fucceed in difgufting us of thofe exprefs or tacit con-

Taxes.

ventions, nor of thofe artificial virtues, which confti-- tute the fecurity and the charm of our focieties.

There are undoubtedly aſſaſſins among us, there are violaters of an aſylum, there are monſters whoſe avidity, indigence, or lazineſs, difguſt the ſocial order. There are other monſters, perhaps more deteſtable, who, poſſeſſed of a plenty which would be fufficient for two or three thouſand families, are only occupied in increaſing the miſery of them. I ſhall not the leſs implore benediction upon the public ſtrength, which moſt commonly inſures my perſon and my property, in return for the contributions which it requires from me.

A tax may be defined, a facrifice of a part of a man's property for the defence of the reſt : it follows from hence, that there ſhould not be any tax either among people in a ſtate of ſlavery, or among ſavages ; for the former no longer enjoy any property, and the latter have not yet acquired any.

But when a nation poſſeſſes any large and valuable property, when its fortune is fufficiently eſtabliſhed, and is conſiderable enough to make the expences of government neceſſary ; when it has poſſeſſions, trade, and wealth capable of tempting the avidity of its neighbours, who may be poor or ambitious ; then, in order to guard its frontiers, or its provinces, to protect its navigation, and keep up its police, there is a neceſſity for forces and for a revenue. It is but juſt and requiſite, that the perſons who are employed in any manner for the public good, ſhould be maintained by all the other orders of the ſociety.

There have been countries and times, in which a portion of the territory was aſſigned for the public expences of the ſtate. The government, not being enabled of itſelf to turn ſuch extenſive poſſeſſions to advantage, was forced to intruſt this charge to adminiſtrators, who either neglected the revenues, or appropriated them to their own uſe. This practice brought on ſtill greater inconveniences. Either the royal do-

mains were too confiderable in time of peace, or in- B O O K
fufficient for the calls of war. In the firft inftance, the   XIX.
liberty of the ftate was oppreffed by the ruler of it;
and in the latter, by ftrangers. It has, therefore, been
found neceffary to have recourfe to the contributions
of the citizens.

Thefe funds were in early times not confiderable.
The ftipends then allowed were merely an indemnification to thofe whom public affairs prevented from attending to thofe employments that were neceffary for
their fubfiftence. Their reward arofe from that pleafing fenfation which we experience from an internal
confcioufnefs of our own virtue, and from the view of
the homage paid to it by other men. This moral
wealth was the greateft treafure of rifing focieties; a
kind of coin which it was equally the intereft of government and of morality not to diminifh the value
of.

Honour held the place of taxes no lefs in the flourifhing periods of Greece, than in the infant ftate of
focieties. The patriot, who ferved his country, did
not think he had any right to deftroy it. The impoft
laid by Ariftides on all Greece, for the fupport of the
war againft Perfia, was fo moderate, that thofe who
were to contribute of themfelves, called it *the happy
fortune of Greece!* What times were thefe, and what
a country, in which taxes made the happinefs of the
people!

The Romans acquired power and empire almoft
without any affiftance from the public treafury. The
love of wealth would have diverted them from the
conqueft of the world. The public fervice was attended to without any views of intereft, even after their
manners had been corrupted.

Under the feudal government, there were no taxes;
for on what could they have been levied? The man
and the land were both the property of the lord. It
was both a real and a perfonal fervitude.

When knowledge began to diffufe its light over Europe, the nations turned their thoughts towards their

BOOK XIX. own fecurity. They voluntarily furnifhed contributions to reprefs foreign and domeftic enemies. But
thofe tributes were moderate, becaufe princes were
not yet abfolute enough to divert them to purpofes of
their own caprices, or to the advantage of their ambition.

The New World was difcovered, and the paffion
for conqueft engaged every nation. That fpirit of aggrandizement was inconfiftent with the flownefs with
which affairs are managed in popular affemblies; and
fovereigns fucceeded without much difficulty in ap-
propriating to themfelves greater rights than they had
ever before enjoyed. The impofition of taxes was the
moft important of their ufurpations; and it is that, the
confequences of which have been the moft pernicious.

Princes have even ventured to render the marks of
fervitude apparent upon all their fubjects, by levying
a poll-tax. Independent of the humiliation it is attended with, can any thing be more arbitrary than
fuch a tax?

Is the tax to be levied upon voluntary information?
But this would require between the monarch and his
fubjects an attachment to each other arifing from a
principle of duty, which fhould unite them by a mutual love of the general good; or, at leaft, a regard to
public welfare, to infpire the one with confidence in
the other, by a fincere and reciprocal communication
of their intelligence and of their fentiments. Even
then, upon what is this confcientious principle to be
founded, which is to ferve as an inftructor, a guide,
and a check in the affairs of government?

Is the fanctuary of families, or the clofet of the citizen, to be invaded, in order to gain by furprife, and
bring to light, what he does not choofe to reveal, what
it is often of importance to him not to difcover? What
an inquifition is this! What an injurious violence!
Though we fhould even become acquainted with the
refources and means of fubfiftence of every individual,
do they not vary from one year to another with the
uncertain and precarious productions of induftry? Are

they not leffened by the increafe of children, by the
decay of ftrength through ficknefs, age, and laborious
occupations? The very faculties of the human fpecies, which are ufeful and employed in laborious occupations, do they not change with thofe viciffitudes
occafioned by time in every thing that depends on nature and fortune? The perfonal tax is a vexation then
to the individual, without being a general benefit. A
poll-tax is a fort of flavery, oppreffive to the man, without being profitable to the ftate.

After princes had impofed this tax, which is a mark
of defpotifm, or which leads to it fooner or later, impofts were then laid upon articles of confumption. Sovereigns have affected to confider this new tribute as
in fome meafure voluntary, becaufe it rifes in proportion to the expences of the fubject, which he is at liberty to increafe or diminifh according to his abilities,
or his propenfities, which are for the moft part factitious.

But if taxation affect the commodities which are of
immediate neceffity, it muft be confidered as an act of
the greateft cruelty. Previous to all the laws of fociety, man had a right to fubfift. And is he to lofe that
right by the eftablifhment of laws? To fell the produce of the earth to the people at a high price is in
reality to deprive them of it: to wreft from them by
a tax the natural means of preferving life, is, in fact, to
affect the very principle of their exiftence. By extort-
ing the fubfiftence of the needy, the ftate takes from
him his ftrength with his food. It reduces the poor
man to a ftate of beggary, and the labouring man to
that of idlenefs: it makes the unfortunate man become a rogue; that is, it is the caufe of bringing the
man who is ready to ftarve to an untimely end, from
the extreme diftrefs to which he is reduced.

If the impofts affect commodities lefs neceffary, how
many hands, loft to tillage and the arts, are employed,
not in guarding the bulwarks of the empire, but in
crowding the kingdom with an infinite number of ufelefs barriers; in embarraffing the gates of towns; in-

fefting the highways and roads of commerce; and fearching into cellars, granaries, and ftorehoufes! What a ftate of war between prince and people, between fubject and fubject! How many prifons, galleys, and gibbets, prepared for a number of unhappy perfons who have been urged on to fraudulent practices, to fmuggling, and even to piracy, by the iniquity of the revenue laws!

The avidity of fovereigns has extended itfelf from the articles of confumption to thofe of traffic carried on from one ftate to another. Infatiable tyrants! will ye never be fenfible, that, if ye lay duties on what ye offer to the ftranger, he will buy at a cheaper rate, he will give only the price demanded by other ftates? if even your own fubjects were the fole proprietors of that produce you have taxed, they ftill would never be able to make other nations fubmit to fuch exactions; for in that cafe the demand would be for a lefs quantity, and the overplus would oblige them to lower the price, in order to find a fale for it.

The duty on merchandife, which one ftate receives from another, is not lefs unreafonable. The price of the goods being regulated by the competition of other countries, the duties will be paid by the fubjects of that ftate which buys commodities for its neighbours. Poffibly, the increafe in the price of foreign produce may diminifh the confumption of it. But if a lefs quantity of merchandife be fold to any country, a lefs quantity will be purchafed of it. The profits of trade are to be eftimated in proportion to the quantity of merchandife fold and bought. Commerce is in fact nothing more than exchange of the value of one commodity for that of another. It is not poffible then to oppofe the courfe of thefe exchanges, without lowering the value of the productions that are fold, by reftraining the fale of them.

Whether, therefore, duties be laid on our own or on foreign merchandife, the induftry of the fubject will neceffarily fuffer by it. The means of payment will be fewer, and there will be lefs raw materials to work up. The greater diminution there is in the annual produce, the greater also will be the decrease of labour. Then all the laws that can be made against beggars will be ineffectual, for man must live on what is given him, if he cannot live by what he earns.

But what then is the mode of taxation the most proper to conciliate the public interest with the rights of individuals? It is the land-tax. An impost is, with respect to the person upon whom it is charged, an annual expence. It can only, therefore, be affessed on an annual revenue; for nothing but an annual revenue can discharge an annual expence. Now there never can be any annual revenue, except that of the land. It is land only which returns yearly what has been bestowed upon it, with an additional profit that may be disposed of. It is but within these few years that we have begun to be sensible of this important truth. Some men of abilities will one day be able to demonstrate the evidence of it: and that government which first makes this the foundation of its system will necessarily be raised to a degree of prosperity unknown to all nations and all ages.

Perhaps there is no state in Europe at present whose situation admits of so great a change. The taxes are everywhere so heavy, the expences so multiplied, the wants so urgent, the treasury of the state in general so much indebted, that a sudden change in the mode of raising the public revenues would infallibly alter the confidence and disturb the peace of the subject. But an enlightened and provident policy will tend, by slow and gradual steps, towards so salutary an end. With courage and prudence it will remove every obstacle that prejudice, ignorance, and private interest, might have to oppose to a system of administration, the advantages of which appear to us beyond all calculation.

In order that nothing may lessen the benefits of this fortunate innovation, it will be necessary that all lands without distinction should be subjected to taxation. The public weal is a treasure in common, wherein every individual should deposit his tribute, his service,

and his abilities. Names and titles will never change
the nature of men and their poffeffions. It would be
the utmoft meannefs and folly to avail ourfelves of di-
ftinctions received from our anceftors, in order to withdraw ourfelves from the burdens of fociety. Every
mark of diftinction that is not of general utility fhould
be confidered as injurious: it can only be equitable,
when it is founded on a formal engagement of devot-
ing our lives and fortunes in a more particular manner
to the fervice of our country.

If in our days the tax were laid for the firft time upon the land, would it not neceffarily be fuppofed that
the contribution fhould be proportioned to the extent
and value of the eftates? Would any one venture to
allege his employments, his fervices, his dignities, in
order to fcreen himfelf from the tributes required for
the public fervice? What connection have taxes with
ranks, titles, and conditions? They relate only to the
revenue: and this belongs to the ftate, as foon as it
becomes neceffary for the public defence.

The manner in which the tax ought to be laid upon
the lands is more difficult to afcertain. Some writers
have imagined, that ecclefiaftical tithes, unfortunately
levied in the greateft part of Europe, would be a proper mode to be adopted. In that fyftem, fay they,
there could be no fraud nor miftake. According as
circumftances fhould require more efforts on the part
of the people, the treafury would take a fourth, a fifth,
a fixth part of the productions at the time of the harveft; and every thing would be fettled without conftraint, without deceit, without miftruft, and without
oppreffion.

But, in this mode of levying, how will the tax be
collected, for objects fo multiplied, fo variable, and fo
little known? Would not the form of adminiftration
require enormous expences? Would not the farming
of the tax give occafion to profits too confiderable?
If this arrangement fhould therefore appear moft fatal
to citizens, would it not be moft fatal to government?
How can any one poffibly doubt, that the intereft of

the individual is the fame as that of the fociety? Can
any one be ftill ignorant of the clofe connection there
is between the fovereign who afks and the fubjects who
grant?

Befides, this impoft, apparently fo equal, would in
fact be the moft difproportioned of all thofe which ignorance hath ever fuggefted. While one contributor
fhould be required to give up only the fourth of his
revenue, one half, and fometimes more, would be taken from others, who, in order to obtain the fame
quantity of productions, will have been obliged, by the
nature of an ungrateful foil, or by the difficulty of
working it, to fupport expences infinitely more confiderable.

Thefe inconveniences have occafioned an idea to
be rejected, which has been propofed or fupported by
men little verfed in political economy, but difgufted,
with reafon, at the arbitrary manner in which they
faw the lands taxed. Suppofe the extent of the domain be admitted as a rule, yet it muft be confidered
that there are fome lands which can pay a great deal,
others which can pay little, and fome, even, which
can pay nothing, becaufe the profits remaining, after
all the expences, are fcarce fufficient to determine the
moft intelligent man to cultivate them. If an exact
ftate of the leafes be demanded, will not the farmers
and proprietors act in concert to deceive the government? and what means are there to difcover a fraud,
planned with confummate art? If you will allow men
to give in the account of their own eftates, for one of
thefe declarations that fhall be honeft, will there not
be a hundred falfe ones? and will not the citizen of
ftrict probity be the victim of him who is deftitute of
principles? In the mode of taking an eftimation of
the value of the lands, will not the agent of the treafury fuffer himfelf to be fuborned by contributors
whofe intereft it is to bribe him? Suppofe the care of
making the repartitions be left to the inhabitants of
each diftrict, it is undoubtedly the moft equitable rule,
the moft conformable to the rights of nature and pro-

B O O K
XIX.
perty; and yet it muft neceffarily produce fo many cabals, altercations, and animofities, fo violent a colli-fion between the paffions, which will interfere with each other, that it cannot be productive of that fyftem of equity which might enfure the public happinefs.

A regifter book, which would cautioufly meafure the lands, which would appreciate, with equity, their value, would alone be capable of effecting this fortu-nate revolution. This principle, fo fimple and fo evi-dent, hath been rarely applied, and then but imper-fectly. It is to be hoped, that this fine inftitution, though warmly oppofed by authority and by corrup-tion, will be improved in thofe ftates where it has been adopted, and that it will be introduced in the empires where it doth not yet exift. The monarch who fhall fignalize his reign by this great benefit, will be bleffed during his life, his memory will be dear to pofterity, and his felicity will be extended beyond ages, if, as it cannot be doubted, there exifts a God, the remunera-tor of good actions.

But let not government, under whatever form it may have been eftablifhed, or ftill fubfifts, ever carry the meafure of impofts to excefs. It is faid, that in their origin they rendered men more active, more fo-ber, and more intelligent; and that they have thus contributed to the profperity of empires. This opi-nion is not deftitute of probability; but it is ftill more certain, that, when the taxes have been extended be-yond the proper limits, they have ftopped the labours, extinguifhed induftry, and produced difcouragement.

Though man hath been condemned by nature to perpetual watchings, in order to fecure a fubfiftence, this urgent care hath not exerted all his faculties. His defires have been extended much beyond this; and the more numerous are the objects which have enter-ed into his plan of happinefs, the more repeated have been his efforts to attain them. If he hath been re-duced, by tyranny, to expect nothing more from ob-ftinate labour than articles of primary neceffity, his activity hath been diminifhed; he hath himfelf contracted the fphere of his wants. Troubled, foured, and exhaufted by the oppreffive fpirit of the treafury, he hath either languifhed by his wretched fire-fide, or hath quitted his country in fearch of a lefs unfortunate deftiny, or hath led a wandering and vagabond life over defolated provinces. Moft focieties have, at different periods, fuffered thefe calamities, and exhibited this hideous fpectacle.

Accordingly, it is an error, and a very great one, to judge of the power of empires by the revenue of the fovereign. This bafis of calculation would be the beft that could be eftablifhed, if the tributes were proportioned to the abilities of the citizens; but when the republic is oppreffed by the weight or the variety of the impofts, thefe riches, far from being a fign of national profperity, are a mark of decay. The people, unable to furnifh any extraordinary affiftance to the mother-country, when threatened or invaded, yield to a foreign yoke, and fubmit to fhameful and ruinous laws. The cataftrophe is haftened, when the treafury has recourfe to the farming of the revenue, in order to collect the taxes.

The contribution of the citizens towards the public treafury is a tribute: they fhould prefent it themfelves to the fovereign; who, on his part, ought prudently to direct the employment of it. Every intermediate agent deftroys thefe connections, which cannot be too nearly united. His influence becomes an unavoidable fource of divifion and ravage. It is under this odious afpect that the farmers of the taxes have always been confidered.

The farmers of the revenue contrive the taxes; and it is their bufinefs to multiply them. They envelope them in obfcurity, in order to give them the degree of extenfion moft fuitable to themfelves. Their interefts are fupported by judges chofen by themfelves. They bribe every accefs to the throne; and they caufe at pleafure their zeal to be extolled, or the people to be calumniated, who are diffatisfied, with reafon, at their vexations. By thofe vile artifices they plunge the province into the lowest degree of misery, while their own coffers regurgitate with riches. Then it is that the laws, manners, honour, and the little remains of the blood of the nation, are sold to them at the vilest price. The contractor enjoys, without shame or remorse, these infamous and criminal advantages, till he hath destroyed the state, the prince, and himself.

Free nations have seldom experienced this terrible destiny. Humane and considerate principles have made them prefer an administration almost always of a paternal kind, to receive the contributions of the citizens. It is in absolute governments that the tyrannical custom of farming out the revenue is peculiarly adopted. Government have sometimes been alarmed at the ravages occasioned by this practice; but timid, ignorant, or indolent administrators, have apprehended, that in the confusion in which things were, a total subversion would be the consequence of the least change. Wherefore, then, should not the time of the disease be that of the remedy? Then it is that the minds of men are better disposed to a change, that opposition is less violent, and that the revolution is more easily accomplished.

It is not, however, sufficient that the impost should be levied with equity, and that it should be collected with moderation; it is further necessary that it should be proportioned to the wants of government, which are not always the same. War hath ever required in all countries, and in every age, more considerable expences than peace. The ancients made a provision for them by their economy in times of tranquillity. Since the advantages of circulation and the principles of industry have been better understood, the method of laying up specie for this purpose has been proscribed, and that of imposing extraordinary taxes has been, with reason, preferred. Every state that should prohibit them would find itself obliged, in order to protract its fall, to have recourse to the methods made use of at Constantinople. The Sultan, who can do every thing but augment his revenues, is constrained

to give up the empire to the extortions of his delegates, B O O K
that he may afterwards deprive them of what they have   XIX.
plundered from his subjects.

That taxes may not be exorbitant, they should be
ordered, regulated, and administered by the representatives of the people. The impost has ever depended
on, and must be proportioned to, the property possessed.
He who is not master of the produce, is not master of
the field. Tributes, therefore, among all nations have
always been first imposed upon proprietors only; whether the lands were divided among the conquerors, or
the clergy shared them with the nobles; or whether
they passed, by means of commerce and industry, into the hands of the generality of the citizens. Everywhere, those who were in possession of them had
reserved to themselves the natural, unalienable, and sacred right of not being taxed without their own consent. If we do not admit this principle, there is no
longer any monarchy or any nation; there is nothing
remaining but a despotic master and a herd of slaves.

Ye people, whose kings command every thing at
pleasure, read over again the history of your own country. You will see that your ancestors assembled themselves, and deliberated, whenever a subsidy was in agitation. If this custom be neglected, the right is not
lost; it is recorded in heaven, which has given the earth
to mankind to possess: it is written on the field you
have taken the pains to enclose, in order to secure to
yourselves the enjoyment of it: it is written in your
hearts, where the Divinity has impressed the love of liberty. Man, whose head is raised towards heaven,
was not made in the image of his Creator to bow before man. No one is greater than another, but by the
choice and consent of all. Ye courtiers, your greatness consists in your lands, and is not to be found in
your attendance on your master. Be less ambitious,
and ye will be richer. Do justice to your vassals, and
ye will improve your fortunes by increasing the general happiness. What advantage can ye propose to
yourselves by raising the edifice of despotism upon the

B O O K ruins of every kind of liberty, virtue, fentiment, and
XIX.   property? Confider that this power will crufh you all.
Around this formidable Coloffus ye are no more than
figures of bronze, reprefenting the nations chained at
the feet of a ftatue.

If the right of impofing taxes be in the prince alone,
though it may not be for his intereft to burden and opprefs his people, yet they will be burdened and oppreffed. The caprices, profufions, and encroachments of the
fovereign, will no longer know any bounds when they
meet with no obftacles. A falfe and cruel fyftem of
politics will foon perfuade him, that rich fubjects will
always become infolent; that they muft be diftreffed,
in order to be reduced to fubjection; and that poverty is the firmeft rampart of the throne. He will proceed fo far as to believe that every thing is at his difpofal; that nothing belongs to his flaves; and that he
does them a favour in leaving them any thing.

The government will appropriate to itfelf all the
means and refources of induftry; and will lay fuch reftraints on the exports and imports of every article of
trade, as will entirely abforb the profits arifing from it.
Commerce will only be circulated by the interference
and for the benefit of the treafury. Cultivation will
be neglected by mercenaries who can have no hopes
of acquiring property. The nobility will ferve in the
army only for pay. The magiftrate will give judgment only for the fake of his fees and his falary.
Merchants will keep their fortunes concealed, in order
that they may convey them out of a land where there
is no fpirit of patriotifm, nor any fecurity left. The
nation, then lofing all its importance, will conceive an
indifference for its kings; will fee its enemies only in
thofe who are its mafters; will be induced to hope
that a change of flavery will tend to alleviate the yoke
of it; will expect its deliverence from a revolution,
and the reftoration of its tranquillity from an entire
overthrow of the ftate.

"This defcription is dreadful," faid a vizier to me,
for there are viziers everywhere. "I am concerned

" at it.　But without contribution, how can I main-
" tain that strength of the state, the necessity and ad-
" vantage of which you yourself acknowledge? This
" strength should be permanent, and always equal;
" otherwise there would be no more security for your
" persons, your property, or your industry.　Happi-
" ness undefended is no more than a chimera.　My
" expences are independent of the variety of seasons,
" of the inclemency of the elements, and of all acci-
" dents.　It is therefore necessary that they should be
" supplied by you, although a pestilence should have
" destroyed your cattle, though insects should have
" devoured your vines, and though the hail should
" have rooted up your harvests.　You must pay, or I
" will turn against you that strength of the state, which
" hath been created for your safety, and which it is
" your business to maintain."

This oppressive system concerned only the propietors
of lands.　The vizier soon informed me of the means
which he employed to render the other members of
the confederacy subservient to the treasury.

" It is chiefly in the cities that the mechanical and
" liberal arts, of utility or ornament, of necessity or
" fancy, are concentrated, or at least their activity,
" their display, or their improvement.　There it is
" that the rich, and consequently indolent citizens,
" attracted or fixed by the charms of society, endea-
" vour to delude the wearisomeness of life by facti-
" tious wants.　There it is, that, in order to gratify
" them, they employ the poor, or, which is the same
" thing, the industrious man; who, in his turn, in order
" to satisfy the wants of primary necessity, which are for
" a long time the only wants with which he is torment-
" ed, endeavours to multiply the factitious wants of the
" rich man; from whence arises between the one and the
" other a mutual dependence, founded upon their re-
" spective interests; for the industrious man wishes to la-
" bour, while the rich man wishes to enjoy.　If, there-
" fore, I can tax the necessary articles of all the inhabi-
" tants of cities, whether industrious or idle, that is to

" fay, if I can raife the price, for the ftate, of all the
" commodities and merchandife which are confumed
" there, by the wants of all the individuals; I fhall
" then have taxed all the fpecies of induftry, and I
" fhall have brought them to the condition of the in-
" duftrious hufbandman. I fhall have done ftill more;
" and efpecially, let not this circumftance efcape your
" notice, I fhall have made the rich pay for the poor,
" becaufe the latter will not fail to raife the price of
" his productions, in proportion to the multiplication
" of his wants."

I conjure thee, vizier, to fpare, at leaft, the air, the
water, the fire, and even the corn, which is not lefs
than thofe three elements, the facred right of every
man, without exception. Deprived of light, no one
can either live or act, and without life or action there
can be no induftry.

" I will think of it. But, attend to me in all the
" different plans, by which I have comprehended all
" the other objects of neceffity, efpecially in the cities.
" In the firft place, being mafter of the frontiers of
" the empire, I fuffer nothing to come from foreigners,
" nor any thing to be conveyed to them, unlefs they
" pay in proportion to the number, weight, and value
" of the thing fent. By this mode, he who hath ma-
" nufactured, or who exports, yields to me a part of
" his profits; and he who receives or confumes, gives
" me fomething above what belongs to the merchant
" or to the manufacturer."

I underftand, vizier; but by interfering thus between the feller and the purchafer, between the manufacturer, or the merchant, and the confumer. without being called upon, and without your interference
being profitable to them; fince, on the contrary, you
keep it up to their detriment, doth it not happen, that
on their parts they endeavour, by deceiving thee fome
how or other, to diminifh thy fhare, or even to fruftrate thee of it?

" Undoubtedly: but of what ufe would the ftrength
" of the ftate be to me then, if I did not employ it in

" finding out the fraud, in guarding againſt it. or in B O O K
" puniſhing it? If they endeavour to-withhold or to XIX.
" diminiſh my ſhare, I take the whole and even ſome-
" times proceed a little further."

I comprehend you: thus it is that wars and exactions are ſtill maintained on the frontiers, and on the
borders of the provinces; and that, in order to preſs
upon that fortunate induſtry, which is the tie of the
moſt diſtant nations, and of the people the moſt ſeparated by their manners and by their religion.

" I am ſorry for it. But every thing muſt be ſacri-
" ficed to the ſtrength of the ſtate, to that bulwark
" which is raiſed againſt the jealouſy and rapaciouſ-
" neſs of neighbouring powers. The intereſt of par-
" ticular individuals doth not always agree with that
" of the greater number. One effect of the proceed-
" ing you complain of is, to preſerve to you commo-
" dities and productions, which perſonal advantage
" would deprive you of by exporting them to foreign
" countries; and I prohibit the importation of foreign
" merchandiſe, which, by the ſuperabundance they
" would occaſion, when united to yours, would lower
" the price of the latter."

I thank thee, vizier: but is it neceſſary that thou
ſhouldſt have troops? Thoſe troops are very inconvenient. And couldſt thou not ſerve me without a military parade?

" If you perpetually interrupt me, you will loſe the
" thread of my ſubtile and marvellous operations.
" After having laid a tax on merchandiſe, on its en-
" trance, and on its going out of the empire, on its
" paſſage from one province to the other, I follow the
" track of the traveller, who goes through my diſtrict
" on account of his affairs, or through motives of cu-
" rioſity. I follow the peaſant who carries to town
" the produce of the fields, or of his farmyard; and
" when thirſt drives him into a public houſe, by means
" of an aſſociation with the maſter....."

What, vizier! An inn-keeper is your aſſociate?

Certainly. Is there any thing deſpicable, when

" the maintenance of the ſtrength of the ſtate, and
" conſequently the wealth of the treaſury, is concern-
" ed? by means of this aſſociation, I receive part of
" the price of the liquor conſumed there."

But, vizier, how does it happen that you come to
be the partner of the keeper of an inn or tavern, in
the ſale of his liquors? Is it poſſible that you ſhould
be his purveyor?

" I his purveyor! this is what I would carefully a-
" void. Where would be the advantage of ſelling the
" wine, which the vine-dreſſer might have given me
" as the tribute of his induſtry? I am better acquaint-
" ed with the management of my affairs. In the firſt
" place, I am in partnerſhip with the vine-keeper or
" proprietor, with the brewer and the diſtiller of bran-
" dy, by which I obtain part of the price for which
" they ſell them to the inn-holders, or keepers of
" public houſes; and I have afterwards another with
" the latter, by which they are accountable to me in
" their turn, for a portion of the price which they
" receive from the conſumer, leaving the ſeller at
" liberty to recover from the conſumer that ſhare of
" the price which belongs to me from the conſump-
" tion."

It muſt be acknowledged that this is very fine. But,
vizier, how do you manage to be preſent at all the ſales
of liquors which are made in your empire? How doth
it happen that you are not pilfered by theſe inn-keep-
ers, who have been notoriouſly diſhoneſt, ever ſince the
times of the Romans, though the queſtors were not in
partnerſhip with them? After what you have intruſted
to me I do not doubt of any thing, but I am curious.

" It is in this inſtance that I ſhall appear bold
" to you, and that you will admire my ſagacity. It
" is impoſſible to aſpire to every kind of merit and
" of glory. Firſt, no man is allowed to move a
" hogſhead of wine, of cyder, bear, or of brandy,
" either from the place where it is produced or pre-
" pared, or from the warehouſe or from the cellar,
" either to ſell or to tranſport, no matter for what

" purpofe, without my permiffion in writing.   By B O O K
" this I know what becomes of them.   If any liquor   XIX.
" be met without this paffport I feize upon it ; and
" the proprietor pays me immediately a third or a
" fourth more than the value.   Afterwards the fame
" agents, who are employed night and day, in all
" parts, to afcertain to me the honefty of the proprie-
" tors, or wholefale merchants, in keeping their com-
" pact of affociation, enter every day twice rather
" than once, into the houfe of each inn or tavern-
" keeper, where they found the veffels, reckon the
" bottles ; and if there be the leaft fufpicion of pil-
" fering upon my fhare, the punifhment is fo fevere
" as to prevent their being tempted a fecond time."

But, vizier, in order to pleafe you, are not your a-
gents fo many petty fubaltern tyrants?

" I make no doubt of it ; and I reward them well
" for it."

Very well ; but, vizier, I have one fcruple.   Thefe
affociations with the proprietor and with the merchants, in wholefale and in retail, have a little the appearance of thofe which the highwayman contracts
with the paffenger whom he robs.

" You do not confider what you fay.   My affocia-
" tions are authorifed by law, and by the facred infti-
" tution of the ftrength of the ftate.   Can no circum-
" ftance then have an influence upon your mind?   But
" let me now perfuade you to come with me to the
" gates of the city, where you will not find me lefs
" admirable.   Nothing enters there without bringing
" fome profit to me.   Should they be liquors, they
" contribute, not in proportion to their value, as in
" my other arrangements, but according to their
" quantity ; and you may be affured that I am not
" the dupe.   The inn-keeper, or the citizen, have no-
" thing to fay, although I have befides fome concern
" with them at the time of the purchafe and of the
" fale, for it is in a different manner.   If they be pro-
" vifions, I have my agents, not only at the gates, but
" at the flaughter-houfes and in the fifh-markets ; and

"no one would attempt to plunder me, without rifk-
"ing more than he could get by the fraud. Lefs pre-
"cautions are neceffary in refpect to wood, forage, or
"paper. Thefe mercantile articles cannot be pilfered
"as a flafk of wine is. I have, however, my emiffa-
"ries on the roads, and in the bye-places; and woe
"be to thofe who fhould be found endeavouring to
"elude my vigilance. You fee, therefore, that who-
"ever dwells in cities, whether he may live by his in-
"duftry, or whether he may employ his income, or a
"part of his profits, in a falary for the induftrious man,
"ftill no one can confume without paying; and that
"all men pay more for the ufual and indifpenfable
"confumptions than for the reft. I have laid every
"kind of induftry under contribution, without its per-
"ceiving it. There are, however, fome branches of it
"with which I have endeavoured to treat more direct-
"ly, becaufe their common refidence is not in towns,
"and that I have imagined they would be more pro-
"fitable to me from a fpecial contribution. For in-
"ftance, I have agents in the forges and furnaces,
"where iron, which is put to fo many different ufes,
"is manufactured and weighed; I have fome in the
"workfhops of the tanners, where the hides, which
"are of fuch general utility, are manufactured; I
"have fome among all thofe perfons who work in
"gold, filver, plate, and jewels; and you will not ac-
"cufe me, in this inftance, of attacking objects of pri-
"mary neceffity. In proportion as my experiments
"fucceed, I extend them. I flatter myfelf that I fhall
"one day be able to fix my fatellites by the fide of
"the linen looms, becaufe they are fo univerfally ufe-
"ful. But do not impart my fecret to any one.
"Whenever my fpeculations get wind, it is always to
"my detriment."

I am truly ftricken, vizier, with your fagacity, or
with that of your fublime predeceffors. They have
digged mines of gold everywhere. They have made
of your country a Peru, the inhabitants of which have,
perhaps, had the fame deftiny as thofe of the other

continent; but of what concern is it to you? But
you fay nothing to me of the falt and the tobacco,
which you fell ten times above their intrinfic value,
though falt be the moft neceffary article in life, after
bread and water. What is the meaning of your filence? Are you fenfible of the contradiction in your
conduct in felling this article, and refufing to collect
the other contributions in kind, under pretence of the
trouble of felling again?

" Not in the leaft. The difference is eafily per-
" ceived. If I received from the proprietor or culti-
" vator his fhare of contribution in kind, in order to
" fell it again afterwards, I become his competitor in
" the markets. My predeceffors have been prudent,
" in referving to themfelves the exclufive diftribution
" of them. This hath been attended with fome diffi-
" culty. In order to bring thofe two ftreams of gold
" into the refervoir of the treafury, it was neceffary to
" forbid the culture and the manufacture of tobacco
" in the nation; which doth not difpenfe me from
" keeping upon the frontiers, and even in the interior
" parts of the empire, an army, to prevent the intro-
" duction and the competition of any other tobacco
" with mine."

Have you found thefe expedients fuccefsful, vizier?
" Not fo fully as I could have wifhed, notwithftand-
" ing the feverity of the penal laws. As for the falt,
" the difficulty was much greater; I cannot but ac-
" knowledge my concern at it. My predeceffors com-
" mitted an irreparable blunder. Under pretence of
" difpenfing a ufeful favour, neceffary to fome of the
" maritime provinces, or, perhaps, induced by the al-
" lurement of a confiderable fum, though a temporary
" one, which other provinces paid, to be allowed to
" furnifh themfelves with falt as they chofe; they
" gave way to exceptions, the confequences of which
" are, that it is not I who fell it, in one third of the
" extent of the empire, or thereabouts. I am indeed
" in great hopes of altering this; but I muft wait for
" the moment of diftrefs."

Independent, therefore, of the armies which you maintain upon the frontiers, to prevent the importation of tobacco and foreign merchandife, you have ftill others in the inland parts of the country, to prevent the fale of the falt belonging to the free provinces from coming into competition with the fale of yours.

" It is true.   However, I muft do juftice to our an-
" cient viziers.   They have left me a very well con-
" trived fyftem of legiflation. For inftance, thofe per-
" fons of the free countries bordering upon thofe pro-
" vinces where I fell, are allowed to fell as little falt as
" poffible, to prevent them from felling it to my pre-
" judice : and by a confequence of the fame wife mea-
" fures, thofe who are to purchafe of me, and who, be-
" ing near the free countries, might be tempted to
" provide themfelves at a cheaper rate, are compelled
" to take more than they can confume."

And is this cuftom confecrated by law ?

" Yes, and fupported by the auguft ftrength of the
" ftate. I am authorifed to number the families ; and
" if any one of them fhould not purchafe the quantity
" of falt that I think neceffary for their confumption,
" they are obliged to pay for it, all the fame as if they
" had."

And every perfon who fhall falt their meat with any other falt than yours will certainly fuffer for it.

" Exceedingly. Befide the feizure of this iniquitous
" falt, it cofts him more than he would expend for fup-
" plying his family for feveral years."

And what becomes of the feller ?

" The feller ! He is of courfe a robber, a plunderer,
" a malefactor, whom I reduce to beggary if he has
" any thing, and whom I fend to the galleys if he has
" nothing."

But are you not, vizier, expofed to inceffant law-fuits ?

" I have many upon my hands ; but there is a par-
" ticular court of juftice, to which the exclufive de-
" termination of them is committed."

And how doft thou extricate thyfelf from them ?

Is it by the interference of thy favourite principle, strength of the state?

" With that and with money."

I can but admire, vizier, thy head and thy courage: thy head, which attends to so many objects, and thy courage, which faces so many enemies. You have been typified in the holy scriptures by Ishmael, whose hands were uplifted against all, and those of all raised against him.

" Alas, I own it! But the importance of the strength " of the state, and the extent of its wants, are such, " that it hath been necessary to have recourse to other " expedients. Besides what the proprietor is annually " indebted to me for the produce of his estate, if he " should resolve to sell it, the purchaser must pay me " a sum above the price agreed on with the seller. I " have rated all human compacts; and no man enters " into any kind of contract without furnishing me a " contribution proportioned either to the object or " the nature of the convention. This examination " implies a set of profound agents. And indeed I am " often in want of them. The pleader cannot take " one single step, either as plaintiff or defendant, with- " out some benefit arising to me from it: and you will " allow that this tribute is very innocent; for no one " is yet disgusted of law-suits."

Suffer me to take breath, vizier, although thy calculation should not be at an end. Thou hast wearied out my admiration; and I know not which circumstance should most excite my astonishment, either that perfidious and barbarous science which extends its influence over every thing, and presses upon every thing, or that patience with which so many repeated acts of subtle tyranny, which spares nothing, are supported. The slave receives his subsistence in exchange for his liberty, while thy wretched contributor is deprived of his liberty by furnishing thee with his subsistence.

Hitherto I have so frequently given way to emotions even of indignation, that I have ventured to think I should be excused for indulging myself for

BOOK XIX. once in ridicule and irony, which have so often decid-ed the most important questions. I resume the cha-racter that suits me, and I say,

There undoubtedly must be a degree of public strength in every government, which shall act both within and without : without, to defend the body of the nation against the jealousy, the cupidity, the am-bition, the contempt, and violence of other nations ; and this protection, or the security which should be the effect of it, requires armies, fleets, fortresses, arse-nals, feeble allies to be kept in pay, and powerful al-lies to be seconded : within, to preserve the citizen, at-tached to the order of society, from the troubles, op-pressions, and injuries he may be exposed to from the wicked man, who suffers himself to be led astray by passions, by personal interest, or by his vices, and who is restrained only by the threats of justice, and by the vigilance of the police.

We shall, moreover, venture to advance, that it is advantageous to the greater number of citizens, that the strength of the state should encourage industry, stimulate talents, and assist those who, from an incon-siderate zeal, unforeseen misfortunes, or false specula-tions, have lost their own ability. It is from this prin-ciple that we trace the necessity of charity-schools and hospitals.

In order to increase the energy of this strength of the state, which, especially in monarchial states, seems to be distinct and separate from the nation, I would even consent that the depositary and director of this public strength should impress awe by a parade of dig-nity, should attract by mildness, and encourage by re-wards, since it is his duty to make it be feared, respect-ed, and cherished.

All these means are expensive. Expences suppose revenue, and a revenue implies contributions. It is just that those who partake of the advantages of the strength of the state should furnish towards its main-tenance. There is a tacit but sacred agreement be-tween the sovereign and his subjects, by which the

former engages to affift, with a degree of that force
proportioned to the portion that has been furnifhed
of it, towards the general mafs of contributions; and
this diftributive juftice would be executed of itfelf by
the nature of things, if it were not inceffantly difturbed by corruption and vice.

But in every convention there is a proportion between the price and the value of the thing acquired;
and this proportion muft neceffarily be in the ratio of
minus on the fide of the price, and in that of *plus* on
the fide of the advantages. I am ready to purchafe a
fword to defend myfelf againft the thief; but if, in order to acquire this fword, I am obliged to empty my
purfe or to fell my houfe, I would rather compound
with the thief.

Now, where then is this analogy, this proportion of
advantages, derived from the ftrength of the ftate, *in
favour of a proprietor*, when compared with the price
which he pays for them, if among the moft civilized
nations of Europe, the leaft expofed to excurfions and
to foreign attacks, after having ceded a part of his poffeffion, he is obliged, when he goes to live in the town,
to purchafe at an advanced price, for the benefit of
this ftrength of the ftate, not only the productions of
other people, but likewife his own, when he choofes
to confume them.

What is this proportion of advantages *for the hufbandman*, if he be compelled, on the one hand, to confume in kind a portion of his time, and of the means
of his induftry, for the conftruction and the repairing
of the roads; and if he be alfo obliged to return in
money a confiderable portion of the productions he
hath acquired from the earth by the fweat of his brow
and by hard labours?

What is this proportion of advantages *for the mechanic*, who cannot work without food, lodging, clothing, light, and firing, and who cannot fupply himfelf
with all thefe articles without contributing, fince thefe
feveral means of fubfiftence are taxed, if he be ftill
obliged to return part of the price of his time and of

his talents to the impoſt which falls directly upon the
productions of his induſtry?

What is this proportion of advantages *for the merchant*, who hath already contributed in a variety of
ways, both by his perſonal conſumption, by the conſumption of his clerks, as well as by the advanced
price of the firſt materials, if he be ſtill obliged to cede
a portion of the price of the merchandiſe which he
ſends out, and from which he may perhaps receive nothing, in caſe of ſome of thoſe numberleſs accidents,
from which this public ſtrength doth not engage either
to ſcreen or indemnify him?

What is this proportion of advantage *for all individuals*, if, after having contributed in every progreſſion
and exertion of our induſtry to the common maſs, on
one hand, by an annual and general impoſt, that of
the poll-tax, which hath no connection, no affinity,
either with property or with induſtry, we ſtill contribute, on the other hand, by the ſalt, a commodity of
primary neceſſity, which is carried to ten times its in-
trinſic and natural value?

Once again, What proportion of theſe advantages
belongs *to all individuals*, if we ſee all theſe quotas, exacted for the maintenance of the ſtrength of the ſtate,
waſted among the extortioners who collect them, while
the remainder, which, after ſeveral expences of circulation, is poured into the king's treaſury, is pillaged in
ſeveral different manners, or diſſipated in extravagance?

We ſhall alſo aſk, what analogy is there between
that ſtrange and complicated variety of contributions,
and the advantages which each of us obtains from the
ſtrength of the ſtate, if it be true, as certain political
calculators pretend, that the ſums of thoſe who contribute are equal to thoſe of the revenue of the proprietors?

We can only ſeek for an anſwer to this queſtion in
the character of the ſovereign. If he be cruel, the
problem will not be ſolved; and time, after a long
ſeries of oppreſſion, will bring about the ruin of the
empire. If the ſovereign ſhould have any ſenſibility,

the problem will be folved in a manner beneficial to his fubjects.

The chief of the nation muft not, however, flatter himfelf with effecting any great or lafting good, if he does not make a judicious choice of the man intrufted with the maintenance of the ftrength of the ftate. It belongs to that great agent of government to diftribute and to render fupportable to every individual the enormous weight of the tribute by his equity and by his fkill, and to divide it according to the relative degrees of ability or non-ability in the contributors. Without thefe two circumftances, the oppreffed people will fall into a ftate of defpair more or lefs diftant, more or lefs alarming. With thefe two circumftances, fupported by the expectation of an immediate or approaching relief, they will fuffer with patience, and will proceed under their burden with fome fhare of courage.

But where is the minifter who will fulfil fo difficult a tafk? Will it be the minifter who, from an odious thirft of wealth, fhall have eagerly fought the management of the public revenues, and who having attained that important poft by dint of fervile intrigue, fhall have abandoned the treafury a prey to his paffions, his friends, his flatterers, and his favourites, and to the detriment of the ftrength of the ftate? Perifh the memory of fuch a minifter!

Will it be he who fhall view, in the power committed to his hands, nothing more but the inftrument of his enmity, or of his perfonal averfions; who fhall confider nothing but how to realize the illufion of his ferocious and difordered imagination; who will treat all meafures differing from his own as abfurdities; whofe anger will be excited againft real or pretended errors, as if they were fo many crimes; to whom the fable of the ftomach and the members fhall be an object of ridicule; who fhall enervate that part of the body politic that fhall be difpleafing to him, by granting almoft exclufive favours to that which his fancy, his intereft, or his prejudices fhall prefer; to whom every

thing fhall bear the ftamp of confufion and diforder
which fhall not be confonant to his fingular ideas;
who, deftitute of the wifdom neceffary to correct what
is defective, fhall fubftitute chimeras to a regular fyftem, perhaps imperfect; and who, in order to correct
pretended abufes, blind to the confequences of an ill-
fuggefted plan of reformation, will fubvert every thing
with a difdainful fmile; an empiric, who is as cruel
as ignorant; who, miftaking poifon for the remedy,
fhall announce a fpeedy cure, when repeated convulfions fhall proclaim the impending diffolution of the
patient? Perifh the memory of fuch a minifter!

Sovereigns, you who are neither exempt from falfehood or feduction, if you have been unfortunate e-
nough to have been directed by fuch minifters, do not
fubftitute to them a weak and pufillanimous man, who,
though well informed, mild, modeft, and perhaps incapable of committing any great faults while he acts for
himfelf, will ftill fuffer himfelf to be mifled by others;
will fall into the fnares that fhall be laid for him; and
will want that neceffary vigour, either to put a ftop
to, or prevent the evil, or to act in oppofition to yourfelves, when his confcience and the general intereft
fhall require it.

Do not fubftitute the morofe, difdainful, and auftere
man, and much lefs the imperious and harfh minifter.
The impoft is a heavy burden; how, therefore, fhall
it be fupported, if the mode of impofing it be aggravated? It is a bitter cup, which all muft fwallow; if
it be prefented haftily or awkwardly, it will certainly
be fpilt.

Do not fubftitute the man who is ignorant of the
law, or who defpifes it, to attend to nothing but finance. It is the intereft of a fovereign, that property
and induftry fhould be protected, againft his own authority, againft the enterprifes of his minifters, often
inconfiderate, and fometimes dangerous. A minifter
who facrifices every thing to finance will often fill the
coffers of his mafter; he will give to the nation, and
to the throne, the fplendour of a formidable power;

but this fplendour will be momentary as lightning. B O O K
Defpair will feize upon the minds of the fubjects. By
reducing induftry to the moft extreme diftrefs, the minifter will have acted the part of the man in the fable,
who killed the hen which brought forth golden eggs.

Do not fubftitute a villain, armed at all points with
the formalities and fubtleties of law, who will keep up
a perpetual quarrel between the treafury and the law,
who will render the former odious. and will relax the
bands of a hard but neceffary obedience.

Do not fubftitute that outrageous philanthropift,
who, giving himfelf up to an ill judged fpirit of patriotifm, fhall forget the treafury, while he indifcreetly
gives way to the feducing impulfe of benevolence and
popularity; an impulfe ever laudable in a philofopher,
but to which a minifter ought not to yield without
great circumfpection. For it muft ftill be acknowledged, that the ftrength of the ftate muft be eftablifhed, and that there muft be a treafury to maintain it.

But above all things, reject the prodigal minifter.
How is it poffible that a man who hath failed in the
management of his own affairs can adminifter thofe of
a great ftate? When he hath diffipated his own eftates,
will he be economical of the public revenue? Let us
fuppofe him to have probity, delicacy, knowledge, and
a fincere defire of being ufeful to the ftate; yet in a
circumftance, and upon an object fo important as that
in queftion, conftitutional virtues are only to be truft-
ed to. How many men are there, who have entered
virtuous into the miniftry, and who, in fix months after their promotion, appeared in a very different light
to others, and even to themfelves? There is, perhaps,
lefs feduction at the foot of the throne, than in the
antichamber of a minifter; and ftill lefs at the foot of
the throne, and in the antichambers of other minifters,
than at the entrance of the clofet of the minifter of finance. But we have dwelt too long on impofts: we
muft now fpeak of what hath been fuggefted to fupply
its place, of public credit.

In general, what is called credit is only a delay granted for payment. This was a cuftom unknown in the firft ages. Every family was fatisfied with what uncultivated nature, and fome coarfe labours, fupplied to them. Some exchanges were foon begun, but only between relations and neighbours. Thefe connections were extended in all places, where the progrefs of fociety multiplied the wants or the pleafures of men. In procefs of time, it was no longer poffible to purchafe provifions of one kind with thofe of another; metals were fubftituted, and became infenfibly the common reprefentative of all things. It happened, that the agents of trade, which were becoming every day more confiderable, wanted the money neceffary for their fpeculations. The merchandife was then delivered, to be paid for at periods more or lefs diftant; and this fortunate cuftom ftill obtains, and will laft for ever.

Credit fuppofes double confidence; confidence in the perfon who is in want of it, and confidence in his abilities to pay. The firft is the moft neceffary. It is too common for a man in debt, who is deftitute of honefty, to break his engagements, though he be able to fulfil them; and to diffipate his fortune by irregularity and extravagance. But the fenfible and honeft man may, by a variety of fchemes well conducted, acquire, or replace the means that have failed him for a time.

The mutual advantage of the purchafer and the feller has given rife to the credit which exifts among the individuals of one fociety, or even of feveral focieties. It differs from public credit in this particular, that the latter is the credit of a whole nation, confidered as forming one fingle body.

Between public and private credit there is alfo this difference, that profit is the end of the one, and expence of the other. From hence it follows, that credit is gain with refpect to the merchant, becaufe it furnifhes him with the means of acquiring riches; but with refpect to governments, it is one caufe of impo-

verifhing them, fince it only fupplies them with the B O O K
means of ruining themfelves. A ftate that borrows XIX.
alienates a portion of its revenue for a capital, which
it fpends. It is therefore poorer after thefe loans, than
it was before it had recourfe to this deftructive expedient.

Notwithftanding the fcarcity of gold and filver, the
ancient governments were unacquainted with public
credit, even at the times of the moft fatal and critical
events. They formed, during peace, a ftock that was
referved for times of diftrefs. The fpecie being by
this method circulated afrefh, excited induftry, and alleviated, in fome meafure, the inevitable calamities of
war. Since the difcovery of the New World has made
gold and filver more common, thofe who have had the
adminiftration of public affairs have generally engaged
in enterprifes above the abilities of the people they
governed, and have not fcrupled to burden pofterity
with debts they had ventured to contract. This fyftem of oppreffion has been continued : it will affect
the lateft generations, and opprefs all nations and all
ages.

It is England, Holland, and France, that is to fay,
the moft opulent nations of Europe, who have given
fo bad an example. Thefe powers have found credit,
for the fame reafon that we do not lend our money to
a man who afks charity, but to him who dazzles us
with his brilliant equipage. Confidence hath given
birth to loans; and confidence arifes of itfelf at the
fight of a country where the richnefs of the foil is increafed by the activity of an induftrious people, and
at the view of thofe celebrated ports which receive all
the productions of the univerfe.

The fituation of thefe three ftates hath alfo encouraged the lender. They are not only the public revenues that are his guarantee, but alfo the incomes of
individuals, in which the treafury finds, in times of
neceffity, its fupport and its refources. In countries
which, like Germany, are open on all fides, and which
have neither barriers, nor natural means of defence, if

the enemy, who can enter into them freely, should
either fix, or only sojourn there for a time, they immediately levy the public revenues for their own benefit, and they even appropriate to themselves, by contributions, a portion of the incomes of individuals.
The creditors of the government then experience the
same thing as happened to those who had annuities in
the Austrian Netherlands, and to whom more than
thirty years arrears were due. With England, France,
and Holland, which are all three somewhat more or
less secured from invasion, there is nothing to fear, except the causes which exhaust them, the effect of which
is slower, and consequently more distant.

But should it not be the province of the indigent
man to borrow, and of the rich to lend? Wherefore,
then, are those states which have the most resources
the most in debt? It is because the folly of nations is
the same as that of individuals: it is because, being
more ambitious, they create to themselves more wants:
it is because the confidence they have in their means
renders them inattentive to the expences they make:
it is because no action at law can be maintained against
them; and that their debts are themselves liquidated,
whenever they have the effrontery to say, we owe nothing: it is because subjects cannot bring their sovereign to justice: it is because a power hath never been,
nor perhaps never will be seen, to take up arms in favour of their citizens, robbed and plundered by a foreign power: it is because a state renders its neighbours in a manner subject to it by loans: it is because
Holland is in constant apprehension, lest the first can-
non-shot which should pierce the side of one of her
ships should acquit England towards her: it is because
an edict dated from Versailles may, without consequences, acquit France to Geneva: it is because these
motives, which it would be shameful to acknowledge,
act secretly in the breasts and in the councils of powerful kings.

The custom of public credit, though ruinous to every state, is not equally so to all. A nation that has

several valuable productions of its own; whose revenue is entirely free; which hath always fulfilled its engagements, which hath not been swayed by the ambition of conquests, and which governs itself; such a
nation will raise money at an easier rate, than an empire, the soil of which is not fertile; which is over-
loaded with debts; which engages in undertakings beyond its strength; which has deceived its creditors,
and groans beneath an arbitrary power. The lender,
who of course imposes the law, will always proportion
the terms to the risks he must run. Thus, a people
whose finances are in a state of confusion, will soon fall
into the utmost distress by public credit: but even the
best-regulated government will also experience the decline of its prosperity from it.

But some political arithmeticians have asserted, that
it is advantageous to invite the specie of other nations
into that of our own country, and that public loans
produce that important effect. It is certain, that it is
a method of attracting the specie of other nations; but
merely, as if it were obtained by the sale of one or
more provinces of the empire. Perhaps it would be a
more rational practice to deliver up the soil to them,
than to cultivate it solely for their use.

But if the state borrowed only of its own subjects,
the national revenue would not be given up to foreigners. It certainly would not: but the state would im-
poverish some of its members, in order to enrich one
individual. Must not taxes be increased in proportion
to the interest that is to be paid, and the capital that
is to be replaced? Will not the proprietors of lands,
the husbandmen, and every citizen, find the burden
greater, than if all the money borrowed by the state
had been demanded from them at once? Their situation is the same, as if they themselves had borrowed
it, instead of retrenching from their ordinary expences
as much as might enable them to supply an accidental
charge.

But the paper-currency which is introduced by the

loans made to government increafes the quantity of
wealth in circulation, gives a great extenfion to trade,
and facilitates every commercial tranfaction. Infatuated men! reflect on the dangerous confequences of
your political fyftem. Extend it only as far as poffible; let the ftate borrow all it can; load it with intereft to be paid; and by thefe means reduce it to the
neceffity of ftraining every tax to the utmoft; ye will
foon find, that, with all the wealth you may have in
circulation, ye will have no frefh fupply for the purpofes of confumption and trade. Money, and the paper which reprefents it, do not circulate of themfelves,
nor without the affiftance of thofe powers which fet
them in motion. All the different figns introduced in
lieu of coin acquire a value only proportionate to the
number of fales and purchafes that are made. Let us
agree with you, in fuppofing all Europe filled with
gold. If it fhould have no merchandife to trade with,
that gold will have no circulation. Let us only increafe commercial effects, and take no concern about
thefe reprefentations of wealth; mutual confidence
and neceffity will foon occafion them to be eftablifhed
without your affiftance. But let your care be principally directed in preventing their increafe, by fuch
means as muft neceffarily diminifh the mafs of your
growing produce.

But the cuftom of public credit enables one power
to give the law to others. Will it never be perceived
that this refource is common to all nations? If it be
a general mode by which a ftate may obtain a fuperiority over its enemies, may it not be ferviceable to
them for the fame purpofes? Will not the credit of
the two nations be in proportion to their refpective
wealth? and will they not be ruined without having
any other advantages over one another, than thofe
they were in poffeffion of, independent of every loan?
When I fee monarchs and empires furioufly attacking
and waging war againft each other, with all their
debts, with their public funds, and their revenue al-

ready deeply mortgaged, it feems to me, fays a philo- fophical writer, as if I faw men fighting with clubs in a potter's fhop furrounded with porcelain.

It would, perhaps, be prefumptuous to affirm, that in no circumftance whatfoever the public fervice can ever require an alienation of part of the public reve- nues. The fcenes that difturb the world are fo vari- ous; empires are expofed to fuch extraordinary revo- lutions; the field of events is fo extenfive; political interefts occafion fuch amazing changes in public af- fairs, that it is not within the reach of human wifdom to forefee and calculate every circumftance. But in this inftance, it is the ordinary conduct of govern- ments that we are attending to, and not an extraordi- nary fituation, which, in all probability, may never prefent itfelf.

Every ftate which will not be diverted from the ruinous courfe of loans, by fuch confiderations as we have juft been offering, will be the caufe of its own deftruction. The facility of acquiring large fums of money at once, will engage a government in every kind of unreafonable, rafh, and expenfive undertaking; will make it mortgage its future expectations for pre- fent exigencies, and game with the prefent ftock to ac- quire future fupplies. One loan will bring on another; and to accelerate the laft, the intereft will be more and more raifed.

This irregularity will caufe the fruits of induftry to pafs into fome idle hands. The facility of obtaining every enjoyment without labour will induce every per- fon of fortune, as well as all vicious and intriguing men, to refort to the capital; who will bring with them a train of fervants, borrowed from the plough; of young girls, deprived of their innocence, and pre- vented from marrying; of perfons of both fexes, de- voted to luxury: all of them the inftruments, the vic- tims, the objects, or the fport, of indolence and volup- tuoufnefs.

The feducing attraction of public debts will fpread more and more. When men can reap the fruits of the earth without labour, every individual will engage in that fpecies of employment which is at once lucrative and eafy. Proprietors of land, and merchants, will all become annuitants. Money is converted into paper-currency, eftablifhed by the ftate, becaufe it is more portable than fpecie, lefs fubject to alteration from time, and lefs liable to the injury of feafons and the rapacity of the farmers of the revenue. The prefe-rence given to the reprefentative paper, above the real fpecie or commodity, will be injurious to agriculture, trade, and induftry. As the ftate always expends what has been wrongfully acquired in an improper manner, in proportion as its debts increafe, the taxes muft be augmented, in order to pay the interest. Thus all the active and ufeful claffes of fociety are plundered and exhaufted by the idle, ufelefs clafs of annuitants. The increafe of taxes raifes the price of commodities, and confequently that of induftry. By thefe means, con-fumption is leffened ; becaufe exportation ceafes, as foon as merchandife is too dear to ftand the competi-tion of other nations. The lands and manufactures are equally affected.

The inability the ftate then finds itfelf in to anfwer its engagements forces it to extricate itfelf by bank-ruptcy ; a method the moft deftructive of the freedom of the people, and of the power of the fovereign. Then the decrees for loans are paid by edicts of re-duction. Then the oaths of the monarch, and the rights of the fubjects, will be betrayed. Then the fureft bafis of all governments, public confidence, will be irrecoverably loft. Then the fortune of the rich man is overthrown, and the poor man is deprived of the fruits of his long-continued labours, which he had intrufted to the treafury, in order to fecure a fubfift-ence in his old age. Then the labour and the falaries are fufpended, and the multitude of laborious perfons fall into a kind of palfy, and are reduced to beggary. Then the manufactures are empty, and the hofpitals are filled, as they are in times of a peftilence. Then the minds of all men are exafperated againft the prince,

while his agents are everywhere loaded with impreca- B o o k
tions. Then the feeble man, who can fubmit to lead XIX
a life of mifery, is condemned to tears; while he to
whom nature has given an impatient and ftronger
mind, arms himfelf with a dagger, which he turns either againft himfelf or againft his fellow-citizen. Then
the fpirit, the manners, and the health of the inhabitants of the nation are deftroyed; the fpirit, by depreffion and affliction; the manners, by the neceffity
of having recourfe to refources which are always criminal or difhoneft; health, by the fame confequences
which would follow a fudden famine. Sovereign minifters, is it poffible that the image of fuch calamity
fhould be prefented to you, without difturbing your
tranquillity, or exciting your remorfe? If there be a
great Judge who waits for you, how will you dare to
appear before him, and what fentence can you poffibly
expect from him? Doubt not but that it will be the
fame as that which thofe wretches whom you have
made, and whofe fole avenger he was, fhall have called
down upon you. Accurfed in this world, you will
ftill be fo in the next.

Such is the end of loans; from whence we may
judge of the principles upon which they are founded.

After having examined the fprings and fupport of Fine arts,
every civilized fociety, let us take a view of the orna- and belles
ments and decorations of the edifice. Thefe are the
fine arts, and polite literature.

Nature is the model of both the one and the other.
To ftudy nature, and to ftudy her with propriety, to
felect her beft appearances, to copy her faithfully, to
correct her defects, and to embellifh or collect her
fcattered beauties, in order to compofe of them one
marvellous object: thefe are fo many talents infinitely
rare. Some of them may accompany the man of genius; others may be the refult of ftudy, and of the labours of feveral great men. Sublimity of thought and
expreffion may prevail, where there is a want of tafte.
Imagination and invention may difplay its powers in a
man who is impetuous and incorrect. Ages pafs away,

before there appears an orator, a poet, a painter, or a
ftatuary, in whom judgment, which reflects upon its
operations, moderates that ardour which is impatient
of advancing in its career.

It is chiefly utility which hath given birth to literature, while the fine arts have owed their origin to the
allurements of pleafure.

In Greece they were the offspring of the foil itfelf.
The Greeks, favoured with the moft fortunate climate,
had a fcene of nature inceffantly before them, replete
with wonderful objects of delight or of horror, rapid
ftreams, craggy mountains, ancient forefts, fertile plains,
agreeable valleys, and delightful flopes; the fea fometimes calm and fometimes agitated; every thing, in a
word, which infufes ardour into the foul, every thing
which awakens fenfibility, and extends the imagination. Thefe people, being fcrupulous imitators, copied nature at firft, fuch as they faw her. They foon
adapted a fpirit of difcrimination to their models. Attention to the principal functions of the limbs pointed
out to them their groffeft defects, which they corrected.
They afterwards difcovered the more trifling imperfections of a figure, which they likewife altered: and thus
they raifed themfelves gradually to the conception of
ideal beauty, that is, to the conception of a being, the
exiftence of which is perhaps poffible, though not real,
for nature makes nothing perfect. Nothing is regular
in it, and yet nothing is out of its place. There are
too many caufes combined at once in the creation, not
merely of an entire animal, but even of the fmalleft fimilar parts of an animal, that we fhould expect to find
exact fymmetry in them. The beautiful of nature
confifts in a precife feries of imperfections. The whole
may be cenfured, but in that whole every part is precifely what it fhould be. The attentive confideration
of a flower, of the branch of a tree, or of a leaf, are
fufficient to confirm this opinion.

It was by this flow and laborious mode that painting and fculpture acquired that degree of perfection
which aftonifhes us, in the Gladiator, the Antinous,

and Venus of Medicis. To thefe forttmate caufes may
be added a language harmonious from its origin, a
poetry fublime and full of agreeable as well as terrible images, previous to the birth of the arts ; the fpirit
of liberty ; the exercife of the fine arts forbidden to
flaves ; the intercourfe of artifts with philofophers ;
their emulation kept up by labours, rewards, and en-
comiums ; the continual view of the human frame in
baths and in the Gymnafia, which is a continual leffon for the artift, and the principle of refined tafte in
the nation ; the large and flowing garments which did
not deform any part of the body, by preffing and confining it ; numberlefs temples to decorate the ftatues
of the gods and goddeffes, and confequently the ineftimable value fet on beauty, which was to ferve as the
model ; and the cuftom of confecrating, by monuments, the memorable actions of great men.

Homer had fet the example of epic poetry. The
Olympic games haftened the progrefs of lyric poetry,
of mufic, and of tragedy. The concatenation of the
arts, one with the other, exerted its influence on architecture. Eloquence affumed dignity and vigour,
while it was difcuffing the public interefts.

The Romans, who copied the Greeks in every thing,
were inferior to their models, having neither the fame
gracefulnefs nor the fame originality. In fuch of their
works as were really beautiful, the efforts of an able
copyift were frequently obferved, a circumftance which
was almoft unavoidable. If the mafterpieces which
they had perpetually before them had been deftroyed,
their genius, left to its own powers and its natural
energy, after fome trials and after fome deviations,
would have foared to a very high degree of perfection,
and their works would have had that character of
truth which they could not poffefs, when executed
partly from nature and partly from the productions
of a fchool, the fpirit of which was unknown to them.
Thefe originals were to them as were the works of the
Creator ; they were ignorant of the manner in which
they were produced.

BOOK
XIX.

A rigid taſte, however, preſided over all the performances of the Romans. It guided equally their
artiſts and their writers. Their works were either the
image or the copy of truth. The genius of invention,
and that of execution, never infringed the proper limits. In the midſt of profuſion and magnificence the
graces were diſtributed with a prudent hand. Every
thing that went beyond the beautiful was ſkilfully re-
trenched.

The experience of all nations and of all ages de-
monſtrates, that whatever hath attained to perfection
is not long before it degenerates. The revolution is
more or leſs rapid, but always infallible. Among the
Romans it was the work of a few ambitious writers,
who, deſpairing to excel, or even equal their predeceſſors, contrived to open to themſelves a new career.
To plans cloſely arranged, to ideas luminous and profound, to images full of dignity, to phraſes of great
energy, and to expreſſions ſuited to every ſubject, were
ſubſtituted the ſpirit of wit, analogies more ſingular
than preciſe, a continual contraſt of words or ideas, a
broken and looſe ſtyle, more ſtriking than natural; in
a word, all the faults that are produced from an habitual deſire of being brilliant and of pleaſing. The arts
were drawn into the ſame vortex; they were carried
to exceſs, too much refined and affected, as eloquence
and poetry were. All the productions of genius bore
the ſame mark of degradation.

They emerged from this, but only to fall into one
ſtill more fatal. The firſt men to whom it was given
to cultivate the arts, intended to make impreſſions that
ſhould be lively and durable. In order to attain their
end with greater certainty, they thought it neceſſary
to enlarge every object. This miſtake, which was a
neceſſary conſequence of their want of experience, led
them to exaggeration. What had been done in the
firſt inſtance from ignorance, was afterwards revived
from flattery. The emperors, who had raiſed an unlimited power upon the ruins of Roman liberty, would
no longer be mere mortals. To gratify this extrava-

gant pride, it was neceſſary to beſtow upon them the
attributes of the Divinity. Their images, their ſtatues,
and their palaces, no longer appeared in their true
proportions, but all of them aſſumed a coloſſal magni-
tude. The nations proſtrated themſelves before theſe
idols, and incenſe was burnt upon their altars. The
people and the artiſts ſeduced the poets, the orators,
and the hiſtorians, whoſe perſons would have been expoſed to inſult, and whoſe writings would have appeared ſatirical, had they confined themſelves within
the boundaries of truth, taſte, and decency.

Such was the deplorable ſtate of the arts and of
letters in the ſouth of Europe, when ſome barbarous
hordes, pouring from the northern regions, annihilated
what had been only corrupted. Theſe people, after
having covered the country-places with human bones,
and after having ſtrewed the provinces with dead bodies, attacked the towns with that fury which was natural to them. They totally demoliſhed ſeveral of
thoſe ſuperb cities, in which were collected all the
moſt perfect productions of the induſtry and genius of
man in books, pictures, and ſtatues. Such of thoſe
precious monuments as had neither been deſtroyed nor
burnt, were either mutilated or devoted to the meaneſt
uſes. The little that had eſcaped the devaſtation was
obſcurely buried under heaps of ruins and aſhes. Even
Rome herſelf, ſo often pillaged by ferocious robbers,
was at length become their reſidence. This miſtreſs
of nations, ſo long the terror and the admiration of
the univerſe, was no more than an object of contempt
and pity. In the midſt of the ruins of the empire, a
few unfortunate perſons, who had eſcaped the ravages
of the ſword or of famine, dragged on a diſgraceful
exiſtence, the ſlaves of thoſe ſavages, to whoſe name
even they were ſtrangers, or whom they had enſlaved
or trampled under foot.

Hiſtory has preſerved the memory of ſeveral warlike people, who, after having ſubdued enlightened
nations, had adopted their cuſtoms, their laws, and

B O O K their knowledge.   At the too fatal period which we
   XIX.   are now defcribing, they were the vanquifhed who
bafely affimilated themfelves to their barbarous conquerors.   The reafon of this is, that thofe mean perfons who fubmitted to the foreign yoke, had loft a
great deal of the knowledge and of the tafte of their
anceftors ; and that the fmall remains of them they
had preferved were not fufficient to enlighten a conqueror plunged in the groffeft ignorance, and who,
from the facility of their conquefts, had accuftomed
themfelves to confider the arts as a frivolous occupation, and as the inftrument of fervitude.

Before this age of darknefs, Chriftianity had deftroyed in Europe the idols of Pagan antiquity, and
had only preferved fome of the arts to affift the power
of perfuafion, and to favour the preaching of the gofpel.   Inftead of a religion embellifhed with the gay
divinities of Greece and Rome, it had fubftituted monuments of terror and gloominefs, fuited to the tragic
events which fignalized its birth and its progrefs.   The
Gothic ages have left us fome monuments, the boldnefs and majefty of which ftill ftrike the eye amidft
the ruins of tafte and elegance.   All their temples
were built in the fhape of the crofs, which was alfo
placed on the top of them ; and they were filled with
crucifixes, and decorated with horrid and gloomy
images, with fcaffolds, tortures, martyrs, and executioners.

What then became of the arts, condemned as they
were to terrify the imagination by continual fpeætacles
of blood, death, and future punifhments?   They became as hideous as the models they were formed upon ; ferocious as the princes and pontiffs that made
ufe of them ; mean and bafe as thofe who worfhipped
the produætions of them ; they frightened children
from their very cradles ; they aggravated the horrors
of the grave by an eternal perfpeætive of terrible
fhades ; they fpread melancholy over the whole face
of the earth.

At length the period arrived for leſſening thoſe ſcaf- B O O K
foldings of religion and ſocial policy; and this was ac- XIX.
compliſhed by the inhabitants of Greece.

This country is at preſent barbarous to a great degree. It groans under the yoke of ſlavery and ignorance. Its climate and ſome ruins are all it preſerves.
There is no veſtige left of urbanity, emulation, or induſtry. There are no more enterpriſes for the public
good, no more objects for the productions of genius,
no more enthuſiaſm for the reſtoration of arts, no more
zeal for the recovery of liberty. The glory of Themiſ-
tocles and of Alcibiades, the talents of Sophocles and
Demoſthenes, the learning of Lycurgus and of Plato,
the policy of Piſiſtratus and of Pericles, and the labours of Phidias and of Apelles, are all forgotten;
every thing hath been deſtroyed; and a profound
darkneſs covers the region, formerly ſo productive of
miraculous events.

The ſlaves who walk over the ruins of ſtatues, columns, palaces, temples, and amphitheatres, and who
blindly trample ſo many riches under foot, have loſt
even the remembrance of the great exploits of which
their country was the ſcene. They have even disfigured the names of the towns and the provinces.
They are aſtoniſhed that the deſire of acquiring knowledge ſhould attract into their country learned men
and artiſts. Become inſenſible to the invaluable remains of their annihilated ſplendour, they would wiſh
that the ſame ſpirit of indifference ſhould be diffuſed
over the whole world. To be allowed to viſit this in-
tereſting ſpot, it is neceſſary to be at great expences,
to run great riſks, and, beſide this, to obtain the protection of government.

Theſe people, though during ten or twelve centuries the interior part of their empire was the prey of
civil, religious, and ſcholaſtic wars, and though expoſed from without to bloody combats, deſtructive invaſions, and continual loſſes, ſtill preſerved ſome taſte
and ſome knowledge; when the diſciples of Mahom-

med, who, armed with the fword and the coran, had
fubdued with rapidity all the parts of fo vaft a dominion, feized upon the capital itfelf.

At this period the fine arts returned with literature
from Greece into Italy by the Mediterranean, which
maintained the commerce between Afia and Europe.
The Hunns, under the name of Goths, had driven
them from Rome to Conftantinople ; and the very
fame people, under the name of Turks, expelled them
again from Conftantinople to Rome. That city, deftined as it was to rule by force or by ftratagem, cultivated and revived the arts, which had been a long
time buried in oblivion.

Walls, columns, ftatues, and vafes, were drawn forth
from the duft of ages, and from the ruins of Italy, to
ferve as models of the fine arts at their revival. The
genius which prefides over defign raifed three of the
arts at once ; I mean architecture, fculpture, and painting. Architecture, in which convenience itfelf regulated thofe proportions of fymmetry that contribute to
give pleafure to the eye ; fculpture, which flatters
princes, and is the reward of great men ; and painting, which perpetuates the remembrance of noble actions, and the examples of mutual tendernefs. Italy
alone had more fuperb cities, more magnificent edifices, than all the reft of Europe. Rome, Florence,
and Venice, gave rife to three fchools of original
painters : fo much does genius depend upon the imagination, and imagination upon the climate. Had
Italy poffeffed the treafures of Mexico and the productions of Afia, how much more would the arts have
been enriched by the difcovery of the Eaft and Weft
Indies ?

That country, of old fo fruitful in heroes, and fince
in artifts, beheld literature, which is the infeparable
companion of the arts, flourifh a fecond time. It had
been overwhelmed by the barbarifm of a latinity corrupted and disfigured by religious enthufiafm. A mixture of Egyptian theology, Grecian philofophy, and

Hebrew poetry; fuch was the Latin language in the B O O K
mouths of monks, who chanted all night, and taught XIX.
by day things and words they did not underftand.

The mythology of the Romans revived in literature
the graces of antiquity. The fpirit of imitation borrowed them at firft indifcriminately. Cuftom introduced tafte in the choice of thofe rich treafures. The
Italian genius, too fertile not to invent, blended its
enthufiafm and caprice with the rules and examples of
its old mafters, and joined even the fictions of fairy
land with thofe of fable. The works of imagination
partook of the manners of the age and of the national character. Petrarch had drawn that celeftial virgin, Beauty, which ferved as a model for the heroines
of chivalry. Armida was the emblem of the coquetry
which reigned in her time in Italy. Ariofto confounded every fpecies of poetry, in a work, which may rather be called the labyrinth of poetry, than a regular
poem. That author will ftand alone in the hiftory of
literature, like the enchanted palaces of his own conftruction in the deferts.

Letters and arts, after croffing the fea, paffed the
Alps. In the fame manner as the Crufades had brought
the oriental romances into Italy, the wars of Charles
VIII. and Lewis XII. introduced into France fome
principles of good literature. Francis I. if he had not
been into Italy in order to contend for the Milanefe
with Charles V. would never, perhaps, have been ambitious of the title of *the Father of letters :* but thefe
feeds of knowledge and improvement in the arts were
loft in the religious wars. They were recovered again,
if I may be allowed the expreffion, in fcenes of war
and deftruction ; and the time came when they were
again to revive and flourifh. Italy was as much diftinguifhed in the 16th century, as France was in the
fucceeding one, which by the victories of Lewis XIV.
or rather by the genius of the great men that flourifh-
ed together under his reign, deferves to make an e-
pocha in the hiftory of the fine arts.

In France all the efforts of the human mind were

BOOK
XIX.

at once exerted in producing works of genius, as they had before been in Italy. Its powers were difplayed in the marble and on the canvas, in public edifices and gardens, as well as in eloquence and poetry. Every thing was fubmitted to its influence, not only the arts of ingenuity, which are mechanical, and require manual labour, but thofe alfo which depend folely on the mind. Every thing bore the ftamp of genius. The colours difplayed in natural objects enlivened the works of imagination; and the human paffions animated the defigns of the pencil. Man gave fpirit to matter, and body to fpirit. But it deferves to be particularly obferved that this happened at a time when a paffion for glory animated a nation, great and powerful by its fituation, and the extent of its empire. The fenfe of honour which raifed it in its own eftimation, and which then diftinguifhed it in the eyes of all Europe, was its foul, its inftinct, and fupplied the place of that liberty which had formerly given rife to the arts of genius in the republics of Athens and of Rome, which had revived them in that of Florence, and compelled them to flourifh on the bleak and cloudy borders of the Thames.

What would not genius have effected in France, had it been under the influence of laws only, when its exertions were fo great under the dominion of the moft abfolute of kings? When we fee what energy patriotifm has given to the Englifh, in fpite of the inactivity of their climate, we may judge what it might have produced among the French, where a moft mild temperature of feafon leads a people, naturally fenfible and lively, to invention and enjoyment. We may conceive what its effects would have been in a country, where, as in ancient Greece, are to be found men of active and lively genius, fitted for invention, from being warmed by the moft powerful and enlivening rays of the fun; where there are men ftrong and robuft in a climate, in which even the cold excites to labour; in which we meet with temperate provinces between north and fouth; fea-ports, together with na-

vigable rivers; vaſt plains abounding in corn; hills
loaded with vineyards and fruits of all ſorts; ſalt pits
which may be increaſed at pleaſure; paſtures covered
with horſes; mountains clothed with the fineſt woods;
a country every where peopled with laborious hands,
which are the firſt reſources for ſubſiſtence; the common materials for the arts, and the ſuperfluities of
luxury; in a word, where we meet with the commerce
of Athens, the induſtry of Corinth, the ſoldiery of
Sparta, and the flocks of Arcadia.   With all theſe advantages, which Greece once poſſeſſed, France might
have carried the fine arts to as great a height as that
parent of genius, had ſhe been ſubject to the ſame
laws, and given a ſcope to the ſame exerciſe of reaſon and liberty, by which great men, and the rulers
of powerful nations, are produced.

Next to the ſuperiority of legiſlation among modern nations, to raiſe them to an equality with the ancients in works of genius, there has, perhaps, been
wanting only an improvement in language.   The Romans, who, like the Greeks, knew the influence of
dialect over the manners, had endeavoured to extend
their language with their arms; and they had ſucceeded in cauſing it to be adopted in all places where
they had eſtabliſhed their dominion.   Almoſt all Europe ſpoke Latin, except only a few obſcure men, who
had taken refuge among inacceſſible mountains: but
the invaſion of the barbarians ſoon changed the nature of this language.   With the harmonious ſounds
of an idiom poliſhed by genius and by delicate organs,
theſe people, who were warriors and hunters, blended the rude accents and the coarſe expreſſions they
brought along with them from their gloomy foreſts
and ſevere climate.   There were ſoon as many different languages as forms of governments.   At the revival of letters, theſe languages muſt naturally have
acquired a more ſublime and a more agreeable pronunciation.   This improvement took place but very
ſlowly, becauſe all thoſe who had any talents for writing, diſdaining a language deſtitute of graces, ſtrength,

B O O K XIX.

and amenity, employed in their performances, with greater or lefs propriety, the language of the ancient Romans.

The Italians were the firft who fhook off this humiliating yoke. Their language, with harmony, accent, and quantity, is peculiarly adapted to exprefs all the images of poetry, and convey all the delightful impreffions of mufic. Thefe two arts have confecrated this language to the harmony of found, it being the moft proper to exprefs it.

The French language holds the fuperiority in profe; if it be not the language of the gods, it is, at leaft, that of reafon and of truth. Profe is peculiarly adapted to convince the underftanding in philofophical refearches. It enlightens the minds of thofe whom nature has bleffed with fuperior talents, who feem placed between princes and their fubjects to inftruct and direct mankind. At a period when liberty has no longer her tribunes nor amphitheatres to excite commotions in vaft affemblies of the people, a language which fpreads itfelf in books, which is read in all countries, which ferves as the common interpreter of all other languages, and as the vehicle of all forts of ideas ; a language ennobled, refined, foftened, and above all, fettled by the genius of writers and the polifh of courts, becomes at length univerfally prevailing.

The Englifh language has likewife had its poets and its profe-writers, who have gained it the character of energy and boldnefs, fufficient to render it immortal. May it be learned among all nations who afpire not to be flaves! They will dare to think, act, and govern themfelves. It is not the language of words, but of ideas ; and the Englifh have none but fuch as are ftrong and forcible ; they are the firft who ever made ufe of the expreffion, *the majefty of the people*, and that alone is fufficient to confecrate a language.

The Spaniards have hitherto properly had neither profe nor verfe, though they have a language formed to excel in both. Brilliant and fonorous as pure gold, its pronunciation is grave and regular like the dances of that nation; it is grand and decent, like the manners of ancient chivalry. This language may claim some diftinction, and even acquire a fuperior degree of perfection, whenever there fhall be found in it many fuch writers as Cervantes and Mariana. When its academy fhall have put to filence the inquifition and its univerfities, that language will raife itfelf to great ideas, and to fublime truths, to which it is invited by the natural pride of the people who fpeak it.

Prior to all other living languages is the German, that mother tongue, that original native language of Europe. From thence the Englifh and French too have been formed, by the mixture of the German with the Latin. However, as it feems little calculated to pleafe the eye, or to be pronounced by delicate organs, it has been fpoken only by the people, and has been introduced but of late into books. The few writers that have appeared in it, feemed to fhow that it belonged to a country where the fine arts, poetry, and eloquence, were not deftined to flourifh. But on a fudden, genius has exerted her powers; and originals, in more than one fpecies of poetry, have appeared rather in confiderable numbers fufficient to enter into competition with other nations.

Languages could not be cultivated and refined to a certain degree, but the arts of every kind muft at the fame time aquire an equal degree of perfection; and indeed the monuments of thefe arts have fo much increafed throughout Europe, that the barbarifm of fucceeding people and of future ages will find it difficult entirely to deftroy them.

But as commotions and revolutions are fo natural to mankind, there is only wanting fome glowing genius, fome enthufiaft, to fet the world again in flames. The people of the Eaft, or of the North, are ftill ready to enflave and plunge all Europe into its former darknefs. Would not an irruption of Tartars or Africans into Italy, be fufficient to overturn churches and palaces, to

B O O K confound in one general ruin the idols of religion and
　XIX.　the master-pieces of art? And as we are so much attached to these works of luxury, we should have the
less spirit to defend them. A city, which it has cost
two centuries to decorate, is burnt and ravaged in a
single day. Perhaps, with one stroke of his axe, a
Tartar may dash in pieces the statue of Voltaire, that
Pigalle could not finish within the compass of ten
years; and we still labour for immortality; vain atoms
as we are, impelled, the one by the others, into that
obscurity from whence we came. Ye nations, whether artisans or soldiers, what are ye in the hands of
nature, but the sport of her laws, destined by turns to
set dust in motion, and to reduce the work again to
dust?

But it is by means of the arts that man enjoys his
existence, and survives himself. Ages of ignorance
never emerge from their oblivion. There remains no
more trace of them after their existence, than before
they began to exist. There is no possibility of indi-
cating the place or time of their passage, nor can we
mark on the ground belonging to a barbarous people,
it is here they lived; for they leave not even ruins to
lead us to collect that they have ever existed. It is invention alone that gives man power over matter and
time. The genius of Homer has rendered the Greek
language indelible. Harmony and reason have placed
the eloquence of Cicero above all the sacred orators.
The pontiffs themselves, polished and enlightened by
the information and attractive influence of the arts,
by being admirers and protectors of them, have assisted the human mind to break the chains of superstition. Commerce has hastened the progress of art
by means of the luxury which wealth has diffused.
All the efforts of the mind, and the exertions of manual labour have been united to embellish and to improve the condition of the human species. Industry
and invention, together with the enjoyments procured by the New World, have penetrated as far as the
polar circle, and the fine arts are attempting to rise

ſuperior to the obſtacles of nature even at Peterſburgh.

Orators, poets, hiſtorians, painters, and ſtatuaries,
are made to be the friends of great men. Heralds of
their fame during their life, they are the eternal pre-
ſervers of it when they no longer exiſt. In rendering
their names immortal, they immortaliſe themſelves.
It is by theſe ſeveral orders of men, that the nations
diſtinguiſh themſelves among contemporary nations.
The arts, after having rendered them illuſtrious, alſo
reſtore wealth to them, when they are become indigent. It is ancient Rome which at preſent ſubſiſts
modern Rome. Let the people whom they honour,
both at the preſent and at future times, if they be not
ungrateful, honour them in their turn. Ye nations,
you will paſs away, but their productions will remain.
The torch of genius, which enlightens you, will be
extinguiſhed if you neglect it ; and after having walk-
ed in darkneſs for ſome ages, you will fall in the abyſs
of oblivion, which hath ſwallowed up ſo many nations
that have preceded you, not becauſe they have been
deſtitute of virtues, but of a ſacred voice to celebrate
them.

Beware eſpecially of adding perſecution to indifference. It is certainly enough for a writer to brave the
reſentment of the intolerant magiſtrate, of the fanatic ſpirit, of the ſuſpicious nobleman, and of all ranks
of men proud of their prerogatives, without being alſo expoſed to the ſeverities of government. To inflict upon a philoſopher an infamous or capital puniſhment, is to condemn him to puſillanimity or to ſilence :
it is to ſtifle or to baniſh genius ; it is to put a ſtop to
national information, and to the progreſs of knowledge.

It will be ſaid, that theſe reflections are thoſe of a
man who is thoroughly determined to ſpeak without
circumſpection of perſons and things ; of perſons,
whom one ſcarce dares to addreſs with frankneſs ; of
things, concerning which a writer endowed with a little ſhare of ſenſe neither thinks nor expreſſes himſelf

as the vulgar, and who yet would wifh to efcape profcription.   This may poffibly be the cafe, and wherefore fhould it not be?   Neverthelefs, whatever may
happen, I will never betray the honourable caufe of
liberty.   If I experience nothing but misfortunes from
it, which I neither expect nor dread, fo much the
worfe for the author of thofe misfortunes.   He will be
detefted during life, for one inftant of my exiftence
which he fhall have difpofed of with injuftice and violence.   His name will be handed down to future ages
branded with ignominy; and this cruel fentence would
be independent of the fmall value, or of the little merit of my writings.

Philofophy.   To the train of letters and fine arts philofophy is an-
nexed, which one would imagine ought rather to di-
rect them; but appearing later than they did, can only be confidered as their attendant.   Arts arife from
the very neceffities of mankind in the earlieft ftate of
the human mind.   Letters are the flowers of its youth;
children of the imagination, being themfelves fond of
ornament, they decorate every thing they approach;
and this turn for embellifhment produces what are properly called the fine arts, or the arts of luxury and elegance, which give the polifh to the primary arts of neceffity.   It is then we fee the winged genii of fculpture fluttering over the porticos of architecture; and
the genii of painting entering palaces, reprefenting the
heavens upon a cieling, fketching out upon wool and
filk all the animated fcenes of rural life, and tracing to
the mind upon canvas the ufeful truths of hiftory, as
well as the agreeable chimeras of fable.

When the mind has been employed on the pleafures
of the imagination and of the fenfes, when governments
have arrived to a degree of maturity, reafon arifes and
beftows on the nations a certain turn for reflection;
this is the age of philofophy.   She advances with gradual fteps, and proceeds filently along, announcing
the decline of empires which fhe attempts in vain to
fupport.   She clofed the latter ages of the celebrated
republics of Greece and Rome.   Athens had no phi-

lofophers till the eve of her ruin, which they feemed B O O K to foretel: Cicero and Lucretius did not compofe their XIX. writings on the nature of the gods, and the fyftem of the world, till the confufion of the civil wars arofe, and haftened the deftruction of liberty.

Thales, Anaximander, Anaximenes, Anaxagoras, had however laid the foundations of natural philofophy in the theories of the elements of matter; but the rage of forming fyftems fucceffively fubverted thefe feveral principles. Socrates then appeared, who brought back philofophy to the principles of true wifdom and virtue: it was that alone he loved, practifed, and taught, perfuaded that morality, and not fcience, was conducive to the happinefs of man. Plato, his difciple, though a natural philofopher, and inftructed in the myfteries of nature by his travels into Egypt, afcribed every thing to the foul, and fcarce any thing to nature; he confounded philofophy with theological fpeculations, and the knowledge of the univerfe with the ideas of the divinity. Ariftotle, the difciple of Plato, turned his inquiries lefs on the nature of the Deity, than on that of man and of animals. His natural hiftory has been tranfmitted to pofterity, though it was holden only in moderate eftimation by his contemporaries. Epicurus, who lived nearly about the fame period, revived the atoms of Democritus; a fyftem, which doubtlefs balanced that of the four elements of Ariftotle: and as thefe were the two prevailing fyftems at that time, no improvements were made in natural philofophy. The moral philofophers engaged the attention of the people, who underftood their fyftem better than that of the natural philofopher. They eftablifhed fchools; for as foon as opinions gain a degree of reputation, parties are immediately formed to fupport them.

In thefe circumftances, Greece, agitated by interior commotions, after having been torn with an inteftine war, was fubdued by Macedonia, and its government diffolved by the Romans. Then public calamities turned the hearts and underftandings of men to mora-

lity. Zeno and Democritus, who had been only natural philofophers, became, a confiderable time after
their death, the heads of two fects of moral philofophers, more addicted to theology than phyfics, rather
cafuifts than philofophers; or it might rather be affirm-
ed, that philofophy was given up and confined entirely
to the fophifts. The Romans, who had borrowed every thing from the Greeks, made no difcoveries in the
true fyftem of philofophy. Among the ancients it
made little progrefs; becaufe it was entirely confined
to morality: among the moderns, its firft fteps have
been more fortunate, becaufe they have been guided
by the light of natural knowledge.

We muft not reckon the interval of near a thoufand
years, during which period philofophy, fcience, arts,
and letters, were buried in the ruins of the Roman
empire, among the afhes of ancient Italy, and the duft
of the cloifters. In Afia, their monuments were ftill
preferved, though not attended to; and in Europe,
fome fragments of them remained which fhe did not
know. The world was divided into Chriftian and Mo-
hammedan, and everywhere covered with the blood of
nations: ignorance alone triumphed under the ftandard of the crofs or the crefcent. Before thefe dreaded figns, every knee was bent, every fpirit trembled.

Philofophy continued in a ftate of infancy, pronouncing only the names of God and of the foul: her attention was folely engaged on matters of which fhe
fhould for ever have remained ignorant. Time, argument, and all her application, were wafted on queftions that were, at leaft, idle; queftions, for the moft
part, void of fenfe, not to be defined, and not to be
determined from the nature of their object; and which,
therefore, proved an eternal fource of difputes, fchifms,
fects, hatred, perfecution, and national as well as religious wars.

In the mean time, the Arabs, after their conquefts,
carried away, as it were in triumph, the fpoils of genius and philofophy. Ariftotle fell into their hands,
preferved from the ruins of ancient Greece. Thefe de-

ſtroyers of empires had ſome ſciences of which they B O O K had been the inventors; among which arithmetic is to be numbered. By the knowledge of aſtronomy and geometry, they diſcovered the coaſts of Africa, which they laid waſte, and peopled again; and they were always great proficients in medicine. That ſcience, which has, perhaps, no greater recommendation in its favour, than its affinity with chemiſtry and natural knowledge, rendered them as celebrated as aſtrology, which is another ſupport of empirical impoſition. Avicenna and Averroès, who were equally ſkilled in phyſic, mathematics, and philoſophy, preſerved the tradition of true ſcience by tranſlations and commentaries. But let us imagine what muſt become of Ariſtotle, tranſlated from Greek into Arabic, and after that, from Arabic into Latin, under the hands of monks, who wanted to adapt the philoſophy of paganiſm to the ſyſtems of Moſes and Chriſt. This confuſion of opinions, ideas, and language, ſtopped for a conſiderable time the progreſs of ſcience, and the reducing of it into a regular ſyſtem. The divine overturned the materials brought by the philoſopher, who ſapped the very foundations laid by his rival. However, with a few ſtones from one, and much ſand from the other, ſome wretched architects raiſed a ſtrange Gothic monument, called the philoſophy of the ſchools. Continually amended, renewed, and ſupported, from age to age, by Iriſh or Spaniſh metaphyſicians, it maintained itſelf till about the time of the diſcovery of the New World, which was deſtined to change the face of the Old one.

Light ſprang from the midſt of darkneſs. An Engliſh monk applied himſelf to the practice of chemiſtry, and paving the way for the invention of gunpowder, which was to bring America into ſubjection to Europe, opened the avenues of true ſcience by experimental philoſophy. Thus philoſophy iſſued out of the cloiſter, where ignorance remained. When Boccacio had expoſed the debauched lives of the regular and ſecular clergy, Galileo ventured to form conjectures upon the figure of the earth. Superſtition was alarmed at it;

BOOK XIX. and its clamours, as well as its menaces, were heard: but philofophy tore off the mafk from the monfter, and rent the vail under which truth had been hidden. The weaknefs and falfehood of popular opinions was perceived, on which fociety was then founded; but in order to put an effectual ftop to error, it was neceffary to be acquainted with the laws of nature, and the caufes of her various phenomena: and that was the object philofophy had in view.

As foon as Copernicus was dead, after he had, by the power of reafon, conjectured that the fun was in the centre of our world, Galileo arofe, and confirmed, by the invention of the telefcope, the true fyftem of aftronomy, which either had been unknown, or lay in oblivion ever fince Pythagoras had conceived it. While Gaffendi was reviving the elements of ancient philofophy, or the atoms of Epicurus, Defcartes imagined and combined the elements of a new philofophy, or his ingenious and fubtile vortexes. Almoft about the fame time, Toricelli invented, at Florence, the barometer, to determine the weight of the air; Pafcal meafured the height of the mountains of Auvergne; and Boyle, in England, verified and confirmed the various experiments of both.

Defcartes had taught the art of doubting, in order to undeceive the mind previous to inftruction. The method of doubting propofed by him was the grand inftrument of fcience, and the moft fignal fervice that could be rendered to the human mind under the darknefs which furrounded, and the chains which fettered it. Bayle, by applying that method to opinions the beft authorifed by the fanction of time and power, has made us fenfible of its importance.

Chancellor Bacon, a philofopher, but unfuccefsful at court, as friar Bacon had been in the cloifter, like him the harbinger rather than the eftablifher of the new philofophy, had protefted equally againft the prejudice of the fenfes and the fchools, as againft thofe phantoms he ftyled the idols of the underftanding. He had foretold truths he could not difcover. In conforinity to the refult of his reafoning, which might be confidered as oracular; while experimental philofophy was difcovering facts, rational philofophy was in fearch of caufes. Both contributed to the ftudy of mathematics, which were to guide the efforts of the mind, and infure their fuccefs. It was, in fact, the fcience of algebra applied to geometry, and the application of geometry to natural philofophy, which made Newton conjecture the true fyftem of the world. Upon taking a view of the heavens, he perceived in the fall of bodies to the earth, and in the motions of the heavenly bodies, a certain analogy which implied an univerfal principle, differing from impulfe, the only vifible caufe of all their movements. From the ftudy of aftronomy he next applied himfelf to that of optics, and this led him to conjecture the origin of light; and the experiments which he made in confequence of this inquiry, reduced it into a fyftem.

At the time when Defcartes died, Newton and Leibnitz were but juft born, who were to finifh, correct, and bring to perfection, what he had begun; that is to fay, the eftablifhing of found philofophy. Thefe two men alone greatly contributed to its quick and rapid progrefs. One carried the knowledge of God and the foul as far as reafon could lead it; and the unfuccefsfulnefs of his attempts undeceived the human mind for ever with refpect to fuch falfe fyftems of metaphyfics. The other extended the principles of natural philofophy and the mathematics much further than the genius of many ages had been able to carry them, and pointed out the road to truth. At the fame time, Locke, preceded by Hobbes, a man on whom nature had beftowed an uncommon underftanding, and who had remained obfcure from the very boldnefs of his principles, which ought to have had a contrary effect; Locke, I fay, attacked fcientific prejudices, even into the intrenchments of the fchools: he diffipated all thofe phantoms of the imagination, which Malebranche fuffered to fpring up again, after he had pointed out

their abfurdity, becaufe he did not attack the foundation on which they were fupported.

But we are not to fuppofe that philofophers alone
have difcovered and imagined every thing. It is the
courfe of events which has given a certain tendency to
the actions and thoughts of mankind. A complication
of natural or moral caufes, a gradual improvement in
politics, joined to the progrefs of ftudy and of the fciences, a combination of circumftances which it was as
impoffible to haften as to forefee, muft have contributed to the revolution that has prevailed in the underftandings of men. Among nations, as among individuals, the body and foul act and react alternately upon
each other. Popular opinions infect even philofophers,
and philofophers are guides to the people. Galileo had
afferted, that as the earth turned round the fun, there
muft be Antipodes; and Drake proved the fact, by a
voyage round the world. The church ftyled itfelf univerfal, and the pope called himfelf mafter of the earth:
and yet, more than two-thirds of its inhabitants did
not fo much as know there was any Catholic religion,
and particularly that there was a pope. Europeans,
who have travelled and trafficked everywhere, taught
Europe that one portion of the globe adopted the vifionary opinions of Mohammed, and a ftill larger one
lived in the darknefs of idolatry, or in the total ignorance and unenlightened ftate of atheifm. Thus philofophy extended the empire of human knowledge,
by the difcovery of the errors of fuperftition, and of
the truths of nature.

Italy, whofe impatient genius penetrated through
the obftacles that furrounded it, was the firft that
founded an academy of natural philofophy. France
and England, who were to aggrandize themfelves even
by their competition, raifed at one time two everlafting monuments to the improvement of philofophy:
two academies, from whence all the learned men of
Europe derive their information, and in which they
depofit all their ftores of knowledge. From hence

have been brought to light a great number of the myf- terious points in nature; experiments, phenomena, dif- coveries in the arts and fciences, the fecrets of electri- city, and the caufes of the Aurora Borealis. Hence have proceeded the inftruments and means of purify- ing air on board of fhips, for making fea-water fit to be drunk, for determining the figure of the earth, and afcertaining the longitudes; for improving agriculture, and for producing more grain, with lefs feed and lefs labour.

Ariftotle had reigned ten centuries in all the fchools of Europe; and the Chriftians, after lofing the gui- dance of reafon, were able to recover it again only by following his footfteps. Their implicit attachment to that philofopher had, for a confiderable time, caufed them to err, in blindly following him through the darknefs of theological doctrines. But at length Def- cartes pointed out the way, and Newton fupplied the power of extricating them out of that labyrinth. Doubt had diffipated prejudices, and the method of analyfis had found out the truth. After the two Ba- cons, Galileo, Defcartes, Hobbes, Locke, and Bayle, Leibnitz and Newton, after the memoirs of the aca- demies of Florence and Leipfic, of Paris and London, there ftill remained a great work to be compofed, in order to perpetuate the fciences and philofophy. This work hath now appeared.

This book, which contains all the errors and all the truths that have iffued from the human mind, from the doctrines of theology to the fpeculations on infects; which contains an account of every work of the hands of men from a fhip to a pin; this repofitory of the in- telligence of all nations, which would have been more perfect, had it not been executed in the midft of all kinds of perfecutions and of obftacles; this repofitory will, in future ages, characterize that of philofophy, which, after fo many advantages procured to mankind, ought to be confidered as a divinity on earth. It is fhe who unites, enlightens, aids, and comforts mankind. She beftows every thing upon them, without exacting

any worſhip in return. She requires of them, not the
ſacrifice of their paſſions, but a reaſonable, uſeful, and
moderate exerciſe of all their faculties. Daughter of
Nature, diſpenſer of her gifts, interpreter of her rights,
ſhe conſecrates her intelligence and her labour to the
uſe of man. She renders him better, that he may be
happier. She deteſts only tyranny and impoſture, becauſe they oppreſs mankind. She does not deſire to
rule; but ſhe exacts of ſuch as govern, to conſider
public happineſs as the only ſource of their enjoyment.
She avoids conteſts, and the name of ſects; but ſhe
tolerates them all. The blind and the wicked calumniate her; the former are afraid of perceiving their
errors, and the latter of having them detected. Ungrateful children, who rebel againſt a tender mother,
when ſhe wiſhes to free them from their errors and
vices, which occaſion the calamities of mankind!

Light, however, ſpreads inſenſibly over a more extenſive horizon. Literature has formed a kind of empire which prepares the way for making Europe be
conſidered as one ſingle republican power. In truth,
if philoſophy be ever enabled to inſinuate itſelf into
the minds of ſovereigns, or their miniſters, the ſyſtem
of politics will be improved, and rendered ſimple. Humanity will be more regarded in all plans; the public
good will enter into negotiations, not merely as an ex-
preſſion, but as an object of utility even to kings.

Printing has already made ſuch a progreſs, that it
can never be put a ſtop to in any ſtate, without lowering the people, in order to advance the authority of
government. Books enlighten the body of the people, humanize the great, are the delight of the leiſure
hours of the rich, and inform all the claſſes of ſociety.
The ſciences bring to perfection the different branches
of political economy. Even the errors of ſyſtematical
perſons are diſpelled by the productions of the preſs,
becauſe reaſoning and diſcuſſion try them by the teſt
of truth.

An intercourſe of knowledge is become neceſſary
for induſtry, and literature alone maintains that com-

munication. The reading of a voyage round the B O O K world has, perhaps, occafioned more attempts of that XIX. kind; for intereft alone cannot find the means of enterprife. At prefent nothing can be cultivated without fome ftudy, or without the knowledge that has been handed down and diffufed by reading. Princes themfelves have not recovered their rights from the ufurpations of the clergy, but by the affiftance of that knowledge which has undeceived the people with refpect to the abufes of all fpiritual power.

But it would be the greateft folly of the human mind to have employed all its powers to increafe the authority of kings, and to break the feveral chains that held it in fubjection, in order to become the flave of defpotifm. The fame courage that religion infpires to withdraw confcience from the tyranny exercifed over opinion, the honeft man, the citizen, and friend of the people ought to maintain, to free the nations from the tyranny of fuch powers as confpire againft the liberty of mankind. Woe to that ftate in which there is not to be found one fingle defender of the public rights of the nation. The kingdom, with all its riches, its trade, its nobles, and its citizens, muft foon fall into unavoidable anarchy. It is the laws that are to fave a nation from deftruction, and the freedom of writing is to fupport and preferve laws. But what is the foundation and bulwark of the laws? It is morality.

Attempts have too long been made to degrade man. Morals. His detractors have made a monfter of him. In their fpleen they have loaded him with outrages; the guilty fatisfaction of lowering the human fpecies hath alone conducted their gloomy pencils. Who art thou then who dareft thus to infult thy fellow-creatures? What place gave thee birth? Is it from the inmoft receffes of thy heart that thou haft poured forth fo many blafphemies? If thy pride had been lefs infatuated, or thy difpofition lefs ferocious and barbarous, thou wouldft have feen only in man a being always feeble, often feduced by error, fometimes carried away by imagination, but produced from the hands of nature with virtuous propensities.

Man is born with the seeds of virtue, although he be not born virtuous. He doth not attain to this sublime state till after he hath studied himself, till after he hath become acquainted with his duties, and contracted the habit of fulfilling them. The science which leads to that high degree of perfection is called morality. It is the rule of actions, and, if one may be allowed the expression, the art of virtue. Encouragements and praises are due for all the labours undertaken to remove the calamities which surround us, to increase the number of our enjoyments, to embellish the dream of our life, to exalt, to improve, and to illustrate our species. Eternal blessings upon those who by their studies and by their genius have procured any of these advantages to human nature! But the first crown will be for that wise man whose affecting and enlightened writings will have had a more noble aim, that of making us better.

The hope of obtaining so great a glory hath given rise to numberless productions. What a variety of useless and even pernicious books! They are in general the work of priests and their disciples, who, not choosing to see that religion should consider men only in the relation they stand in to the Divinity, made it necessary to look for another ground for the relations they bear to one another. If there be an universal system of morality, it cannot be the effect of a particular cause. It has been the same in past ages, and it will continue the same in future times: it cannot then be grounded on religious opinions, which, ever since the beginning of the world, and from one pole to the other, have continually varied. Greece had vicious deities, the Romans had them likewise: the senseless worshipper of the Fetiches adores rather a devil than a god. Every people made gods for themselves, and gave them such attributes as they chose: to some they ascribed goodness, to others cruelty, to some immorality, and to others the greatest sanctity and severity of

manners. One would imagine, that every nation in-B O O K
tended to deify its own paffions and opinions. Not- XIX.
withftanding this diverfity in religious fyftems and
modes of worfhip, all nations have perceived that
men ought to be juft ; they have all honoured as virtues, goodnefs, pity, friendfhip, fidelity, paternal tendernefs, filial refpect, fincerity, gratitude, patriotifm ;
in a word, all thofe fentiments which may be confidered as fo many ties adapted to unite men more
clofely to one another. The origin of that uniformity
of judgment, fo conftant, fo general, ought not then
to be looked for in the midft of contradictory and
tranfient opinions. If the minifters of religion have
appeared to think otherwife, it is becaufe by their fyftem they were enabled to regulate all the actions of
mankind, to difpofe of their fortunes and command
their wills, and to fecure to themfelves, in the name
of Heaven, the attributary government of the world.

Their empire was fo abfolute, that they had fucceeded in eftablifhing that barbarous fyftem of morality, which placed the only pleafures that make life
fupportable in the rank of the greateft crimes ; an abject morality, which impofed the obligation of being
pleafed with humiliation and fhame ; an extravagant
morality, which threatened with the fame punifhments
both the foibles of love and the moft atrocious actions ; a fuperftitious morality, which enjoined to murder, without compaffion, all thofe who fwerved from
the prevailing opinions ; a puerile morality, which
founded the moft effential duties upon tales equally
difgufting and ridiculous ; an interefted morality,
which admitted no other virtues than thofe which
were ufeful to priefthood, nor no other crimes than
thofe which were contrary to it. If priefts had only
encouraged men to obferve natural morality by the
hope or the fear of future rewards and punifhments,
they would have deferved well of fociety ; but in endeavouring to fupport by violence ufeful tenets, which
had only been introduced by the mild way of perfua-

fion, they have removed the vail which concealed the
depth of their ambition : the maſk is fallen off.

It is more than two thouſand years ſince Socrates,
ſpreading out a vail above our heads, had declared,
that nothing of what was paſſing beyond that vail
concerned us ; and that the actions of men were not
good becauſe they were pleaſing to the gods, but that
they were pleaſing to the gods becauſe they were
good : a principle which ſeparated morality from religion.

Accordingly, at the tribunal of philoſophy and reaſon, morality is a ſcience, the object of which is the
preſervation and common happineſs of the human ſpecies. To this double end all its rules ought to be referred. Their natural, conſtant, and eternal principle
is in man himſelf, and in a reſemblance there is in the
general organization of men, which includes a ſimilarity of wants, of pleaſures and pains, of force and weakneſs ; a ſimilarity from whence ariſes the neceſſity of
ſociety, or of a common oppoſition againſt ſuch dangers as are equally incident to each individual, which
proceeds from nature herſelf, and threatens man on all
ſides. Such is the origin of particular connections and
domeſtic virtues : ſuch is the origin of general duties
and of public virtues : ſuch is the ſource of the notion
of perſonal and public utility, the ſource of all compacts between individuals, and of all laws.

There is, properly ſpeaking, only one virtue, which
is juſtice, and only one duty, to make one's ſelf happy.
The virtuous man is he who hath the moſt exact notions of juſtice and happineſs, and whoſe conduct con-
forms moſt rigorouſly to them. There are two tribunals, that of nature, and that of the laws.

The law chaſtiſes crimes, nature chaſtiſes vices. The
law preſents the gallows to the aſſaſſin, nature preſents
dropſy or conſumption to intemperance.

Several writers have endeavoured to trace the firſt
principles of morality in the ſentiments of friendſhip,
tenderneſs, compaſſion, honour, and benevolence, be-

cause they found them engraven on the human heart. But did they not also find there hatred, jealousy, revenge, pride, and the love of dominion? For what reason, therefore, have they founded morality on the former principles rather than on the latter? It is because they have underftood that the former were of general advantage to fociety, and the others fatal to it. Thofe philofophers have perceived the neceffity of morality, they have conceived what it ought to be, but have not difcovered its leading and fundamental principle. The very fentiments, indeed, which they adopt as the ground-work of morality, becaufe they appear to be ferviceable to the common good, if left to themfelves, would be very prejudicial to it. How can we determine to punifh the guilty, if we liften only to the pleas of compaffion? How fhall we guard againft partiality, if we confult only the dictates of friendfhip? How fhall we avoid being favourable to idlenefs, if we attend only to the fentiments of benevolence? All thefe virtues have their limits, beyond which they degenerate into vices; and thofe limits are fettled by the invariable rules of effential juftice, or, which is the fame thing, by the common interefts of men united together in fociety, and the conftant object of that union.

Is it on its own account that valour is ranked among the number of virtues? No; it is on account of the fervice it is of to fociety. This is evident from the circumftance of its being punifhed as a crime in a man who makes ufe of it to difturb the public peace. Wherefore is drunkennefs a vice? Becaufe every man is bound to contribute to the common good; and, to fulfil that obligation, he muft maintain the free exercife of his faculties. Wherefore are certain actions more blameable in a magiftrate or general than in a private man? Becaufe greater inconveniencies refult from them to fociety.

The obligations of the man feparated from fociety are unknown to me, fince I can neither perceive the fource nor the end of them. As he lives by himfelf, he is certainly at liberty to live for himfelf alone. No being has a right to require fuccours from him which he does not implore for himfelf. It is quite the contrary with refpect to a perfon who lives in the focial ftate. He is nothing by himfelf, and is fupported only by what furrounds him. His poffeffions, his enjoyments, his powers, and even his own exiftence, all belong entirely to the body of the ftate : he owes them all to the body politic, of which he is a member.

The misfortunes of fociety become thofe of the citizen ; he runs the rifk of being crufhed, whatever part of the edifice may fall down. If he fhould commit an injuftice, he is threatened with a fimilar one. If he fhould give himfelf up to crimes, others may become criminal to his prejudice. He muft therefore tend conftantly to the general good, fince it is upon this profperity that his own depends.

If one fingle individual fhould attend only to his intereft, without any concern for thofe of the public ; if he fhould exempt himfelf from the common duty, under pretence that the actions of one individual cannot have a determined influence upon the general order, other perfons will alfo be defirous of indulging their perfonal propenfities. Then all the members of the republic will become alternately executioners and victims. Every one will commit and receive injuries, every one will rob and be robbed, every one will ftrike and receive a blow. A ftate of warfare will prevail between all forts of individuals. The ftate will be ruined, and the citizens will be ruined with the ftate.

The firft men who collected themfelves into fociety were undoubtedly not immediately fenfible of the whole of thefe truths. The idea of their ftrength being moft prevalent in them, they were probably defirous of obtaining every thing by the exertion of it. Repeated calamities warned them in procefs of time of the neceffity of forming conventions. Reciprocal obligations increafed in proportion as the neceffity of them was felt : thus it is that duty began with fociety.

Duty may therefore be defined to be the rigid obli-

gation of doing whatever is fuitable to fociety. It in-BOOK
cludes the practice of all the virtues, fince there is not XIX.
one of them which is not ufeful to a civilized body;
and it excludes all the vices, becaufe there is not one
which is not prejudicial to it.

It would be reafoning pitifully to imagine, with
fome corrupt perfons, that men have a right to defpife all the virtues, under pretence that they are only inftitutions of convenience. Wretch that thou art,
wouldft thou live in a fociety which cannot fubfift without them; wouldft thou enjoy the advantages which
refult from them, and wouldft thou think thyfelf dif-
penfed from practifing, or even from holding them in
eftimation? What could poffibly be the object of them
if they were not connected with man? Would this
great name have been given to acts that were merely
barren? On the contrary, it is their neceffity which
conftitutes their effence and their merit. Let me once
more repeat, that all morality confifts in the maintenance of order. Its principles are fteady and uniform,
but the application of them varies fometimes according to the climate, and to the local or political fituation of the people. Polygamy is in general more natural to hot than to cold climates. Circumftances,
however, of the times, in oppofition to the rule of the
climate, may order monogamy in one ifland of Africa,
and permit polygamy in Kamtfchatka, if one be a
means of putting a ftop to the excefs of population at
Madagafcar, and the other of haftening its progrefs
upon the coafts of the frozen fea. But nothing can
authorife adultery and fornication in thofe two zones,
when conventions have eftablifhed the laws of marriage or of property in the ufe of women.

It is the fame thing with refpect to all the lands
and to property. What would be a robbery in a ftate,
where property is juftly diftributed, becomes fubfiftence for life in a ftate where property is in common.
Thus it is that theft and adultery were not permitted
at Sparta; but the public right allowed what would
be confidered elfewhere as theft and adultery. It was

BOOK XIX.

not the wife or the property of another perſon that was then-taken, but the wife and the property of all, when the laws granted as a reward to dexterity every advantage it could procure to itſelf.

It is everywhere known what is juſt and unjuſt; but the ſame ideas are not univerſally attached to the ſame actions. In hot countries, where the climate requires no clothing, modeſty is not offended by nakedneſs; but the abuſe, whatever it may be, of the intercourſe between the ſexes, and premature attempts upon virginity, are crimes which muſt diſguſt. In India, where every thing conſpires to make a virtue even of the act itſelf of generation, it is a cruelty to put the cow to death which nouriſhes man with her milk, and to deſtroy thoſe animals whoſe life is not prejudicial, nor their death uſeful, to the human ſpecies. The Iroquois, or the Huron, who kill their father with a ſtroke of a club, rather than expoſe him to periſh of hunger, or upon the pile of the enemy, think they do an act of filial piety in obeying the laſt wiſhes of their parent, who aſks for death from them as a favour. The means the moſt oppoſite in appearance tend all equally to the ſame end, the maintenance and the proſperity of the body politic.

Such is that univerſal morality, which, being inherent in the nature of man, is alſo inherent in the nature of ſocieties; that morality which may vary only in its application, but never in its eſſence; that morality, in a word, to which all the laws muſt refer and be ſubordinate. According to this common rule of all our public and private actions, let us examine whether there ever were, or ever can be, good morals in Europe.

We live under the influence of three codes, the natural, the civil, and the religious code. It is evident, that as long as theſe three ſorts of legiſlations ſhall be contradictory to each other, it will be impoſſible to be virtuous. It will ſometimes be neceſſary to trample upon nature in order to obey ſocial inſtitutions, and to counteract ſocial inſtitutions to conform to the precepts of religion. The confequence of this will be, that while we are alternately infringing upon thefe feveral authorities, we fhall refpect neither of them, and that we fhall neither be men, nor citizens, nor pious perfons.

Good morals would therefore require previous reform, which fhould reduce thefe codes to identity. Religion ought neither to forbid nor to prefcribe any thing to us but what is prefcribed or forbidden by the civil law; and the civil and religious laws ought to model themfelves upon natural law, which hath been, is, and will always be the ftrongeft. From whence it appears, that a true legiflator hath not yet exifted; that it was neither Mofes, nor Solon, nor Numa, nor Mohammed, nor even Confucius; that it is not only in Athens, but alfo over all the globe, that the beft legiflation they could receive hath been given to man, not the beft which could have been given to them; that in confidering only morality, mankind would perhaps be lefs diftant from happinefs had they remained in the fimple and innocent ftate of fome favages; for nothing is fo difficult as to eradicate inveterate and fanctified prejudice. For the architect who draws the plan of a great edifice, an even area is better than one covered with bad materials, heaped upon one another without method and without plan, and unfortunately connected together by the moft durable cements of time, of cuftom, and of the authority of fovereigns and of priefts. Then the wife man advances in his work only with timidity; he is expofed to greater rifks, and lofes more time in demolifhing than in conftructing.

Since the invafion of the barbarians in this part of the world, almoft all governments have had no other foundation than the intereft of one fingle man, or of a fingle corporate body, to the prejudice of fociety in general. Founded upon conqueft, the effect of fuperior ftrength, they have only varied in the mode of keeping the people in fubjection. At firft war made victims of them, devoted either to the fword of their

enemies or to that of their masters. How many ages
have passed away in scenes of blood and in the carnage of nations, that is to say, in the distribution of
empires, before the terms of peace had deified that
state of intestine war, which is called society or government?

When the feudal government had for ever excluded
those who tilled the ground from the right of posses-
sing it; when, by a sacrilegious collusion between the
altar and the throne, the authority of God had been
enforced by that of the sword; what effect had the
morality of the gospel, but to authorise tyranny by the
doctrine of passive obedience, but to confirm slavery
by a contempt of the sciences; in a word, to add to
the terror of the great, that of evil spirits? And what
were morals with such laws? What they are at present
in Poland, where the people, being without lands and
without arms, are left to be massacred by the Russians,
or enlisted by the Prussians, and having neither courage
nor sentiment, think it is sufficient if they are Christians, and remain neutral between their neighbours
and their lords palatine.

To a similar state of anarchy wherein morals had
no distinguishing character, nor any degree of stability, succeeded the epidemic fury of the holy wars,
by which nations were corrupted and degraded, by
communicating to each other the contagion of vices
with that of fanaticism. Morals were changed with
the change of climate. All the passions were inflamed and heightened between the tombs of Jesus and
Mohammed. From Palestine was imported a principle of luxury and ostentation, an inordinate taste for
the spices of the East, a romantic spirit which civilized
the nobility, without rendering the people more happy, consequently more virtuous: for if there be no
happiness without virtue, virtue, on the other hand,
will never support itself without a fund of happiness.

About two centuries after Europe had been depopulated by Asiatic expeditions, its transmigration in
America happened. This revolution introduced an

universal confusion, and blended the vices and productions of every climate with our own.   Neither
was any improvement made in the science of morality, because men were then destroyed through avarice,
instead of being massacred on account of religion.
Those nations which had made the largest acquisitions
in the New World, seemed to acquire at the same
time all the stupidity, ferociousness, and ignorance of
the Old.   They became the channel through which
the vices and diseases of their country were communicated.   They were poor and dirty in the midst of
their wealth, debauched though surrounded with temples and with priests; they were idle and superstitious
with all the sources of commerce, and the facility of
acquiring information.   But the love of riches likewise corrupted all other nations.

Whether it be war or commerce which introduces
great riches into a state, they soon become the object
of public ambition.   At first men of the greatest power seize upon them : and as riches come into the hands
of those who have the management of public affairs,
wealth is confounded with honour in the minds of the
people ; and the virtuous citizen, who aspired to employments only for the sake of glory, aspires, without
knowing it, to honour for the sake of advantage.
Neither lands nor treasure, any more than conquests,
are obtained with any other view but to enjoy them ;
and riches are enjoyed only for pleasure and the ostentation of luxury.   Under these different ideas, they
equally corrupt the citizen who possesses them, and the
people who are seduced by their attraction.   As soon
as men labour only from a motive of gain, and not
from a regard to their duty, the most advantageous si-
tuations are preferred to the most honourable.   It is
then we see the honour of a profession diverted, ob-
scured, and lost in the paths that lead to wealth.

To the advantage of that false consideration at which
riches arrive, are to be added the natural conveniences
of opulence, a fresh source of corruption.   The man
who is in a public situation is desirous of having peo-

ple about him; the honours he receives in public are not sufficient for him; he wants admirers, either of his talents, his luxury, or his profusion. If riches be the means of corruption, by leading to honours, how much more will they be so, by diffusing a taste for pleasure! Misery offers its chastity to sale, and idleness its liberty; the prince sets the magistracy up to auction, and the magistrates set a price upon justice: the court sells employments, and placemen sell the people to the prince, who sells them again to the neighbouring powers, either in treaties of war, or subsidy; of peace, or exchange of territory. But in this sordid traffic, introduced by the love of wealth, the most evident alteration is that which it makes in the morals of women.

There is no vice which owes its origin to so many other vices, and which produces a greater number of them, than the incontinence of a sex, whose true attendant, and most beautiful ornament, is bashfulness and modesty.

I do not understand by incontinence, the promiscuous of women; the wise Cato advised it in his republic; nor do I mean a plurality of them, which is the result of the ardent and voluptuous countries of the East; neither do I mean the liberty, whether indefinite or limited, which custom in different countries, grants to the sex, of yielding to the desires of several men. This, among some people, is one of the duties of hospitality, among others, a means of improving the human race, and in other places an offering made to the gods, an act of piety consecrated by religion. I call incontinence, all intercourse between the two sexes forbidden by the laws of the state.

Why should this misdemeanour, so pardonable in itself, this action of so little consequence in its nature, so much confined in the gratification, have so pernicious an influence upon the morals of women? This is, I believe, a consequence of the importance we have attached to it. What will be the restraint of a woman, dishonoured in her own eyes, and in those of her fellow-citizens? What support will other virtues find in her soul, when nothing can aggravate her shame? The contempt of public opinion, one of the greatest efforts of wisdom, is seldom separated, in a feeble and timid mind, from the contempt of one's self. This degree of heroism cannot exist with a consciousness of vice. The woman who no longer respects herself, soon becomes insensible to censure and to praise; and without standing in awe of these two respectable phantoms, I know not what will be the rule of her conduct. There remains nothing but the rage of voluptuousness, that can indemnify her for the sacrifice she has made. This she feels, and this she persuades herself of; and thus, free from the constraint of the public consideration, she gives herself up to it without reserve.

Women take their resolution with much more difficulty than men, but when once they have taken it, they are much more determined. A woman never blushes when once she has ceased to blush. What will she not trample upon, when she hath triumphed over virtue? What idea can she have of that dignity, that decency, and that delicacy of sentiment, which, in the days of her innocence, directed and dictated her conversation, constituted her behaviour, and directed her dress? These will be considered only as childishness, as pusillanimity, or as the little intrigue of a pretended innocent person, who has parents to satisfy, and a husband to deceive; but a change of times brings on a change of manners.

To whatever degree of perversity she may have attained, it will not lead her to great enormities. Her weakness deprives her of the boldness to commit atrocious acts; but her habitual hypocrisy, if she hath not entirely thrown off the mask, will cast a tint of falsity upon her whole character. Those things which a man dares to attempt by force, she will attempt and obtain by artifice. A corrupt woman propagates corruption. She propagates it by bad example, by insidious counsels, and sometimes by ridicule. She hath

begun by coquetry, which was addreſſed to all men ;
ſhe hath continued by gallantry, ſo volatile in its propenſities, that it is more eaſy to find a woman who
hath never had any paſſions, than to find one who
hath only been once impaſſioned ; and at laſt ſhe
reckons as many lovers as ſhe hath acquaintances,
whom ſhe recals, expels, and recals again, according
to the want ſhe hath of them, and to the nature of
intrigues of all kinds into which ſhe hath plunged herſelf. This is what ſhe means by having known how
to enjoy her beſt years, and to avail herſelf of her
charms. It was one of theſe women, who had entered into the depths of the art, and who declared upon
her death-bed, that ſhe regretted only the pains ſhe
had taken to deceive the men ; and that the moſt honeſt among them were the greateſt dupes.

Under the influence of ſuch manners, conjugal love
is diſdained, and that contempt weakens the ſentiment
of maternal tenderneſs, if it doth not even extinguiſh it.
The moſt ſacred and the moſt pleaſing duties become
troubleſome ; and when they have been neglected or
broken, nature never renews them. The woman who
ſuffers any man but her huſband to approach her, hath
no more regard for her family, and can be no more
reſpected by them. The ties of blood are ſlackened ;
births become uncertain ; and the ſon knows no more
his father, nor the father his ſon.

I will therefore maintain it, that connections of gallantry complete the depravity of manners, and indicate it more ſtrongly than public proſtitution. Religion is extinct, when the prieſt leads a ſcandalous life ;
in the ſame manner virtue hath no aſylum, when the
ſanctuary of marriage is profaned. Baſhfulneſs is under the protection of the timid ſex. Who is it that
ſhall bluſh, when a woman doth not ? It is not proſtitution which multiplies acts of adultery ; it is gallantry which extends proſtitution. The ancient mo-
raliſts, who pitied the unfortunate victims of liber-
tiniſm, condemned without mercy the infidelity of
married women ; and not without reaſon. If we were

to throw all the shame of vice upon the class of common women, other women would not fail soon to take honour to themselves from a limited intercourse, although it would be so much more criminal, as it was more voluntary and more illicit. The honest and virtuous women will no more be distinguished from the women of strong passions ; a frivolous distinction will be established between the woman of gallantry and the courtezan ; between gratuitous vice, and vice reduced by misery to the necessity of requiring a stipend ; and these subtleties will betray a system of depravation. O fortunate and rude times of our forefathers, when there were none but virtuous or bad women ; when all who were not virtuous were corrupted ; and where an established system of vice was not excused by persevering in it.

But finally, what is the source of those delicate passions, formed by the mind, by sentiment, and by sympathy of character? the manner in which these passions always terminate, shows plainly, that those fine expressions are only employed to shorten the defence and justify the defeat. Equally at the service of reserved and dissolute women, they are become almost ridiculous.

What is the result of this national gallantry? A premature libertinism, which ruins the health of young men before they are arrived to maturity, and destroys the beauty of the women in the prime of their life ; a race of men without information, without strength, and without courage ; incapable of serving their country ; magistrates destitute of dignity and of principles; a preference of wit to good sense ; of pleasures to duty ; of politeness to the feelings of humanity ; of the art of pleasing, to talents, to virtue ; men absorbed in self-consideration, substituted to men who are serviceable ; offers without reality ; innumerable acquaintances, and no friends ; mistresses, and no wives ; lovers, and no husbands ; separations and divorces ; children without education ; fortunes in disorder ; jealous

B O O K mothers, and hyfterical women; nervous diforders;
XIX. peevifh old age, and premature death.

It is with difficulty that women of gallantry efcape
the dangers of the critical period of life. The vexation at the neglect which threatens them, completes
the depravation of the blood and of the humours, at
a time when the calm which arifes from confcioufnefs
of an honeft life might be falutary. It is dreadful
to feek in vain, in one's felf, the confolations of virtue, when the calamities of nature furround us.

Let us therefore, talk no more of morality among
modern nations; and if we wifh to difcover the caufe of
this degradation, let us fearch for it in its true principle.

Gold doth not become the idol of a people, and virtue
does not fall into contempt, unlefs the bad conftitution of the government leads on to fuch a corruption.
Unfortunately it will always have this effect, if the government be fo conftituted, that the temporary intereft of a fingle perfon, or of a fmall number, can with
impunity prevail over the common and invariable intereft of the whole. It will always produce this corruption, if thofe in whofe hands authority is lodged
can make an arbitrary ufe of it; can place themfelves
above the reach of juftice: can make their power adminifter to plundering, and their plunder to the continuance of abufes occafioned by their power. Good
laws are maintained by good morals, but good morals
are eftablifhed by good laws. Men are what government makes them. To modify them, it is always
armed with an irrefiftible force, that of public opinion; and the government will always make ufe of
corruption, when by its nature it is itfelf corrupt. In
a word, the nations of Europe will have good morals
when they have good governments. Let us conclude.
But let us previoufly give a rapid fketch of the good
and of the evil produced by the difcovery of the Eaft
and Weft Indies.

Reflections   This great event hath improved the conftruction of
upon the
good and   fhips, navigation, geography, aftronomy, medicine, na-

tural hiftory, and fome other branches of knowledge; and thefe advantages have not been attended with any known inconvenience.

B O O K XIX.

the evil which the difcovery of the New World hath done to Europe.

It hath procured to fome empires vaft domains, which have given fplendour, power, and wealth, to the ftates which have founded them. But what expences have not been lavifhed to clear, to govern, or to defend thefe diftant poffeffions? When thefe colonies fhall have acquired that degree of culture, knowledge, and population, which is fuitable for them, will they not detach themfelves from a country which hath founded its fplendour upon their profperity? We know not at what period this revolution will happen, but it muft certainly take place.

Europe is indebted to the New World for a few conveniencies and a few luxuries. But before thefe enjoyments were obtained, were we lefs healthy, lefs robuft, lefs intelligent, or lefs happy? Are thefe frivolous advantages, fo cruelly obtained, fo unequally diftributed, and fo obftinately difputed, worth one drop of that blood which hath been fpilt, and which will ftill be fpilt for them? Are they to be compared to the life of a fingle man? And yet, how many lives have hitherto been deftroyed, how many are at prefent devoted, and how many will not hereafter be facrificed, to fupply chimerical wants, which we fhall never be perfuaded to get rid of, either by authority or reafon.

The voyages undertaken upon all the feas have weakened the principle of national pride; they have infpired civil and religious toleration; they have revived the ties of original fraternity; have infpired the true principles of an univerfal fyftem of morality, founded upon the identity of wants, of calamities, of pleafures, and of the analogies common to mankind under every latitude; they have induced the practice of benevolence towards every individual who appeals to it, whatever his manners, his country, his laws, and his religion may be. But at the fame time, the minds of men have been turned to lucrative fpeculation. The

B O O K fentiment of glory hath been weakened ; riches have
XIX.   been preferred to fame ; and every thing which tended to the elevation of mankind hath vifibly inclined to
decay.

The New World hath multiplied fpecie amongft us.
An earneft defire of obtaining it hath occafioned much
exertion upon the face of the globe ; but exertion is
not happinefs. Whofe deftiny hath been meliorated
by gold and filver ? Do not the nations who dig them
from the bowels of the earth languifh in ignorance,
fuperftition, and pride, and all thofe vices which it is
moft difficult to eradicate, when they have taken deep
root ? Have they not loft their agriculture and their
manufactures ? Their exiftence, is it not precarious ?
If an induftrious people, proprietors of a fertile foil,
fhould one day reprefent to the other people that they
have too long carried on a lofing trade with them, and
that they will no longer give the thing for the reprefentation, would not this fumptuary law be a fentence
of death againft that region, which hath none but riches
of convention, unlefs the latter, driven by defpair,
fhould fhut up its mines, in order to open furrows in
the ground ?

The other powers of Europe may perhaps have acquired no greater advantage from the treafures of A-
merica. If the repartition of them hath been equal
or proportionate between them, neither of them have
decreafed in opulence or increafed in ftrength. The
analogies which exifted in ancient times ftill exift. Let
us fuppofe that fome nations fhould have acquired a
greater quantity of metals than the rival nations, they
will either bury them, or throw them into circulation.
In the firft inftance, this is nothing more than the barren property of a fuperfluous mafs of gold. In the fecond, they will acquire only a temporary fuperiority,
becaufe in a fhort fpace of time all vendible commodities will bear a price proportionate to the abundance
of the figns which reprefent them.

Such are then the evils attached even to the advantages which we owe to the difcovery of the Eaft and

West Indies.   But how many calamities, which can- B O O K
not be compenfated, have not attended the conqueft XIX.
of thefe regions?

Have the devaftators of them loft nothing by depopulating them for a long feries of ages?   If all the
blood that hath been fpilt in thofe countries had been
collected into one common refervoir, if the dead bodies had been heaped up in the fame plain, would not
the blood and the carcafes of the Europeans have occupied a great fpace in it?   Hath it been poffible fpeedily to fill up the void which thefe emigrants had left
in their native land, infected with a fhameful and cruel
poifon from the New World, which attacks even the
fources of reproduction?

Since the bold attempts of Columbus and of Gama,
a fpirit of fanaticifm, till then unknown, hath been
eftablifhed in our countries, which is that of making
difcoveries.   We have traverfed, and ftill continue to
traverfe, all the climates from one pole to another, in
order to difcover fome continents to invade, fome
iflands to ravage, and fome people to fpoil, to fubdue,
and to maffacre.   Would not the perfon who fhould
put an end to this frenzy deferve to be reckoned a-
mong the benefactors of mankind?

The fedentary life is the only favourable one to population.   The man who travels leaves no pofterity
behind him.   The land forces have created a multitude of perfons devoted to celibacy.   The naval forces
have almoft doubled them, with this difference, that
the latter are deftroyed by illneffes on board of fhip,
by fhipwrecks, by fatigue, by bad food, and by the
change of climate.   A foldier may return to fome of
the profeffions ufeful to fociety.   A failor is a failor for
ever.   When he is difcharged from the fervice, he is
of no further ufe to his country, which is under the
neceffity of providing an hofpital for him.

Long voyages have introduced a new fpecies of a-
nomalous favages: I mean thofe men who traverfe fo
many countries, and who in the end belong to none;
who take wives wherever they find them, and that

only from motives of animal neceffity; thofe amphibious creatures, who live upon the furface of the waters; who come on fhore only for a moment; to whom every habitable latitude is equal; who have, in reality, neither fathers, mothers, children, brothers, relations, friends, nor fellow-citizens; in whom the moft pleafing and the moft facred ties are extinct; who quit their country without regret; who never return to it without being impatient of going out again; and to whom the habit of living upon a dreadful element gives a character of ferocioufnefs. Their probity is not proof againft the croffing of the line; and they acquire riches in exchange for their virtue and their health.

This infatiable thirft of gold hath given birth to the moft infamous and the moft atrocious of all traffics, that of flaves. Crimes againft nature are fpoken of, and yet this is not inftanced as the moft execrable of them. Moft of the European nations have been ftained with it, and a bafe motive of intereft hath extinguifhed in their hearts all the fentiments due to our fellow-creatures. But, without thefe affiftances, thefe countries, the acquifition of which hath coft fo dear, would ftill be uncultivated. Let them then remain fallow, if, in order to cultivate them, it be neceffary that man fhould be reduced to the condition of the brute, in the perfon of the buyer, of the feller, and of him who is fold.

Shall we not take into our account the complication which the fettlements in the Eaft and Weft Indies have introduced in the machine of government? Before that period, the perfons proper to hold the reins of government were infinitely fcarce. An adminiftration more embarraffed, hath required a more extenfive genius, and greater depth of knowledge. The cares of fovereignty, divided between the citizens placed at the foot of the throne, and the fubjects fettled under the equator, or near the pole, have been infufficient for both the one and the other. Every thing hath fallen into confufion. The feveral ftates have languifhed under the yoke of oppreffion; and endlefs wars, or fuch

as were inceffantly renewed, have haraffed the globe, B O O K
and ftained it with blood.   XIX.

Let us ftop here, and confider ourfelves as exifting
at the time when America and India were unknown.
Let me fuppofe that I addrefs myfelf to the moft cruel
of the Europeans in the following terms : There exift
regions which will furnifh thee with rich metals, a-
greeable clothing, and delicious food ; but read this
hiftory, and behold at what price the difcovery is promifed to thee. Doft thou wifh or not that it fhould
be made ? Is it to be imagined that there exifts a being infernal enough to anfwer this queftion in the af-
firmative ? Let it be remembered, that there will not
be a fingle inftant in futurity when my queftion will
not have the fame force.

Nations, I have difcourfed to you on your deareft
interefts. I have placed before your eyes the benefits
of nature, and the fruits of induftry. As ye are too
frequently the occafion of your mutual unhappinefs,
you muft have felt how the jealoufy of avarice, how
pride and ambition, remove far from your common
weal the happinefs that prefents itfelf to you by peace
and commerce. I have recalled that happinefs which
has been removed from you. The fentiments of my
heart have been warmly expreffed in favour of all mankind, without diftinction of fect or country. Men are
all equal in my fight, by the reciprocal relation of the
fame wants and the fame calamities, as they are all
equal in the eyes of the Supreme Being through the
connection between their weaknefs and his power. I
have not been ignorant that, fubject, as ye were, to
mafters, your deftiny muft principally depend upon
them ; and that while I was fpeaking to you of your
calamities, I was cenfuring them for their errors or
their crimes. This reflection hath not depreffed my
courage. I have never conceived, that the facred refpect due to humanity could poffibly be irreconcileable with that which is due to thofe who fhould be its
natural protectors. I have been tranfported in idea
into the councils of the ruling powers. I have fpoken

BOOK
XIX.
without difguife and without fear, and have no reafon to accufe myfelf of having betrayed the great caufe I have ventured to plead. I have informed princes of their duties, and of the rights of the people. I have traced to them the fatal effects of that inhuman power which is guilty of oppreffion, and of that whofe indolence and weaknefs fuffers it. I have fketched all around them portraits of your misfortunes, and they cannot but have been fenfibly affected by them. I have warned them, that if they turned their eyes away, thofe true but dreadful pictures would be engraven on the marble of their tombs, and accufe their afhes, while pofterity trampled on them.

But talents are not always equal to our zeal. Undoubtedly I have ftood in need of a greater fhare of that penetration which difcovers expedients, and of that eloquence which enforces truth. Sometimes, perhaps, the fentiments of my heart have contributed to raife my genius; but moft frequently I have perceived myfelf overwhelmed with my fubject, and confcious of my own inability.

May writers, on whom nature has beftowed greater abilities, complete by their mafterpieces what my effays have begun! Under the aufpices of philofophy, may there be one day extended, from one extremity of the world to the other, that chain of union and benevolence which ought to connect all civilized people! May they never more carry among favage nations the example of vice and oppreffion! I do not flatter myfelf that, at the period of that happy revolution, my name will be ftill in remembrance. This feeble work, which will have only the merit of having brought forth others better than itfelf, will doubtlefs be forgotten. But I fhall, at leaft, be able to fay, that I have contributed as much as was in my power to the happinefs of my fellow-creatures, and pointed out the way, though perhaps at a diftance, to improve their deftiny. This agreeable thought will ftand me in the ftead of glory. It will be the delight of my old age, and the confolation of my lateft moments.

INDEX.

N. B. *The Roman Numerals refer to the Volume, and the Figures to the Page.*

ture and models, 302. Character of their rhubarb, 305. Inquiry into the gold and silver trade with, ib. Their treatment of the Portuguese at Macao, 306. Present state of their intercourse with the Dutch, 307. Their trade with the English, 308. With France, ib. With the Danes and Swedes, 309. Summary view of the a-mount of their commercial dealings with Europeans, ib. General remarks on, 310. Political inquiry into the merits of the trade with China, and into the proper mode of conducting it, 311.

Chivalry, reflections on the tendency of the spirit of, i. 110.

Chocolate, description of the tree and the nuts from which it is made, iii. 53.

Christianity, causes which favoured the re-ception of, among the Romans, vi. 216. Sources of its corruption, 218. Leading causes of the Reformation, 219. Requires support from the civil magistrate, 221. Historical view of the system of ecclesiastical policy founded upon, 284. Ought to be subordinate to the civil power, 295.

Christopher's, St. the island settled jointly by the English and French, iii. 408. The native Caribs expelled, 409. Is resigned to the English by the peace of Utrecht, iv. 384. Occasion of the dissensions between the first French and English inhabitants, v. 27. Is long neglected by the English after the expulsion of the French, 28. The island and its inhabitants described, ib. Its produce, 29. Anecdotes of Negro slaves there, ib.

Cinnabar, the constituent parts of that mine-ral, iii. 122. Quicksilver, how separated from it, 123.

Cinnamon tree, botanical description of, i. 222. Methods of taking off the bark, and its qualities, 223.

Cities made free by commerce, i. 15, 16. The support of, derived from agriculture, vi. 383. Origin of, 403.

Civil Law of Great Britain, cause of its dif-fuseness and perplexity, vi. 116.

Civil wars, the origin of, iii. 32. The issues of, when victorious, suitable to the mo-tives, 37.

Clergy, inquiry into the best mode of main-taining them, iii. 378. Must be made sub-ordinate to the civil magistrate, to pre-vent the subversion of a state, 379. A set of men useless, at best, to the earth, and the most dreadful enemies to a nation when they disgrace their profession, vi. 384. The most respectable of them, those who are most despised, and burdened with duty, 385. Their unalienable domains an ob-struction to population, 404.

Climate, its influence on religion, i. 36, 37, Philosophical remarks on, and inferences from, v. 293. Forms the character, com-plexion, and manners of nations, vi. 393. Determines the species of manufactures in a country, ib. Is improved by agriculture, 399.

Cloves, first discovered in the Molucca Islands by the Chinese, i. 109. Botanical descrip-tion of the tree, and its culture, 196. Pro-perties of the clove, 197. Are cultivated at Amboyna, under Dutch authority, ib.

Cloisters, anciently the seats of manufactures, ii. 3. Naturally tend to accumulate wealth, 4.

Cochin, on the Malabar coast, account of that kingdom, i. 364.

Cochin-china, French account of that em-pire and its inhabitants, ii. 51. Produc-tions and manufactures of the country, 52. Amiable disposition of the natives, ib. Equity of their first system of government, 53. Progress of corruption in their go-vernment, 54. View of their trade, 55. Causes of the French losing the advan-tages of this market, 56.

Cochineal, a production peculiar to Mexico, ii. 433. Natural history of, 434. De-scription of the shrub on which they breed, ib. How cultivated, ib. How gather-ed, 436. Method of killing and preserving them, 437. Is introduced in St. Domingo, 438.

Cocoa tree, natural history of, i. 106. Its fruit, and the properties of it, 107.

Cod, the fish described, v. 329. A fishery for, carried on in the northern seas of Europe, ib. Account of the fishery at Newfound-land, 330. Method of curing the cod, 336. Rise of the English, and decline of the French fisheries, 343.

Coffee, where originally found, with an ac-count of the discovery of its properties, i. 336. Where now cultivated, 339. Much used in, and great exports of from, Arabia, 340. Introduced into the Caribbee Islands from the East, iv. 141. The tree and its berries described, 142. Method of culti-vating it, ib. Manner of preparing the berries for sale, 143.

Coffee-houses, the origin of, i. 336. Ineffec-tual attempt to suppress them at Constan-tinople, 337. Are opened in London, 339.

Colbert, M. forms a French East India Com-pany, ii. 10. His character as a financier, 71. Mistakes in his administration point-ed out, iv. 276. Subjects the French co-lonies to the oppressions of an exclusive company, 277.

Cold, the various effects produced by, in Hudson's Bay, v. 303, 304.

THE END.